DANCE WORLD

1971

by

JOHN WILLIS

1970-1971 SEASON

Volume 6

CROWN PUBLISHERS, INC.

419 Park Avenue South

New York, N. Y. 10016

TO
ISADORA BENNETT

with love and gratitude, and with deep admiration for her tremendous expenditure of self for dance and dancers—

and to all other devoted press agents and managers of dance, past and present, whose gracious cooperation and generous assistance have made these volumes of dance history possible. For this volume, the following are also acknowledged with special thanks:

Philip Bell
Mary Colquhoun
Judith Daykin
Virginia Donaldson
Murray Farr
Martin Feinstein
Meg Gordean

Thomas Kerrigan
Seymour Krawitz
LeRoy Leatherman
Doris Luhre
Samuel Lurie
Arks Smith
Leila Sturm

left: *Helen Morison Photo*

Bettie De Jong, Eileen Cropley, Carolyn Adams, Paul Taylor
in "Big Bertha" (Premiere Feb. 9, 1971)

CONTENTS

EDITOR: JOHN WILLIS
Assistant Editor: Stanley Reeves
Staff: Frances Crampon, Frances Harwood, Jack Moore, Lucy Williams
Staff Photographers: Louis Melancon, Lyn Smith, Van Williams, Ted Yaple

NEW YORK STATE THEATER
Opened Tuesday, June 16, 1970.*
Ballet Theatre Foundation (Sherwin M. Goldman, President) in association with City Center of Music and Drama, Inc. (Norman Singer, General Administrator) presents.

AMERICAN BALLET THEATRE

Directors, Lucia Chase, Oliver Smith; Musical Director, Jaime Leon; Conductor, Akira Endo; Guest Conductor, Kenneth Schermerhorn; Regisseur, Dimitri Romanoff; Assistant to the Directors, John Kriza; Ballet Master, Enrique Martinez; General Manager, Daryl Dodson; Press, Doris Luhrs, Arks Smith, Judi Jedlicka; Company Manager, Phillipe de Conville; Technical Supervisor, George Bardyguine; Lighting, Nananne Porcher; Stage Manager, Ben Janney

COMPANY

PRINCIPALS: Toni Lander, Royes Fernandez, Bruce Marks, Sallie Wilson, Eleanor D'Antuono, Gayle Young, Cynthia Gregory, Ted Kivitt, Mimi Paul, Ivan Nagy, Michael Smuin, Alexandra Radius, Han Ebbelaar, and Lupe Serrano
PERMANENT GUEST ARTISTS: Carla Fracci, Erik Bruhn
SOLOISTS: Diana Weber, Terry Orr, Roni Mahler, John Prinz, Gail Israel, Paul Nickel, Karena Brock, Rosanna Seravalli, Paula Tracy, Susan Casey, Marcos Paredes, Betsy Erickson, William Carter, Robert Gladstein, Ian Horvath, Zhandra Rodriguez, Dennis Nahat
CORPS: Buddy Balough, Amy Blaisdell, Robert Brassel, Carol Bryan, Christine Busch, Richard Cammack, Betty Chamberlin, David Coll, Zola Dishong, Deborah Dobson, Helyn Douglas, Jan Fisher, Carol Foster, Ingrid Fraley, Nanette Glushak, Rhodie Jorgenson, Sue Knapp, Keith Lee, Rosamond Lynn, Jacquelyn Marshall, Ruth Mayer, Christine Motzkus, Richard Rein, Stephen Shaw, Frank Smith, Naomi Sorkin, Bojan Spassoff, Marianna Tcherkassky, Gaudio Vacacio, Vane Vest, Luis Villanueva, Patricia Wesche, Stephanie Wolf, Maria Youskevitch, James Zynda

REPERTOIRE

"At Midnight" (Mahler, Feld), "Brahms Quintet" (Brahms, Nahat), "Caprichos (Bartok, Ross), "Concerto" (Shostakovich, MacMillan), "Dark Elegies" (Mahler, Tudor), "Etudes" (Riisaager after Czerny, Lander), "Fancy Free" (Bernstein, Robbins), "Gala Performance" (Prokofieff, Tudor), "Gartenfest" (Mozart, Smuin), "Harbinger" (Prokofieff, Feld), "Les Noces" (Stravinsky, Robbins), "Miss Julie" (Rangstrom, Cullberg), "Pillar of Fire" (Schoenberg, Tudor), "Pulcinella Variations" (Stravinsky, Smuin), "The Eternal Idol" (Chopin, Smuin), "Theme and Variations" (Tchaikovsky, Balanchine), "Giselle" (Adam, Blair after Coralli), "La Sylphide" (Cosma-Loewenskjold, Lander after Bournonville), "Swan Lake" (Tchaikovsky, Blair after Petipa-Ivanov), "Gaiete Parisienne" (Offenbach, Massine), "Petrouchka" (Stravinsky, Benois, Diaghilev, Fokine), "The Traitor" (Schuller, Limon), "Fall River Legend" (Gould, deMille), "Jardin aux Lilas" (Chausson, Tudor), World Premiere June 25, 1970 of "The River" (Ellington, Ailey; Costumes, Frank Thompson; Lighting, Nicholas Cernovitch), "The Moor's Pavane" (Purcell, Limon)

* Closed July 12, 1970 after 32 performances.

Top Right: Royes Fernandez, Lucia Chase in "Swan Lake"

Ivan Nagy, Carla Fracci in "Giselle"

John Prinz in "The River"Top Left: Sallie Wilson, Keith Lee in "The River" (Premiere June 25, 1970) Top Right: Robert Gladstein, Michael Smuin, Cynthia Gregory in "Gaiete Parisienne"

"Les Noces" Top Left: Roni Mahler, Paula Tracy in "Swan Lake"
Right: Eleanor D'Antuono, Royes Fernandez in "Giselle"

AMERICAN BALLET THEATRE

Carla Fracci, Ted Kivitt in "Coppelia" Top: Terry Orr, Michael Smuin, Dennis Nahat in "Fancy Free"

Sallie Wilson, Ted Kivitt in "Petrouchka"

9

METROPOLITAN OPERA HOUSE
Opened Tuesday, July 7, 1970.*
S. Hurok presents:

MOISEYEV DANCE COMPANY

Artistic Director, Igor Moiseyev; Musical Director and Conductor, Nikolai Nekrassov; Conductor, Sergei Kolobkov; Choreography, Igor Moiseyev; Guest Conductor, Arthur Lief; Wardrobe Mistress, Vera Stalnaya; Coordinator, Simon Semenoff

SOLOISTS

Mikhail Alexandrov, Yuri Alexandrov, Boris Berezin, Nelly Bondarenko, Anatoli Fyodorov, Lev Golovanov, Rudi Khodzhoyan, Nikolai Kosogorov, Stanislav Kulikov, Olga Moiseyeva, Boris Petrov, Nenel Samsonova, Boris Sankin, Vassily Savin, Galina Yeliseyeva, Alfat Yenikeyev

PROGRAM

"Suite of Old Russian Dances," "Yurochka," "Khorumi," "Polyanka," "Zhok," "Old City Quadrille," "Partisans," "Sicilian Tarantella," "Gaucho," "Sunday," "Dance of the Buffoons," "Gypsies," "Two Boys in a Fight," "Gopak"

General Manager:Naum Levinson
Company Manager:John H. Wilson
Press:Martin Feinstein, Dale Heapps, James Murtha, Edward Parkinson
Stage Manager:Nicholas Russiyan

* Closed July 25, 1970 after limited engagement of 21 performances. Returned Oct. 6-18, 1970 for 14 additional performances at Madison Square Garden's Felt Forum.

Vladimir Zhmikhov
Top: Vasily Savin

"Sicilian Tarantella"
Above: Nikolai Brovkin

Victor Dolgov Above: Olga Moiseyeva, Viktor
Lavrukhin Top: Yuri Shumilin

"Sicilian Tarantella"
Above & top: "Dance of the Buffoons"

NEW YORK STATE THEATER

Opened Tuesday, August 25, 1970.*
City Center of Music and Drama presents:

NEW YORK CITY BALLET

Directors, George Balanchine, Lincoln Kirstein; Choreographer, George Balanchine; Ballet Masters, George Balanchine, John Taras, Una Kai; Assistant, Rosemary Dunleavy; Musical Director and Principal Conductor, Robert Irving; Associate Conductor, Hugo Fiorato; Pianists, Gordon Boelzner, Harry Fuchs, Jerry Zimmerman; Costumes, Karinska; Wardrobe, Cornelie De-Brauw, Arthur Craig; Lighting, Ronald Bates, Peter Harvey, Jean Rosenthal, Rouben Ter-Arutunian, Jules Fisher, David Hays, Nananne Porcher; Scenery, Jean Rosenthal, Rouben Ter-Arutunian, Peter Harvey, David Hays, Esteban Frances, Raoul Pene DuBois, Cecil Beaton, Georges Rouault, Horace Armistead, Jo Mielziner, John Boyt

COMPANY

PRINCIPALS: Jacques d'Amboise, Anthony Blum, Melissa Hayden, Conrad Ludlow, Patricia McBride, Nicholas Magallanes, Peter Martins, Kay Mazzo, Arthur Mitchell, Francisco Moncion, Suki Schorer, Violette Verdy, Edward Villella, Jean-Pierre Bonnefous, Helgi Tomasson
SOLOISTS: Karin von Aroldingen, John Clifford, Gloria Govrin, Deni Lamont, Sara Leland, Teena McConnell, Robert Maiorano, Marnee Morris, Shaun O'Brien, Frank Ohman, Richard Rapp, Earle Sieveling, Bettijane Sills, Carol Sumner, William Weslow
CORPS DE BALLET: Merrill Ashley, James Bogan, Stephen Caras, Gail Crisa, Hermes Conde, Richard Dryden, Rosemary Dunleavy, Suzanne Erlon, Renee Estopinal, Elise Flagg, Deborah Flomine, Elizabeth Geyer, Kathleen Haigney, Susan Hendl, Gloriann Hicks, Linda Homek, Gail Kachadurian, Gelsey Kirkland, Johnna Kirkland, Deborah Koolish, Suzette Mariaux, Linda Merrill, Karen Morell, Catherine Morris, Colleen Neary, Karen O'Sullivan, Leslie Peck, Delia Peters, Carolyn Peterson, Roger Pietrucha, Susan Pilarre, Bryan Pitts, Terry Port, Christine Redpath, David Richardson, Giselle Roberge, Cam La Rondeau, Donna Sackett, Paul Sackett, Polly Shelton, Francis Sackett, Marjorie Spohn, Michael Steele, Lynne Stetson, Marilee Stiles, Virginia Stuart, Sheryl Ware, Robert Weiss, Bruce Wells, Carielle Whittle

REPERTOIRE

(All choreography by George Balanchine except where noted) "Jewels", "Afternoon of a Faun" (Debussy, Jerome Robbins), "Agon" (Stravinsky), "Allegro Brillante" (Tchaikovsky), "Apollo" (Stravinsky), "Ballet Imperial" (Tchaikovsky), "Brahms-Schoenberg Quartet", "Bugaku" (Mayuzumi), "The Cage" (Stravinsky), "Concerto Barocco" (Bach), "Dances at a Gathering" (Chopin, Robbins), "Dim Lustre" (Strauss), "Divertimento" (Mozart), "Don Quixote" (Nabokov), "Episodes" (Webern), "Fantasies" (Ralph Vaughan Williams, John Clifford), "Firebird" (Stravinsky), "Four Temperaments" (Hindemith), "Harlequinade" (Drigo), "Haydn Concerto" (Haydn, Taras), "Illuminations" (Britten, Ashton), "In The Night" (Chopin, Robbins), "Irish Fantasy" (Saint-Saens, d'Amboise), "Ivesiana" (Ives), "Jeux" (Debussy, Taras), "Jewels" (Faure-Stravinsky-Tchaikovsky), "La Sonnambula" (Rieti), "La Valse" (Ravel), "Liebeslieder Walzer" (Brahms), "A Midsummer Night's Dream" (Mendelssohn), "Monumentum Pro Gesualdo" (Stravinsky), "Movements for Piano and Orchestra" (Stravinsky), "The Nutcracker" (Tchaikovsky), "Pas de Deux" (Tchaikovsky), "Prodigal Son" (Prokofiev), "Raymonda Variations" (Glazounov), "Reveries" (Tchaikovsky, John Clifford), "Scotch Symphony" (Mendelssohn), "Serenade" (Tchaikovsky), "Slaughter on Tenth Avenue" (Rodgers), "Stars and Stripes" (Sousa), "Stravinsky Symphony" (Stravinsky, Clifford), "Swan Lake" (Tchaikovsky, Balanchine after Ivanov), "Symphony in C" (Bizet), "Tarantella" (Gottschalk), "Tchaikovsky Suite" (d'Amboise), "Trois Valses Romantiques" (Chabrier), "Western Symphony" (Kay), "Who Cares?" (Gershwin)

Company Manager: Zelda Dorfman
Press: Virginia Donaldson
Stage Managers: Ronald Bates, Kevin Tyler, Roland Vazquez

Martha Swope, Fred Fehl Photos

**Top Right: Jacques d'Amboise, Melissa Hayden
in "The Nutcracker" Below: Violette Verdy,
Conrad Ludlow in "The Nutcracker"**

* Closed Sept. 6, 1970 after 16 performances. Returned for winter season from Nov. 18, 1970 through Feb. 14, 1971 (103 performances) with premieres of "Suite Number 3" (Tchaikovsky, George Balanchine; Scenery and Costumes, Nicolas Benois; Lighting, Ronald Bates) on Thursday, Dec. 3, 1970; "Kodaly Dances" (Zoltan Kodaly, John Clifford; Costumes, Stanley Simmons; Lighting, Ronald Bates) on Thursday, Jan. 14, 1971; "Four Last Songs" (Richard Strauss, Lorca Massine; Scenery, John Braden; Costumes, Joe Eula; Lighting, Ronald Bates), and "Concerto for Two Pianos" (Stravinsky, Richard Tanner) both on Thursday, Jan. 21, 1971. During the spring season from Apr. 27 through June 27, 1971 (71 performances) premieres of "Octandre" (Edgard Varese, Richard Tanner) on Thursday, May 13, 1971; "The Goldberg Variations" (J. S. Bach, Jerome Robbins; Costumes, Joe Eula; Lighting, Thomas Skelton) on Thursday, May 27, 1971; "PAMTGG" (Roger Kellaway, George Balanchine; Scenery and Lighting, Jo Mielziner; Costumes, Irene Sharaff) Thursday, June 17, 1971. On Thursday, May 6, 1971 for the Spring Benefit the Dance Theatre of Harlem joined NYC Ballet for one performance of "Concerto for Jazz Band and Orchestra" (Rolf Lieberman, Balanchine-Arthur Mitchell)

Frank Ohman, Susan Hendl in "Slaughter on Tenth Avenue" Above: Helgi Tomasson Top: Edward Villella, Gelsey Kirkland in "Suite No. 3" (Premiere)

"In the Night" Above: "Jewels" Top: Conrad Ludlow, Johnna Kirkland in "Reveries"

14

Johnna Kirkland, Anthony Blum
in "Kodaly Dances" (Premiere)

Edward Villella, Patricia McBride in "Symphony in C"
Top: John Prinz, Anthony Blum, Patricia McBride, Robert
Maiorano, Sara Leland in "Dances at a Gathering"

Lorca Massine in "Four Last Songs" (Premiere) Top: (L) "Who Cares?" (R) Jacques d'Amboise, Gelsey Kirkland in "Firebird"
NEW YORK CITY BALLET

"Concerto for Two Pianos" (Premiere) Top: (L) Premiere and only performance of "Concerto for Jazz Band and Orchestra" in collaboration with Dance Theatre of Harlem (R) Patricia McBride, Conrad Ludlow in "A Midsummer Night's Dream"

Kay Mazzo, Conrad Ludlow, Sara Leland,
Anthony Blum in "Fantasies" Top: Edward
Villella in "Prodigal Son"

Jacques d'Amboise, Kay Mazzo
in "Afternoon of a Faun"

NEW YORK CITY BALLET

Gelsey Kirkland, John Clifford
in "Concerto for Two Pianos" (Premiere)

Susan Hendl and top: "The Goldberg Variations"
(Premiere)

"Octandre" (Premiere) Above: "PAMTGG" (Premiere)
NEW YORK CITY BALLET

"Harlequinade" Top: (L) Conrad Ludlow, Violette Verdy in "Raymonda Pas de Deux" (R) Sara Leland, John Clifford, Patricia McBride in "Dances at a Gathering"

"Brahms-Schoenberg Concerto" Top: (L) Melissa Hayden, Jacques d'Amboise in "Swan Lake" (R)
Patricia McBride, Edward Villella in "Jewels"
NEW YORK CITY BALLET

ALICE TULLY HALL

Saturday & Sunday, October 3, 4, 1970.
S. Hurok presents:

CIRO
and his
BALLET FLAMENCO

Choreography and Costumes Designed by Ciro; Lighting, Andie Wilson Kingwell; Stage Manager, Grant Logan; Press, Martin Feinstein, Dale Heapps, James Murtha

COMPANY

Ciro, Rosa Montoya (Special Guest Artist), Luisa Escobar, Roberto Amaral, Juana Ortega, Oscar Nieto, Mariana Maduel, Domingo Alvarado (singer), Benito Palacios (guitar), Bunyan Webb (classical guitar)

PROGRAM

"Rumores de la Caleta" (Albeniz), "Guajira," "Solea," "Lo Flamenco y Lo Clasico" (Sor), "Zorongo Gitano," "Caracoles," "Verdiales," "Leyenda" (Albeniz), "Alegrias, " "Por Farruca," "Tanguillo, Rumba and Bulerias"

Cecil Thompson Photos

Right: Ciro and Rosa Montoya

Ciro (L) and Rosa Montoya

ALICE TULLY HALL

Opened Monday, December 21, 1970.*
Columbia Artists Festivals Corp. presents:

BAYANIHAN
Philippine Dance
Company

Produced by Bayanihan Folk Arts Center; Company Director and Music Director, Lucrecia R. Kasilag; Choreographer and Dance Director, Lucrecia Reyes Urtula; Assistant Company Director, Costumes, Isabel A. Santos; Artistic Director, Jose Lardizabal; Technical Director, Cesar Roberto Roces; Technical Consultant, Teodoro L. Hilado; Road Production Manager, William Mullaney; Production Coordinator, Barbara Tuck; International Representative, John M. Reed.

COMPANY

Maria Lolita V. Adea, Erlynn R. Bernardez, Melannie R. Bernardez, Judy P. Caldoza, Mary Joan V. Fajardo, Fe. V. Flores, Enya C. Gabor, Mary Anne E. Garcia, Zenaida M. Lopez, Ma. Fatima Manuel Viveca R. Medrano, Ma. Cristina V. Ocampo, Carmencita Santos, Mercedes J. Teves, Orlando Bartolome, Reynaldo A. Feleo, Leoncio Grajo III, Earl M. Janairo, Edgardo Lualhati, Tomas O. Matias, Ramon Obusan, Ely C. Rogado, Fernando Sison III, Antonio C. Sol, Dennis J. Tan, Glicerio R. Tecson, Roberto Tongko, Vocalists Miriam C. Odejar, Roberta Topacio

REPERTOIRE

"Dances of the Mountain Province," "Ecos de La Ermita," "Mindanao Tapestry," "Tagabili," "Bayanihan"

*Company Manager:*Charles K. Jones
*Press:*Richard O'Harra

* Closed Jan. 3, 1971 after limited engagement of 16 performances.

Charles W. Miller Photos

"The Hat Dance"
Above: Rickie Nicolas

"Tagabili" Above: "Dove Dance"
Top: "Indarapatra"

METROPOLITAN OPERA HOUSE
Opened Monday, April 19, 1971.*
S. Hurok presents:

STUTTGART BALLET

Director-Choreographer, John Cranko; General Administrator, Dr. Walter Erich Schafer; Assistant, Hurt May; Assistant Director, Anne Woolliams; Ballet Master, Alan Beale; Musical Director, Ashley Lawrence; Conductors, Friedrich Lehn, Kenneth Klein; General Manager, Dieter Grafe; Assistant Ballet Master, Edward Dutton; Technical Director, Herbert Grohmann; Lighting, Gilbert V. Hemsley, Jr.

COMPANY

PRINCIPALS: Marcia Haydee, Birgit Keil, Judith Reyn, Susanne Hanke, Egon Madsen, Richard Cragun, Heinz Clauss, Bernd Berg, Jan Stripling, Ruth Papendick, Jane Landon, Leigh-Ann Griffiths, Gudron Lechner, Kyoko Ishimatsu, Hella Heim, David Sutherland, Vladimir Klos, Jiri Kylian, Reid Anderson, Dieter Ammann
SOLOISTS AND CORPS DE BALLET: Pamela Ainsworth, Wendy Auton, Rosine Bena, Trudie Campbell, Joyce Cuoco, Barbara Dunlop, Kristine Elliot, Emilietta Ettlin, Fiona Fairrie, Cherylanne Gillam, Ursula Hageli, Christine Hasting, Lucia Lisenring, Elisabeth King, Sabine Kupferberg, Deirdre O'Donhoe, Kevyn O'Rourke, Lourdja Peixoto de Mesquita, Catherine Prescott, Norma Restier Gonsalves, Hedda Twiehaus, Elma Wege, Peter Connell, Joel Dabin, Ulf Esser, Christian Fallanga, Urs Frey, Zoltan Imre, Marcis Lesins, Jusuf Mailovic, Mark Neal, Andrew Oxenham, Michael Sanchez, Kurt Specker, Michael Wasmund, Steven Wistrich

REPERTOIRE

(All choreography by John Cranko) "Eugene Onegin" (Tchaikovsky), "Romeo and Juliet" (Prokofiev), "Carmen" (Bizet) U.S. premiere, "Opus One" (von Webern), U.S. premieres of "Brouilliards" (Debussy), "Ebony Concerto" (Stravinsky), and "The Seasons" (Glazounov), "The Taming of the Shrew" (Kurt-Heinz Stolze after Domenico Scarlatti), "The Catalyst" (Shostakovich), "Jeu de Cartes" (Stravinsky), U.S. premiere of "Salade" (Milhaud), "Mozart Concerto" (Mozart), "Divertissements: Russian and Ludmilla Pas de Quatre, Grand Pas de Deux from Coppelia, Mirror Pas de Deux from Eugene Onegin"

Company Manager: John H. Wilson
Press: Martin Feinstein, Dale Heapps, James Murtha, Edward Parkinson

* Closed May 29, 1971 after limited engagement of 48 performances. Returned July 20-Aug. 1, 1971 with Margot Fonteyn as guest artist in "Poeme De L'Extase."

**Marcia Haydee, and above with Heinz Clauss
in "Eugene Onegin"**

**Marcia Haydee, Jan Stripling
in "Eugene Onegin"**

Richard Cragun Top: (L) Marcia Haydee, Egon Madsen (R) Richard Cragun, Marcia Haydee in "Carmen"

Marcia Haydee, Richard Cragun, also above and top in "Taming of the Shrew"
STUTTGART BALLET

Heinz Clauss Above: Susanne Hanke, Richard Cragun, Marcis Lesins, Marcia Haydee Top: Egon Madsen, Susanne Hanke in "Taming of the Shrew"

Hella Heim, Marcia Haydee Above: Marcia
Haydee Top: Richard Cragun, Marcia Haydee

David Sutherland, Egon Madsen, Richard Cragun,
Jan Stripling Top: Birgit Keil

in "Romeo and Juliet"

Richard Cragun
in "The Catalyst"

"Mozart Concerto"
Top: "Jeu des Cartes"

STUTTGART BALLET

Richard Cragun, Egon Madsen, Margot Fonteyn in "Poeme de L'Extase" (Premiere) Top: (L) Heinz Clauss, Marcia Haydee, Egon Madsen in "Ebony Concerto" (R) Egon Madsen in "Jeu des Cartes"

NEW YORK CITY CENTER DANCE PROGRAMS

Norman Singer, General Administrator

NEW YORK CITY CENTER

Opened Wednesday, August 19, 1970.*
North American Productions Ltd. in association with
the City Center of Music and Drama presents:

LES BALLETS AFRICAINS

Artistic Directors, Hamidou Bangoura, Italo Zambo;
General Manager, Mamadou Lamine Sane; Assistant
General Manager, Mohamed Lamine Camara; Exclusive
Direction, Kolmar-Luth Entertainment Inc.

COMPANY

Mariama Sadio Bah, Oumou Bangoura, Mariama Barry,
Aly Camara, Faouly Camara, Ibrahima Camara, Lan-
sana Dede Camara, Maia Camara, Mossokoura Camara,
Manana Cisse, Damany Conde, Sekou Conde, Ibrahima
Conte, Aissata Dabo, Koca Sale Diabate, Mariama
Diallo, Almamy Dioubate, Bintou Dioubate, Sekou
Dioubate, Karamoke Fofana, Malene Fofana, Vomo
Gbamou, Fanta Kaba, Mabinty Keita, Noumody Keita,
Famoudou Konate, Mamadi Kourouma, M'Bady Kouy-
ate, Nakani Kouyate, Jeanne Macauley, Mamady Man-
sare, Bakary Mara, Goundo Souare, Bintou Soumah,
Salifou Sylla, Jean Tonia, Aissatou Toure, Arafan Toure,
Guila Traore

PROGRAM

"Overture," "Evolution of Africa," "Tiranke," "Initiation," "Night of the Cora," Finale

Company Manager: Oscar Abraham
Press: James Hughes
Stage Manager: Salifou Bangoura

* Closed Aug. 23, 1970 after limited engagement of 7
performances. Returned for one performance on Dec.
13, 1970 at the Fashion Institute.

NEW YORK CITY CENTER

Opened Tuesday, September 29, 1970.*
Foundation for American Dance in association with
City Center of Music and Drama, Inc. presents:

CITY CENTER JOFFREY BALLET

Artistic Director-Choreographer, Robert Joffrey; Assistant Director-Choreographer, Gerald Arpino; General Administrator, Omar K. Lerman; Music Director, Walter Hagen; Guest Conductor, Seymour Lipkin; Lighting, Thomas Skelton; Production Supervisor, Jennifer Tipton; Ballet Master, Basil Thompson; Assistant to Mr. Arpino, James Howell

COMPANY

Charthel Arthur, Zelma Bustillo, Diana Cartier, Lili Cockerille, Francesca Corkle, Donna Cowen, Starr Danias, Erika Goodman, Alaine Haubert, Denise Jackson, Pamela Johnson, Sue Loyd, Victoria More, Diane Orio, Barbara Remington, Nancy Robinson, Dana Sapiro, Donna Silva, Martine Van Hamel, Gay Wallstrom, Rebecca Wright Scott Barnard, Frank Bays, Henry Berg, Dermot Burke, Gary Chryst, James Dunne, Robert Estner, Luis Fuente, Randal Harris, Phillip Hoffman, Christian Holder, George Montalbano, Haynes Owens, Robert Talmage, Burton Taylor, Robert Thomas, Edward Verso, Dennis Wayne, Glenn White, William Whitener

REPERTOIRE

"Petrouchka" (Stravinsky, Massine after Fokine), "Confetti" (Rossini, Arpino), "Green Table" (Cohen, Joos), "Viva Vivaldi!" (Vivaldi, Arpino), "Clowns" (Kay, Arpino), "Konservatoriet" (Paulli, Brenaa after Bournonville), "Fanfarita" (Chapi, Arpino), "Pineapple Poll" (Sullivan, Blair after Cranko), "Moves" (Jerome Robbins), "Pas des Deesses" (Field, Joffrey), "Facade" (Walton, Ashton), "William Tell Variations" (Rossini, Brenaa after Bournonville), "Astarte" (Crome Syrcus, Joffrey), "Olympics" (Mayuzumi, Arpino), "Cakewalk" (Gottschalk-Kay, Boris), "Cello Concerto" (Vivaldi, Arpino), "Solarwind" (Druckman, Arpino), "Three-Cornered Hat" (de Falla, Massine), "Secret Places" (Mozart, Arpino)
NEW PRODUCTIONS of "Still Point" (Debussy, Todd Bolender), and "Time Cycle" (Foss, Bolender)
PREMIERE of "Trinity" (Alan Raph-Lee Holdridge, Gerald Arpino) in three sections titled "Sunday," "Summerland," and "Saturday" (October 9, 1970)

Company Manager: Donald Antonelli
Press: Isadora Bennett
Stage Managers: Andre St. Jean, Diana Banks

* Closed Nov. 8, 1970 after 48 performances. Returned for a spring season of 42 performances from Tuesday, Feb. 16 through Mar. 28, 1971. On leave were Barbara Remington and Edward Verso; Zelma Bustillo and Luis Fuente were not with the company.
   Added to the repertoire were "Reflections" (Tchaikovsky, Arpino) premiered on Feb. 24, 1971, "Valentine" (Jacob Druckman, Arpino) premiered on Mar. 10, 1971 with Rebecca Wright and Christian Holder, and new productions of "Abyss" (Richter, Hodes), and "Square Dance" (Corelli-Vivaldi, Balanchine)

Fred Fehl, James Howell, Herbert Migdoll Photos

"Olympics"
Top Right: "Viva Vivaldi!"

"The Green Table" Above: Zelma Bustillo,
Luis Fuente in "Fanfarita"

**Dennis Wayne, Pamela Johnson
in "Still Point"**

**Nancy Robinson, Christian Holder
in "Astarte" Top: "Time Cycle"**

Christian Holder in "Trinity" (Premiere) Top: (L) Rebecca Wright, Dermot Burke in "Trinity"
(Premiere Oct. 9, 1970) (R) Luis Fuente in "Facade"
CITY CENTER JOFFREY BALLET

Rebecca Wright, Glenn White, Sue Loyd, Gary Chryst in "Confetti" Top: (L) Paul Sutherland, Charthel Arthur in "The Lesson" (R) Starr Danias, Dennis Wayne in "Reflections"

CITY CENTER JOFFREY BALLET

Francesca Corkle, Paul Sutherland in "Square
Dance" Top: Rebecca Wright, Christian Holder
in "Valentine" (Premiere Mar. 10, 1971)

Dennis Wayne, Lili Cockerille
in "Abyss"

Dermot Burke, Christian Holder, Gary Chryst in "Solarwind" Above: "Moves" Top: "Konservatoriet"

Edward Verso, Alaine Haubert in "Three-Cornered Ha[...]
Above: Dermot Burke, Rebecca Wright, Yurek Lazows[...]
Gary Chryst in "Petrouchka" Top: Gary Chryst in "The Clo[...]

CITY CENTER JOFFREY BALLET

NEW YORK CITY CENTER

Opened Tuesday, November 10, 1970.*
S. Hurok under the auspices of the City Center of
Music and Drama (Norman Singer, Executive
Director) presents:

BALLET FOLKLORICO OF MEXICO

General Director-Choreographer, Amalia Hernandez;
Director, Norma Lopez Hernandez; Artistic Coordinator,
Guillermo Keys Arenas; Musical Director, Ramon No-
ble; Costumes, Dasha, Delfina Vargas; Scenery, Robin
Bond, Covarrubias Lopez-Mancera, Delfina Vargas;
Lighting, Louise Guthman; General Manager, Victor
Altamirano; Coordinator of Chorus, Pedro Munoz;
Wardrobe, Mario Sosa

COMPANY

Letitia Cazares, Marcia Cravioto, Elsa Garcia, Maria
Elia Gonzalez, Maria Luisa Gonzalez, Brisa Guilarte,
Guillermina Lopez, Maria Elia Macias, Josefina Maldo-
nado, Teresa Padilla, Evangelina Pola, Aida Polanco,
Ana Maria Tapia, Monica Vial, Juan Jose Burgos,
Rolando Cano, Alfredo Espinoza, Fidel Herrera, Anto-
nio Lizaola, Enrique Martinez, Juan Medellin, Rafael
Mendizabal, Juan Munoz, Jose Santacruz, Humberto
Trevino, Jorge Tyller, Eduardo

PROGRAM

"Guelaguetza," "Sugar Harvest in Tamaulipas," "The
Revolution," "Games," "Mocambo," "The Aztecs,"
"Dance of the Little Old Men of Jaracuaro," "Wedding
on the Isthmus of Tehuantepec," "Deer Dance of the
Yaqui Indians," "Guadalajara"

*Company Manager:*Kurt Neumann
*Press:*Martin Feinstein, Dale Heapps, James Murtha,
Lilian Libman
*Stage Manager:*Louise Guthman

* Closed Nov. 15, 1970 after limited engagement of 8
performances.

NEW YORK CITY CENTER

Opened Tuesday, December 8, 1970.*
City Center of Music and Drama in association with
America-Israel Cultural Foundation and Gil Shiva by
arrangement with Sherman Pitluck presents:

BATSHEVA DANCE
COMPANY OF ISRAEL

Founder, Bethsabee De Rothschild; Artistic Adviser,
Martha Graham; Artistic Director, Norman Walker;
Rehearsal Director, Moshe Romano; Guest Conductor,
Simon Sadoff; Music Adviser, Gary Bertini; Lighting
Adviser, Haim Tchelet; Manager, Pinhas Postel; Stage
Supervisor, Joseph Bastien; Sound, Akiba Melamed;
Technical Manager, Yaacov Erlich

COMPANY

Rina Schenfeld, Moshe Efrati, Ehud Ben-David, Rena
Gluck, Rahamim Ron, Nurit Stern, Tselila Goldstein,
Yaakov Sharir, Bruce Becker, Dalya Levy, Laurie Freed-
man, Esther Nadler, Pamela Sharni, Yair Vardi, Avner
Vered, Marcus Schulkind

REPERTOIRE

American premiere of "Baroque Concerto 5" (Vivaldi,
Norman Walker), "Errand into the Maze," (Menotti,
Graham), "The Mythical Hunters" (Partos, Tetley),
American Premiere of "Sin Lieth at the Door" (Naom
Sherif, Moshe Efrati), American Premiere of "Re-
hearsal!..(?)" (Moncayo-Revueltas, Norman Morrice),
"Diversion of Angels" (Dello-Joio, Graham), American
Premiere of "Percussion Concerto" (Leonard Salzedo,
Norman Morrice), "The Exiles" (Schoenberg, Limon),
"Cave of the Heart" (Barber, Graham), American Pre-
miere of "Ein-Dor" (Zvi Avni, Moshe Efrati), "Moves"
(Jerome Robbins), American Premiere of "Curtains"
(Naom Sherif, Rina Schenfeld)

Company Manager: Frank Wicks
Press: Meg Gordean, Joseph Frenkel, D. Belkin
Stage Manager: Moshe Romano

* Closed Dec. 20, 1970 after limited engagement of 16
performances.

Mula & Haramaty Photos

"Moves" Above: "Baroque Concerto No. 5" also
at top

Rena Gluck
in "Cave of the Heart"

Tselila Goldstein, Moshe Efrati in "Ein-Dor" Top: (L) Rina Schenfeld, Moshe Efrati
in "The Mythical Hunters" (R) Nurit Stern, Rahamim Ron in "The Exiles"

Rena Gluck
in "Rehearsal!...(?)"

Moshe Efrati, Rina Schenfeld, Ehud Ben-David in
"Sin Lieth at the Door" Top: "Curtains"

Yael Lavi, Rena Gluck, Tselila Goldstein, Laurie Freedman in "Diversion of Angels" Top: (L) Rina Schenfeld in "Errand into the Maze" (R) Rina Schenfeld, Rahamim Ron, Tselila Goldstein in "Curtains"

BATSHEVA DANCE COMPANY

NEW YORK CITY CENTER

Opened Tuesday, December 8, 1970.*
Ballet Theatre Foundation (Sherwin M. Goldman, President) in association with City Center of Music and Drama (Norman Singer, Executive Director) presents:

AMERICAN BALLET THEATRE

Directors, Lucia Chase, Oliver Smith; Musical Director, Jaime Leon; Conductor, Akira Endo; Regisseur, Dimitri Romanoff; Ballet Master, Enrique Martinez; General Manager, Daryl Dodson; Company Manager, Phillipe de Conville; Press, Doris Luhrs; Stage Manager, Ben Janney; Technical Supervisor, George Bardyguine

COMPANY

Erik Bruhn, Eleanor D'Antuono, Royes Fernandez, Carla Fracci, Cynthia Gregory, Ted Kivitt, Toni Lander, Natalia Makarova, Bruce Marks, Ivan Nagy, Mimi Paul, Lupe Serrano, Michael Smuin, Sallie Wilson, Gayle Young Karena Brock, William Carter, Betsy Erickson, Alexander Filipov, Ian Horvath, Gail Israel, Roni Mahler, Dennis Nahat, Paul Nickel, Terry Orr, Marcos Paredes, John Prinz, Zhandra Rodriguez, Rosanna Seravalli, Naomi Sorkin, Paula Tracy, Diana Weber
Buddy Balough, Amy Blaisdell, Robert Brassel, Carol Bryan, Christine Busch, Richard Cammack, Betty Chamberlin, David Coll, Zola Dishong, Deborah Dobson, Helyn Douglas, Jan Fisher, Carol Foster, Rory Foster, Nanette Glushak, Rhodie Jorgenson, Sue Knapp, Keith Lee, Jacquelyn Marshall, Ruth Mayer, Christine Motzkus, Richard Rein, Janet Shibata, Frank Smith, Bojan Spassoff, Marianna Tcherkassky, Gaudio Vacacio, Martine van Hamel, Vane Vest, Luis Villanueva, Patricia Wesche, Stephanie Wolf, Maria Youskevitch

REPERTOIRE

"Giselle" (Adam, David Blair after Coralli-Perrot) introducing Natalia Makarova, "Coppelia" (Delibes, Martinez), "Les Sylphides" (Chopin, Fokine), "The Moor's Pavane" (Purcell, Limon), "The River" (Ellington, Ailey), "Theme and Variations" (Tchaikovsky, Balanchine), "Brahms Quintet" (Brahms, Nahat), New York Premiere of "A Rose for Miss Emily" (Alan Hovhaness, Agnes deMille; Scenery and Costumes, A. Christina Giannini) on Dec. 30, 1970 with Sallie Wilson and Bruce Marks, "Gaiete Parisienne" (Offenbach, Massine), "Les Patineurs" (Meyerbeer, Ashton), "Miss Julie" (Ranstrom, Cullberg), "Fancy Free" (Bernstein, Robbins), "At Midnight" (Mahler, Feld), World Premiere Jan. 1, 1971 of "Schubertiade" (Schubert, Michael Smuin; Scenery, William Pitkin; Costumes, Marcos Paredes) with Cynthia Gregory, Gayle Young, Eleanor D'Antuono, Terry Orr, Diana Weber, John Prinz, Zola Dishong, Frank Smith, Helyn Douglas, Richard Cammack, Paula Tracy, Vane Vest, Sallie Wilson, Marco Paredes, Laurie Sheppard, Danny Ray, World Premiere Jan. 6, 1971 of "Ontogeny" (Karel Husa, Dennis Nahat; Set and Costumes, Willa Kim; Lighting, Nananne Porcher) with Naomi Sorkin, William Carter, Gaudio Vacacio, Robert Brassel, Ian Horvath, Martine van Hamel, Karena Brock, Terry Orr, Helyn Douglas, Zola Dishong, "The Traitor" (Schuller, Limon)

* Closed Jan. 10, 1971 after limited engagement of 24 performances.

Top Left: Natalia Makarova, Erik Bruhn, Eleanor D'Antuono in "Les Sylphides" Below: Ivan Nagy, Natalia Makarova in "Swan Lake"

Erik Bruhn, Carla Fracci
in "Giselle"

Premiere of "Schubertiade" (Jan. 1, 1971) Top: (L) Gayle Young, Sallie Wilson in "A Rose for Miss Emily"
(Premiere Dec. 30, 1970) (R) Natalia Makarova, Erik Bruhn in "Giselle"

Bruce Marks, Eleanor D'Antuono, Ted Kivitt in
"Petrouchka" Above: "Gala Performance"

John Prinz, Natalia Makarova in "Jardin aux Lilas"
Top: Premiere of "Ontogeny" (Jan. 6, 1971)

"Brahms Quintet" Top: (L) Bruce Marks, Mimi Paul in "Gaiete Parisienne"
(R) Carla Fracci, Ivan Nagy in "Giselle"
AMERICAN BALLET THEATRE

NEW YORK CITY CENTER
Opened Tuesday, January 26, 1971.*
S. Hurok by arrangement with The Australian Ballet
Foundation presents:

THE AUSTRALIAN BALLET

Artistic Directors, Dame Peggy Van Praagh, Sir Robert Helpmann; Administrator, Peter F. Bahen; Music Director, Dobbs Franks; Guest Conductor, John Lanchbery; Assistant to Artistic Directors, Bryan Ashbridge; Ballet Master, Ray Powell; Production Director and Lighting, William Akers

COMPANY

PRINCIPALS: Alan Alder, Kelvin Coe, Elaine Fifield, Marilyn Jones, Marilyn Rowe, Garth Welch
SOLOISTS: Patricia Cox, Francis Croese, Josephine Jason, Gary Norman, Robert Olup, Colin Peasley, Graham Powell, Carolyn Rappel, Gailene Stock, Janet Vernon
ARTISTS:Roslyn Anderson, Don Asker, Ronald Bekker, Lesley Billing, John Brice, David Burch, Alida Chase, Julie da Costa, Susan Dains, Roma Egan, Jo-Anne Endicott, Gail Ferguson, Gillian Francis, Gary Hill, Graeme Hudson, Joseph Janusaitis, Michela Kirkaldie, Shelley Linden, Cheryl Mallinson, Rex McNeill, John Meehan, Wendy Moyle, Graeme Lloyd-Murphy, Leigh Rowles, Paul Saliba, Lucyna Sevitsky, Margaret Smith, Juliette Solley, Ian Spink, Robin Thomson, Wendy Walker, Leigh Warren, Frederic Werner
GUEST ARTISTS: Lucette Aldous, Robert Helpmann, Rudolf Nureyev, Ray Powell

REPERTOIRE

"Don Quixote" (Minkus, Nureyev after Petipa), "Les Rendezvous" (Auber, Ashton), "The Display" (Williamson, Helpmann), "Raymonda" (Glazounov, Nureyev after Petipa), "Divertissements," "Sun Music" (Peter Sculthorpe, Helpmann)

*Company Manager:*John H. Wilson
*Press:*Noel Pelly, Martin Feinstein, Lilian Libman, Dale Heapps, James Murtha
*Stage Managers:*John Moulton, Terry Martin, Gilbert Hemsley

* Closed Feb. 7, 1971 after limited engagement of 16 performances.

"Don Quixote" Top Left: Lucette Aldous, Rudolf
Nureyev in "Don Quixote"

Garth Welch, Lucette Aldous Above: Rudolf Nureyev, Lucette Aldous in "Don Quixote"

"Raymonda, Act III"

NEW YORK CITY CENTER

Opened Tuesday, January 12, 1971.*
S. Hurok presents under the auspices of City Center
of Music and Drama:

MAZOWSZE
POLISH SONG AND
DANCE COMPANY

Founder, Tadeusz Sygietynski; Artistic Director, Ar-
rangements, Costumes, Staging, Folk Song Adaptations,
Mira Ziminska-Sygietynska; Lighting, Wojciech Nasio-
rowski

SOLOISTS

Maria Bedlicka, Ryszard Brozek, Jan Dybul, Zdzislawa
Grabkowska, Krystyna Jarczyk, Michal Jarczyk, Jozef
Oledzki, Stanislaw Paduchowski, Jerzy Rozycki, Andrzej
Tatarewicz, Urszula Wnuk, Henryk Wrobel, Witold
Zapala, Stanislaw Jopek (vocal)

PROGRAM

"Chodzony: Round and Round," "Oberek from
Opoczno," "Dances and Songs from Rozbar," "Court-
ship of Krzemienice," "Rzeszow Dances and Songs,"
"Dances from Biskupizna Wielkopolska," "Shepherds'
Songs and Dances from Jurgow," "Kaszuby Dances and
Songs," "Dances from Lublin," "Carnival in Wil-
amowice," "Stub," "Jokes and Dances from Podegrod-
zie," "Cracow Dances and Songs," "Krakowiak," "Polo-
naise and Mazurka," "Polka Mazurka," "Cieszyn
Songs," "Kujawiak," "Tatra Dances and Songs,"
"Dances from Zywiec," "Polish Songs," "The Lowicz
Maiden," "Mazurka," "Oberek," Finale

General Manager: Marianna Sygietynska
Company Manager: Kurt Neumann
Press: Martin Feinstein, Dale Heapps, James Murtha,
Edward Parkinson, Leila Sturm
Stage Managers: Waclaw Zukowski, Jeffery Longe

* Closed Jan. 24, 1971 after limited engagement of 16
performances.

NEW YORK CITY CENTER
Opened Tuesday, February 9, 1971.*
Sheldon Soffer presents:

INBAL DANCE THEATRE OF ISRAEL

Founder-Director-Choreographer, Sara Levi-Tanai; Administrative Director, Gila Toledano; Musical Consultant, Shulamit Vibal; Sets, Z. Halperin, M. Cohen, Dani Karavan, Arnon Adar, Naftali Besem; Costumes, Ofra Burla, Anatol Gurevitch

COMPANY

Lea Avraham, Lea Ben David, Ilana Cohen, Yehudith Debi, Nissim Garame, Aviva Haziz, Ruth Razabi, Sara Shikarchi, Malka Zuberi, and singers Hannah Benyamini, Dina Yefet, Dani Ben-Moshe, Zadok Zuberi

PROGRAM

New York premiere of "Ruth in the Field" (Ovadia Tuvia, Levi-Tanai), "Shabbat Shalom" (Mordechai Zeira, Levi-Tanai), New York premiere of "Wild Rose" (Tuvia, Levi-Tanai), "Yemenite Wedding" (Traditional, Levi-Tanai), "Women" (Yemenite-Oriental melodies, Levi-Tanai), "Carry Us to the Desert" (Israeli Folk Songs, Levi-Tanai)

General Manager: Mary Lou Tuffin
Company Manager: Tennent McDaniel
Press: Seymour Krawitz, Patricia McLean Krawitz, Bruce Silke
Stage Managers: Raphael Cohen, Moshe Cohen

* Closed Feb. 14, 1971 after limited engagement of 9 performances.

Mula & Haramaty Photos

Top Right: Schlomo Haziz, Lea Avraham in "Shabbat Shalom"

"Carry Us to the Desert"

Ilana Cohen, Schlomo Haziz in "Wild Rose"
Above: "Yemenite Wedding"

NEW YORK CITY CENTER
Tuesday, April 13, 1971.*
Howard Dando in association with City Center of
Music and Drama presents:

LES GRANDS BALLETS
CANADIENS

Founder-Director, Ludmilla Chiriaeff; Associate Artis-
tic Director, Fernand Nault; General Manager, Uriel G.
Luft; Resident Choreographers, Fernand Nault, Brydon
Paige; Ballet Mistress, Linda Stearns; Assistant Ballet
Master, Daniel Jackson; Conductor, Paul Duplessis;
Costumes, Nicole Martinet, Francois Barbeau; Lighting,
Nicholas Cernovitch; Sets, David Jenkins; Sound, Mi-
chel Beaulieu; Technical Director, Jean Fananas

COMPANY

Richard Beaty, Alexandre Belin, Erica Jayne, Hilda
Morales, Vincent Warren, William Josef, Hae Shik Kim,
Heinz Spoerli, John Stanzel Russell Chambers, Leslie-
May Downs, Judith Karstens, Mannie Rowe, Laszlo
Tamasik, James Bates, Richard Bouchard, Francine
Boucher, Barbara Bourget, James Boyd, Lorna Cameron,
Louise Dore, John Gardner, Gerry Gilbert, Eileen
Heath, Barbara Jacobs, Carole Landry, Manon Larin,
Maurice Lemay, Helen McKergow, Reva Pincusoff,
Renald Rabu, Cathy Sharp, Janet Snyder, Andris Toppe,
Lorne Toumine, Douglas Wassell, Bruce Weavil,
Laeleen Winchiu, Barbara Withey, David Graniero

PROGRAM

"Hip and Straight" (Paul Duplessis, Fernand Nault),
"Tommy" (Peter Townshend-John Entwistle-Keith
Moon, Fernand Nault)

*General Manager:*George Elmer
*Company Managers:*Alfred Fischer, Guy Lamarre
*Press:*Seymour Krawitz, Martin Shwartz,
Yolande Rivard
*Stage Managers:*G. Allison Elmer, Maxine Glorsky,
Felix Smith

* Closed Apr. 25, 1971 after limited engagement of 16
performances.

Heinz Spoerli
Above: Erica Jayne

Alexandre Belin

Alexandre Belin, Hilda Morales
Top: Alexandre Belin in "Tommy"

Hilda Morales, Alexandre Belin
in "Tommy"

NEW YORK CITY CENTER

Opened Tuesday, April 27, 1971.*
City Center of Music and Drama (Norman Singer, Executive Director) presents:

THE ALVIN AILEY AMERICAN DANCE THEATER

Artistic Director-Choreographer, Alvin Ailey; Associate Director-Ballet Master, Ramon Segarra General Manager, Ivy Clarke; Production Manager, William Hammond; Lighting, Chenault Spence; Administrator, Mary Colquhoun; Press, Meg Gordean, Samuel Lurie; Conductor, Ronald Isaac.

COMPANY

Dudley Williams, Judith Jamison, Kelvin Rotardier, Consuelo Atlas, Linda Kent, Clive Thompson, Sylvia Waters, Ramon Segarra, Morton Winston, John Parks, Hector Mercado, Leland Schwantes, Mari Kajiwara, Kenneth Pearl, Rosamond Lynn, Gail Reese, Lee Harper, Ronald Dunham

GUEST ARTIST: Lynn Seymour of The Royal Ballet

REPERTOIRE

"Blues Suite" (Traditional, Ailey), "Flowers" (Pink Floyd-Pink Faith-Janis Joplin, Ailey), "Revelations" (Traditional, Ailey), Premiere Apr. 28, 1971 of "Choral Dances" (Benjamin Britten, Alvin Ailey; Costumes, A. Christina Giannini; Lighting, Nicola Cernovitch) with company, "Gymnopedies" (Satie, Ailey), "Streams" (Kabelac, Ailey), "Dance for Six" (Vivaldi, Trisler), Premiere May 4, 1971 of "Cry" (Alice Coltrane, Laura Nyro, The Voice of East Harlem; Alvin Ailey; Lighting, Chenault Spence) danced by Judith Jamison, "Knoxville: Summer of 1915" (Barber, Ailey), "Icarus" (Matsushita, Hoving), New York Premiere May 5, 1971 of "Child of the Earth" (Hugh Masekela, Kelvin Rotardier; Lighting, Chenault Spence) danced by Consuelo Atlas, Kelvin Rotardier

* Closed May 9, 1971 after limited engagement of 16 performances.

Jack Mitchell, Rosemary Winckley Photos

Top Left: Alvin Ailey, Judith Jamison

Judith Jamison in Premiere of "Cry"
(May 4, 1971)

Consuelo Atlas, Judith Jamison, Kelvin Rotardier, Hector Mercado in "Revelations"

Judith Jamison, Kelvin Rotardier in "Masekela Langage"
Top: Dudley Williams, Hector Mercado, Sylvia
Waters in "Streams"

THE CITY CENTER AMERICAN DANCE MARATHON

January 18 through March 13, 1971

ANTA THEATRE

Opened Monday, January 18, 1971.*
City Center of Music and Drama (Norman Singer, Executive Director) presents The American Dance Season (Charles Reinhart, Executive Producer) featuring:

THE ALVIN AILEY AMERICAN DANCE THEATER

Artistic Director-Choreographer, Alvin Ailey; Associate Director-Ballet Master, Ramon Segarra; General Manager, Ivy Clarke; Production Manager, William Hammond; Lighting, Jennifer Tipton, Chenault Spence; Administrator, Mary Colquhoun; Press, Meg Gordean, Samuel Lurie.

COMPANY

Dudley Williams, Judith Jamison, Kelvin Rotardier, Linda Kent, Consuelo Atlas, Michele Murray, Clive Thompson, John Parks, Ramon Segarra, Renee Rose, Sylvia Waters, Mari Kajiwara, Leland Schwantes, Morton Winston, Hector Mercado, Alfonso Figueroa, Kenneth Pearl, Rosamond Lynn, Gail Reese, Lee Harper, Ronald Dunham Brother John Sellers and The Howard Roberts Chorale and Jazz Ensemble

GUEST ARTIST: Lynn Seymour of The Royal Ballet

REPERTOIRE

"Toccata" (Schiffrin, Beatty), "Reflections in D" (Ellington, Ailey), "Blues Suite" (Traditional, Ailey), Premiere (Jan. 18, 1971) of "Archipelago" (Andre Boucourechliev, Ailey; Costumes, Evadne Giannini) with the company, "Revelations" (Traditional, Ailey), "Streams" (Kabelac, Ailey), "Masekela Langage" (Masakela, Ailey), "Congo Tango Palace" (Davis-Evans, Beatty), "The Beloved" (Hamilton, Horton), Premiere Jan. 25, 1971 of "Flowers" (Big Brother & The Holding Company, Pink Floyd, Blind Faith, Janis Joplin; Alvin Ailey; Costumes, Christina Giannini) with Lynn Seymour, Ramon Segarra, and Leland Schwantes, Hector Mercado, Kenneth Pearl, Morton Winston, John Parks, Ronald Dunham, "The Road of the Phoebe Snow" (Ellington-Strayhorn, Beatty), "Journey" (Ives, Trisler).

* Closed Jan. 30, 1971 after limited engagement of 16 performances.

Jack Mitchell, Rosemary Winckley Photos

"Revelations"

Consuelo Atlas, Clive Thompson in "Revelations"
Above: Clive Thompson, Judith Jamison in "Blues Suite"

Judith Jamison, Dudley Williams, Kelvin Rotardier in "Icarus"

Lynn Seymour, Kelvin Rotardier in "Flowers" (Premiere Jan. 25, 1971) Top: Lynn Seymour in "Flowers"

Ramon Segarra in "Archipelago" (Premiere Jan. 18, 1971) Top: (L) "The Road of the Phoebe Snow" (R)
Consuelo Atlas, Clive Thompson in "Child of the Earth" (Premiere May 5, 1971)
ALVIN AILEY AMERICAN DANCE THEATER

Dudley Williams in "Reflections in D"
Top: "Toccata"

Linda Kent, Judith Jamison, Sylvia Waters
in "Revelations"

ANTA THEATRE

Monday, February 1, 1971.*
City Center of Music and Drama presents the
American Dance Marathon with:

LOUIS FALCO COMPANY OF FEATURED DANCERS

Artistic Director-Choreographer, Louis Falco; Artistic
Adviser, William Katz; Associate Directors, Jennifer
Muller, Juan Antonio; Lighting, Edward Effron

COMPANY

Louis Falco, Jennifer Muller, Juan Antonio, Carla Maxwell, Georgiana Holmes, Matthew Diamond, Mary Jane
Eisenberg, Clyde Morgan

PROGRAM

World Premiere of "Ibid" (Maatthews Kheaann Khris-
tiaann, Louis Falco; Decor and Costumes, Stanley
Landsman), "Huescape" (Pierre Schaeffer-Lasry-
Baschet), World Premiere of "The Sleepers" (Decor and
Costumes, William Katz) danced by Jennifer Muller,
Georgiana Holmes, Matthew Diamond, Juan Antonio;
"Caviar" (Pot), "Timewright"

* Repeated on Wednesday matinee, Feb. 3, and Friday,
Feb. 5, 1971.

Jack Mitchell Photos

Left: Louis Falco in "Timewright"

Louis Falco, Carla Maxwell, Jennifer Muller, Juan Antonio, Mary Jane Eisenberg, Matthew Diamond, Georgiana Holmes in "Caviar"

Juan Antonio, Jennifer Muller, Louis Falco in "Huescape" Top: Carla Maxwell, Jennifer Muller, Louis Falco in "Timewright"

Georgiana Holmes
in "Caviar"

ANTA THEATRE

Opened Tuesday, February 2, 1971.*
City Center of Music and Drama presents the
American Dance Season with:

PEARL LANG AND
DANCE COMPANY

Director-Choreographer, Pearl Lang; Conductor, Simon Sadoff; Sets, Nina Yankowitz; Costumes, Christina Giannini, Francois Barbeau; Lighting, Gerald Rothman, Tom Skelton; Production Supervisor, Ken Billington; Production Assistant, Hugh Harvey; Representative, Philip Bell

COMPANY

Marcia Plevin, Tonia Shimin, Elisa Monte, Dorothy Zito, Traci Musgrove, Sherry Sable, Eleanor McCoy, Mary Price, Patricia Jones, Daniel Maloney, Lar Roberson, David Roche, Aaron Osborne, Phillip J. Jonson, Darrell Barnett

GUEST ARTIST: Richard Gain

PROGRAM

"Sharjuhm" (a work in progress; Alan Hovhaness, Lang), "Persephone" (Kupferman, Lang), "Piece for Brass" (Alvin Etler, Lang), "The Brood" (Pierre Schaefer, Richard Kuch)

* Repeated Feb. 3, and Feb. 6, 1971.

Right: Daniel Maloney, Pearl Lang in "Shirah"

Kenneth Pearl, Pearl Lang in "Shirah"
Above: "Piece for Brass"

Lar Robinson, Daniel Maloney, Kenneth Pearl in
"Piece for Brass"

ANTA THEATRE

Thursday & Saturday, February 4, 6, 1971.
City Center of Music and Drama presents The
American Dance Marathon with:

ELEO POMARE DANCE COMPANY

Artistic Director and Choreographer, Eleo Pomare;
Managing Director, Michael E. Levy; Lighting, Gary
Harris; Costumes and Props, James Snodgrass; Business
Manager, Press, William Moore, Jr.

COMPANY

Frank Ashley, Shawneequa Baker-Scott, Lillian
Coleman, Dyane Harvey, Carole Johnson, Strody
Meekins, Dianne Nelson, Jacques Patarozzi, Roberta
Pikser, Eleo Pomare, Ernest Royaster, Shirley Rushing,
James Snodgrass, assisted by Chantal Belhumeurt, Su-
san Congdon, Gertrude Sherwood

PROGRAM

"Las Desenamoradas" (Coltrane, Pomare), World Premiere of "Movements" (Morton Subotnick, Eleo Pomare), "Two Excerpts from Black on Black" (Sound
Collage, Pomare), "Blues for the Jungle" (Traditional,
Pomare), "Narcissus Rising" (Collage, Pomare), Premiere of "Burnt Ash" (Collage by Michael Levy, Eleo
Pomare), "Climb" (Kelemen, Pomare)

Camera Associates Photos

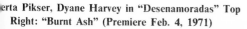
…erta Pikser, Dyane Harvey in "Desenamoradas" Top
Right: "Burnt Ash" (Premiere Feb. 4, 1971)

Jacques Patarozzi, Strody Meekins, Frank Ashley
in "Movements" (Premiere Feb. 4, 1971)

JACK MITC

ANTA THEATRE

Opened Monday, February 8, 1971.*
City Center of Music and Drama (Norman Singer, Executive Director) presents the American Dance Season (Charles Reinhart, Producer) with:

PAUL TAYLOR DANCE COMPANY

Director-Choreographer, Paul Taylor; Conductor, Simon Sadoff; Lighting, Jennifer Tipton; Costumes, George Tacit, Alec Sutherland, Alex Katz, John Rawlings

COMPANY

Paul Taylor, Bettie De Jong, Daniel Williams, Carolyn Adams, Jane Kosminsky, Eileen Cropley, Senta Driver, Earnest Morgan, Britt Swanson, Nicholas Gunn

REPERTOIRE

"Lento" (Hayden), new version of "Agathe's Tale" (Surinach), "Post Meridian" (Evelyn Lohoefer DeBoeck), "Foreign Exchange" (Subotnick; Set, Alex Katz; Costumes, Alec Sutherland; Premiere May 5, 1970), "Big Bertha" (St. Louis Melody Museum-John Herbert McDowell, Paul Taylor; Set and Costumes, Alec Sutherland; Premiere Feb. 9, 1971), "Public Domain" (McDowell), "Churchyard" (Cosmos Savage, Taylor; Costumes, Alec Sutherland; Premiere Dec. 10, 1969), "From Sea to Shining Sea" (McDowell), "Aureole" (Handel), "Private Domain" (Iannis Xenakis, Taylor; Costumes, Alex Katz; Premiere May 7, 1969)

General Manager: Alec Sutherland
Press: Samuel Lurie
Stage Managers: Judith Daykin, Rick Thorkelson

* Closed Feb. 20, 1971 after limited engagement of 16 performances

Jack Mitchell Photos

Carolyn Adams, Daniel Williams, Eileen Cropley, Paul Taylor, Bettie De Jong in "Churchyard"
Top: (L) Carolyn Adams, Daniel Williams in "Lento"

Paul Taylor, Daniel Williams, Eileen Cropley,
Earnest Morgan in "Agathe's Tale" Top: Paul
Taylor, Eileen Cropley in "Churchyard"

Paul Taylor in "Aureole"

Bettie De Jong, Eileen Cropley, Paul Taylor, Carolyn Adams in "Big Bertha" (Premiere Feb. 9, 1917) Top: (L) Bettie De Jong, Paul Taylor, Daniel Williams, Carolyn Adams, Britt Swanson, Nicholas Gunn, Jane Kosminsky, Eileen Cropley, Senta Driver in "From Sea to Shining Sea" (R) Jane Kosminsky, Carolyn Adams, Eileen Cropley, Senta Driver, Nicholas Gunn in "Post Meridian" (Premiere May 5, 1971)

Paul Taylor, Bettie De Jong in "Post Meridian"
Top: Daniel Williams, Earnest Morgan, Nicholas
Gunn in "Churchyard"

Paul Taylor, Bettie De Jong, Senta Driver, Carolyn Adams
in "Public Domain"   Top: Eileen Cropley, Paul Taylor,
Bettie De Jong in "Churchyard"

PAUL TAYLOR DANCE COMPANY

ANTA THEATRE
Opened Monday, February 22, 1971.*
The City Center American Dance Marathon
presents:

NIKOLAIS DANCE THEATRE

Artistic Director, Choreographer, Sound Scores, Costumes, Lighting by Alwin Nikolais; Company Managing Director, Murray Farr; Technical Director, George Gracey; Stage Manager, Ruth Grauert; Sound Engineer, John Davis; Costume Director, Frank Garcia; Administrative Director, Betty Young; Press, Meg Gordean, Samuel Lurie; Technical Assistants, David Logan, James Teeters.

COMPANY

Tandy Beal, Rick Biles, Suzanne McDermaid, Claudia Melrose, Wanda Pruska, Bob Beswick, Emery Hermans, Thea Martinez, Gerald Otte, Robert Solomon

UNDERSTUDIES: Kathleen Gaskin, James Teeters

REPERTOIRE

"Divertissement II: Quintet from Sanctum, Trio from Vaudeville of the Elements, Group Dance from Sanctum," "Structures," "Tent," "Divertissement I: Quintet from Sanctum, Trio from Vaudeville of the Elements, Noumenom and Tensile Involvement from Masks, Props, and Mobiles," "Echo," "Tower from Vaudeville of the Elements," "Somniloquy," World Premiere Feb. 25, 1971 of "Scenario"

* Closed March 6, 1971 after limited engagement of 16 performances.

Brynn Manley, Susan Schiff-Faludi Photos

"Somniloquy" (also Top Left)

"Tent" (also above)

"Echo"
Above: "Tent"

"Tower" Above: "Structures"
Top: "Noumenom"

NIKOLAIS DANCE THEATRE

ANTA THEATRE

Monday, March 8, 1971.*
City Center of Music and Drama (Norman Singer, Executive Director) presents The American Dance Season (Charles Reinhart, Executive Producer) with:

DANCE THEATRE OF HARLEM

Executive and Artistic Director, Arthur Mitchell; Associate Artistic Director, Karel Shook; Musical Director, Tania Leon; Administrative Director, Kathleen Stanford-Grant; Production Manager and Lighting Designer, G. V. Lowther; Pianists, Tania Leon, Edward Muller; Sets, James French; Costumes, Bernard Johnson

COMPANY

Lydia Abarca, Olinda Davis, Yvonne Hall, Virginia Johnson, Pamela Jones, Susan Lovelle, Gayle McKinney, Melva Murray, Cassandra Phifer, Patricia Ricketts, Sheila Rohan, Ronda Sampson, Roslyn Sampson, Llanchie Stevenson Gerald Banks, Homer Bryant, Lazar Dano, Clover Mathis, Edward Moore, Ronald Perry, Walter Raines, William Scott, Samuel Smalls, Derek Williams

PROGRAM

"Concerto Barocco" (Bach, Balanchine), "Afternoon of a Faun" (Debussy, Robbins), Premiere of "Fun and Games" (Piero Piccioni, Arthur Mitchell), "Rhythmetron" (Marlos Nobre, Arthur Mitchell)
*Wednesday matinee, March 10, 1971 the company performed "Design for Strings" (Tchaikovsky, Taras), "Afternoon of a Faun," "Biosfera" (Nobre, Mitchell), "Fete Noire" (Shostakovich, Mitchell). On Friday, March 12, 1971 the company danced "Fete Noire," "Fun and Games," "Rhythmetron"

"Rhythmetron" Top Right: Arthur Mitchell (C) and company

ANTA THEATRE

Tuesday, March 9, 1971.*
City Center of Music and Drama presents The
American Dance Season with:

ERICK HAWKINS DANCE COMPANY

Artistic Director-Choreographer, Erick Hawkins; Conductor, Gerald Schwarz; Lighting, Robert Engstrom; Costumes, Ralph Lee; Designs, Ralph Dorazio; Associate Managers, Mary Jane Spencer, Bradford W. Lewis; Music, Lucia Dlugoszewski.

COMPANY

Beverly Grown, Darrell Barnett, Carol Conway, Bill Groves, Erick Hawkins, Natalie Richman, Lillo Way, Robert Yohn

PROGRAM

"Lords of Persia" (Dlugoszewski, Hawkins), "Naked Leopard" (Zoltan Kodaly, Hawkins), "Black Lake" (Dlugoszewski, Hawkins), World Premiere of "Of Love" (Lucia Dlugoszewski, Erick Hawkins) danced by Beverly Brown, Carol Conway, Lillot Way, Bill Groves, Erick Hawkins, Robert Yohn

* Repeated Wednesday evening and Saturday matinee, March 10, 13, 1971.

Ted Yaple Photos

Right: Lillo Way in "Black Lake"

"Black Lake" (also above)

Erick Hawkins, Robert Yohn in "Black Lake"
Above: Natalie Richman, Robert Yohn
in "Black Lake"

70

ANTA THEATRE
Thursday & Saturday, March 11, 13, 1971.
City Center of Music and Drama presents The
American Dance Marathon with:

DON REDLICH DANCE COMPANY

Artistic Director-Choreographer, Don Redlich; Lighting, Jennifer Tipton; Costumes, Sally Ann Parsons; Film, Jackson Tiffany; Stage Manager, Fred Barry; Press, Meg Gordean, Samuel Lurie.

COMPANY

Don Redlich, Elina Mooney, Luly Santangelo, Irene Feigenheimer, William Siegenfeld

PROGRAM

"Jibe" (Norma Dalby), "Air Antique" (Lukas Foss), "Cahoots" performed in silence, "Implex: Tabloid (Radio Collage), "Poco Curante" (Tom Boutilier), World Premiere of "Tristan, Isolde, Aida, Hansel and Gretel" (John Herbert McDowell, Don Redlich), "Earthling" (Debussy), "Slouching Towards Bethlehem" (Essays by Joan Didion)

Jack Mitchell Photos

Right: Elina Mooney, Luly Santangelo, Don Redlich, Irene Feigenheimer, Billy Siegenfeld in Premiere of "Tristan, Isolde, Aida, Hansel and Gretel" (Mar. 11, 1971)

Don Redlich in "Earthling"

Luly Santangelo, Irene Feigenheimer, Billy Siegenfeld, Elina Mooney

NEW YORK DANCE FESTIVAL
Delacorte Theater, Central Park
August 26 through Sept. 6, 1970

Presented by the New York Shakespeare Festival in association with the Lepercq Foundation; Executive Producer, Donald Saddler; Lighting, Martin Aronstein; Technical Director, Michael Hopper; Stage Manager, R. Derek Swire; Press, Merle Debuskey, Faith Geer

Wednesday, August 26, 1970.
LOUIS FALCO & COMPANY OF FEATURED DANCERS: Jennifer Muller, Juan Antonio, Carla Maxwell, Charles Phipps, Georgiana Holmes, Matthew Diamond, Mary Jane Eisenberg in "Timewright" and "Caviar" (Pot, Falco)
AMERICAN BALLET COMPANY: Eliot Feld (Director), Olga Janke, Elizabeth Lee, Christine Sarry, John Sowinski, Marilyn D'Honau, Karen Kelly, Christine Kono, Cristina Stirling, Eve Walstrum, Kerry Williams, Larry Grenier, Edward Henkel, Kenneth Hughes, Daniel Levins, James Lewis, Richard Munro, Lance Westergard in "Harbinger" (Prokofieff, Field), and "Intermezzo" (Brahms, Feld)
LUIS RIVERA & COMPANY: Luis Rivera, Marta Castillo, Moraima Munos, Domingo Alvarado, Emilio Prados, Nino Garcia in "Fandango," "Aires de Cadiz," "Fantasia Madrilena," "Con mi Soledad"

Thursday, August 27, 1970.
AMERICAN BALLET COMPANY in "Harbinger" and "Early Songs"
LOUIS FALCO & COMPANY OF FEATURED DANCERS in "Huescape" and "Caviar"
DONALD McKAYLE DANCE COMPANY: Roger Briant, Rodney Griffin, Sally Neal, John Parks, Clay Taliaferro, David Hatch-Walker in "Rainbow 'Round My Shoulder"

Friday, August 28, 1970.
AMERICAN BALLET COMPANY in "Harbinger," and "Intermezzo"
LOUIS FALCO & COMPANY in "Argot," and "Timewright"
LUIS RIVERA & COMPANY in Spanish dances

Saturday, August 29, 1970.
AMERICAN BALLET COMPANY in "Harbinger" and "Early Songs"
LOUIS FALCO & COMPANY in "Timewright," and "Caviar"
DONALD McKAYLE DANCE CO. in "Rainbow 'Round My Shoulder"

Sunday, August 30, 1970.
AMERICAN BALLET COMPANY in "Harbinger," and "Intermezzo"
THE BLACK DANCE UNION: Loretta Abbott, Ronald Dunham, Winston Hemsley, Elinor McCoy, Michael Peters, Arlene Rolant, Morton Winston in "π r = Love," and "Where to Go?"
MURRAY LOUIS DANCE COMPANY: Murray Louis, Michael Ballard, Raymond Johnson, Lyn Levene, Sarah Shelton, Francis Tabor in "Go-6," and "Proximities"

Monday, August 31, 1970.
THE BLACK DANCE UNION in "π r = Love," and "Where to Go?"
MURRAY LOUIS DANCE COMPANY in "Go-6," and "Proximities"
AMERICAN BALLET COMPANY in "Harbinger," and "Early Songs"

Tuesday, September 1, 1970.
BALLET BRIO: Sandra Balestracci, Rosemarie Menes, Carlyn Muchmore, Mario Ignisci, Dale Muchmore, Anthony Salatino, Ellen Glemby, Candace Itow, Jacqueline McKannay, Jennifer Potts, Laura Rzasa, Christine Varjan in "Images in Five" (Elgar, Thomas Andrew), and "The Snare" (Bartok, Andrew)
MURRAY LOUIS DANCE COMPANY in "Go-6," and "Proximities"
BONNIE MATHIS and DENNIS WAYNE in "After Eden" (Hoiby, Butler)
MURA DEHN'S TRADITIONAL JAZZ DANCE COMPANY: Avon Long, Cook and Brown, Chuck Green, Albert Gibson, Baby Laurence, Louise Parks, Bubber Gaines, Sandra Gibson, Buster Brown, Letitia Jay, Bill Washington, Big Stomp, James Cross, Zizi Richards in "From Rag to Rock"

Jack Mitchell Photos

Milton Oleaga Photo

Top Right: Juan Antonio, Mary Jane Eisenberg, Matthew Diamond, Georgia Holmes in "Caviar" (Louis Falco Co.) Below: Luis Rivera

Murray Louis, Frances Tabor, Michael Ballard, Sara Shel Raymond Johnson, Phyllis Lamhut in "Proximities" (Murray Louis Co.)

Wednesday, September 2, 1970.
BALLET BRIO in "Images in Five," and "Battered Bacchanal" (Ponchielli, Andrew)
DONALD McKAYLE DANCE COMPANY in "Rainbow 'Round My Shoulder"
MURA DEHN'S TRADITIONAL JAZZ DANCE COMPANY in "From Rag to Rock"
LAR LUBOVITCH AND COMPANY: Takako Osakawa, Teresa Hill, Judith Liefer, Martha Ingle, David Hatch-Walker, Kenneth Hughes, Lar Robeson in "Ecstasy" (Messian, Lubovitch)

Thursday, September 3, 1970.
DONALD McKAYLE DANCE COMPANY in "Rainbow 'Round My Shoulder"
MURA DEHN'S TRADITIONAL JAZZ DANCE COMPANY in "From Rag to Rock"
LAR LUBOVITCH AND COMPANY in "Ecstasy"
MATTEO AND THE INDO-AMERICAN DANCE COMPANY: Holly Armstrong, Bella Birnbaum, Dennis Diamond, Matthew Diamond, Corinne Dieli, Janet Krause, Larry Landau, Dina Manhim, Wendy Mansfield, Socorro Santiago, Terry Yorysh, Dawn Young in "Durbar" (Traditional, Matteo), and "Bharata Natya Vrinda" (Arranged, Matteo)

Friday, September 4, 1970.
BALLET BRIO in "Images in Five," and "Battered Bacchanal"
LAR LUBOVITCH AND COMPANY in "Ecstasy"
BONNIE MATHIS AND DENNIS WAYNE in "After Eden"
THE DANCE COMPANY OF THE NATIONAL CENTER OF AFRO-AMERICAN ARTISTS: Dolores Browne, Annette Brown, Jacque Lynne Curry, Charles Augins, Danny Sloan in "Bring My Servant Home" (Folk, Talley Beatty)

Saturday matinee, September 5, 1970.
THE DANCE COMPANY OF THE NATIONAL CENTER OF AFRO-AMERICAN ARTISTS in "Bring My Servant Home"
BALLET TEAM: Beverley Brown, Mariano Garcia, Danny Giagni, Christina Hamm, Teresa Hill, Judith Jenkins, Alex Kotimsky, Clay Taliaferro, Alan Tung, Dana Wolfe, Armando Zetina in "Ballet Crossroads" (Choreographers, Percival Borde, Vincente Nebrada, Gary Rambach, Stuart Hodes)

Saturday between matinee and evening, September 5, 1970.
ELLEN KLEIN'S MIME TROUP AND MEDICINE SHOW: Thomas Appell, Chris Collins, Dick Daley, Nathaniel Eskin, Carol Hollett, Katie Kelly, Stephanie Kesten, Ellen Klein, Marilyn Lerner, Eve Murray, Kevin Quinn, Lincoln Scott, Alan Shields, Jack Smith, Alice Tarantal, Richard Van Buren, Joe White, Wendy Wray, The Apostolic Family (David Ames, Genie Ames, John Townley)

Saturday evening, September 5, 1970.
BALLET TEAM in "Love Play" (originally "responsive Reading" with music by Sandy Bull; Choreography, Stuart Hodes), and "Dance for a Film Whale Trip" (Susan Berger, Hodes) danced by Dana Wolfe and Clay Taliaferro
RUDY PEREZ DANCE THEATER: Barbara Roan, Anthony Lagiglia, Leonard Hanitchak, Ellen Jacobs, Rudy Perez, Paul Plumidore, Ellen Robbins, Wendy Summit in "Annual, Part II" (Perez), and "Coverage" (Perez) danced by Rudy Perez
TWYLA THARP AND COMPANY: Willma Davis, Doug Dunn, Isabel Garcia-Lorca, Rael Lamb, Sara Rudner, Rose Marie Wright in "Fugue Is a Trio," and "100's"
CLIFF KEUTER with Irene Feigenheimer, Elina Mooney, Karla Wolfangle in "The Game Man and the Ladies" (Ezra Sims, Keuter), and "Dream a Little Dream of Me, Sweetheart" (John Herbert McDowell, Keuter)
DANCE THEATRE WORKSHOP COMPANY: Ze'eva Cohen, Jeff Duncan, Lenore Latimer, Aaron Osborne, Lillo Way in "Resonances" (Pierre Henry, Jeff Duncan)

Sunday, September 6, 1970.
BALLET TEAM in "Ballet Crossroads"
MATTEO AND THE INDO-AMERICAN DANCE COMPANY IN "Durbar", and "Bharata Natya Vrinda"

Top Right: Indo-American Dance Company in "Durbar" Below: Lar Lubovitch, Takako Asakawa in "Ecstasy"

John Littlewood Photo

Jack Mitchell Photo

Edward Effron Photo

Janet Aaron, Irene Feigenheimer, Cliff Keuter, in "The Game Man and the Ladies"

CHARLES WEIDMAN
and
THEATRE DANCE COMPANY

EXPRESSION OF TWO ARTS THEATRE

Every weekend during the season; Charles Weidman, Director-Choreographer; Administrative Assistant, Maya Doray; Lighting, Charles Attard, Murray Van Dyke; Press, Janet Towner, Margaret O'Sullivan.

COMPANY

Selby Beebe, Maya Doray, Marjie Havelin, Myra Hushansky, Donna Mondonara, Margaret O'Sullivan, Janet Towner, Janice Wodynski, Max Schufer, Charles Wilson, Michael Wodynski

REPERTOIRE

"Christmas Oratorio" (Bach), "Easter Oratorio" (Bach), "Brahms Waltzes," "Lynchtown" (Engle), "Bargain Counter" (Engle), "Opus 51" (Fine), "Diabelli Variations" (Diabelli), "Submerged Cathedral" (Debussy), "Saints, Sinners and Scriabin" (Scriabin), "Kinetic Pantomime" (Debussy), "Images" (Debussy, Peter Hamilton), "Children Are Crying" (Betsy Chapman, Donna Mondanaro), "Palms" (Bach), "Our Hearts and Eyes Overflow" (Bach), "Dialogues" (Bloch), "Et Vous Mer" (Pierce), "Letter to Mrs. Bixby" (Hindemith), "Study" (Novak), "In the Beginning" (Debussy), "Three Gymnopedias" (choreography by Janet Towner, Donna Mondanaro)

Frank Derbas Photos

Charles Weidman (also top left) in "Bargain Counter"

"Bargain Counter"
Top: "Lynchtown"

"Opus 51"

DANCE PROGRAMS AT THE CUBICULO

Philip Mesiter, Artistic Director   Elaine Sulka, Managing Director

THE CUBICULO
Monday, June 8, 1970.
The Cubiculo presents:

INDRA-NILA
in
"Portrait of Shiva"

Choreography, Indra-Nila; Lighting, V. Ramamurthy;
Technical Director, William Lambert.

PROGRAM

"Ganesh Stuti," "Natanam Adinar," "Jagat Janani,"
"Suddha Paityakaran," "Gowri Kalyanam," "Sringara
Lahari," "Maha Ganapati," "Kartikeya Music," "Pea-
cock," "Adavum Solluval Aval," "Kurathi," "Thillana"

Indra-Nila

THE CUBICULO
Monday, June 22, 1970.*
The Cubiculo presents:

RUDY PEREZ DANCE THEATER

Director-Choreographer, Rudy Perez; Choreographers, Barbara Roan, Anthony LaGiglia

COMPANY

Rudy Perez, Barbara Roan, Anthony LaGiglia, Tom
Borek, Ellen Robbins, Wendy Perron, Wendy Summit,
Harold Silver, Wayne Adams

PROGRAM

"Annual: Part 2" (Perez), and premieres (commissioned
by The Cubiculo) of "Coverage" (Perez), "(Ocean)"
(Roan), "If there is a garden..." (LaGiglia)

* Repeated June 23, 24, 1970.

Herbert Migdoll Photo

THE CUBICULO
Sunday, June 28, 1970.*
The Cubiculo presents:

ROBERT STREICHER
PEGGY CICIERSKA

PROGRAM: Premieres of "Implode" and "Device"
choreographed and danced by Robert Streicher,
"Seascape" choreographed and danced by Peggy Cicierska, "Birth Space" choreographed by Miss Cicierska,
danced by Dana Mann, Joan Ann Mendel, Mary Miller,
Zoey Noyes, Luanna Reid, Katie Sakol, Ann Vachon,
Marris Wolff

* Repeated June 29, 30, 1970.

**Barbara Roan, Wendy Summit, Stephen Buck,
Rudy Perez in "Annual"**

THE CUBICULO

Monday and Tuesday, July 20, 21, 1970.
The Cubiculo presents:

ASHA DEVI
Court and Temple Dances
of India, Bali, Japan

Narrator, Barbara Seddon; Demonstration of Kishi No Yanagi, Margaret Newman; Tabla, Bihari Sharma; Flute, Suresh Shukla; Lighting, V. Ramamurthy; Technician, William Lambert; Stages Manager, Ellen Schwartz

PROGRAM

"Khamba Thoibi," "Jatiswaram," "Shabdam," "Padam," "The Lotus and the Bee," "Kathac," "Chandra Metu," "Pung Cholam," "Kishi No Yanagi"

Asha Devi, Bihari Sharma

THE CUBICULO

Monday & Tuesday, July 27, 28, 1970.
The Cubiculo presents:

GERDA ZIMMERMANN
KAMMERTANZ THEATRE

A solo dance recital of "Lot's Wife," "Contrasts," and premieres of "Episode 4," and "Sidewalk Interlude."

Richard Kalven Photo

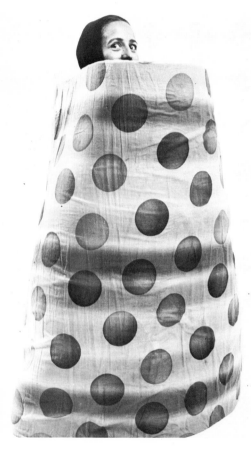

Gerda Zimmermann in "Sidewalk Interlude"

THE CUBICULO

Opened Thursday, July 30, 1970.*
The Cubiculo presents:

TWO MIMES & ONE
DISEUSE

PERFORMERS: Bert Houle and Sophie Wibaux, Elaine Sulka
PROGRAM: Mimes, Songs, and Pantomimes

* Closed Aug. 1, 1970 after limited engagement of 3 performances.

Bert Houle, Sophie

Peggy Cicierska in "Seascape"

Clyde Morgan, Carla Maxwell in "Function"

THE CUBICULO

Monday, August 3, 1970.*
The Cubiculo presents its annual retrospect dance concert with the outstanding dancers of the season in:

CUBICULO DANCE THEATRE II

PART I: Toby Armour, Peggy Cicierska, Chuck Davis, Kei Takei, Movements Black, Phoebe Neville, Rod Rodgers, Bert Houle and Sophie Wibaux

* Repeated on Aug. 4, 5, 1970. Part II opened on Monday Aug. 10, and was repeated on Aug. 11, 12, 1970.
PART II: Chuck Davis, Kei Takei, Joan Miller, Movements Black, Phoebe Neville, Barbara Roan, The Rudy Perez Dance Theatre, and Michael Henry.

THE CUBICULO

Monday, October 5, 1970.*
The Cubiculo presents:

CLIFF KEUTER DANCE COMPANY

Director-Choreographer, Cliff Keuter; Lighting and Stage Manager, Nicholas Wolff Lyndon; Technical Assistant, Robert Freund; Costumes and Sets, Ronald Bowen, Karla Wolfangle, Cliff Keuter; Props and Liaison, James Kearns

COMPANY

Janet Aaron, Christopher Beck, Edward Effron, Irene Feigenheimer, Cliff Keuter, Elina Mooney, Karla Wolfangle

PROGRAM

"Dream a Little Dream of Me, Sweetheart" (McDowell), "Letter to Paul" (Keuter), Premieres of "Sunday Papers" (Ivanovitch-McDowell), and "Twice" (Stephen Smoliar)

* Program repeated Oct. 6 and 7, 1970. On Monday, Tuesday, and Wednesday, Oct. 12, 13, 14, 1970 the company performed "The Game Man and the Ladies" (Ezra Sims), "Twice," and Premiere of "Three for Four Plus One" (McDowell, Keuter), "Sunday Papers," "Letter to Paul."

THE CUBICULO

Opened Thursday, October 8, 1970.*
The Cubiculo Theater presents:

CLYDE MORGAN CARLA MAXWELL

Program Director, Maurice Edwards; Stage Manager and Lighting, David Krohn; Technical Assistants, Paul Molnar, Robert Freund; Costumes, Judi Dearing, Carla Maxwell, Clyde Morgan
GUEST ARTISTS: John Parks, Bob Carmany, Lee Connor, Ryland Jordan, Charles Hayward

PROGRAM

New York Premiere of "Duets for Unaccompanied Cello" (Bach-Xenakis, Anna Sokolow) danced by Carla Maxwell and Clyde Morgan, New York Premiere of "Function" (Carla Maxwell) performed by Lee Connor, Ryland Jordan, Clyde Morgan, Carla Maxwell, "With My Eye and with My Hand" (Harris-Colgrass, Daniel Nagrin) danced by Clyde Morgan, New York Premiere of "Triptych" (Primus Fountain III, Clyde Morgan) danced by the company, "The Exiles" (Schoenberg, Limon) danced by Carla Maxwell, Clyde Morgan

* Program repeated on Oct. 9, 10, 1970.

Dagmar Photo

THE CUBICULO

Friday & Saturday, October 16, 17, 1970.
The Cubiculo presents

LONNY JOSEPH GORDON
BARBARA GARDNER

PROGRAM: "Phrases, Fields--Breath Groups, Kanda, 6 P.M., Number 4 from 'Seasons from This Heart'" (Toshi Ichiyanagi) choreographed and danced by Lonny Joseph Gordon; "Vignettes: Requiem, Epitaph, Song, and Yell" (Leadbelly-Howard Roberts, Lonny Joseph Gordon) performed by Susan Lundberg, Mary Ann Serowski, Gale Ormiston, Lonny Joseph Gordon; "Duet from Alice, or Babsie Boy and the Undance Kid" choreographed by Barbara Gardner and performed with Charles Stanley; Premiere of work in progress "Cloudrifts and Winterivers" (Katsutoshi Nagasawa, Gordon) performed by Hidako Tano, Janet Markovitz, Howard Hormann, Susan Lundberg, Luise Wykell, Gale Ormiston, Mary Ann Serowski, Margarete Tsuai, Billy Siegenfeld, Clare Johnson; "Tama-Furi, Tama-Shizume" (Kazuo Yura-Gordon) choreographed and danced by Lonny Joseph Gordon.

John Van Lund Photo

Lonny Joseph Gordon in "Phrases, Fields..."

THE CUBICULO

Monday, October 19, 1970.
The Cubiculo presents:

SACHI DEVI MALLEGOWDA
MALINI SRIRAMA

Lighting Designer, V. Ramamurthy; Narrator, Glenda Taylor; Technical Director, William Lambert

PROGRAM

"Invocation: Varnam," "Githa Govinda," "Thaye Yashode," "Natanam Adinar," "Tillana"

Malini Srirama, Sachi Devi Mallegowda
in "Tillana"

THE CUBICULO

Monday, November 3, 1970.*
The Cubiculo presents:

ELINA MOONEY &
COMPANY

Choreography by Elina Mooney

COMPANY

Elina Mooney, Luly Santangelo, Christopher Beck, Arlene Schloss, Ray Kelly

PROGRAM

"Play Dance," "Figure," "Hard Edge"

* Repeated Nov. 4, 5, 1970.

THE CUBICULO

Monday, November 9, 1970.*
The Cubiculo presents:

AN EVENING OF
BARBARA ROAN THINGS

with Barbara Roan, Anthony LaGiglia, Ellen Robbins, Leonard Hanichak, Wendy Perron, Wendy Summit, Aaron Osborne. All choreography by Barbara Roan.

* Repeated on Nov. 10, 11, 1970.

THE CUBICULO
Monday & Tuesday, November 16, 17, 1970.
The Cubiculo presents:

SUSAN MATHEKE
JOEL HARRISON

with Anne Koren, Elizabeth Laze, Lee Harper, Theodore Rotante, Philip Jonson, Michele Levine

PROGRAM

"Interspace," "Chamber Piece," "HebSed," "To Mix to Blend"

THE CUBICULO
Sunday, November 22, 1970.*
The Cubiculo presents:

ROBERT STREICHER
JAN VAN DYKE

PROGRAM: "Achyllus in Three Stages" (Pink Floyd) choreographed and danced by Robert Streicher; "Two" (Choreography, Jan Van Dyke) danced by Jean Jones, Cathy Paine; "Camp Lilies" (Monkees- Ussachevsky, Jan Van Dyke) danced by Jean Jones, Cathy Paine, Jan Van Dyke; "3 Ringling" (Fred Jewell, Jan Van Dyke) danced by Jean Jones, Jan Van Dyke, Leonard Hanitchak; "Implode" (Alvin Lucier) choreographed and danced by Robert Streicher

* Repeated Monday and Tuesday, Nov. 23, 24, 1970.

Jan Van Dyke, Cathy Paine, Jean Jones
in "Camp Lilies"

THE CUBICULO
Monday & Tuesday, Nov. 30, Dec. 1, 1970.
The Cubiculo presents:

GERDA ZIMMERMANN
KAMMERTANZ III

A solo recital of "Contrasts," "Sidewalk Interlude," and premiere of "Salute to a Gorgon" in seven parts.

Gerda Zimmermann

THE CUBICULO
Monday, December 7, 1970.*
The Cubiculo presents:

TINA CROLL
& DANCE COMPANY

Director-Choreography-Tapes, Tina Croll; Lighting, and Stage Manager, David Krohn; Technical Director, William Lambert

COMPANY

Tina Croll, Ted Striggles, Barbara Ensley, Toni Lacativa

PROGRAM

"In the Back of the Closet," "One Space, One Figure and Occasional Sounds," "Red Chair Film," premiere of "Farm"

* Repeated Dec. 8, 9, 1970.

THE CUBICULO
Tuesday & Wednesday, December 22, 23, 1970.
The Cubiculo presents:

LONNY JOSEPH GORDON
GALE ORMISTON

with Hidako Tano, Margarate Tsuai, Yung Yung Tsuai; Choreography, Lonny Joseph Gordon, Gale Ormiston; Decor, Michael Green; Lighting Design, Stage Manager, William Lambert

PROGRAM

"Mu" choreographed and danced by Hideko Tano; "Solo" choreographed and danced by Gale Ormiston; "Where Some Never Travel," and "Fractures" choreographed and danced by Lonny Joseph Gordon.

V. Sladon Photo

Tony Lacativa, Ted Striggles, Barbara Ensley,
Tina Croll in "Farm"

THE CUBICULO

Monday, January 25, 1971.*
The Cubiculo presents:

THE BARD COLLEGE THEATRE OF DRAMA AND DANCE

COMPANY: Albert Reid (Choreographer), Ruth Alpert, Michael Bloom, Susan Cohen, Arli Epton, Gail Gilkey, Charles Grant, Ned Griefen, Ilse Gruber, John Juhl, Eugenia Marshall, Phillip Terry.

PROGRAM

"Ethnic Dance" choreographed and danced by Toby Armour; "Eclipse" (Chopin-Nancarrow-Mendelssohn-Mozart-Berlin, Albert Reid) danced by the company; "The Abyss" (Judy Collins) choreographed and danced by Margie Farnogli; "Harriet" choreographed and danced by Peggy Cicierska; "For Janis Joplin" choreographed and danced by Laura Glenn; "Minus Eros" (Choreography Albert Reid) danced by the company.

* Repeated on Jan. 26, 27, 1971.

Top Right: Charles Grant, Phillip Terry, John Juhl, Ned Griefen, Susan Cohen, Ruth Alpert, Ilse Gruber, Gail Gilkey in "Eclipse"

THE CUBICULO

Monday & Tuesday, February 1, 2, 1971.
The Cubiculo presents:

PAUL PLUMADORE DANCE COMPANY

with Paul Plumadore, Ted Rotante, Nora Guthrie, Chris Bigelow, Vicki Uris

PROGRAM

Premiere of "Circa: A Journey" (Harry Partch, Gunter Hampel, Louis Armstrong, and others; Choreography, Paul Plumadore; Costumes, Theodora Skipitares) a full length piece in two parts.

Right Center: Paul Plumadore

THE CUBICULO

Monday & Tuesday, February 8, 9, 1971.
The Cubiculo presents:

CHUCK DAVIS DANCE COMPANY

PROGRAM

"The Embodiment of One" (Choreography, Chuck Davis), "Fere Kordaba" (Choreography, Italo Zambo), "I Am Africa," "Yesterday's Spirituals-Today's Moods" (Choreography, Chuck Davis)

THE CUBICULO

Monday, February 22, 1971.*
The Cubiculo presents:

MERLE LISTER DANCE COMPANY

Director-Choreographer, Merle Lister

COMPANY

Merle Lister, Carolynne Kast, Pablo Lubera, Phyllis Distler, Renee Binger

PROGRAM

"The Chemistry of Consciousness," "Seatrans," "Time Is a Dimension," "Remembrance of Time Past"

Chuck Davis

Gale Picard Photo

Monday & Tuesday, March 8, 9, 1971.
The Cubiculo presents:

CHRISTINE LOIZEAUX
LAURA PAWEL

PROGRAM

"Hug" and other works choreographed by Christine Loizeaux, and danced by Jessica Traum and Paul Corman. Laura Pawel presented "Mumbledumb," "Sic," "What Must the Lions Think?" assisted by Pamela Finney and Emily Kistler

THE CUBICULO
Monday & Tuesday, March 15, 16, 1971.*
The Cubiculo presents:

SUKHENDU DUTT
in
Classical Indian Dances

PROGRAM: "Puspavilas," "The Glory of Spring," "Yugma Nrittya," "Krishna Abhisar," "Vasanta Bihar," "Street Dancer," "Kathak," "Mana Bana Bhavene," "Himalay," "Gandharva" Commentary read by Maurice Edwards, Lloyd Kay

*Repeated Friday and Saturday, May 21, 22, 1971, at Museum of Modern Art.

Left: Sukhendu Dutt

THE CUBICULO
Monday, March 29, 1971.*
The Cubiculo presents:

MARGARET BEALS
in
"IMPULSES"

A concept of dance improvisations with musicians, conceived and directed by Margaret Beals, assisted by Sam Rivers (winds), Bill Wood (bass), Gwendolyn Watson (cello), Sheila Jordan (voice), Joel Press (winds), Gary Harris (lights)

* Repeated on March 30, 31, and Monday, May 17, 1971. For the last performance Miss Beals was assisted by Daniel Carter (flute), Carol Tenny (voice), Collin Walcott (sitar), Gwendolyn Watson (cello), Bill Wood (bass), Ken Billington (lights)

THE CUBICULO
Monday & Tuesday, April 5, 6, 1971.

Suzette Martinez
Jan Van Dyke
Lillo Way

PROGRAM: "Study in Repetitious Time Phrases" (Suzette Martinez) danced by Nada Diachenko Reagan, Kenneth Rinker; "Going On" choreographed and danced by Jan Van Dyke; "from where the giant lives to where you always face" choreographed and danced by Lillo Way; "Dance for Two Dancers" (Choreography, Suzette Martinez) danced by Nada Diachenko Reagan and Kenneth Rinker; "Duet I" choreographed and danced by Jan Van Dyke with Wendy Gross, Jean Jones, John Moore; "Duet II" (Choreography, Jan Van Dyke) danced by Jean Jones, John Moore

Lillo Way in "from where the giant lives to where you always face"

THE CUBICULO
Monday & Tuesday, April 12, 13, 1971.*
The Cubiculo in association with Dance Theater
Workshop presents:

ZE'EVA COHEN
in
Solo Dances

PROGRAM: "Harriet" (Sounds-Songs of the Humpback
Whale, Peggy Cicierska), "Contrasts" (Tape by Rich
O'Donnell, Gerda Zimmermann), "Green River Road
(Summer)) (Sandy Bull, Deborah Jowitt), "Three Ex-
cerpts from Resonances" (Pierre Henry, Jeff Duncan),
"Cloud Song" (Rev. Gary Davis-Jimi Hendrix-The
United States of America, Ze'eva Cohen)

* Repeated Friday & Saturday, June 4, 5, 1971.

THE CUBICULO
Sunday & Monday, May 2, 3, 1971.*
The Cubiculo presents:

VIJA VETRA
in
An Evening of Modern Dance

* On Tuesday, May 4, 1971 Miss Vetra performed "An
Evening of Dances of India"

Left: Ze'eva Cohen

Left Center: Vija Vetra

THE CUBICULO
Wednesday & Thursday, May 5, 6, 1971.
The Cubiculo presents:

CARE OF THE BODY

Written by Daniela Gioseffi; Read by Miss Gioseffi; A
mixed-media poem by Daniela Gioseffi; Read by Miss
Gioseffi; Choreography, Jan Van Dyke; Performed by
Miss Van Dyke, Jean Jones, Kenneth Rinker; Slides,
Richard Kearney; Overall Production, Maurice Edwards.

THE CUBICULO
Monday, May 10, 1971.*
The Cubiculo presents:

ELINA MOONEY
DANCES

Choreography, Elina Mooney.

COMPANY

Elina Mooney, Janet Aaron, Christopher Beck, Phoebe
Neville, Bill Siegenfeld, Arleen Schloss, Ray Kelly

PROGRAM

"Sawing-in-Half Dance," "Figure," "Region"

* Repeated May 11, 12, 1951.

Kenneth Rinker, Jan Van Dyke
in "Care of the Body"

THERESA L. KAUFMANN CONCERT HALL DANCE PROGRAMS

92nd Street YM-YWHA, New York City

KAUFMANN CONCERT HALL

Wednesday, June 17, 1970.
The Martha Graham Center of Contemporary Dance
presents:

NEW WORKS BY BERTRAM ROSS

COMPANY: Bertram Ross, Mary Hinkson, Richard
Kuch, Takako Asakawa, Phyllis Gutelius, Judith Leifer,
Hugh Appet, Joanne Blucher, Patricia Jones, Linda
Kettel, Lucinda Mitchell, Kenneth Pearl, David Roach,
David Hatch Walker, Rebecca West

PROGRAM

"El Penitente" (Horst, Graham), Premieres choreo-
graphed by Bertram Ross: "Oases" (Walter Caldon),
"See You Around" (tape) danced by Bertram Ross,
Phyllis Gutelius, "Yellow Roses" (John Wallowitch)
danced by Takako Asakawa, Richard Kuch, David
Hatch Walker.

Martha Swope Photo

Milton Oleaga Photo

Bertram Ross and company in "Oases"

KAUFMANN CONCERT HALL

Saturday, October 17, 1970.

DOWNTOWN BALLET COMPANY

Artistic Director, Paschal Guzman; Assistant Director,
Robert Christopher; Lighting, Peter Brown; Costumes,
Phoebe Franke; Administrative Director, Robert
Shuster; Press, Bruce Blugerman, Jo-Ann Geffin

COMPANY

Karen Battell, Phoebe Franke, Christiana Ham, Jill
Malamud, Christopher Frey, Paschal Guzman, Anne
Kennedy, Robert Raimondo

PROGRAM

"Scherzo Capricioso" (Dvorak, Guzman), "Toccata for
Percussion" (Chavez, Guzman), "Pas de Deux Scher-
zando" (Lalo, Guzman), "The Mystic" (Holtz, Guzman),
"The Web" (Brown, Guzman), "Wassermusik" (Handel,
Guzman)

Ed Franke Photos

Jill Malamud, Paschal Guzman in "The Web"

84 Above: Christopher Frey, Christiana Ham in "Mystic"

EUGENE JAMES DANCE COMPANY

Director-Choreographer, Eugene James; Artistic Director, Liz Williamson; Lighting, Leonid Levine; Costumes, Stanze Peterson, Alice Gilbert

COMPANY

Larl Becham, Beverley Brown, Joyce Griffen, Lucinda Ransom, Eugene James, Gail Reese, Delphine Oravetz, June Segal, Ernest Andrews, Jack Cunningham, Scott Michaels, Tommy Pinnock, Philip Stamps, Claretta Fremon (singer), and the Ralph Dorsey Musicians

PROGRAM

"Carnival Sketches: Summer Samba (Valle), Yellow Days (Carillo), Samba de Orpheu," "Color of Tears" (Ortolani), "Drums at Dawn" (Folk), "Silent Men--Silent Spring" (Otix-Pearson-Hartburg-Arlen), "Lagniappe: A Little Something Extra" (McMahan-Bachrach-Legrand, Liz Williamson)

Jack Mitchell Photos

"Silent Men--Silent Spring" Above: Lucinda Ransom, Eugene James in "Carnival"

MANUEL ALUM

with members of the Sanasardo Dance Company: Willa Kahn, Yon Martin, Georgiana Holmes, Judith Blackstone, Gerri Houlihan, Matthew Diamond, and guest artist Jennifer Muller

Choreography, Manuel Alum; Lighting, Gary Harris; Costumes and Decor, Robert Natkin; Stage Managers, Irvin Cook, Diana Smith

PROGRAM

"Nightbloom" (Serocki), "The Cellar" (Kilar), "Palomas" (Oliveros), and premieres of "Era" (Penderecki), "Roly-Poly" (Berio)

Manuel Alum in "The Cellar"
Above: "Era"

Leonard Fowler Photo

Paul Keller, Sarah Coolidge, Judith Jenkins, Gail Visentin, Cheryl Hartley, Michele Ellis, Phillip Filiato in "French Suite"

KAUFMAN CONCERT HALL
Sunday, November 22, 1970.

LEONARD FOWLER BALLET

Artistic Director-Choreographer, Leonard Fowler; Coordinator, Betty Fowler; Decor and Lighting, Gary Harris; Stage Managers, Judith Hayser, Irvin Cook, Diana Smith

COMPANY

David Billheimer, Sarah Coolidge, Michele Ellis, Phillip Filiato, Cheryl Hartley, Judith Jenkins, Paul Keller, Jacques Patarozzi, Mary Price, Thomas Stevens, Tatiana, Gail Visentin

PROGRAM

Premieres of "Pictures for Six" (Sauguet), "Extensions" (Robert Ward), "French Suite" (Francaix), "Mandala" (Bax-Berkeley)

KAUFMANN CONCERT HALL
Saturday, January 23, 1971.

JOY BOUTILIER DANCE COMPANY

Director-Choreogapher, Joy Boutilier: Lighting, Don Abrams; Costumes, Frank Garcia; Sound, Thomas Boutilier; Stage Managers, Irvin Cook, Diane Smith

COMPANY

Joy Boutilier, Linda Adamson, Santa Aloi, Louis Bartlett, Carol Chalik, Margery Halpern, Susan Papert, Charles Stuart, Hanna Takashige, Penelope Walker, Timothy Williams

PROGRAM

"Sortilegy" (Xenakis), "Variations on a Sigh" (Henry, Gladys Bailin), "Box Suite" (Praetorius), "Colony" (Wilson), "Lines by Lewis Carroll" (Davidovsky), "In Grandma's House" (Thomas Boutilier), premiere of "A Sequel to Her Visit" (Visee-Beethoven-Fados), "Chorus" (Thomas Boutilier)

Milton Oleaga Photo

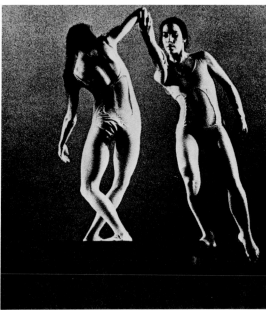

Joy Boutilier, Phoebe Neville in "A Sequel to Her Visit"

KAUFMANN CONCERT HALL
Saturday, February 27, 1971.
Sheldon Soffer presents:

LUIS RIVERA SPANISH DANCE COMPANY

Program Conceived, Directed, and Choreographed by Luis Rivera; Lighting, Beverly Emmons; Stage Managers, Irvin Cook, Diane Smith

COMPANY

Luis Rivera, Marta Castillo, Moraima Munoz, Domingo Alvarado (singer), Steven Rosenthal, Donald Foster (pianists), Emilio Prados (guitarist)

PROGRAM

"Fandango" (Vives), "Aires de Cadiz," "Feria en Malaga," "Cante Flamenco," "Tiempo de Zapateado" (Suris), "Castilla" (Albeniz), "Danza 1" (DeFalla), "Viva La Jota!" (Montorio-Olmedo), "Cerebrum" (Rodrigo), "Orgia" (Turina), "Encuentro en la Noche," "Fantasia Madrilena," "Son Mi Soledad"

Moraima Munoz, Luis Rivera, Marta Castillo

Jack Mitchell Photo

KAUFMANN CONCERT HALL
Sunday, March 7, 1971.

YURIKO & DANCE COMPANY

Choreography and Costumes, Yuriko; Lighting, Gary Harris; Personal Representative, Clara Clayman; Tape, Deryck Waring; Stage Manager, Gary Harris; Technicians, Irvin Cook, Charles O'Connor, Diane Smith

COMPANY

Yuriko, Frank Ashley, Ymme Dahlberg, Susan Kikuchi, Mari Ono, Rebecca West, Tina Yuan

GUEST ARTIST: Bess Saylor

PROGRAM

Premiere of "Quintet" (Andre Jolivet), "Wanderers" (Hovhaness), "The Cry" (Jolivet), "Events I," Premiere of "Events II" (Joel Press-Gwendolyn Watson), New York premiere of "Celebrations" (Antonio Vivaldi)

Right: Yuriko, Frank Ashley (C), Ymme Dahlberg, Susan Kikuchi, Tina Yuan, Mari Ono, Rebecca West in "Events II"

KAUFMANN CONCERT HALL
Sunday, March 28, 1971.

LEONARD FOWLER BALLET

Artistic Director-Choreographer, Leonard Fowler; Coordinator, Betty Fowler; Decor and Lighting, Gary Harris; Stage Manager, Judith Kayser; Technicians, Irvin Cook, Charles O'Connor, Diane Smith

COMPANY

David Billheimer, Robert Bowyer, Irene Buchinskas, Robert Dicello, Michele Ellis, Phillip Filiato, Cheryl Hartley, Judith Jenkins, Phillip Jonson, John Melof, Thomas Stevens, Gail Visentin

PROGRAM

Premieres of "Extensions" (Robert Ward), "Festival" (Richard Mohaupt), "The Gate" (Andrzej Panufnik), "Serenata Concertante" (Juan Orrego-Salas)

Leonard Fowler Photo

Phillip Filiato, Thomas Stevens, Robert Dicello, Robert Bowyer, John Melof in "The Gate"

(Leonard Fowler Ballet)

KAUFMANN CONCERT HALL
Saturday, May 1, 1971.
Lalit-Kala Kendra presents Kalidasa's:

SHAKUNTALA

Choreography, Maya Kulkarni; Music, Suresh Shukla; Decor, India Nepal, Inc.; Lighting, Frank Wicks; Stage Design, Bihari Sharma.

COMPANY

Maya Kulkarni, Bihari Sharma, Veera Dalal, Asha Devi, Geeta Vashi, Geeta Singh, Birendra Barot, Devendra Sharma, Alyosh Aggarwal

Vocalists: Virendra Barot, Padmini Kamat, Kanu Patel, Brij Saxena

Musicians: Anand Joshi, Devi Kamat, Harshad Parekh, Badal Roy Choudary, Ranjit Saxena, Sanjit Saxena, Suresh Shukla

Bihari Sharma, Maya Kulkarni in "Shakuntala"

KAUFMANN CONCERT HALL
Tuesday, May 4, 1971
92nd Street YM-YWHA presents:

ON TAP!
JERRY AMES &
JIMMY SLYDE

Narrated by Sandra Hochman; Musical Direction, Paul Shelley; Vocalist, Jo-Anne Engel

PROGRAM

"Just in Time," "Bluesette," "Chitty Chitty Bang Bang," "Latin Flavor," "The Old Soft Shoe," "From Out of Nowhere," "Too Close for Comfort," "Medley of Requests," "The Challenge"

Jack Mitchell Photo

Left: Jerry Ames

KAUFMANN CONCERT HALL
Saturday, May 8, 1971.

CARLOS IBANEZ
COMPANY

Executive Director, Howard Monlneux; Artistic Director, Mariquita Flores; Company Manager, John Caranci; Lighting, Bob Edmonds; Costumes, Enrique Arteaga, Helena; Stage Managers, Irvin Cook, Diane Cook; Entire production under direction of Mariquita Flores.

COMPANY

Carlos Ibanez, Mariquita Flores, Domingo Alvarado, Daniel DeCordoba, Luis Liciaga, Alicia Laura, Lucila, Cecilia Torres, Esperanza Celi, Chela, Michele, Lisette Palacio, Constanza Piccirillo, Guitarists Guillermo Rios, Guillermo Montes, Pianist Conchita Villar

PROGRAM

"Prologue," "Farruca de Jerez," "Leyenda," "An 18th Century Suite," "Holy Week and the Fair in Sevilla," "La Verbena de la Paloma," "Wedding at Luchon, Aragon," "La Guitarra Suena, " "Estampas Flamencas"

Left Center: Carlos Ibanez (C) and company

KAUFMANN CONCERT HALL
Saturday, May 15, 1971.

SHAPMOCHON, KING
OF THE DARK CHAMBER

ARTISTS: Bhaskar, Polly Roy, Bihari Sharma, and Musical Director Dr. Brij Saxena

Sal Terracina Photo

Bhaskar

HUNTER COLLEGE DANCE PROGRAMS
Omus Hirshbein, Administrator

HUNTER COLLEGE
Friday, September 18, 1970.*
The Herbert Barrett Management in association with
the Hunter College Concert Bureau present:

THE CLAUDE KIPNIS MIME THEATRE

Director, Claude Kipnis; Sets and Costumes, Dina
Kipnis; Stage Manager, Mike Hendricks

COMPANY

Claude Kipnis, Rudy Benda, Rita Nachtmann, Doug
Day, Mike Hoit, Chris Swing, Robert Giffard, Donna
Gibbons, Marty Sausser, John Stravinsky

PROGRAM

"Opus Blue...Is Pink" (Ben Johnson), "Au Clair de La
Lune" (Neely Bruce), "Point of View" (Edwin London),
"The Miraculous Mandarin" (Bela Bartok), "Histoire du
Soldat and Renard" (Stravinsky), "Men and Dreams"
(Noam Sheriff)

**Right and Below: Kipnis Company
in "Opus Blue Is Pink"**

HUNTER COLLEGE
Saturday & Sunday, October 10, 11, 1970.
Hunter College Concert Bureau in association with
Albert Morini presents:

OLAETA BASQUE FESTIVAL OF BILBAO

Founder-Director, Victor Olaeta; Co-Director, Lide
Olaeta; Company Manager, Harry Rand; Stage Technicians, Joseph Londin, Leonard Suib

COMPANY

Begona Irarrogorri, Isabel Alberdi, Margarita Calvo,
Miquel Escudero, Juan Antonio Menica, Miren Terese
Olaeta, Ana Maria Crespo, Javier Olaeta, Jesus Altuna,
Jose Luis Garaizabel, Marisa Zuniga, Rosario Benguria,
Eduardo Irisarri, Luis Echaburu, Inaki Erekatxo

PROGRAM

"Agur Jaunak," "Mikel Deuna," "Binbili," "Uso Txuria,"
"Makil Dantza," "Arku Dantza," "Oi Euskalerri," "Con-
trapasa Eta Museta," "Zuberoaka Dantza," "Sagar
Dantza," "Txistu Solo," "Balkarlosko-Yauntziak," "Lar-
rain-Dantza," "Alboka eta Zaldabe," "Intermezzo,"
"Dantza Guerra," "Village Life in the Basque Country,"
"Vandango eta Arin Arin"

**Olaeta Basque Festival
also above**

HUNTER COLLEGE
Sunday, October 25, 1970.
Hunter College Concert Bureau (Omus Hirshbein, Administrator) presents:

LADO--THE YUGOSLAV NATIONAL DANCE AND FOLK ENSEMBLE

Artistic Leader, Zvonko Ljevakovic; Director, Ivo Vuljevic; Herbert Barrett Management.

PROGRAM

"Ladarke, A Midsummer Day Custom" (Emil Cossetto, Zvonko Ljevakovic), "Dances from Dupljaja" (Bozidar Potocnik, Ivan Sulina), "Duj-Duj" (Potocnik, Hanival Dundovic), "Ring Dance from Vrlika" (Ljevakovic), "Bunjevac Bachelor's Dance" (Potocnik, Ljevakovic), "Osogovka" (Dimcevski, Mitke Aleksov), "Wedding in Podravina" (Ivan Ivancan), "Dances of East Serbia" (Bojan Adamic, Ljevakovic), "Dance from Valpovo" (Potocnik, Ljevakovic), "Dances from Posavina" (Ljevakovic), "Komitas Dance" (Cossetto, Ljevakovic), "Dances from Prigorje" (Ljevakovic)

Lado, also above and top

HUNTER COLLEGE
Wednesday, November 25, 27, 28, 1970.
Hunter College of the City University of New York presents:

KERALA KALAMANDALUM KATHAKALI COMPANY

PRINCIPALS: Kunchu Nair, Ramankutty Nair, Padmanabhan Nair, V. M. Govindan, Madavoor Vasudevan Nair, Nelliyode Vasudevan Namboodiri, Kattakkal Sivaraman, Neelakantan Nambissan, Appukutty Poduval, Chandra Mannadiar

PROGRAM

"Mahabharata," "Ramayana," "Kalyana Saugandhikam"

Kerala Kalamandalum Kathakali Co.

HUNTER COLLEGE

Sunday, December 6, 1970.
Hunter College of the City University of New York
by arrangement with Harold Shaw presents:

THE AFRO-AMERICAN DANCE COMPANY

Director, Arthur Hall; Production Manager, Dan Thomas; Costumers, Arthur Hall, Elizabeth Roberts, Melvin Purnell; Lighting, Judith Haynes.

COMPANY

James Crawford, Melvin Purnell, Arthur Hall, Paul Roberts, John Jones, Evangeline Brown, Carol Butcher, LaVerne McBride, Karen Steptoe, Elizabeth Roberts, Dolores Jones, Betty Joseph, Delphine Mantz, Shirley Phelps, Barbara Kinney

PROGRAM

"High Life," "The Queen Is Dead," "Obatala," "Calabash," "Court Dance of the Royal Watusi," "Moon Song," "Satyr at Noon," "Harvest and Fertility Rites, "Premiere of "Three Wives," "Agbaja"

Right: Arthur Hall, and below: Afro-American Dance Company

HUNTER COLLEGE

Saturday & Sunday, February 20, 21, 1971.
Hunter College Concert Bureau presents:

TAMBURITZANS

Managing Director, Walter Kolar; StageTechnician, Joseph Londin

PROGRAM

"Volim Diku," "Songs and Dances from Baranja," "Dva Su Cvijeta," "Iz Stare Bosne," "Dedeckovo Solo," "Dances from Muntenia," "Dalmatian Sea Songs," "Vrlicko Kolo," "Slovenian Polkas," "Nocoj, Le Se Nocoj," "Slovenian Mountain Dances," "Macedonian-Bulgarian Dance Airs," "S'one Strane Morave," "Dances of Dobrudja," "Songs and Dances from Nisava River Valley," "Melodies for Frula," "Jablani Se Povijaju," "Dances from Hungary," "Jedno Momce Malo," "Baranjska Humoreska," "Kryzacok," "Russian Folk Songs," "Suite of Russian Dances"

Tamburitzans, also above

91

CLARK CENTER
Saturday & Sunday, October 3, 4, 1970.
Clark Center for the Performing Arts presents:

THE CONTEMPORARY BALLET ENSEMBLE OF NEW YORK

Directors, Margaret Black, Morris Donaldson, Jay Norman; Costumes, Ann Roth, Susan Houseknecht; Lighting, George Vaughn Lowther; Stage Manager, Susan Beckerman.

COMPANY

Loretta Abbott, Margaret Black, Mary Jane Eisenberg, Marti Ingle, Barbara Kravitz, Robert Bowyer, Roger Briant, Morris Donaldson, Louis Solino

PROGRAM

"Ionization" (Varese, Seamus Murphy), and premieres of "Montage" (Arranged by Nice, Jay Norman), "Thru the Edge" (Samuel Barber, Michael Lopuszanski), "Grass Roots-Up Roots" (Archie Shepp, Morris Donaldson), "Encounter" (Isaac Hayes-Tenwheel Drive, Jay Norman)

Left and above: Contemporary Ballet Ensemble in "Encounter"

CLARK CENTER
Sunday, November 8, 1970.
Interboro Civic Ballet, Inc., presents:

FRED BENJAMIN DANCE COMPANY

Director-Choreographer, Fred Benjamin; Lighting, Kenny Hamilton; Program Director, Barbara Sedlar; Wardrobe, Benny Wakefield; Stage Manager, John Williams; Costumes, Bernard Johnson, Benny Wakefield

COMPANY

Karen Burke, Eleanor McCoy, Cynthia Ashby, Arlene Rolant, Michael Peters, George Faison, Andy Torres, Ronald Dunham, Winston DeWitt Hemsley, Bryant Baker

PROGRAM

"Movin'" (Quincy Jones, Fred Benjamin), "Journey" (Copeland, Bryant Baker), "902 Albany Street" (Contemporary, Benjamin), "Pi R Square = Love" (Contemporary, Michael Peters), "New Work" (Bryant Baker), "Mountain High" (Simpson-Ashford, Benjamin)

Diane Conway, George Faison, Ronald Dunham in "Mountain High"

CLARK CENTER

Saturday & Sunday, December 12, 13, 1970.
Clark Center for the Performing Arts presents:

ROD RODGERS DANCE COMPANY

Choreography, Rod Rodgers; Technical Director, Karen DeFrancis; Lighting, Marshall Williams; Costumes, B. Fuller; Stage Manager, Karen DeFrancis

COMPANY

Rod Rodgers, Marilyn Atkinson, Morris Donaldson, Tommy Pinnock, Shirley Rushing, Ronald Pratt, Barbara Roan, Ellen Robbins

PROGRAM

"Percussion Suite," premiere of "Now! Nigga..." (L. Tristano), "Tanjents", "Sketches for Projected Space," "Dances in Projected Space(Gwendolyn Watson-Joel Press; Slide Environment, Bill Longcore)

Right: Rod Rodgers in "Percussion Suite"
Above: "Projected Space"

CLARK CENTER

Thursday, May 6, 1971.
Clark Center for the Performing Arts with Dance Vectors Inc. presents the debut concert of:

PHYLLIS ROSE DANCE COMPANY

Director-Choreographer, Phyllis Rose; Costumes, Terri Leong; Lighting, Gary Harris; Stage Manager, Lawrence Eichler; Production Assistant, Mel Rosen

COMPANY

Susan Cherniak, Erick Hodges, Pat Kornhauser, Adele Latour, Nada Diachenko Reagan, Steven Van Pelt

PROGRAM

"Spread a Little Joy Around" (Richard Bunn), "Diversions 1, 2, 3, 4, 5, 6, 7," "Trio for Four" (Jimmy Erwin), "Pollution" (Eric Salzman), "Ho!"

Right: The Phyllis Rose Dance Company in "Spread a Little Joy Around"

CLARK CENTER

Saturday & Sunday, May 15, 16, 1971
Clark Center for the Performing Arts in association with Concert Artists Guild presents:

SEAMUS MURPHY DANCE COMPANY

Director-Choreographer, Seamus Murphy

COMPANY

Seamus Murphy, Robert Bowyer, Ernesta Corvino, Eileen Feigay, Adriana Keathley, Louis Solino

PROGRAM

"Forsaken" (Monteverdi), "And the Fallen Petals" (Wne-Chung), "Manfire" (Avni), "Ionization" (Varese), and premiere of "Sunshine" (rock)

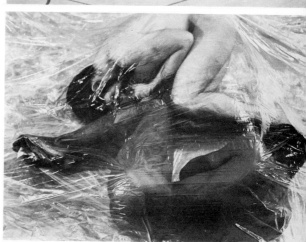

Seamus Murphy, Philip Jonson in "Dust"

93

WESTBETH DANCE SERIES

New York City

WESTBETH
Sunday, March 14, 1971.
Video Exchange presents:

SUKANYA
in
Indian Classical Dances

PROGRAM: "Sringara Lahari," "Krishnani," "Kudu-saivaitu," "Karunaini," "Sariga Kongu," "Tillana," "Mangala Charanam," "Raga Lakshana," "Natangi"

Sukanya in "Bharata Natyam"

WESTBETH
Friday & Saturday, March 19, 20, 1971.
Video Exchange presents:

DAN WAGONER
AND DANCERS

Choreography, Dan Wagoner; Program Coordinator, Blondell Cummings; Production Staff, Andrea Giambrone, Sam Ashe, Steve Majewski

PROGRAM

"Brambles" spoken and written by George Montgomery, danced by Dan Wagoner; "Duet" (Purcell) danced by Dan Wagoner and Mirjam Berns; "Iron Mountain" (Hindemith) danced by Cathy Boyd, Emmy Devine, Sally Hess, Judith Moss, Dan Wagoner

Left: Dan Wagoner, Mirjam Berns in "Duet"

WESTBETH
Friday & Saturday, April 2, 3, 1971.
Video Exchange presents:

RUDY PEREZ DANCE
THEATER

Director-Choreographer, Rudy Perez; Assistants, Barbara Roan, Anthony LaGiglia; Stage and Lighting Director, John Moore; Sound Collages, Rudy Perez; Press, Linda Phillips

COMPANY

Alice Coughlin, Stephen Deutsch, Dick Dickinson, Dennis Florio, Sandra Genter, Linda Hayes, Raymond Johnson, Linda Kennaman, Anthony LaGiglia, Ginger Lyons, Dianne McIntyre, Susan Montanye, John Moore, Jerianne Niebergall, Rudy Perez, Daniel Press, Harriet Ravitz, Barbara Roan, Susan Sandler, Harold Silver, Betsy Sullivan, Wendy Summit, Frances Tabor

PROGRAM

"Monumental Exchange," "Arcade," "Coverage"

Robert Rogers Photo

**Rudy Perez Dance Theater
in "Monumental Exchange"**

Wednesday, April 28, 1971.
The Video Exchange presents:

EDITH STEPHEN THEATRE DANCE COMPANY

Artistic Director-Choreographer, Edith Stephen; Design Consultant, Athos Zacharries; Production Assistant, Ben Jennings; Visuals, Maxine Haleff; Sound, Morris J. Morkowitz

COMPANY

Edith Stephen, Sydney Lee Brooks, Larry Bailey, Frederick Courtney, Douglas Gourley, Ellen Holmes, Lillie Prebel, Diana Reutter

PROGRAM

"The Wrecked Tangle" (Dylewski, Stephen), "Concrete Heart" (Subotnick, Stephen), "Celebration for Myself" (Tape collage, Stephen)

Right Top: Edith Stephen Theatre Dance Company in "The Wrecked Tangle"

Vija Vetra

Rudy Perez
in "Coverage"

Ted Wester Photo

Wednesday, April 28, 1971
Video Exchange presents:

VIJA VETRA
in
Dances of India

PROGRAM: "Shlokam," "Puja," "Pujarini," "Alarippu," "Tillana"

ChoreoConcerts
New School
Laura Foreman, Director
October 6-27, 1970

A series of modern dance concerts/lecture demonstrations/discussions, presented by the New School in association with Choreographers Theatre, Lighting, Barry Suttin; Sound, Hank O'Neal, John Watts; Special Technician, Charles Hyman; Stage Managers, Arnold Aronson, Robert Jackson, Susan Scott; Discussion Coordinators, Richard Bull, Laura Foreman, Stuart Hodes, Kelly Holt, Phyllis Lamhut, Gus Solomons, Jr.; Program Coordinators, Marilynn Danitz, Dee Dee Eversley, Cynthia Read, Julie Sandler, Blondine Singer; Press, Harold Klein, Arthur Raybin.

TUESDAY, OCTOBER 6, 1970: Premiere of "Save a Kiss for Wally" (Ortman-Whiting, Choreography and costumes, Margot Parsons, danced by Sandra Roll); Premiere of "This room gives one a sense of confusion. It shows poor taste in the selection and the arrangement of the furniture and decorative objects. Such a room would have a bad influence upon the people who might live in it, for it would tend to dull their sense of beauty" (Choreography, Shawn Avrea; Art and Costumes, Richard Banks) danced by Shawn Avrea, Margot Colbert; Premiere of "Whelk Woman" (Eleanor Hovda Gilbert) choreography, costumes, poetry, and danced by Beverly Brown; Premiere of "Audio Visual" (Black Box, Stuart Hodes; Projections, Alfred Gescheidt; Readings by Marshall McLuhan) danced by Beverly Brown, Mariano Garcia, Daniel Giagni, Teresa Hill, Judith Henkins, Allan Tung, Lance Westergard, Dana Wolfe)

TUESDAY, OCTOBER 13, 1970: Premiere of "Warm-up Piece" (Movement structure, Tape, Gus Solomons, Jr.) danced by Darrell Barnett, Susan Cherniak, Carol Conway, Charlotte Honda, Gus Solomons, Jr., Gene Stulgaitis, Steven Van Pelt, Ethel Winter; Premiere of "Quote...Unquote" (Bahnfahrt) choreographed and danced by Charlotte Honda; Premiere of "One Three" (Peter Hyde, Carol Conway) danced by Susan Cherniak, Steven Van Pelt, Carol Conway; Premiere of "Cat. CCS70-1013NSSR-GSJ9M" choreographed and danced by Gus Solomons, Jr.; Premiere of "An Age of Innocence" danced by Darrell Barnett, Gene Stulgaitis, Ethel Winter

TUESDAY, OCTOBER 20, 1970: "Solo from Palomas" (Oliveros, Manuel Alum) danced by Willa Kahn; Premiere of "New trio for Shungopovi Shade" (Shinichi Yuize, Kelly Holt) danced by Nora Guthrie, Paul Plumadore, Red Rotante; Premiere of "Pass Fe White II" (Gwendolyn Watson), choreographed and danced by Joan Miller; "Big Feature" (Arranged, Phyllis Lamhut) danced by Phyllis Lamhut, Raymond Clay

TUESDAY, OCTOBER 27, 1970: Premiere of "Quilt" (Traditional, Elizabeth Keen) danced by Elizabeth Keen, Davidson Lloyd, Judy McCilligin; Premiere of "Signals" (John Watts, Laura Foreman) danced by Margot Parsons, Dana Wolfe, Christian Singer, Sean Singer; Premiere of "Poem in October" (Tape by Ratter, Cliff Keuter) danced by Janet Aaron, Cliff Keuter; Premiere of "Sing-Along Sun King" (The Beatles, Richard Bull) danced by Joan Consroe, Irma Pylyshenko, Kathy Simons, Richard Bull, and the audience

Peter Moore Photos

Lance Westergaard, Beverly Brown, Teresa Hill, Dana W
Judith Jenkins, Allan Tung, Mariano Garcia in "Audio V

Joan Consroe, Irma Pylyshenko, Kathy Simons,
Richard Bull in "Sing-Along Sun King"

Ethel Winter, Gene Stulgaitis, Darrell Barnett
in "An Age of Innocence"

Beverly Brown
in "Whelk Woman"

Paul Plumadore, Nora Guthrie, Ted Rotante
in "New Trio for Shungopovi Shade"

ChoreoConcerts
EXPERIMENTAL
WORKSHOP

Video Exchange Dance Series
Friday, March 5, 6, 7, 1971

PHYLLIS LAMHUT AND DANCE COMPANY: Phyllis Lamhut, Raymond Clay, Donald Blumenfeld, Rosalind E. Dance, Bob Diaz, Patrice Evans, Rick Fite, Kathleen Gaskin, Joan Gedney, Deborah Gerson, Mason Klein, Victoria Larrain, Candy Lerman, Menlo McFarlane, Elaine McHugh, Susan Papert, Rolaondo Pena, Lynn Pyle, Karen Rimmer, Natasha Simon, Joan Friedman, John Fox, Leslie Levinson, Ron Roseli, Jim Teeters. Lee Wasserwald in premiere of full-length work "Field of View" choreographed by Phyllis Lamhut with music by Christian Wold, Phil Werren; Costumes, Frank Garcia, Anne Datson, Lighting, Barry Suttin; Sound, Hank O'Neal; Stage Manager, Jay Poswolski.

ChoreoConcerts
EXPERIMENTAL
WORKSHOP

Wollman Hall Dance Series
Friday & Saturday, March 12, 13, 1971.

Lighting, Barry Suttin; Sound, Hank O'Neal; Stage Manager, Miguel Romero; Coordinators, Marilynn Danitz, Dee Dee Eversley, Susan Norton, Joy Javits, Julie Sandler
PROGRAM: Premiere of "The Little Prince" (Text from De Saint-Exupery, Aviva Stern) danced by Aviva Stern, Paul Corman; Premiere of "Flowerleaf I-III" (Choreography, Elza Tiner) danced by Amy Horowitz; Premiere of "Sic" (Choreographic revision by Laura Pawel) danced by Pamela Finney, Raymond Healy, Emily Kistler; Premiere of "Point of Reference" (Tape and choreography by Blondell Cummings) danced by Blondell Cummings, Anya Allister; Premiere of "Stencil" (Joan Friedman, Henry Smith, Carolyn Carlson) danced by Bob Diaz, Rick Fite, Joan Friedman, Karen Levin, Gale Ormiston, Ron Roseli, Henry Smith

ChoreoConcerts
REPERTORY
COMPANY

Washington Square Church
Friday, March 26, 1971.

Presented by Free Music Store; Lighting, Barry Suttin; Sound, Hank O'Neal; Stage Manager, Charles Gilbert; Coordinators, DeeDee Eversley, Roselee Moskowitz, Rhea Needleman, Susan Norton, Sara Yohai

COMPANY

Richard Bull, Esther Chaves, Gus Solomons, Jr., Clay Taliaferro, Dana Wolfe, Jennifer Anton, Susan Burton, Ellen Charles, Lynette Chun, Jane Cirker, Kathy Duncan, Catherine Rowe, Christian Singer, Sean Singer, Ilana Snyder, Karen Soroca, Elza Tiner, Graciela Torino, Judy Yardley

PROGRAM: "Cat. CCS70-1013NSSR-GSJ9M" choreographed and danced by Gus Solomons, Jr.; "Signals" (ARP Synthisizer with Text by John Watts, Laura Foreman) danced by Esther Chaves, Dana Wolfe, Christian Singer, Sean Singer, Catherine Rowe (vocalist); "Dance for a Film/Whale Trip" (Susan Berger, Stuart Hodes) danced by Dana Wolfe, Clay Taliaferro; "Save a Kiss for Wally" (Ortman-Whiting, Margot Parsons) danced by Esther Chaves; "War Games: Strategies, Tactics, Diversions, and Delights" (Director, Richard Bull; Conductor, Thomas Johnson; Text written and spoke by Richard Bull) danced by Jennifer Anton, Susan Burton, Ellen Charles, Lynette Chun, Jane Cirker, Kathy Duncan, Ilana Snyder, Karen Soroca, Elza Tiner, Graciela Torino, Judy Yardley

Peter Moore Photos

Top Right: Raymond Clay, Phyllis Lamhut in "Big Feature" Below: Margot Colbert, Shawn Avrea in "This room gives one a sense of confusion. . . ."

Christian Singer, Sean Singer in "Signals"

Clay Taliaferro, Dana Wolfe
in "Dance for a Film/Whale Trip"   **97**

ChoreoConcerts
EXPERIMENTAL
WORKSHOP

Wollman Hall Dance Series
Friday, April 2, 1971

GUS SOLOMONS, JR.

Lighting, Barry Suttin; Sound, Hank O'Neal; Stage Managers, Miguel Romero, Charles Gilbert; Technicians, David Boyce, Su Burns; Coordinators, DeeDee Eversley, Susan Norton, Blondine Singer, Judy Yardley; Choreography, Gus Solomons, Jr.

PROGRAM: "Notebook," "Two Reeler," "Kinesia 5," "Cat. CCS70-1013NSSR-GSJ9M," "Visual Collage Film and Slides from 1968-9," "we don't know only how much time we have..."

SATURDAY, APRIL 3, 1971: "we don't know only how much time we have...," "Two Reeler," "Kinesia 5," "Stencil" (Joan Friedman-Henry Smith, Carolyn Carlson) danced by Bob Diaz, Rick Fite, Joan Friedman, Karen Levin, Gale Ormiston, Ron Roseli, Henry Smith

AMERICAN THEATRE LAB

Friday, May 7, 8, 9, 1971.

Lighting, Barry Suttin; Sound, Hank O'Neal; Stage Managers, Arnold Aronson, Phil Haultcoeur; Coordinators, Marilynn Danitz, DeeDee Eversley, Susan Norton, Julie Sandler, Bernard Singer, Blondine Singer

PROGRAM: Premiere of "Love Only Me, For There Is None Other" choreographed and danced by Shawn Avrea; Premiere of "Transitions" danced by Gale August, Cookie Drayton, Charlotte Honda, Lorna Lable; Premiere of "The Honor of Your Presence Is Requested" (Mahler, Stuart Hodes) danced by Beverly Brown, Mariano Garcia, Jane Jaffe, Judith Jenkins, Louis Montes de Oca, Dale Talley, Allan Tung, Dana Wolfe; Premiere of "I Never Loved Anybody and I Never Will" (Tape by Dana Wolfe-Hank O'Neal, Dana Wolfe) danced by Dana Wolfe, Sandra Roll; Premiere of "glass and shadows" (Tape by Hank O'Neal-John Watts, Laura Foreman) danced by Esther Chaves, Lynette Chun, Barbara Coyne, Judith Jenkins, Elza Tiner, Graciela Torino, Judy Yardley

ChoreoConcerts
REPERTORY
COMPANY

Wollman Hall
Friday, May 14, 1971

Lighting, Barry Suttin; Sound, Hank O'Neal; Stage Managers, Arnold Aronson, Charles Gilbert; Composers Theatre Director, John Watts; Coordinators, Marilynn Danitz, Blondine Singer, Ilana Snyder

COMPANY

Richard Bull, Esther Chaves, Margot Parsons, Teresa Hill, Charlotte Honda, Gus Solomons, Jr., Clay Taliaferro, Dana Wolfe, Catherine Rowe, Christian Singer, Sean Singer
PROGRAM: "Making and Doing" (Bull-Coryell, Richard Bull) danced by Esther Chaves, Teresa Hill Charlotte Honda, Margot Parsons, Richard Bull; "Cat. CCS70-1013NSSR-GSJ9M" choreographed and danced by Gus Solomons, Jr.; "Signals" (ARP Synthesizer-John Watts, Laura Foreman) danced by Esther Chaves, Dana Wolfe, Christian Singer, Sean Singer, Catherine Rowe (vocalist); "You Can't Get There from Here" (Jo Jones) choreographed and danced by Margot Parsons; "Dance for a Film/Whale Trip" (Susan Berger, Stuart Hodes) danced by Dana Wolfe, Clay Taliaferro

Peter Moore Photos

Top Right: Gus Solomons, Jr. in "Cat. CCS70-1013NSSR-GSJ9M" Below: Judith Jenkins, Esther Chaves, Barbara Coyne, Judy Yardley, Lynette Chun, Graciela Torino, Elza Tiner in "glass and shadows"

Dana Wolfe, Sandra Roll in "I Never Loved Anybody and I Never Will"

Judy McCilligin, Davidson Lloyd, Elizabeth Keen in "Quilt"

DANCE THEATER WORKSHOP
New York, N.Y.
Jeff Duncan, Director,   Jack Moore, Associate Director

DANCE THEATER WORKSHOP
SERIES 1
New York, N. Y.
Jeff Duncan, Director, Jack Moore, Associate
Director

Assistant Director, Art Bauman; Lighting, Nick Lyndon; Stage Manager, David Usitalo; Crew, John Moore, Ken Mills

DANCE THEATER WORKSHOP
November 6 through December 12, 1970
Fridays and Saturdays only

PROGRAM
Fridays: "The One of No Way" (Tony Scott-Shimichi and Hozan Yamamoto) choreographed and performed by Frances Alenikoff; "Beginning" Carl Michaelson, Betsy Wetzig) performed by Hideko Tano, Betsy Wetzig, Louise Harrison, Cynthia Read; "Harriet" (Roger S. Payne) choreographed and performed by Peggy Cicierska; "Primer & Disposable Dances for November 20 & 27, December 4 & 11, 1970" (Tape Collages by Mark Seiden) performed by Gay Delanghe and extras; "Olympic for Three" (Susan Ain, Wendy Perron) performed by Sherry Sable, Wendy Summit, Anthony LaGiglia

Saturdays: "Circus Minimums" (Merle Evans) choreographed and performed by Toni Lacativa; "Light Part III" (Choreography, Kei Takei) performed by Carmen Beauchat, Elsi Miranda, Noemi Ramirez, Kei Takei, Maldwyn Pate; "Episode I #4" (Pierre Henry) choreographed and performed by Gerda Zimmermann; "Going On" choreographed and performed by Jan Van Dyke; "Turnips and Down" (Choreographed by Holly Rosenwald) performed by Wendy Summit and Leonard Hanitchak

DANCE THEATER WORKSHOP
February 12 through March 20, 1971
Fridays and Saturdays only

PROGRAM
Fridays: "Pyrothonium" (Choreography, Gus Solomons, Jr.) performed by Su Burns, David Boyce, Gus Solomons, Jr.; "Empty Sky" choreographed and performed by Judy Rekert; "Please" choreographed and danced by Wendy Summit; "Circle Solo" by Nancy Topf; "The One of No Way" (choreography, Frances Alenikoff) performed by Wendy Perron; "In Between" choreographed and danced by Betsy Wetzig

Saturdays: "Parentheses" choreographed and danced by Elizabeth Keen (or Laura Pawel); "Suicide Remarks" choreographed and danced by Peter Sparling; "A Work by Barbara Roan" danced by Miss Roan; "Hooliwhar" (Paul Hindes, Whitney Bergman) danced by Pam Fiala, Hannah Kahn, Peter Sparling, "Cloud Song" (Rev. Gary Davis-Jimi Hendrix) choreographed and danced by Ze'eva Cohen.

Irene Vilhar Photos

Wendy Summit, Anthony LaGiglia, Sherry Sable
in "Olympic for Three"

Betsy Wetzig in "In Between"

**Hannah Kahn, Pam Fiala, Peter Sparling
in "Hooliwhar"**

**Elsi Miranda, Noemi Ramirez, Carmen Beuchat,
Maldwyn Pate, Kei Takei in "Light: Part III"**

99

WESTBETH

Thursday, April 15 through Sunday, April 18, 1971.
Thursday, April 22 through Sunday, April 25, 1971.
Video Exchange (David Schiller, Michael Temmer, Co-Directors) presents:

DANCE THEATER WORKSHOP

Director, Jeff Duncan, Assistant Director, Art Bauman; Associate Director, Jack Moore; Press, John Vinton; Company Manager, Harold Silver; General Assistant, Cynthia Read; Technical Director, John Moore; Stage Managers, Karen De Francis, Lettie Battle; Sound, Gary and Timmy Harris

PROGRAM

"Act without Words 2" (Samuel Beckett, Elizabeth Keen) performed by Ben Hendrickson and Jim Moody; "DTW Improvisation Group" (Art Bauman, Coordinator) performed by Frances Alenikoff, Connie Allentuck, Art Bauman, Carol Boggs, Peggy Cicierska, Jeff Duncan, Wendy Gross, Deborah Jowitt, Lenore Latimer, John Moore, Wendy Perron, Cynthia Read, Barbara Roan, Harold Silver, Wendy Summit, Jan Van Dyke, Betsy Wetzig; "In the Salt Range" (Sound Collage, Frances Alenikoff) performed by Connie Allentuck, Wendy Gross, John Moore, Wendy Perron, Judy Rekert, Harold Silver, Wendy Summit; "Judith Dunn/Bill Dixon" (Bill Dixon, Judith Dunn) with performers Judith Dunn, Barbara Ensley, Erika Bro, Megan Bierman, Cheryl Niederman; "Kinesia 5" by Gus Solomons, Jr.; "L'Aigrette" (Stephen Horenstein) choreographed and danced by Linda Tarnay; "Light Part III-- Rain Puddle Reflections" (Choreography, Kei Takei) performed by Miss Takei, Carmen Beuchat, Elsi Miranda, Noemi Ramirez, Maldwyn Pate; "New Work in Progress" (Choreography, Alice Condodina) performed by Jim May, Dorothy Hershkowitz, Alice Coughlin, Nancy Salmon, Larry Clark; "Pyrothonium" (choreography, Gus Solomons, Jr.) performed by David Boyce, Su Burns, Mr. Solomons; "Roan's Parade 1: Woolworth's" with Irene Feigenheimer, Wendy Perron, Spider Kedelsky, Ellen Robbins, Wendy Summit, Ellen Jacobs, Connie Allentuck, Dick Dickinson, Gene Stulgaitis, Dennis Florio, Amy Berkman, Joanna Tankel, Wendy Gross, John Moore, Barbara Roan, Anthony LaGiglia, Fran Tabor, Tom Spence, Emily Smith; "Space Test" (Taped Sounds) choreographed and performed by Jeff Duncan; "Upriver" (Incredible String Band-Tzvi Avni, Deborah Jowitt) performed by Dorothy Hershkowitz, Jim May, Wendy Perron, Wendy Summit, Connie Allentuck, Cynthia Read, Nancy Salmon

V. Sladon Photos

Judith Dunn, Barbara Ensly, Bill Dixon in "Improvisations"

Jeff Duncan, John Moore in "Space Test" Top Right: Frances Alenikoff and company in "In the Salt Range"

Barbara Roan and company in "Roan's Parade 1: Woolworth's" Above: Linda Tarnay in "L'Aigrette"

AMERICAN THEATRE LABORATORY

Thursday through Sunday, March 4-7, 1971.
Dance Theatre Workshop, Inc. presents

FOUR EVENINGS OF DANCE

Choreographers, Art Bauman, Jack Moore, Kathryn
Posin; Lighting, Richard W. Kerry; Stage Managers,
Harry Brauser, Karen DeFrancis; Production Coordina-
tor, Harold Silver

PROGRAM

Thursday and Saturday: "Errands" (The Ventures-
Beethoven, Art Bauman) performed by Phillip Jonson,
Jim May, Louis Solino; "Block" (Bartok-Krohn) choreo-
graphed and danced by Kathryn Posin; Premiere of
"Ode" (Toru Takemitsu, Jack Moore) performed by
Connie Allentuck, Anthony LaGiglia, Karen Lierly, John
Moore, Wendy Perron, Barbara Roan, Gene Stulgaitis,
Wendy Summit, Linda Wilder; "Headquarters" (Barry,
Bauman) performed by Barbara Roan, Anthony
LaGiglia; Premiere of "Fantaisie Pour Deux" (Choreo-
graphy and Sound, Jack Moore) performed by Linda
Tarnay, Gene Stulgaitis; Premiere of "Three Country-
sides" (Led Zeppelin-Jethro Tull, Kathryn Posin) per-
formed by Laura Glenn, Lenore Latimer, Kathryn
Posin, Jim May, Phillip Jonson, Aaron Osborne, Lar
Roberson

Friday and Sunday: "Burlesque/Black & White" (Choreography, Art Bauman) performed by Laura Glenn,
Lenore Latimer, Wendy Perron; Premiere of "Days"
choreographed and performed by Kathryn Posin; "Fantaisie Pour Deux" (Jack Moore); "Residue 1" (Stockhausen, Jack Moore) performed by Rudy Perez; "Residue 4" (Nancarrow, Moore) danced by Barbara Roan;
"Dialog" arranged and performed by Art Bauman;
"Three Countrysides" (Zeppelin-Tull, Kathryn Posin)

V. Sladon, Irene Vilhar Photos

Eric Reiner Photos

**Barbara Roan in "Residue 4" Above: Barbara Roan,
Wendy Perron, Connie Allentuck,
Anthony LaGiglia in "Ode"**

**Jim May, Dorothy Hershkowitz, Wendy Summit
in "Upriver" Above: Hideko Tano in "Beginning"**

**Improvisation Group Above: Gene Stulgaitus,
Linda Tarnay in "Fantaisie Pour Deux"**

MISCELLANEOUS NEW YORK DANCE PROGRAMS

(Failure to submit material necessitated omission of several programs)

UNIVERSALIST-UNITARIAN CHURCH
Saturday, September 26, 1970.
Murray Grove Association presents:

SACRED DANCE GUILD OF MIAMI

Director, Diana Avery; Choreography, Diana and Paul Avery; Press, Clarene Caplan

COMPANY

Judy Bennett, Helen Marie Gordich, Lyn Pletts, Jan Richardson, Jeanne Ruddy

PROGRAM

"One Royal Mantle of Humanity" with music by Ric Masten, and libretto arranged by Geoffrey P. Selth from the writings of William Blake, John Murray, Carl Sandburg, Herman Melville, St. Paul, Walt Whitman, Don Marquis, William Shakespeare, Edna St. Vincent Millay, Robert Burns

Right: Jan Richardson, Diana Avery of Sacred Dance Guild

29 WOOSTER STREET
Friday and Saturday, October 2, 3, 1970.

BATYA ZAMIR JUDY PADOW

PROGRAM: "Circles," "Turns," "Forward and Backward Walks," "Open and Closed Turns," "Direction Changes," "Runs"

Below: Batya Zamir

FASHION INSTITUTE
Saturday, October 10, 1970.

MARY ANTHONY DANCE THEATRE

Director-Choreographer, Mary Anthony; Assistant, Ross Parkes; Sets and Lighting, Tom Munn; Costumes, Leor Curtiss Warner II, Bernard Johnson, Susan McPherson

COMPANY

Ross Parkes, Yuriko Kimura, Daniel Maloney, Tonia Shimin, Ellen Robbins, Muriel Cohan, Carole Simpson, David Roche, Marcia Plevin

PROGRAM

Premiere of work in progress "Dream Flights" (Luigi Nono), New York premiere of "In the Beginning: I. Adam, II. Eve" (Peter Sculthorpe).. "To Jose Clemente Orozco from 'Dedications in Our Time' " (Kenneth Klaus, James Truitte after Lester Horton), New York premiere of "Antiphon" (Louis Calabro), "Threnody" (Benjamin Britten)

Ross Parkes, Mary Anthony in "Threnody" Left Center: Ross Parks, Yuriko Kimura in "In the Beginning: Eve"

COOPER UNION

Friday, October 23, 1970
The Cooper Union for the advancement of Science and Art presents:

VIJA VETRA
in
Dances of India

Artistic Direction, Choreography, Costumes, Vija Vetra; Associate Artists, Glenda Taylor (reading poetry), Rama Murphy (vocalist), Henry Levin (tabla), Lynn Levin (tamboura)

PROGRAM

"Shlokam," "Devotional Poems," "Puja," "Pijarini," "Alarippu," "Tillana," "Radha," "Kurati"

V. Sladon Photo

Right: Vija Vetra

DONNELL AUDITORIUM

Saturday, October 24, 1970.*
The Donnell Library Center of the New York Public Library presents:

PHILIPPINE DANCE COMPANY
OF NEW YORK

Founder-Executive Director, Bruna Seril; Director-Choreographer, Ronnie G. Alejandro; Artistic Director, Jamin Alcoriza; Music Director, Jerry Dadap; Assistant Dance Director, Ching Valdez; Assistant Music Director, Divinagracia Montalban; Technical Director, Mel Chionglo; Stage Manager, Gil T. Santos; Costumes, Gang Gomez; President, Jesse Gamboa

COMPANY

Ronnie G. Alejandro, Reilly Afable Alip, Mel Chionglo, Pete Concepcion, Ruben Delagana, Jr., Jesse Gamboa, Gang Gomez, Rei Llorente, Ed Oreta, Jorge Ortol, Gil T. Santos, Jerry Dadap, Honey Barredo, Brenda Duque, Cynthia Evangelista, Sita Gomez, Linda Mananghaya, Nini Mendoza, Divinagracia Montalban, Agnes Montalban, Loreta Pasion, Anita Soria, Odie Tablit, Ching Valdez, Gilda Yap

PROGRAM

"Salidom-Ay Suite," "Bailes de Ayer," "Sarimanok Suite," "Sa Kabukiran"

* Program repeated on Saturday, May 1, 1971.

Gil Resureccion Photo

Right: "Salidom-Ay Suite"

CARNEGIE HALL

Sunday, November 1, 1970.
Arthur Shafman International, Ltd. presents:

JOSE MOLINA BAILES
ESPANOLES

Choreography, Jose Molina, Luis Montero; Musical Director, Silvio Masciarelli; Production Manager, Richard Ivey; Technical Adviser, Jack Bates; Costumes, Anita of Madrid, Ricardo Vargas of Madrid

COMPANY

Jose Molina, Antonia Martinez, Luis Montero, Carmen Dominguez, Maria Carmen Villena, Manolo Rivera, Azucena Flores, Felix Granados, vocalist La Trianera, guitarists Francisco Espinosa, Beltran Espinosa

PROGRAM

"La Boda de Luis Alonso" (Gimenez), "El Vito" (Infante), "Dolores," "La Noche," "Leyenda" (Albeniz), "Lagarteranos" (Guerrero), "Zapateado" (Sarasate), "Cana," "Espana" (Chabrier), "Juan Romero" (Turina), "Goyescas" (Granados), "Taberna"

**Jose Molina (L) and company
in "Espana"**

James Cunningham

BARNARD GYMNASIUM
Friday & Saturday, November 6, 7, 1970.
Dance Uptown (Janet Soares, Director) presents:

VIOLA FARBER & COMPANY
JAMES CUNNINGHAM
& COMPANY

PROGRAM

PART I: "Passage," and premieres of "Three Duets," and "Trio" choreographed by Viola Farber, and danced by Viola Farber, June Finch, Anne Koren, Rosalind Newman, Andre Peck, Jeff Slayton, Dan Wagoner
PART II: New York premiere of James Cunningham's "The Junior Birdsmen" performed by Lauren Persichetti, Candice Lerman, Joel Harrison, Ted Striggles, and company of eighty.

Ted Wester Photo

CHAPEL OF THE INTERCESSION
Sunday, November 29, 1970.*

HUJER DANCE COMPANY

Director-Choreographer, Flower Hujer; Artistic Direction and Design, Miller Richardson

COMPANY

Michael Herter, Michael Traven, Robert Bowyer, Deborah Wood, Flower Hujer, Karen McGarven, Nancy Salmon, John Valley, Darryl Stipek

PROGRAM

"The Juggler of Our Lady" a medieval dance drama based on the legend of Saint Barnabus, presented in 9 scenes without intermission

* Repeated for two performances on Wednesday, Dec. 16, 1970 at Trinity Church.

Flower Hujer, Deborah Wood
in "The Juggler of Our Lady"

TRINITY CHURCH
Wednesday, December 2, 1970.

DOWNTOWN BALLET
COMPANY

Director-Choreographer, Paschal Guzman; Assistant Director, Robert Christopher

COMPANY

Karen Battell, Phoebe Frank, Christina Ham, Jill Malamud, Christopher Frey, Paschal Guzman, Anne Kennedy, Robert Raimondo

PROGRAM

Premiere of "Recollections: La Nativite, The Heavens Declare, Kleine Praeludien und Intermezzi, Arioso, Poco Vivace, Toccata in G Major, La Nativite"

Downtown Ballet
in "Recollections"

Robert Rogers Photo

Rudy Perez Dance Theater
in "Monumental Exchange"

PRATT INSTITUTE

Friday, December 11, 1970.
Pratt Institute Dance Workshop and Graduate Art present:

RUDY PEREZ DANCE THEATER

Choreography and Sounds by Rudy Perez

COMPANY

Rudy Perez, Barbara Roan, Anthony LaGiglia, Tom Borek, Wendy Summit, Steven Buck

PROGRAM

"A Monumental Work" (assisted by Pratt students), "Arcade," "Coverage"

CHILDREN'S THEATRE

Saturday, December 5, 1970.*

BHASKAR & SHALA DANCES OF INDIA

PROGRAM: "Natanan Adinar," "Krishna," "Thala Nirtham," "Maya," "Naga Nirtham," "Surya Nirtham"

* Additional performances at Bushwick High School (Dec. 9, 1970), Children's Theatre (Dec. 20), PS 171 (Feb 1, 1971), Chelsea High School (Feb. 17), PS115 (Feb.27), as well as throughout the United States

Bhaskar and Shala

ISADOR STRAUS THEATRE

Sundays, December 13, 20, 1970.
The Educational Alliance presents:

MARIAN SARACH AND DANCE COMPANY

Choreography, Marian Sarach; Costumes, Charles Stanley, Vivian Steinberg; Lighting, Charles Atlas; Stage Manager, Frank Lilly; Press, Doris Gubernick

COMPANY

Marian Sarach, Janet Markovitz, Billy Siegenfeld, Marcia Wardell, Steven Malkus, Bryan Hayes

PROGRAM

Premiere of "Facets" (Roy Harris), "Etude for a March" (Tape collage), "My Secret Life" (John Herbert McDowell), Premiere of "Bread and Butter" (Rudy Crosswell); Narrator, Kristina Olsczer)

Bryan Hayes, Steven Malkus, Janet Markovitz
in "Facets"

105

COOPER UNION

Friday, December 18, 1970.
The Cooper Union for the Advancement of Science and Art (Johnson E. Fairchild, Director) presents:

JEAN ERDMAN
THEATER OF DANCE

Artistic Director-Choreographer, Jean Erdman; Administrative Assistant, Marcia Sherman; Guest Artist-Composer, Jimmy Giuffre

COMPANY

Jean Erdman, Ari Darom, Edward Henkel, Elizabeth Kagan, Rachel Lampert, Michelle Levine, Susan Matheke, Andrea Stark, Aviva Stern, Byron Wheeler

PROGRAM

"Promenade," "The Double Spiral," "Four Classes of Natural Action," "Salutatio" (Mozart) solo danced by Jean Erdman, "Jimmy Giuffre on the Theme of Spontaneity in Music," "Facets of the Interrelationship of Dance and Music," "Excerpts from the Castle" (Giuffre)

Lyn Smith Photos

Jean Erdman (R) and above with
Jimmy Giuffre in "The Castle"

Indra-Nila

PHILOSOPHICAL RESEARCH SOCIETY
Saturday, December 19, 1970.*

INDRA-NILA

PROGRAM: "Alarippu," "Thaye Yashoda," "Jagath Janani," "Natanam Adinar," "Suddha Paithyakaran," "Adavum Solluval Aval," "Thillanna," "Krishnani Begane Baro," "Sringara Lahari," "Madura Nagarilo," "Telisenura," "Mayura Nritta"

* This program entitled "Introduction to Indian Dance" was in three parts, with second and third performances on Jan. 30, and Mar. 13, 1971.

PUBLIC THEATER

Sunday, December 20, 1970.*
WBAI Free Music Store presents:

DANIEL NAGRIN

in

THE PELOPONNESIAN WAR

Choreography, Daniel Nagrin; Music, Eric Saltzman, Archie Shepp; Tape, Saltzman-Nagrin; Voice, Frank Langella; Costumes, Sally Ann Parsons; Presented in 2 parts and 15 sequences: Waltz, Arise, Miscellaneous, Falls, Turning Dance, National Dance I, National Dance II, Johnny Dance, Indentity, Decision, The World Game, Culture, In Memoriam, The Survivor, Power Play, Answer

* Repeated Dec. 25, 27, 1970, and Jan. 1, 3, 1971, and at WBAI Church on Jan. 1, 4, 11, 18, 25, Feb. 2, 8, Mar. 1, 8, 15, 22, 29, Apr. 5, 12, 19, 26, 1971.

Daniel Nagrin in "The Peloponnesian War"

Les Ballets Africains (also above)

BROOKS ATKINSON THEATRE

Opened Saturday, December 26, 1970.*
Kolu Productions, Inc. presents:

LES BALLETS AFRICAINS

Artistic Directors, Hamidou Bangoura, Italo Zambo; General Manager, Mamadou Lamine Sane; Assistant General Manager, Mohamed Lamine Camara; Exclusive Booking Direction, Kolmar-Luth Entertainment, Inc.

COMPANY

Mariama Sadio Bah, Oumou Bangoura, Mariama Barry, Aly Camara, Faouly Camara, Ibrahima Camara, Lansana Dede Camara, Maia Camara, Mossokoura Camara, Manana Cisse, Damany Conde, Sekou Conde II, Ibrahima Conte, Aissata Dabo, Koca Sale Diabate, Mariama Diallo, Almamy Dioubate, Bintou Dioubate, Sekou Dioubate, Karamoke Fofana, Malene Fofana, Vomo Gbamou, Mabinty Keita, Noumody Keita, Famoudou Konate, Mamadi Kourouma, M'Bady Kouyate, Jeanne Macauley, Mamdy Mansare, Bakary Mara, Mama Somano, Goundo Souare, Bintou Soumah, Salifou Sylla, Jean Tonia, Aissatou Toure, Arafan Toure, Guila Traore

PROGRAM

"The Evolution of Africa," "Tiranke," "Initiation," "Night of the Cobra," Finale

Company Manager: Murray Luth
Press: Max Eisen, Warren Pincus
Stage Manager: Salifou Bangoura

* Closed Jan. 17, 1971 after limited engagement of 26 performances.

Mariana Parra, Barbara Martos, Mariano Parra,
Jerane Michel, Ines Parra

METROPOLITAN MUSEUM
Friday, January 1, 1971.*
Springtime Festival and Musical Artists present:

MARIANO PARRA
SPANISH DANCE COMPANY

Artistic Director, Mariano Parra; Assistant Director,
Jerane Michel; Choreographers, Mariano Parra, Jerane
Michel, Mercedes de Leon, Maria Rosa Mercede, La
Meri

COMPANY

Mariano Parra, Jerane Michel, Ines Parra, Mariana
Parra, Barbara Martos, Dominico (singer), Guillermo
Montes (guitarist)

PROGRAM

"Seguidillas" (Albeniz), "Baile Para Dos," "Las Tres
Mujeres de Cadiz," "Farruca," "Danza Prima" (De-
Falla), "Evocacion" (Albeniz), "Romanza Gitana," "Za-
pateado" (Sarasate), "La Cana," "Playeras," "Jota
Valenciana," "Fiesta Flamenca"

* Repeated on Saturday, March 20, and Tuesday, April
  13, 1971.

Van Williams Photo

BORDEN AUDITORIUM
Friday, January 15, and Saturday, January 16, 1971.
The Manhattan School of Music presents:

ALABAMA BALLET
COMPANY

PRINCIPALS: Helen Dexter, Larry McMillian, Sasha
Gosic, Larry James Bailey, Jo Ann Baker, Gregg Freeman, Radamir Vuchic (Belgrade National Ballet)

PROGRAM

"Le Monde de Lautrec" (Flagello, Josef Gregory),
"Estancia" (Ginastera, Robert Davis), "Don Quixote Pas
de Deux" (Minkus, Petipa), "Black Swan Pas de Deux"
(Tchaikovsky, Parlic), "Gospel Suite" (Flagello, Wilma
Curley)

Al Levine Photo

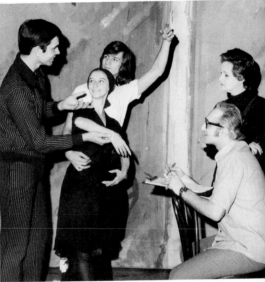

Joseph Gregory, Sasha Gosic, Larry James Bailey,
Martin Streicher, Wilma Curley of Alabama Ballet

NYU EDUCATION AUDITORIUM
Wednesday, January 20, 1971.
NYU School of Continuing Education presents:

PAUL SANASARDO
DANCE COMPANY

Artistic Director-Choreographer, Paul Sanasardo; Assistant Artistic Director, Manuel Alum; Musical Director,
Eugene Lester; Lighting, Gary Harris

COMPANY

Manuel Alum, Judith Blackstone, Diane Germaine,
Willa Kahn, Joan Lombardi, Gerri Houlihan, Georgina
Holmes, Yon Martin, Matthew Diamond, Joseph Fon-
tano, Paul Sanasardo

PROGRAM

"Metallics" (Cowell-Badings), "The Cellar" (Kilar, Manuel Alum), "Cut Flowers" (Serocki), "Roly-Poly" (Berio,
Alum), "Fatal Birds" (Ginastera)

**Yon Martin, Gerri Houlihan, Diane Germaine
in "Cut Flowers"**

Fred Fehl Photo

Opened Thursday, January 28, 1971.*
Columbia Artists Management and J. H. Zarovich present:

SIBERIAN DANCERS & SINGERS OF OMSK

Founder-Artistic Director, Elena Kalugina; Director, Yuri Yurovsky; Choir Leader, Iraida Ivanova; Chief of Choir, Georgi Pantukov; Choreographer, Yakov Kolomeisky; Company Manager, John Scott; Stage Manager, Hans Hortig; Personal Direction, Chris Schang

PROGRAM

"Carnival" (Pronin), "Green Field" (Ivanova), "Coachman's Dance" (Folk), "When the Moon" (Folk), "Peddlers" (Folk), "From Behind the Island into the Bay" (Folk), "Love Song," "Tea" (Pantukov-Pronin), "Let's Dance," "Siberian Fun" (Folk), "My Hut" (Folk), "My Husband Forced Me To.." (Folk), "The Spooners" (Rud), "Little Widow" (Ponomarenko), "Moon Song," "Love Grass" (Folk), "Siberian Troika" (Folk), "Prairie Song," "Down Hill" (Folk)

* Closed Saturday, Feb. 6, 1971 after limited engagement of 12 performances.

Top Left and Below: Siberian Dancers

CHELSEA LANE STUDIO THEATRE

Friday and Saturday, January 29, 30, 1971.*

THE ALONSO CASTRO DANCE COMPANY

Director-Choreographer, Alonso Castro; Costumes, Bill Orzack; Masks, A. Mathieu; Lighting, S. Vincent

COMPANY

Marc Dico, Rickey Edmondson, Trudy Emanuel, Robert Ghigliotty, Ina Kahn, Lynn Matlock, Diana Scher, Wendy Stein, Israel Valle, Sergio Vicencio, Alonso Castro, Tanna Hunter, Clifton Jones, Govinda

PROGRAM

"Concerto 5" (Bach), Sacred Grapes" (Sati), "The Grand Grand Grand Pas de Deux" (Sati), "Varnam," "Tillana," "Eat a Puss Rex" (Rameau), "Flower High" (Donizetti), "Vignettes of Carmina Burana" (Orff)

* Program repeated Friday and Saturday, Feb. 5, 6, 1971.
Friday and Saturday, March 12, 13, 1971.*

PROGRAM

"Concerto 5," "Afternoon of a Faun" (Debussy), "Vignettes of Carmina Burana," "The Inquisitors" (Bloch, Bach, Britten)

* Repeated on March 19 and 20, 1971.

Ina Kahn Photo

Marc Dico of Alonso Castro company in "Afternoon of a Faun"

FERRIS BOOTH HALL
Sunday, January 31, 1971.*
Columbia University presents:

SHAKUNTALA

Choreographer, Maya Kulkarni; Music, Suresh Shukla; Stage Design, Bihari Sharma

COMPANY

Maya Kulkarni, Bihari Sharma, Veera Dalal, Asha Devi, Geeta Vashi, Geeta Singh, Virendra Barot, Devendra Sharma, Alyosh Aggarwal

PROGRAM

"Shakuntala" an Indian Classical Dance drama in three acts

* Repeated Saturday, Feb. 6, 1971.

Right: Maya Kulkarni

NYU EDUCATION AUDITORIUM
Wednesday, February 3, 1971.
The Martha Graham Center of Contemporary Dance presents:

NEW WORKS BY BERTRAM ROSS

COMPANY: Bertram Ross, Matt Turney, Mary Hinkson, Clive Thompson

PROGRAM: "Embattled Garden" (Surinach, Graham), Premieres of "A Small Book of Poems" (David Walker, Bertram Ross), and "Still Life" (Bertram Ross)

Left: Bertram Ross

NYU EDUCATION AUDITORIUM
Wednesday, February 10, 1971.
NYU School of Continuing Education presents:

ROD RODGERS DANCE COMPANY

Artistic Director-Choreographer, Rod Rodgers; Administrative and Production Assistant, Helen Cash; Lighting, William Marshall; Technical Assistant, William Boone; Costumes, B. Fuller; Slide Environment, Bill Longcore; Set, Jane Stein

COMPANY

Rod Rodgers, Blondell Cummings, Morris Donaldson, Quincey Edwards, Leona Johnson, Thomas Pinnock, Ronald Pratt, Barbara Roan, Ellen Robbins, Joanne Robinson, Shirley Rushing
MUSICIANS: Gwendolyn Watson, Joel Press, Bill Wood, Rod Rodgers, Danny Barrajamos, Chief Bey, E. Calvin, Bernice Reagan

PROGRAM

Premiere of "Trajectories E" (Castiglioni), "Now! Nigga..." (L. Tristano), "Dances in Projected Space" (Watson-Press), "Harambee!"

Rod Rodgers company in "Harambee"

Sichi Ko Photo

HALL OF FAME PLAYHOUSE

Wednesday, February 17, 1971.
The Student Union Board of New York University presents:

DOWNTOWN BALLET COMPANY

Director, Paschal Guzman; Assistant Director, Robert Christopher; Choreographer, Paschal Guzman; President, Robert Shuster

COMPANY

Karen Battell, Phoebe Franke, Christiana Ham, Jill Malamud, Christopher Frey, Paschal Guzman, Anne Kennedy, Robert Raimondo

PROGRAM

"Scherzo Capriciose" (Dvorak), "Toccata and Percussion" (Chavez), "Wassermusik" (Handel), "Peasant Pas de Deux from Giselle," and premiere of "Beethovanesque" (Beethoven, Paschal Guzman)

Paschal Guzman rehearsing Downtown Ballet

ASIA HOUSE

Sunday, February 28, 1971.

SUNG HAE OH

in a program of traditional, folk, court, and religious dances of Korea

Left: Sung Hae Oh

Fibich company in a "Hora"

BROOKLYN MUSEUM

Saturday, March 21, 1971.

FELIX FIBICH DANCE COMPANY

Director-Choreographer, Felix Fibich

COMPANY

Felix Fibich, Judith Fibich, Philip Johnson, Charles Karp, Bruce Bloch, Karen Marcus, Aviva Passow, Irene Buochinsakas

PROGRAM

"The Sabbath Mood" (Kon), "Celebration," "Matchmaking" (Kon), "Wedding Dance" (Press), "The Shepherd and the Girl," "Bocharian Dance," "Debka" (Folk), "The Hora" (Folk)

Thurday and Friday, March 25, 26, 1971.
The Judson Dance Theater presents:

CAROLYN BILDERBACK

Choreographed and performed by Carolyn Bilderback; Lighting, Shirley Pendergast; Environment, Paul Swedenberg; Costumes, Carolyn Bilderback; Stage Manager, Paul Swedenberg; Recorder, Jeff Simmons; Flute, Gary Johnson; Percussion, Nick Hodsdon.

PROGRAM

"Mystery of Growth," "Lake of Fire," "Stone Listening to the Rain," " The Beginning of Love in an Ancient Eternal Place," "Design," "Design Repeated," "Thread of the Universe," "Snail's Foot, Rabbit's Prayer, Newborn," "Yawn to Afternoon Sunlight," "Figure of Misery," "Untitled," "Horse in Moonlit Field"

Left: Carolyn Bilderback in "Mystery of Growth"

EMANU-EL MIDTOWN YM-YWHA
Saturday, March 27, 1971.

DANCES BY
BATYA ZAMIR

COMPANY: Kenneth Fishman, Angela Frascone, Thomas Henner, Eileen Kasofsky, Naomi Landau, Al Loving, Nelson Richardson, Jan Sarkisian, Richard Van Buren, Batya Zamir

PROGRAM

"Trio Release," "Trio Exchange," "Individual Turns," "Circles to Turn," "Circle Exchange," "Slot Exchanges," "Direction Changes"

Batya Zamir (C)

EMANUEL YW-YMHA
Sunday, March 28, 1971.

MARY FULKERSON
AND COMPANY

Director-Choreographer, Mary Fulkerson; Sound and Stage Manager, James Fulkerson

COMPANY

Margot Bassett, Tim Butler, Phillip Heinegg, Alice Lusterman, John Rolland, Judy Savage, David Woodberry

PROGRAM: "In Passing"

**Philip Heinegg, Mary Fulkerson, Margot Bassett
in "In Passing"**

MUSEUM OF NATURAL HISTORY
Tuesday, March 30, 1971.
BHASKAR'S DANCES OF INDIA
PROGRAM: "Natanan Adinar," "Krishna," "Thala Nirtham," "Naga Nirtham," "Surya Nirtham"

Left: Bhaskar

NYU EDUCATION AUDITORIUM
Friday, April 9, 1971.
The Dance Program of the Division of Creative Arts in conjunction with its 1971 College Dance Symposium presents:
NANCY MEEHAN DANCE COMPANY

Director-Choreographer, Nancy Meehan; Lighting, Stage Manager, Chenault Spence; Technical Assistants, Bruce King, David Guthrie, Susan Burton, Maria Sturm; Costumes, Anthony Candido; Percussionist, Richard Fitz

COMPANY

Nancy Meehan, Kay Gilbert, Shelly Goldklank, Trude Link, Susan Lundberg, Nina Sprecher

PROGRAM

"Whitip", "Hudson River Seasons: Spring, Summer, Autumn, Winter" (Jeffrey Levine)

Nancy Meehan in "Whitip"

BROOKLYN MUSEUM
Monday, April 12, 1971.
PERCIVAL BORDE AND COMPANY

Director-Choreographer, Percival Borde; Research and Choreography, Pearl Primus; Drummer-Accompanist, Alphonse Cimber

COMPANY: names not submitted

PROGRAM: "Talking Drums of Africa," "Drums of the Caribbean"

**Percival Borde
in "Drums of the Caribbean"**

THE CROSBY PROJECT
Friday and Saturday, April 16, 17, 1971.

DANCES BY
BATYA ZAMIR

COMPANY: Kenneth Fishman, Angela Frascone, Thomas Henner, Eileen Kasofsky, Naomi Landau, Al Loving, Nelson Richardson, Jan Sarkisian, Batya Zamir

PROGRAM

"Trio Release," "Trio Exchange," "Individual Turns," "Trio Exchange," "Circles to Turn," "Circle Exchange," "Direction Changes"

Batya Zamir Company

Jean-Leon Destine in "Spider Dance"

MOFFETT CENTER
Saturday, April 17, 1971.

JEAN-LEON DESTINE
and his
Afro-Haitian
Dance Company

Artistic Director-Choreographer, Jean-Leon Destine; Costumes, Ellie Antoine; Lighting, Judie Scott

COMPANY

Jean-Leon Destine, Edouard Walrond, Shirley Spiceur, Joan Atigbi, Benjamin Sterlin, Marianne Marvellia, Louines Louinis, and drummers Alphonse Cimer, Louis Celestin

PROGRAM

"Village Festival," "Creole Songs," "Baptism of the Drum," "Slave Dance," "Yoruba/Bakas," "Serenade Tropicale," "Drums," "Witch Doctor," "Caribbean Bamboche," "Fantasie Musicale," "Spider Dance," "Drum Conversation," "Ceremony Bembe"

Louis Mélançon Photo

JUDSON MEMORIAL CHURCH
Monday, April 19, 1971.*
Judson Dance Theater presents:

MARIAN SARACH
AND DANCE COMPANY

Choreography, Marian Sarach; Costumes, Charles Stanley, Norvie Bullock; Lighting, Earl Eidman, Susan Bauer; Stage Manager, Nancy Stover

COMPANY

Marian Sarach, Joan Baker, Janet Markovitz, Bryan Hayes, Antoine McCoy

PROGRAM

"Openers" (Persichetti), "Elements I" (Pauline Oliveros), "Elements II" (Oliveros), "Cambridge Memories" (Stephen Smoliar), "Oriental Poppy" (Rudy Crosswell), "Concertante" (John Herbert McDowell)

* Repeated on April 20, 21, 1971.

Ted Wester Photo

**Marian Sarach
in "Etude for a March"**

PUBLIC THEATER

Friday, April 23, 1971.*
New York Shakespeare Festival in association with
Lepercq Foundation presents:

LAR LUBOVITCH
AND COMPANY

Director-Choreographer, Lar Lubovitch; Manager,
Gary Lindsey; Costumes and Lighting, Lar Lubovitch;
Stage Manager, Jon Brittain; Management Shaw Concerts

COMPANY

Louis Bartlett, George Coleman, Diane Duffy, Tom
Ellicott, Teresa Hill, Marti Ingle, Bonnie Mathis, Michele
Murray, Mari Ono, Ernest Pagnano, Jeanne Solan, Sally
Trammell, Marcus Williamson, Janet Wong, Armando
Zetina, and Lar Lubovitch

PROGRAM

"Ecstasy" (Olivier Messiaen), "Whirligogs" (Luciano
Berio), "Some of the Reactions of Some of the People
Some of the Time upon Hearing the Reports of the
Coming of the Messiah" (Handel)

* Repeated Apr. 24, 25, 26, 1971.

Dina Makarova Photo

Lar Lubovitch in "Some of the reactions. . . ."

Tina Croll in "Groundwork"

WASHINGTON SQUARE CHURCH

Tuesday, April 27, 1971.*
WBAI Free Music Store presents:

TINA CROLL
& DANCE COMPANY

Director-Choreographer, Tapes, Tina Croll; Lighting,
and Stage Manager, David Krohn; Sound, Paul Rosal

COMPANY

Tina Croll, Barbara Ensley, Micki Goodman, Ted Striggles, Toni Lacativa, John Moore

PROGRAM

"Ground-Work," "Farm," and premiere of "The Limestone Room"

* Repeated Apr. 28, and Sunday, May 2, 1971.

Ted Wester Photo

DONNELL LIBRARY CENTER

Wednesday, April 28, 1971.

ASHA DEVI
Dance and Music of India

Narrator, Barbara Seddon; Sitar, Mira Benedict;
Tabla and Dholak, Bihari Sharma; Sarangi, Kim Woodruff; Violin, Ranjit Saxena; Clarinet, Sanjit Saxena

PROGRAM

"Jatiswaram," "Karunaini," "Thaye Yashodha," "The
Lotus and the Bee," "Kathak," "Lai Harouba," "Chandra Metu"

Asha Devi, Bihari Sharma

RIVERSIDE THEATRE
Saturday & Sunday, May 1, 2, 1971.

TOBY ARMOUR
& COMPANY

Director-Choreographer, Toby Armour; Music Direc-
tor, Ezra Sims, Lighting, Jennifer Tipton; Production
Manager, Lois Ginandes; Technical Director-Stage
Manager, Harvey Spevak.

COMPANY

Toby Armour, Lois Ginandes, Jan Houston, Leslie Innis,
Mari Jackman, Christina Jackmauh, Mike Mao, Bruce de
Satin Crois, Marlene Wallin, Alex MacRae (guitarist)

PROGRAM

"Brick Layers" (Tape), "Pastorale" (Sims), "Abalone
Co."

Charles Fatone Photo

Left: Toby Armour

SAINT PETER'S GATE
Monday, May 17-21, 1971
Cabaret Theatre at Noon presents:

VIJA VETRA
in
Dances of India

Director-Choreographer, Production Coordinator,
Howard Girven; Managing Director, Donna Seigfried

PROGRAM

"Shlokam," "Devotional Poems," "Puja," "Puarini,"
"Alarippu," "Tillana"

Henry Levy Photo

Vija Vetra

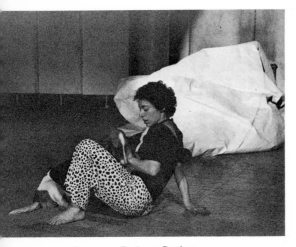

JUDSON MEMORIAL CHURCH
Opened Tuesday, May 18, 1971.*
The Judson Dance Theater presents:

THE BARBARA GARDNER
CONSTRUCTION COMPANY

Director-Choreographer, Barbara Gardner; Lighting,
John P. Dodd; Sound, John Herbert McDowell; Stage
Manager, Jamison R. Kinkaid; Masks, Tom Gardner;
Crew, J. R. Kinkaid, Scott Markham, Mike Weinstein

COMPANY

Susan Bluestein, Jacques Browers, Marcia Dubetsky,
William Dunas, Barbara Gardner, Martin Gleitsman,
Carolyn Lord, Phoebe Neville, Betsy Polatin, Edward
Spena, Charles Stanley

PROGRAM

"Slope: How to Kill a Tiger" "Tank"

* Closed May 21, 1971 after limited engagement of 4
performances.

Papagena, Barbara Gardner
in "Slope: How to Kill a Tiger"

Mirjam Berns, Dan Wagoner in "Duet"

STAGE CITY
Saturday & Sunday, May 22, 23, 1971.
Frank Wicks presents:

DAN WAGONER
AND DANCERS

Choreography, Dan Wagoner; Lighting, Earl Eidman;
Assistant, Susan Zwarman

COMPANY

Mirjam Berns, Cathy Boyd, Emmy Devine, Sally Hess,
Karen Levey, Judith Moss, Dan Wagoner, and George
Montgomery

PROGRAM

"Brambles," "Night Duet", Premiere of "Cows and
Ruins" (Traditional Country-Western, Dan Wagoner)
danced by Mirjam Berns, Cathy Boyd, Emmy Devine,
Sally Hess, Dan Wagoner, "Iron Mountain" (Hindemith), "Westwork" (Purcell), "Duet" (Purcell) danced
by Mirjam Berns and Dan Wagoner.

WASHINGTON SQUARE
METHODIST CHURCH

Thursday & Friday, May 27, 28, 1971.
The WBAI Free Music Store presents: +

ROBERT STREICHER
SOLO DANCES

PROGRAM: "Device" (Robert Ashly, Streicher), "Achil-
les in Three Stages" (Pink Floyd, Streicher), and premiere of "Winterloss" (Steve Reich, Streicher)

Robert Streicher

GENEROSO POPE AUDITORIUM

Friday & Saturday, May 28, 29, 1971.
The Department of the Arts of Fordham at Lincoln
Center presents:

LARRY RICHARDSON
AND DANCE COMPANY

Director-Choreographer, Larry Richardson; Costumes,
DeBenedetti; Lighting, Gary Harris; Press, J. Antony
Siciliano; Sets and Properties, Paolo.

COMPANY

Honey Barredo, Barbara Bernhardt, Angel Betancourt,
Jose Coronado, Marina Keijzer, Mario Delamo, Jeri
McAndrews, Mary Price, Pat Taylor, Christine Varjan,
Dorothy Zito

PROGRAM

"Fusion" (Copland), "The Walking Wounded" (Mache-
Collage), Premieres of "Epoch" (Stockhausen, Richardson) with the company, and "Santa Claus" (Collage)

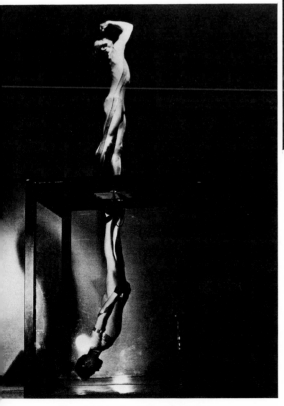

Larry Richardson, Lar Roberson
in "The Walking Wounded"

BROOKLYN ACADEMY OF MUSIC

Festival of Dance 1970-1971
Harvey Lichtenstein, Director

BROOKLYN ACADEMY OF MUSIC
Opened Friday, October 2, 1970.*
The Brooklyn Academy of Music in cooperation with
The Martha Graham Center of Contemporary
Dance, Inc., by arrangement with Harold Shaw
presents:

MARTHA GRAHAM DANCE COMPANY

Founder-Director-Choreographer, Martha Graham;
Co-Director, Bertram Ross; Conductor, Eugene Lester;
Associate Conductor, Stanley Sussman; Settings, Isamu
Noguchi, Arch Lauterer, Philip Stapp; Lighting, Jean
Rosenthal, William H. Batchelder; Rehearsal Director,
Patricia Birch; Producer, LeRoy Leatherman; Production
Manager, William H. Batchelder; Costume Supervisor,
Ursula Reed

COMPANY

Bertram Ross, Helen McGehee, Richard Gain, Mary
Hinkson, Robert Powell, Patricia Birch, Matt Turney,
Richard Kuch, Takako Asakawa, Moss Cohen, Judith
Hogan, Yuriko Kimura, David Hatch Walker, Phyllis
Gutelius, Diane Gray, Judith Leifer, Dawn Suzuki, Lar
Roberson

GUEST ARTISTS: Jane Dudley, Pearl Lang, Jean
Erdman

REPERTOIRE

"El Penitente" (Louis Horst), "Deaths and Entrances"
(Hunter Johnson), "Every Soul Is A Circus" (Paul Nor-
doff), "Oases" (Walter Caldon, Bertram Ross), "Letter to
the World" (Hunter Johnson), "Phaedra" (Robert
Starer),"Appalachian Spring" (Copland), "Cave of the
Heart" (Barber)

*Press:*Isadora Bennett, Tom Kerrigan
*Stage Managers:*Jane Clegg, Howard Crampton-Smith

* Closed Oct. 8, 1970 after limited engagement of 8
performances.

Martha Swope, Ron Protas Photos

Mary Hinkson
in "Deaths and Entrances"

Bertram Ross, Mary Hinkson, Richard Hutch
Above: Mary Hinkson, Bertram Ross
in "El Penitente"

"Oases" Above: Diane Gray, Robert Powell, Phyllis Gutelius, Yuriko Kimura
in "Every Soul Is a Circus"

Martha Swope Pho

Takako Asakawa, Richard Gain in "Cave of the Heart"

Bertram Ross, Yuriko Kimura in "Cave of the Heart" Top: Jean Erdman, Pearl Lang, Bertram Ross in "Letter to the World"

"Phaedra" Top: (L) Mary Hinkson (R) Bertram
Ross, Patricia Birch in "Every Soul Is a Circus"
MARTHA GRAHAM DANCE COMPANY

BROOKLYN ACADEMY OF MUSIC
Opened Wednesday, October 21, 1970.*
The Brooklyn Academy of Music in association with
The American Dance Foundation presents:

THE AMERICAN BALLET COMPANY

Director-Choreographer, Eliot Feld; Ballet Mistress,
Barbara Fallis; Musical Director, Christopher Keene;
Associate Conductor, Isaiah Jackson; Administrative
Director, William Crawford; Lighting, Jules Fisher;
Production Assistant, David Bixler; Stage Managers,
Ellen Wittman, Randall Brooks; Pianist, Gladys Celeste
Mercader; Wardrobe, Elonzo Dann; Press, Thomas
Kerrigan, Anne Goodrich

COMPANY

Olga Janke, Elizabeth Lee, Christine Sarry, Eliot Feld,
John Sowinski Marilyn D'Honeau, Cristina Stirling,
Larry Grenier, Daniel Levins, Karen Kelly, Eve Wal-
strum, Edward Henkel, James Lewis, Christine Kono,
Kerry Williams, Kenneth Hughes, Richard Munro

REPERTOIRE

"Harbinger" (Prokofieff, Feld), World Premiere Oct. 21,
1970 of "A Poem Forgotten" (Wallingford Riegger, Eliot
Feld; Scenery and Costumes, Jose-Luis Cuevas), World
Premiere Oct. 21, 1970 of "Cortege Parisien" (Emmanuel
Chabrier, Eliot Feld; Costumes, Frank Thompson) with
Christine Sarry, John Sowinski, Elizabeth Lee, Richard
Munro, Cristina Stirling, Kenneth Hughes, "Early
Songs" (Srauss, Feld), World Premiere Oct. 23, 1970 of
"Clockwise" (Jean Francaix, Bruce Marks; Costumes,
Stanley Simmons), "The Maids" (Milhaud, Herbert
Ross), World Premiere Apr. 20, 1970 of "Romance"
(Johannes Brahms, Eliot Feld; Costumes, Stanley Sim-
mons; Lighting, Jennifer Tipton) with Anna Laerkesen,
Elizabeth Lee, John Sowinski, Daniel Levins, Christine
Sarry, Cristina Stirling, Richard Munro, Kenneth
Hughes, "The Consort" (Dowland-Neusidler-Morley-
Anonymous, Feld), World Premiere Apr. 24, 1970 of
"Theatre" (Richard Strauss, Eliot Feld; Costumes, Frank
Thompson; Lighting, Jennifer Tipton) danced by the
company.

* Closed Nov. 1, 1970 after limited engagement of 14
performances.

Martha Swope Photos

"Consort" Top Left: Elizabeth Lee *Terry Middleton Photo*

John Sowinski, Christine Sarry Top: Elizabeth
Lee, John Sowinski in "Harbinger"

Christine Sarry, Larry Grenier

"Early Songs"
Above: Eliot Feld, Christine Sarry, John
Sowinski, Elizabeth Lee in "Early Songs"

Terry Middleton Photo

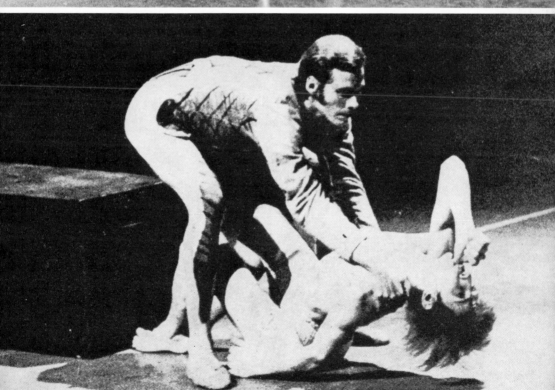

Edward Henkel, Daniel Levins in "A Poem Forgotten"
Above: Elizabeth Lee, John Sowinski in
"Meadowlark"
AMERICAN BALLET COMPANY

Ron Protas Photo

BROOKLYN ACADEMY

Friday & Saturday, October 16, 17, 1970.
The Brooklyn Academy of Music in association with
Dance Theatre Workshop presents:

TWO EVENINGS OF DANCE
BY JEFF DUNCAN

Choreography, Jeff Duncan; Lighting, Gary Harris;
Costumes, Leor C. Warner, Jack Moore

COMPANY

Ze'eva Cohen, Jeff Duncan, Phillip J. Jonson, Deborah
Jowitt, Leonore Latimer, Daniel Maloney, Susan
Matheke, Jim May, Aaron Osborne, Ross Parkes, Rudy
Perez, Wendy Perron, Kathryn Posin, Linda Tarnay,
John Wilson, with Leonard Hanitchak, Andres Mannik,
Robert Michie, Ted Striggles

PROGRAM

Friday: "Vinculum" (Andrew Rudin), Premiere of "The
Glade" (Oliver Messiaen), danced by Ross Parkes,
Daniel Maloney, "Winesburg Portraits" (Folk) Saturday:
"The Glade", "Diminishing Landscape" (Bayle-Mache-
Carson), "Statement" (Donald Lybbert), "Resonances"
(Pierre Henry)

V. Sladon Photos

Kenn Duncan Photo

Daniel Maloney, Ross Parkes in "The Glade"
Below: "Vinculum"

Jeff Duncan
in "Winesburg Portraits"

"Statement"
Above: "Resonances"

BROOKLYN ACADEMY OF MUSIC

Opened Tuesday, November 3, 1970.*

The Brooklyn Academy of Music in cooperation with the Cunningham Dance Foundation presents:

MERCE CUNNINGHAM AND DANCE COMPANY

Director-Choreographer, Merce Cunningham; Artistic Adviser, Jasper Johns; Lighting, Richard Nelson; Production Manager, James Baird; Administrators, Jean Rigg, David Vaughan, David Schiller

COMPANY

Merce Cunningham, Carolyn Brown, Sandra Neels, Valda Setterfield, Meg Harper, Susana Hayman-Chaffey, Louise Ann Burns, Chase Robinson, Mel Wong, Douglas Dunn, Ulysses Dove

REPERTOIRE

"Rainforest" (David Tudor), "Second Hand" (John Cage), "Tread" (Christian Wolff), "Canfield" (Oliveros), premiere of "Signals" (Behrman-Cage-Mumma-Tudor), "Walkaround Time" (Behrman), "How to Pass, Kick, Fall and Run" (Cage), premiere of "Objects" (Alvin Lucier), "Scramble" (Ichiyanagi)

*Press:*Thomas Kerrigan, Anne Goodman
*Stage Managers:*Charles Atlas, Richard Nelson

* Closed Nov. 15, 1970 after limited engagement of 11 performances.

James Klosty Photos

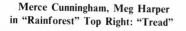

Merce Cunningham, Meg Harper in "Rainforest" Top Right: "Tread"

"Canfield" Above: Carolyn Brown, Merce Cunningham in "Second Hand"

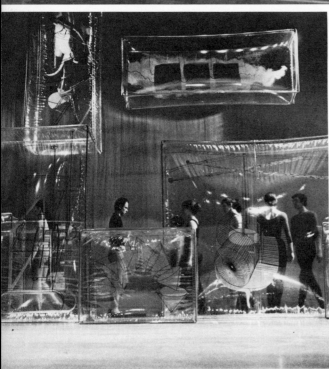

"Walkaround Time"

Carolyn Brown in "How to Pass, Kick. . . ."
Top: Merce Cunningham, Douglas Dunn, Valda
Satterfield, Mel Wong in "Signals" (Premiere)

128

MERCE CUNNINGHAM AND DANCE COMPANY

Jack Mitchell Photo

Chase Robinson, Sandra Neels, Carolyn Brown,
Douglas Dunn in "Objects" (Premiere)

Carolyn Brown, Sandra Neels in "Scramble"
Top: Douglas Dunn, Susana Hayman-Chaffey, Louise
Ann Burns, Sandra Neels in "Objects" (Premiere)

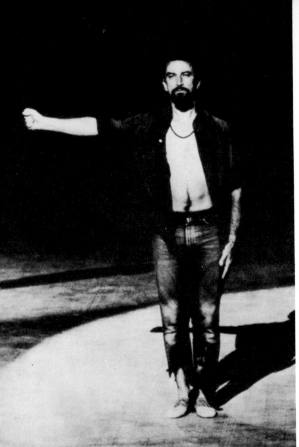

BROOKLYN ACADEMY OF MUSIC

Opened Monday, January 25, 1971.*
The Brooklyn Academy of Music in association with
International Telephone and Telegraph Corp., and
Theatre Royal de la Monnaie--National Opera of
Belgium (Maurice Huisman, Director) presents:

BALLET OF THE 20TH CENTURY

Artistic director-Choreographer, Maurice Bejart; Adminstrator, Anne Lotsy; Ballet Masters, Pierre Dobrievich, Jorg Lanner; Pianist, Claire Paulet; Stage Director, Maurice Bivort; Sound, Leo Van Horenbeeck; Wardrobe Mistress, Simone Renglet

COMPANY

Paolo Bortoluzzi, Jorge Donn, Suzanne Farrell, Maina Gielgud, Beatriz Margenat, Daniel Lommel, Micha Van Hoecke, Victor Ullate, Robert Thomas, Paul Mejia, Woytek Lowski, Jorg Lanner, Floris Alexander, Krystyna Schubert, Angele Albrecht, Gerard Wilk, Jaleh Kerendi, Catherine Verneuil, Gunter Kranner, Louba Dobrievich, Tania Bari, Jorge Lefebre, Christiane Velle, Guy Brasseur, Dyane Gray-Cullert, Lise Pinet, Madeleine Stierli, Denise Vanderhoeft, Robert Denvers Franco Romano, Jean Roland, Franky Arras, Eisaku Udagawa, Jean-Paul Balmer, Karl Schreck, Rene Portenart, Jean Francois Bouchard, Bryan Poer, Antonio Cano, Guy Mathys, Daniel Lambo

REPERTOIRE

World Premiere of "Choreographic Offering" (Bach), U. S. premieres of "Erotica" (Tadeusz Baird), "Bhakti" (Hindu themes), "Actus Tragicus" (Bach), "Nomos Alpha" (Iannis Xenakis), "Les Vainqueurs" (Richard Wagner), "Bach Sonata", "Le Sacre du Printemps" (Stravinsky), "Messe Pour Le Temps Present" (Pierre Henry, percussion, and sound effects), "Four Last Songs" (Strauss), "Firebird" (Stravinsky), "Romeo and Juliet Suite" (Berlioz), "Opus 5" (Webern)

*Press:*Thomas Kerrigan, Anne Goodrich
*Stage Managers:*Marie Deville, Daniel Toussaint

* Closed Feb. 14, 1971 after limited engagement of 22 performances.

Robert Kayaert Photos

Lyn Smith Pho[...]

**Laura Proenca, Jorge Donn
in "Messe Pour Le Temps Present"**

**Paolo Bortoluzzi, Itomi Asakawa
in "Bhakti"
Top Left: Maurice Bejart**

"Sacre du Printemps" Top: (L) Jorge Donn,
Suzanne Farrell (R) Maina Gielgud

131

Itomi Asakawa, Jorge Donn, Maina Gielgud in "Actus Tragicus"
Above: "Les Vainqueurs"

BEJART'S BALLET OF THE 20TH CENTURY

BROOKLYN ACADEMY OF MUSIC

Saturday, March 6, 1971.

EGLEVSKY BALLET COMPANY

Artistic Director-Choreographer, Andre Eglevsky; Co-Director, Salvatore Aiello; Sets, Joseph Bares; Costumes, Dosi Sorokin; Stage Manager, Philip Kaesen

COMPANY

Diane Duffy, Marina Eglevsky, Alexis Hoff, Bonnie Mathis, Robin Welch, Salvatore Aiello, Fernando Bujones, Brian Pitts, Bill Thompson, Robert Vickrey, Judith Carlson

GUEST ARTISTS: Elisabeth Carroll, Leo Ahonen

PROGRAM

"Grand Pas Espagnol" (Moszkowski, Benjamin Harkarvy), "Little Improvisations" (Schumann, Tudor), "A La Francaix" (Francaix, Balanchine), Premiere of "Sleep on, Beauty!" (Gary McFarland, Jay Norman), "Glinka Pas de Trois" (Glinka, Eglevsky), "Paquita Pas de Deux" (Minkus, Petipa), Premiere of "The Sorcerer's Apprentice" (Dukas, Aiello)

Dania Makarova Photos

Right: Marina Eglevsky, Fernando Bujones, Diane Duffy in "Grand Pas Espagnole" Above: "The Sorcerer's Apprentice"

Edith Stephen, Rita Brosh, William Farrell in "Forbidden Playground"

BROOKLYN ACADEMY OF MUSIC

Saturday, April 24, 1971.

EDITH STEPHEN THEATRE DANCE COMPANY

Director-Choreographer, Edith Stephen; Artistic Consultant-Designer, Helen Daphanis Avlon; Projections, Maxien Haleff, Francis Nieto

COMPANY

Edith Stephen, Frederick Courtney, Susan Gill, Marilyn Worrell, Jean Morris, Lynne Von Egidy

PROGRAM

"Forbidden Playground" (Feldman), "The Wrecked Tangle" (Joseph Dylewski), and premieres of "Celebration for Myself" (Feldman-Bach-Debussy-Moondog, Stephen), "Concrete Heart" (Morton Subotnick, Edith Stephen)

133

Jack Mitchell Photo

BROOKLYN ACADEMY OF MUSIC

Thursday, May 20, 21, 22, 1971.
The Brooklyn Academy of Music in association with
Modern Dance Artists presents the:

SANASARDO DANCE COMPANY

Artistic Director-Choreographer, Paul Sanasardo; Assistant Artistic Director, Manuel Alum; Musical Director, Eugene Lester; Lighting and Sound, Gary Harris; Costumes, Linda Lumsden; Press, William Weaver; Stage Managers, Judy Welsh, Karen de Francis; Accompanist, Gwendolyn Watson; Pianist, David Holzman

COMPANY

Manuel Alum, Diane Germaine, Judith Blackstone, Willa Kahn, Joan Lombardi, Gerri Houlihan, Georgiana Holmes, Yon Martin, Matthew Diamond, Martin Bland, Joseph Fontano, Jacques Patarozzi, Paul Sanasardo

REPERTOIRE

"Metallics" (Cowell-Badings, Sanasardo), Premiere of "Sight Seeing" (Eugene Lester, Paul Sanasardo; Costumes, Lois Bewley), "Footnotes" (Lester, Sanasardo), "Pain" (Lutoslawski, Sanasardo), "Fatal Birds" (Ginastera, Sanasardo), "Era" (Penderecki, Manuel Alum), "Cut Flowers" (Serocki, Sanasardo), "Palomas" (Oliveros, Alum)

Gerri Houlihan, Manuel Alum, Judith Blackstone, Yon Martin in "Footnotes"
Top Left: Paul Sanasardo in "Metallics"

Fred Fehl Photo

James Gladden Photo

Judith Blackstone, Paul Sanasardo in "Pain"
Above: "Fatal Birds"

Willa Kahn, Diane Germaine in "Fatal Birds"
Top: "Footnotes"

JACOB'S PILLOW DANCE FESTIVAL
Lee, Massachusetts
TED SHAWN, ARTISTIC DIRECTOR
June 25, through August 29, 1970
Thirty-eighth Year

Founder-Artistic Director, Ted Shawn; Executive Director, John Christian; Business Manager, Grace Badorek; Press, Sarah Jeter; Musical Director, Jess Meeker; Stage Manager, Robert Powell

Thursday June 25, through Saturday, June 27, 1970

NORTH CAROLINA DANCE THEATRE

Director, Robert Lindgren; Ballet Mistress, Sandra Williams; Assistant to Director, Elizabeth John; Costumes, A. Christina Giannini; Lighting, Gene Lowery; Sets, Peter Larkins, William Greene

COMPANY

Christine Spizzo, Jeannde Ford, Nancy Thueson, Lee Provancha, Rebecca McLain, Nancy Muller, Diane Winter, Melinda Lawrence, Susan McKee, Eric McCullough, Dale Talley, Jordeen Ivanov, Victor Barbee, James Boyd, Deneen Ford, Sharon Filone, David Graniero, Denise Pence, Lynne Hedrick, Becky Slifkin, Michael Sanders, Tom Kovaleski, Sergio Lopez, John Fisher, Evelyn Shepard, Anton Ness, Kathleen Fitzgerald, Gina Vidal, Gyula Pandi, Cathy Wheeler, Lynne Keeton

PROGRAM

"Symphony 13" (Haydn, Duncan Noble), "Closed Door" (Webern, Valerie Bettis), "Summernight" (Schoenberg, Job Sanders)

GUEST ARTISTS: Patricia McBride and Edward Villella in "Tchaikovsky Pas de Deux" (Balanchine)
Thursday, July 2-4, 1970

NORTH CAROLINA DANCE THEATRE in "Concertino" (Pergolesi, Pauline Koner), "Poeme" (Barber, Koner), "Fugitive Visions" (Prokofiev, Job Sanders) , "Flick-Flack" (Britten, Duncan Noble)
GUEST ARTIST: Pauline Koner in "The Farewell" (Mahler, Koner)

North Carolina Dance Theatre in "Symphony 13", and above in "Closed Door"

Patricia McBride, Edward Villella

Pauline Koner in "The Farewell"

JACOB'S PILLOW
Tuesday, July 7-11, 1970

LES GRANDS BALLETS CANADIENS

Artistic Director, Ludmilla Chiriaeff; Associate Director, Fernand Nault; Ballet Mistress, Linda Stearns; Resident Choreographer, Brydon Paige; Assistant Ballet Master, Daniel Jackson; General Manager, Uriel G. Luft; Production Manager, Guy Savard; Company Manager, Roger Rochon; Scenery, Claude Berthiaume

COMPANY

ARTISTS: Richard Beaty, Erica Jayne, Veronique Landory, Sonia Taverner, Alexandre Belin, Linda Stearns, Nicole Vachon, Haeshik Kim, Bryan Poer
CORPS DE BALLET: James Bates, Barbara Bourget, Russel Chambers, Lorna Cameron, Leslie-May Downs, Manon Larin, Stephen Lockser, Mannie Rowe, Cathy Sharp, Laszlo Tamasik, Lorne Toumine, Andris Toppe, Bruce Weavil, Laeleen Winchiu, Barbara Withey

PROGRAM

"Allegro Brillante" (Tchaikovsky, Balanchine), "The Brood" (Pierre Henry, Richard Kuch), "Catulli Carmina" (Carl Orff, John Butler), "Symphony of Psalms" (Stravinsky, Nault)
RITHA DEVI in "Kuchipudi Dance", "Odissi Dances"

JACOB'S PILLOW
Tuesday, July 14-18, 1970

THE AMERICAN MIME THEATRE (Paul J. Curtis, Director) with Paul J. Curtis, Rick Wessler, Charles Barney, Sherry Halle, Bridget Leicester, Neil Lippe, Nina Petrucelli in "The Lovers," "Hurly Burly," "Dreams"
BARTON MUMAW in "Pierrot in the Dead City" (Eric Korngold, Ted Shawn), and "Cutting Sugar Cane" (Ernesto Lecuona, Ted Shawn)
LUPE SERRANO and ROYES FERNANDEZ dancing "Les Sylphides Pas de Deux" (Chopin, Fokine), and "La Esmeralda Pas de Deux" (Pugni, after Petipa)

John Van Lund Photos

Les Grands Ballets Canadiens in "Catulli Carmina", and above in "The Brood"

**Barton Mumaw
in "Cutting the Sugar Cane"**

Ritha Devi

JACOB'S PILLOW
Tuesday, July 21-25, 1970

PEARL LANG
AND DANCE COMPANY

Director-Choreographer, Pearl Lang; Assistant, Baya Weisman; Rehearsal and Technical Assistant, Ellen Tittler; Lighting, Gerald Rothman; Costumes, Pearl Lang, Christina Giannini; Sets, Pearl Lang, Nina Yankowitz; Press, Philip Bell

COMPANY

Pearl Lang, Marcia Plevin, Daniel Maloney, Christina Parker, Lar Roberson, Tonia Shimin, Kenneth Pearl, Georgiana Holmes, Frank Ashley, Elisa Monte, Dorothy Zito, Traci Musgrove, David Roach, Tony Catanzaro (guest artist)

PROGRAM

Premier of work in progress "Moonways and Dark Tides" (Subotnick-Takemitsu, Lang), "Piece for Brass" (Etler, Lang), "Shirah" (Hovhaness, Lang)

JACOB'S PILLOW
Tuesday, July 28-August 1, 1970

BHASKAR with SHALA and Asha Devi, Bihari Sharma, Polly Roy in "Natanam Adinar," "Krishna," "Pung Cholam," "Thala Nirtham," "Maya," "Naga Nirtham," "Surya Nirtham"
LONNY JOSEPH GORDON in "Phrases, Fields, Breath Groups, Kanda, 6 P. M." (Ichiyanagi, Gordon), and "Tama-Furi, Tama-Shizume" (Yura, Gordon)
JOYCE CUOCO and BILL MARTIN-VISCOUNT dancing "Black Swan Pas de Deux" (Tchaikovsky, Petipa), and "William Tell Pas de Deux" (Rossini, Bournonville)

Pearl Lang, Daniel Maloney in 'Shirah'

Joyce Cuoco, Bill Martin-Viscount
Above: Pearl Lang in "Shirah"

John Van Lund Photos

Lonny Joseph Gordon in "Phrases, Fields. . . ."
Above: Asha Devi, Bhaskar, Polly Roy

138

JACOB'S PILLOW
Tuesday, August 4-8, 1970

THE FIRST CHAMBER DANCE COMPANY

Director, Charles Bennett; Assistant Director, Michael Uthoff; Stage Manager, Michael Judson; Wardrobe Master, Alan Madsen

COMPANY

Charles Bennett, Lisa Bradley, Bonnie Mathis, Marjorie Mussman, Michael Uthoff

PROGRAM

"Recollection of an Age" (Boieldieu, Bennett), "Shadowed Heart" (Brahms, Bennett), "Windsong" (Elgar, Uthoff), "Where...To?" (Baird, Sokolow), "The Judgment of Paris" (Weill, Tudor)," Promenade" (Pergolesi, Uthoff), "Dusk" (Satie, Uthoff), "Contrasts" (Louis, Jay Norman), "Reflections" (Kabalevsky, Uthoff), "Legong" (Balinese, Bennett), "By Candlelight" (Buffy St. Marie-Traditional, Bennett)

LUIS RIVERA & COMPANY

Director-Choreographer, Luis Rivera; Assistant Choreographer, Maria Walling; Costumes, Vargas, Quintero, Sevilla

COMPANY

Luis Rivera, Marta Castillo, Moraima Munoz, Emilio Prados (guitar), Domingo Alvarado (singer), Nino Garcia (pianist)

PROGRAM

"Fandango" (Vives), "Aires de Cadiz" (Popular), "Fantasia Madrilena" (Popular), "Con Mi Soledad" (Popular), World Premier of "Cerebrum" (Rodrigo) dedicated to Ted Shawn

John Lindquist Photos

Charles Bennet, Marjorie Mussman in "By Candlelight"

Luis Rivera   *Jack Mitchell Photo*

Luis Rivera Above: Lisa Bradley, Marjorie Mussman, Bonnie Mathis in "Judgment of Paris"

139

JACOB'S PILLOW
Tuesday, August 11-15, 1970

MURRAY LOUIS DANCE
COMPANY

Director-Choreographer, Murray Louis; Technical
Director, James Van Abbema; Costumes, Frank Garcia;
Assistant Technical Director, Carl Reinhart; Decor, Nick
Loper, Murray Stern

COMPANY

Murray Louis, Michael Ballard, Raymond Johnson, Lyn
Levene, Sara Shelton, Frances Tabor

PROGRAM

"Landscapes" (Walker), "Intersection" (Farberman),
"Proximities" (Brahms), "Junk Dances" (Arranged)

JACOB'S PILLOW
Tuesday, August 18-22, 1970

DANCE THEATRE
OF HARLEM

Artistic Director, Arthur Mitchell; Assiciate Artistic
Director, Karel Shook; Stage Manager and Lighting,
George Vaughn Lowther; Assistants, Gerald Francis,
Richard Tsukada; Pianist-Conductor, Tania Leon Viera;
Administrative Director, Kathleen Stanford Grant

COMPANY

Llanchie Stevenson, Lydia Abarca, Virginia Johnson,
Clover Mathis, Walter Raines, Samuel Smalls, Sheila
Rohan, Ronda Sampson, Lazar Dano, William Scott,
Gayle McKinney, Ronald Perry, Olinda Davis, Patricia
Ricketts, Gerald Banks, Roslyn Sampson, Cassandra
Phifer

PROGRAM

"Holberg Suite" (Grieg, Mitchell), "Biosfera" (Nobre,
Mitchell), "Ode to Otis" (Perkinson, Mitchell) "Rhythmetron" (Nobre, Mitchell)

Milton Oleaga Photo

John Van Lund Photos

Dance Theatre of Harlem in "Holberg Suite"
Top Right: Murray Louis and company in "Intersection", and "Proximities" below

JACOB'S PILLOW

Tuesday, August 25-29, 1970

JEAN-LEON DESTINE AND COMPANY

Artistic Director-Choreographer, Jean-Leon Destine; Costumes, Ellie Antoine, Édouard Walrond; Lighting, Judie Scott

COMPANY

Jean-Leon Destine, Shirley Spiceur, Marianne Marvellia, Benjamin Sterlin, Louines Louinis, Joan Sharon, drummers Alphonse Cimber, Jacques Succes, and flutist, Louines Louinis.

PROGRAM

"Cafe Coumbite," "Fantaisie," "Baptism of the Drum," "Slave Dance," "Yoruba Baka, " "Drums," "Transition," "Fetiche," "Drum Conversation," "Le Legende de L'Assotor"

JACOB'S PILLOW DANCERS

Richard Powell, Pamela Richard, Denise Houle, Suzanne Sausner, Louise Latreille, Carla Wessel, Shelley Washington, Beth Haberer, Annette Brooks, Lillian Anne Colby, Ernest Pysher, David Wanstreet, Gabrielle Taylor, Patrick van Asdalan, Sheila Atwood, Michele Deschamps, Richard Hoskinson,Francine Burnet, Jackie Chester, Jack Yantis, Andrew Charles Skalko, Andrew Harris in World Premier of work in progress "Alice in the Garden" (Van Grove-Bizet-Rossini-Delibes-Gottschalk, Ruth Page; Costumes, Andre Delfau; Masks, Athos)
GUEST ARTISTS: Joyce Cuoco, Patricia Klekovic, Lonny Joseph Gordon, Kenneth Johnson

Right: Jean-Leon Destine and company in "Cafe Cumbite" and above in "Yoruba Bakas"

John Van Lund Photo

John Lindquist Photo

Joyce Cuoco and Richard Powell with Jacob's Pillow Dancers in "Alice in the Garden"

AMERICAN DANCE FESTIVAL

Connecticut College, New London, Conn.

Charles Reinhart, Director

July 11 through Aug. 8, 1970

Administrator, Olive Johns; Press, Ellen Jacobs, Marianne Handy; Technical Director, Fred Grimsey; Technical Assistants, Steven Detmold, Ceil Halstead, Lawrence Loewinger, Tom Schmitt; Assistant to Director, Marie Meachum

Saturday, July 11, 1970.

LUCAS HOVING DANCE COMPANY

Margaret Beals, Sandra Brown, Randall Faxon, Gay DeLanghe, Eugene Harris, Seamus Murphy, Charles Phipps, Lucas Hoving

PROGRAM

"Aubade II," "Uppercase," "Opus '69," "Icarus," "Satiana," all choreographed by Mr. Hoving (No other details available)

Friday, July 17, 1970.

JAMES CUNNINGHAM AND DANCERS

PROGRAM: "Lauren's Dream October 8, 1969," and World Premiere of "The Junior Birdsmen," both choreographed by Mr. Cunningham. (No other details available)

Saturday, July 18, 1970.

MEREDITH MONK/THE HOUSE

PROGRAM: "Needle-brain Lloyd and the System's Kid--A Live Movie," choreographed by Miss Monk and performed by "The House," a group of 100 performers. (No other details available)

Saturday, July 25, 1970.

MARTHA GRAHAM DANCE COMPANY

Mary Hinkson, Matt Turney, Helen McGehee, Bertram Ross, Takako Asakawa, Patricia Birch, Diane Gray, Yuriko Kimura, Richard Gain, Moss Cohen, Robert Powell, Phyllis Gutelius, Judith Leifer, Dawn Suzuki

PROGRAM

"Deaths and Entrances," "Cave of the Heart," "Diversion of Angels," all choreographed by Miss Graham. Saturday, August 1, 1970, the company performed "El Penitente" and "Deaths and Entrances" by Miss Graham, and "Oases" by Bertram Ross. (No other details available)

Saturday, August 8, 1970, the company performed "Every Soul Is A Circus," "El Penitente," and "Diversion of Angels" by Miss Graham.
Friday, July 31, 1970.

SPECIAL PERFORMANCE Premieres of "Genesis 3" choreographed by Ray Cook, "Trio" by June Lewis," and "Time-Stop" by Martha Myers.(no other details available)

Friday, August 7, 1970.

SPECIAL PERFORMANCE New Works by Lucas Hoving, Peter Saul, Dorothy Vislocky, and "Crazy Quilt" by Richard Englund. (No other details available)

Top Right: Gay Delanghe, Lucas Hoving in "Uppercase"

Ted Wester Photo

James Cunningham and company

Philip Biscuti Photo

Lauren Perscetti in "Lauren's Dream
Oct. 8, 1969"

Meredith Monk Top: Martha Graham Dance
Company in "Oases"

FESTIVAL OF ETHNIC DANCE
Barnstable, Massachusetts
La Meri, Artistic Director
July 9 through August 29, 1970

Administrative Assistant, William Adams; Press, Lawrence Humphries, Barbara Arbo; Lighting, Al Wendel, Jr., Jack Vetorino; Stage Manager, Joan Condit; Presented by Ethnic Dance Arts, Inc.

PROGRAMS

Thursday, July 9-11, 1970.
MARIANO PARRA AND THE BALLET ESPANOL (Producer-Director-Choreographer, Mariano Parra) with Mariano Parra, Mariana Parra, Ines Parra, Barbara Martos, Jerane Michel, Guillermo Montes (guitarist), Dominico (singer) performing "Seguidillas" (Albeniz), "Baile Para Dos," "Las Tres Muheres de Cadiz," "Farruca," "Danza Prima," "Envocacion," "Romanza Gitana, " "Zapateado," "La Cana," "Playeras," "Jota Valenciana," "Fiesta Flamenca"
Thursday, July 23-25, 1970
NALA NAJAM with THAMBAL YAIMA in "Dances of India" including "Alarippu," "Jatiswaram," "Leima Jago," "Shabdam," "Maibi Priestess Dance," "Pushpanjali and Jati," "Nrit and Tatkar," "Homage to Vivaldi"
Thursday, August 6-8, 1970

SUNG HAE OH and NOBUKO SHIMAZAKI in "Dances of the Far East: including "Chang Dan Moo," "Musume-Dojoji," "Boo Che Choom," "Harusame," "Mok Dong," "Hwang Chini," "Kurokame," "Taell Choom," "Mitsumen Komori," "Moo Dang," "Soon Moo"
Thursday, August 27-29

MATTEO and the ETHNO-AMERICAN DANCE COMPANY with guest artist CAROLA GOYA performing "Kalvayshaki," world premiere of "Ganesha-Shiva Stutti," "Shari Dance," "Dasi Attam," "Natanam Adinar," "Durbar," "Polynesian Suite," "Okame to Gombei," "Castanuelas," "Goyescas Suite," "Latin-American Suite," "Spanish Suite"

Right: Matteo and Indo-American Dance Co.
Above: Mariano Parra and Company

La Meri   Nala Najan   Nobuko Shimazaki

SCHOOL OF MODERN DANCE
Spa Summer Theatre Dance Festival
Saratoga Springs, N. Y.
Paul Sanasardo, Artistic Director
August 1 through August 16, 1970

Assistant Artistic Director, Manuel Alum; Administrator, Sally Sears Mack; Executive Director, Richard P. Leach; Sponsored by Saratoga Performing Arts Center, Capital Area Modern Dance Council

PROGRAM

Saturday & Sunday, August 1, 2, 1970.

DANCE THEATRE OF HARLEM (Arthur Mitchell, Karel Shook, Artistic Directors) with Lydia Abarca, Virginia Johnson, Gayle McKinney, Roslyn Sampson, Llanchie Stevenson, Cassandra Phifer, Clover Mathis, Walter Raines, William Scott, Susan Lovelle, Gerald Banks, Samuel Smalls, Sheila Rohan, Ronald Perry, Rodney Swan performing "Holberg Suite" (Grieg, Mitchell), U.S. Premiere of "Biosfera" (Nobre, Mitchell), "Tones (Leon, Mitchell), "Rhythmetron" (Nobre, Mitchell), "Concerto Barocco" (Bach, Mitchell), World premiere of "Pas de Deux from Fun and Games" (Piccioni, Mitchell), "Ode to Otis" (Perkinson, Mitchell)

Saturday & Sunday, August 8, 9, 1970

MURRAY LOUIS DANCE COMPANY (Director-Choreographer, Murray Louis) with Murray Louis, Michael Ballard, Raymond Johnson, Lyn Levene, Sara Shelton, Frances Tabor performing "Go 6" (Heinrich), "Landscapes" (Walker), "Proximities" (Brahms), "Junk Dance" (Arranged)

Saturday & Sunday, August 15, 16, 1970

PAUL SANASARDO DANCE COMPANY (Director-Choreographer, Paul Sanasardo) with Paul Sansardo, Judith Blackstone, Diane Germaine, Gerri Houlihan, Yon Martin, Manuel Alum, Joan Lombardi, Martin Bland, Willa Kahn, Charles Hayward performing "Metallics" (Henk-Badings-Cowell), "Footnotes" (Lester), "Pain" (Lutoslawski), "Fatal Birds" (Ginastera)

Murray Louis and company in "Proximities"
Above: Dance Theatre of Harlem in "Ode to Otis"

Yon Martin, Judith Blackstone, Diane Germaine, Mark Franko, Willa Kahn in "Fatal Birds"

Fred Fehl Photo

Paul Sanasardo and company in "Pain"

145

REGIONAL AND PROFESSIONAL DANCE COMPANIES IN THE U.
(Failure to meet deadline necessitated omission of several companies)

AL HUANG DANCE THEATRE

Director-Choreographer-Set Designer, Al Huang; Costume Designer, Suzanne Pierce; Artists-in-residence at Krannert Center for the Performing Arts, Urbana, Illinois.

REPERTOIRE

"Invitation to the Dance," "Yin and Yang," "Cicade Song," "Dandelions and Sunflowers," "O, Vaporous Heart!," "Owari," "Ssu Fan," "Phantom Landscape," "A Cloud Passed," "Dragon Play," "The Monkey and the Moon," "Flower in the Mirror," "Butterfly Dream," "Change"

PREMIERES OF: "Tai Chi," "A Shadow's Flight," "Yulan," "The Golden Flower"

THE AMERICAN MIME THEATRE
New York, N. Y.
Paul J. Curtis, Founder-Director

COMPANY: Jean Barbour, Charles Barney, Paul J. Curtis, Anita Morris, Nina Petrucelli, Bill Stavers, Rick Wessler

REPERTOIRE

"The Lovers," "Dreams," "Birds," "Hurlyburly," "The Pinball Machine," "The Scarecrow"

ANDAHAZY BALLET BOREALIS COMPANY
St. Paul, Minnesota

Lorand and Anna Adrianova Andahazy, Directors, Choreographers, Lorand Andahazy, Anna Adrianova Andahazy; Conductors, Max Metzger, Emmett Stark; Designers, Lorand and Anna Andahazy, Cornelis A. Bartels, Helen Beaverson, Victor Hubal; Press, Edith Finholt, Carol Hone; Stage Manager, Emmett Stark; Scenic Artist, Victor Hubal

COMPANY

PRINCIPALS: Anna Adrianova Andahazy, Lorand Andahazy, Marius Andahazy, Linda Finholt, Jane Keyes
SOLOISTS: Lisa Abrahamson, Robin Barke, Michelle Davidek, Laurie Edwards, Mona Finholt, Susan Hines, Kay Page, Karen Rasmussen, Lois Rosenberg, Eric Shellum

CORPS DE BALLET: Celeste Anderson, Gilbert Bauman, Wilor Bluege, Gina Brown, Susan Dooley, Reiko Ito, Cherie Kaspar, Roxanne Krass, Sandra Lochen, Loretta Miller, Sarah Mooney, Sarah Napier, Jamie Olson, Mitzi Olson,, Kathleen Quick, Leah Rosch, Constance Scheurer, Duane Shellum, Kirk Shellum, Richard Shellum, Vernon Stryker, Nancy Zuber

GUEST ARTISTS: Alan Howard, Judanna Lynn, Desiree Thalley, George Zoritch

REPERTOIRE

"Aurora's Wedding" (Tchaikovsky, Petipa), "Scheherazade" (Karsakoff, Fokine), "Cargo of Lost Souls" (Hadley, Andahazy), Slavonic Scenes" (Alpheraky-German, Andahazy-Adrianova), "Swan Lake" (Tchaikovsky, Petipa-Ivanov), "Serenade" (Tchaikovsky, Balanchine), "Les Sylphides" (Chopin, Fokine), "Nutcracker Grand Pas de Deux" (Tchaikovsky, Ivanov), "Suite of Dances to Harpsichord" (Handel, Andrianova), "Le Spectre de la Rose" (Weber, Fokine), "Bluebird Pas de Deux" (Tchaikovsky, Petipa), "Snow Maidens" (Mumma-Tarenghi-Rimsky Korszkov, Andahazy-Adrianova), "Szuret" (Keler, Andahazy), "The Rose Adagio" (Tchaikovsky, Petipa), "Dying Swan" (Saint–Saens, Fokine), "Romanian Rhapsody" (Enesco, Lazowsky), "Carmina Burana" (Orff, Andahazy-Adrianova), "Aubade" (Poulenc, Andahazy), "Los Seises" (Rodrigo-Albeniz, Adrianova), "Stabat Mater" (Poulenc, Adrianova), "The Miraculous Stag" (Kodaly-Karoly, Andahazy-Adrianova), "Pas de Quatre" (Pugni, Dolin), "Le Foyer de la Danse a L'Opera" (Puccinni-Verdi-Weber-Gluck-Balakirev-Adam-Pugni, Adrianova), "Opus II" (Menotti, Barbon) "Petrouchka" (Stravinsky, Fokine)

Al Huang Dance Company
in "The Golden Flower"

American Mime Theatre
in "The Lovers"

Linda Finholt, Lorand Andahazy, Kay Page
in "Les Sylphides" (Andahazy Ballet)

ANN ARBOR CIVIC BALLET
Ann Arbor, Michigan
Sylvia Hamer, Co-Founder/Artistic Director

Co-Director/Choreographer, Pamela Rutledge; Muscial Director, Georgia Bliss; Concert Manager, Paul Cloke; Administrator, Edgar Brennan; Stage Director, Jay King; Sets, Tobina Lake Studio; Wardrobe, Vicki Susan

COMPANY

Kathryn Adams, Ruth Adams, Aleyn Airey, Karen Aseltine, Susan Beneteau, Linda Bennett, Kathy Birchmeier, Patty Bodine, Gail Brenan, Gina Capalbo, Christine Colvin, Helen Guzman, Lee Ann King, Nancy Kooi, David Carlyon, Cindy McCollum, David Roeger, Pamela Schutz, Bonnie Sue Smith, Lisa Ann Smith, Pamela Rutledge, Mary Jane Williams, Marilyn Young

REPERTOIRE

"Coppelia," "Swan Lake," "Gayne Ballet Suite," "Konzertstuck" (Choreography, Nathalie Branitzka), "Jewels" (Choreography, Marjorie Hassard), "Cirque Royale" (Choreography, Sylvia Hamer), "Brahms Variations," "Giselle," "Grape Festival"

PREMIERES OF: "A La Foire" (Choreography, Dom Orejudos), "Ballet Blanc" (Choreography, Sulvia Hamer), "Aurora's Wedding" (Producer-Director, Christine DeBoulay)

Top Right: Cindy McCollum, Alyne Airy, Lynn Brennan

ANN ARBOR DANCE THEATRE
Ann Arbor, Michigan
Colby Schneider Wertenberg, Producer

Choreographers, Nancy Armandariz, Alan Barter, Elizabeth Weil Bergmann, Taya Bergmann, Gretchen Chua, Christine Dakin, Dianne Elliott, Alice Hinterman, Margot Hull, LoRainne Jones, Pat Knowles, Selma Odom, Linda Ellis Peck, Catherine Quick Spingler, Pat Tate; Lights, Charles Vornberger, Peter Wilde; Press, Ellen Miller, Rusty Schumacher

COMPANY

Nancy Armandariz, Alana Barter, Bunita Berg, Elizabeth Weil Bergmann, Taya Bergmann, Ellen Brown, Gretchen Chua, Jennifer Cole, Christine Dakin, Ann Deloria, Dianne Elliot, Amy Ellsworth, Ann Gallup, Amy Grossman, Tuck Hejna, Alice Hinterman, Margot Hull, Wendy Kisken, Pat Knowles, Philip Lewis, Selma Odom, Jo Parkus, Linda Ellis Peck, Appleseed Robinson, Wendy Shifrin, Catherine Quick Spingler, Pat Tate

REPERTOIRE

"Collage," "Incessance," "Circles and Approaches," "Energies," "Stasis," "Scraps 2," "Spart III," "Currents," "Polite Conversations," "Canticle of Peace," "Break-up," "Celebration"

Eck Stanger Photo

Right Center: Ann Arbor Dance Theatre

ANNE WILSON DANCE COMPANY
New York, N. Y.
Anne Wilson, Artistic Director

COMPANY: Anne Wilson, Robert Christopher, Alonso Castro, Rosalind Pierson, David Gleaton

REPERTOIRE

"Pre Classic Suite" (Boccherini-Gretry, Anne Wilson), "Coppelia Excerpts" (Delibes, St. Leon), "Giselle Excerpts" (Adam, Coralli), "Shapes" (Varese, Wilson), "Billy the Kid Excerpts" (Copland, Loring), "Waltzes, Opus 39" (Brahms, Weidman), "Psalm" (Handel, Castro), "Offering" (Handel, Castro), "The Return" (Villa-Lobos, Pierson), "Thud" (Rosenbloom, Wilson) Premiere of "Chagall" (Traditional, Anne Wilson)

**Anne Wilson
in "Billy the Kid"**

THE ATLANTA BALLET
Atlanta, Georgia
Robert Barnett, Director

Associate DIrectors, Carl Ratcliff, Virginia Barnett, Merrilee Smith; Executive Secretary, Blanche A. Bevins; Production Manager, Charles Fishl; Scenic Designers, Luis Maza, Carl Ratcliff; Costumes, Luis Maza, Robert Barnett, Margaret Shepherd, A. Christina Gianinni, Carl Ratcliff; Founder-Consultant, Dorothy Alexander; Guest Conductors, Lewis Dalvit, Simon Sadoff, Michel Perrault

COMPANY

PRINCIPALS: Anne Burton, Robert Barnett, Virginia Barnett, Carl Ratcliff, Sharon Long, Terrell Paulk, Wendy Lane, Joey Carman
SOLOISTS AND CORPS DE BALLET: Pennie Abel, Lindy Agel, Melissa Beale, Andrea Berta, Susan Eldridge, Angelique Grayson, Susan Hall, Renee Hallman, Leslie Hughes, Leslie Jones, Teena Kahle, Mary Ann Kellogg, Melissa Logan, Mary Ann Lupton, Rebecca Prater, Connie Prince, Ellen RIchard, Kathi Smith, Linda Spriggs, Nancy Tabaka, Vicki Tabaka, Debbie Thwaites, Ellyn Yeung, John Fisher, Tom Moore, Thomas Pazik, Chester Roberts, John Walker, Jerome Weiss
GUEST ARTISTS: Richard Beaty, Manuel Maldonado

REPERTOIRE

"Nutcracker" (Tchaikovsky, Balanchine), "Raymonda Variations" (Glazounov, Victoria Simon after Balanchine), "Bach Impressions" (Bach, Robert Barnett), "Concertino" (Pergolesi, Koner), "Giselle Peasant Pas de Deux" (Burgmuller, Coralli-Perrot), "Sleeping Beauty" (Tchaikovsky, Robert Barnett and Merrilee Smith after Petipa), "Young Persons Guide to the Orchestra" (Britten, Joanne Lee), "La Boutique Fantasque" (Rossini-Respighi, Joanne Lee)
PREMIERES: "Joey and Friends" (The Beatles, Robert Barnett), "To Heloise and Abelard" (Josef Suk, Carl Ratcliff), "Shubert Fifth Sumphony" (Shubert, R. Barnett)

Charles Rafshoon Photos

Top Right: Anne Burton, Robert Barnett, Pennie Abel, Joey Carman in "Shubert-5th Symphony"

**Virginia Barnett, Carl Ratcliff
in "To Heloise and Abelard"**

**Joey Carman, Wendy Lane in "Joey and Friends"
Above: Terrell Paulk, Anne Burton in "Giselle"**

AUGUSTA BALLET COMPANY
Augusta, Georgia
Ronald Colton, Artistic Director

Sets and Costumes, Michael Hotopp; Lighting-Production Manager, Jim Thomas; Wardrobe, Joan McKenney; Ballet mistress, Merry Clark

COMPANY

Lynn Boucher, Karen Brown, Merry Clark, Alice Everett, Cammy Fisher, Sheila Gracey, Peggy Howard, Melinda Jordon, Marjorie Kemp, Joanne McKenney, Thom Moore, Jo Pirkle, Pam Willingham
GUEST ARTIST: Zanne Beaufort

REPERTOIRE

"The Sorcerer's Apprentice" (Dukas, Kathy Calhoun), "Sixty Years Ago" (Elton John, Calhoun), "Pictures at an Exhibition" (Moussorgsky-Ravel, Sallie Carlson), "Design" (Varese, Ronald Colton), "Pageant" (Douglas Moore, Colton), "Poems" (Ravel, Colton), "Presentation" (Britten, Colton), "Reflections with Voice" (Stockhausen, Colton), "Sleeping Beauty Waltz" and "Waltz of the Flowers" (Tchaikovsky, Colton), "Classical Gas" (Schifrin-Williams, Calhoun-Colton), "Trio" (Mozart, Zompakos)
PREMIERES: "Mystere" (Albinoni, Duncan Noble), "Symphony in D" (Mozart, Stanley Zompakos), "Chance Dance" (Cage, Thom Moore), "Mac and the Polys" (Tape, Moore), "Praise Ye the Lord" (Handel, Kathy Calhoun)

Augusta Civic Ballet in "Design"

AUSTIN CIVIC BALLET
Austin, Texas
Stanley Hall, Artistic Director-Choreographer

Artistic Adviser, Nora White Shattuck; Regisseur, Kirsten Perry Barrera; Sets and Costumes, Kathleen Harter Gee

COMPANY

PRINCIPALS: Mary Kay von Bieberstein, Judy Myer, Tyra Menzie Bevers, King Douglas
SOLOISTS: Johanna Bartosh, Ricardo Garcia, Irish Hill, Suzanne Miller, Eileen Price, Buddy Smith, Sylvia Stewart, Ron Thornhill
CORPS DE BALLET: Diane Aldis, Cindy Bauhof, Jonie Bergquist, Gail Brown, Lucia Bryan, Byron Johnson, Jean Lemens, Maurine Mills, Diane Moore, Terri Lynn Wright, Tani Adams, Mary Barbash, Oscar Elizondo, Janet Grobe, Sharon Hurst, Lea Johnson, Louise Knobler, Dave Larson, Melissa Owens, Sharon Schwenke, Rosemary Thomas, Charles Wohletz, Ken Yoder
GUEST ARTISTS: Judy Kendall, Sarah Wisdom, Renata Powers Sanford

REPERTOIRE

"Flower Festival Pas de Deux" (Helsted, Hall after Bournonville), "The Nutcracker" (Tchaikovsky, Hall after Ivanov)
PREMIERES: "Eternal Return" (Arnold Bax, Hall), "Song of the City" (Frederick Delius, Hall), "Love" (Arranged, Hall), "Pastiche a L'Empire" (Emmanuel Chabrier, Hall), "Tregonell" (Jerry Goldsmith-Vladimir Ussachevsky, Hall), "Divertissement Romantique" (Burgermuller-Drigo-Minkus, Hall), "Rites for Joseph Byrd" (Joe Byrd, Hall)

Judy Kendall, Mary Kay von Bieberstein, Judy Myer, Sarah Wisdom in "Pastiche a L'Empire"

BALLET CELESTE INTERNATIONAL
San Francisco, California
Merriem Lanova, Artistic Director

Tour Director, Mercedes Hamblen; Costumes, James Kerber; Music, John Bishchof, Jr.; Stage Manager, C. Hugh Hamblen.

COMPANY

PRINCIPALS: Benjamin Reyes, Josefa Villaneuva, Kimberly Graves, Laura Brunnell, Daniel Copich, Holly Hamblen
SOLOISTS: Sonette Dhanda, James Kerber, Katherine Ivanoff, WIlliam Starrett, and guests Koichi Fujimo, Hiroshi Nishikawa
CORPS DE BALLET: Stephanie Ballard, Brigette Beggs, Dorothy Bong, Alice Brydges, Marta Daya, Beth Deenihan, Sandra Drury, Glenn Hasstedt, Margorite Jarmarillo, Frances Katsimbras, Lyra Katsimbras, Becca Ligh, Patti McGoush, Linda Montaner, Julian Montaner, Jennifer Palo, Maria Tijano, Sandra Sciford, Jeanne Walker, Heidi Young, Jennifer Young
GUEST ARTISTS: Marina Eglevsky, Salvatore Aiello

REPERTOIRE

"Swan Lake," "Nutcracker," "Giselle," "Coppelia," "Sleeping Beauty," "Les Sylphides," "Six Princess," "Creole Trio," "Grand Pas de Quatre," "Le Lecon," "Pleasures of Paris," "Chinese Cinderella," "Light and Shadow," "Peter and the Wolf," "Philippine Festival," "Three Pavlova Solos," "Scheherazade," "Verdiana," "Tales of the Tzar-Sultan"
PREMIERES: "The WInd and the Rose," "Fear and Anne Frank," "Saint by Flame," all choreographed by Merriem Lanova, "Les Patineurs" by Benjamin Reyes.

Sonette Dhanda and Ballet Celeste corps in "The Nutcracker"

Dulce Anaya and Ballet Concerto corps in
"Giselle"

Carlos Photo

BALLET CONCERTO
Coral Gables, Florida

Directors, Sonia Diaz, Martha del Pino, Eduardo
Recalt; Choreographers, Sonia Diaz, Martha del Pino,
Eduardo Recalt, Haydee Gutierrez; Conductor, Paul
Csonka; Costumes, Óscar Kare; Stage Manager, Sets,
Lighting, Demetrio.

COMPANY

PRINCIPALS: Dulce Anaya, Eduardo Recalt
SOLOISTS: Haydee Gutierrez, Hilda Maria Revente,
Silvia Blanco, Addy Castellanos, Leticia Mederos, Su-
sana Prieto, Mariana Alvarez
CORPS DE BALLET: Martha Acosta, Regla Angulo,
Patricia Diaz, Maria Elena Mencia, Bertha Martinez,
Loundes Oquendo, Maria Elena Olivera, Mayda Ro-
driguez, Lourdes Rabell, Mary Torres, Maria Esther
Valiente, Susy Garcia, Carmen Luisa More, Gilberto
Almaguer, Juan de la Fe, Nelson Someillan, Delfin Diaz,
Orland Manaure, Dulce Cruz
GUEST ARTISTS: Ivan Nagy, Lupe Serrano, Royes
Fernandez, Ramon Segarra, Terry Orr, Desmond Kelly,
Lolita Monreal, Antonio Jimenez, Eleanor D'Antuono

REPERTOIRE

"Giselle" (Adam, Diaz after Petipa), "Swan Lake Act II"
(Tchaikovsky, Diaz-del Pino after Petipa), "Coppelia"
(Delibes, Diaz-del Pino after St. Leon), "Les Sylphides"
(Chopin, Diaz-del Pino after Fokine), "Nutcracker"
(Tchaikovsky, Diaz-del Pino after Petipa), "Grand Pas
de Quatre" (Pugni, Diaz-del Pino after Lester), "Don
Quixote Pas de Deux" (Minkus, Diaz after Petipa),
"Aurora's Wedding" (Tchaikovsky, Diaz after Petipa),
"Latin American Symphony" (Gould, Diaz), "Gradua-
tion Ball" (Strauss, Diaz-del Pino), "Triptych" (Debussy,
Recalt), "Adagio" (Grieg, Recalt), "Cain and Abel"
(Shostakovitch, Recalt), "Autumn" (Glazounov, Diaz),
"El Amor Brujo" (Falla, Lolita Monreal), "Evocacion"
(Lecuona, Diaz-del Pino)
PREMIERE: "Aria" (Stravinsky, Haydee Gutierrez)

BALLET DES JEUNES
Philadelphia, Pa.
Ursula Melita, Director
COMPANY

Maureen Reynolds, Trude Cone, Sally Jackson, Marianne Sherman, Mindy Marko, Janice Kates

REPERTOIRE

"Concerto Grosso, Opus 6" (Handel), "La Vida Breve"
(DeFalls), "Sevilla" (Albeniz), "Slavonic Dances: (Dvo-
rak), "Hoe Down from Rodeo" (Copeland), "Search for
Spring" (Shostakovitch), "Serenade Eine Kleine Nacht-
musik" (Mozart), "Hello World" (Mayer), "Roumanian
Rhapsody" (Enesco), "Golden Slippers" (Haydn), "Pas
de Quatre" (Pugni)
PREMIERE: "Snow Queen" (William Mayer, Ursula
Melita)

Right Center: Ballet des Jeunes

Gilbert Mack Photo

BALLET ETUDES
Norwalk, Connecticut
Russell Fratto, Artistic Director

Co-Directors, Jeannette Lauret, James Zynda; Managing Director, Deborah Rudman; Choreographers, Jeannette Lauret, James Zynda, Charles Nicoll; Sets, Leo
Meyer; Costumes, James Zynda; Stage Manager, James
Leonard; Production Assistant, John Howlett

COMPANY

Jennifer Barton, Catherine Barribal, Sonja Bukvic, Susan
Carney, Patricia Cherry, Anna Daniel, Toni-Ann Gar-
della, Linde Gibb, Linda Gilbertie, Kristie Hannum,
Marrianne Hartmayer, Sherree Kassuba, Charlotte Law,
Nancy Love, Tedde Lowry, Nancy Lushington, Eliza-
beth Mac Cormack, Dione Mason, Marianne Maggiore,
Revel Paul, Constance Stine, Anastasia Vallas, Miguel
Garcia, John Howlett, Dennis Kocjan, Miguel Lopez,
Patrick Madden, Antonio Mendez, Marcus Williamson
GUEST ARTISTS: Beth Fritz, James Zynda

REPERTOIRE

"The Nutcracker" (Tchaikovsky, Zynda), "Coppelia"
(Delibes, Lauret)

James Zynda, Beth Fritz and Ballet Etudes corps
in "Coppelia"

Frank Debias Photo

Ballet Guild of Jacksonville

BALLET GUILD OF JACKSONVILLE
Jacksonville, Florida
Mervyn Rickard, Artistic Director

Choreographer, Mervyn Rickard; Guest Ballet Master, Bill Martin-Viscount; Technical Director, Norman Rickard; Junior Director, Donna Freyberg; Artist Members, Frances Anderson Cooke, Phyllis Picus, Dorothy Willard, Jean Tepsic

COMPANY

Jill Blanchard, Mary Kay Collins, Pam Cooper, Angela Edens, Risa Edwards, Monique Field, Melodye Fraker, Betty Ann Gordon, Becky Hazouri, Alice Holden, Jean-Ellen Kelley, Elizabeth Kimsey, Eda McConnell, Susan Nichols, Arlene Sandler, Debbie Sidbury, Karen Steere, Christi Thomas, Terri Johnson, Jan Willyoung, Kathi Garland, Susan Poland, Lynn Whitehurst, Lisa Clarson, Julie Turner

REPERTOIRE

"Carmina Burana" (Orff, Rickard), "Spirituals for Dancers" (Gould, Freyberg), "Scarlatti 5/3" (Scarlatti, Tepsic), "Tryst in a Garden" (Ralke, Willard), "Salute to Strauss" (Strauss, Rickard)

BALLET ROYAL
Winter Park, Florida
Edith Royal, Artistic Director

Choreographer, Edith Royal; Business Manager and Technical Director, William Royal; Costume Design and Wardrobe, Phyllis Watson

COMPANY

Monique Barker, Susan Burwell, Denise Carlson, Kathy Coburn, Connie Colquitt, Lindsay Coulter, Elizabeth Cramer, Kethy Donaldson, Christy Donohoe, JoEllen Durhan, Dana Flick, Jeanette Gurinskas, Tinker Gipson, Pam Harned, Vicky Harvey, Teri Hinton, Julie Jaeb, Robin Knisely, Pamela Lab, Mitzi Maxwell, Robin McGarry, Kim McKinney, Julie Mesmer, Maureen Murray, Suzy O'Hara, Jane Odum, Tricia Page, Carol Sue Palmer, Susan Polaski, Suzannah Read, Cindy RIchards, Kim Rodenberry, Suzanne Rogers, Pam Smith, Viki Smith, Suzanne Staton, Kim Sulleau, Myra Tang, Elizabeth Mengel, Kent Barker, Gary Coburn, Mike Hall, Jeff Nolle Erik Petersen, Tony Busman

REPERTOIRE

"Badinage" (Lecocq), "Ah One and Ah Two" (Bernstein), "Pas de Trois" (Glinka), "Hallelujah" (Traditional Gospel), "The Firebird" (Stravinsky)
PREMIERES: "Paendora" (Richard Martorano, Edith Royal), "Four Sketches for Ballet" (O. A. Lowe, Edith Royal)

Jane Odum, Jeff Nolle, Monique Barker
of Ballet Royal

BALLET OF SAN DIEGO
San Diego, Calif.

Artistic Directors, Deborah Hadley, Bill Edward; Artistic Adviser, Jillana; Technical Adviser, Bruce Kelley; Business Manager, Lisa Gonzalez; Chairman of the Board, Mrs. Michael I. Gonzalez

COMPANY

PRINCIPALS: Deborah Hadley, Bill Edward
SOLOISTS: Darcy Curran, Renee Dufallo, Judy Emile, Tamara Hadley, Colleen Robertson, Laurence Robertson, Robin Sherertz
CORPS DE BALLET: Lee Braly, Cathy Chigos, Sue Connor, Colleen McCoy, Shawn Miles, Anna Spelman
GUEST ARTIST: Jillana

REPERTOIRE

"A La Francaix" (Francaix, Balanchine), "Bach Suite" (Bach, Johnson), "Classical Symphony" (Prokofiev, Carter), "Con Amore" (Rossini, L. Christensen), "Episodes" (Harrison, Davis), "Filling Station" (Thomson, L. Christensen), "Holberg Suite" (Grieg, Carter), "Huapango" (Moncayo, Edward), "Jinx" (Britten, L. Christensen), "Le Gourmand" (Mozart, L. Christensen), "Les Sylphides" (Chopin, Fokine), "Masque of the Red Death" (Liszt, Carter), "Now Was the Time" (Bartok, Davis), "Nutcracker" (Tchaikovsky, Carter-L. Christensen), "Prisms" (Poulenc, Loring), "Renard," (Stravinsky, Carter) "Romeo and Juliet" (Tchaikovsky, Johnson), "Simple Symphony" (Britten, Carter, "Sisters" (Ruggles, Loring) ("Swan Lake Act II" (Tchaikovsky, Petipa), "Variations 8 + 2" (Gould, Carter, "Western Orpheus" (Ward-Steinman, Carter), "Blue Bird Pas de Deux," "Grand Pas de Deux from Don Quixote," "Le Corsaire Pas de Dux," "Nutcracker Grand Pas de Deux," "Giselle Peasant Pas de Deux"
PREMIERES: "Bolero '71" (Ravel, Edward), "Pas de Trois" (Tchaikovsky, Edward), "Variaciones Concertantes" (Ginastera, Edward)

Deborah Hadley   Bill Edward
San Diego Ballet

151

BALLET WEST
Salt Lake City, Utah
William P. Christensen, Artistic Director

Ballet Mistress, Bene Arnold; Manager, Richard W. Cooper; Company Manager, Steven Horton, Press, Terry R. Twitchell; Stage Manager, Gary Horton; Costume Mistress, Sara Price; Musical Director, Ardean Watts

PRINCIPALS: Janice Rule, Tomm Ruud, Barbara Hamblin, John Hiatt, Vicki Hutten

ARTISTS: Christopher Fair, Bruce Caldwell, John Nelson, Michael Onstad, Richard Spoelstra, Mary Brid, Mary Ellen Davis, Lorna Erker, Charles Fuller, Philip Fuller, Merribeth Habegger, Vicki Morgan, Jacqueline Price, Patricia Rozow, Cathy Soctt, Mary Lynne Shupe, Sondra Sugi, Christine Surba, Nancy Taverna, Frank Hay, Kristine Miller, Michael Rozow, Norman Shelburne, Suzanne Sattler, Marsha Stygar

REPERTOIRE

(All choreography by William P. Christensen except where noted) "Black Swan Pas de Deux" (Petipa), "Le Cour d'Azur," "Blue Bird Pas de Deux" (Petipa), "Bravura," "Chaos" (Richard Kuch), "Con Amore" (Lew Christensen), "Cinderella," "Concerto Barocco" (Balanchine) "Coppelia," "Creatures of Prometheus," "Cycle" (Bene Arnold), "Filling Station" (L. Christensen), "Firebird," "Giselle" (Coralli), "Irish Fantasy" (d'Amboise), "La Bayadere," "La Fille Naive," "La Valse," "Les Bijoux du Mal," "Mobile" (Tomm Ruud), "Nothing Doing Bar," "Nutcracker," "Paquita Pas de Deux," "Pas de Six," "Quartet" (Ruud), "Romeo and Juliet Fantasy," "Serenade" (Balanchine), "Swan Lake," "Symphony in C" (Balanchine), "The Lady of Shalott" (L. Christensen), "Til Eulenspiegel's Merry Pranks," "Three Movements for the Short Haired" (L. Christensen), "Toxcatl"

Right: Janice James, Tomm Ruud in "La Bayadere" Below: Vickie Hutten in "Con Amore"

Tomm Ruud, Janice James in "Cinderella"
Above: Craig Smith, Philip Fuller, Charles Fuller in "Nutcracker"

John Hiatt, Barbara Hamblin in "Firebird"

BALLET SPECTACULAR
Miami, Florida

Conceived, Created, and Directed by Francis Mayville; Conductors, Simon Sadoff, Kenneth Schermerhorn, Richard Dunn, Dean Ryan; Press, A. Robert Owens; Stage Manager, Kevin Tyler

ARTISTS: Jacques d'Amboise, Melissa Hayden, Lupe Serrano, Scott Douglas, Lois Smith, Earl Kraul, Dean Crane, Robert Scevers, Earle Sieveling, Marina Svetlova, Grace Doty, David Anderson, Thatcher Clarke, Estrellita and Raul, Allegra Kent, Mimi Paul, Patricia Neary, Ramon Segarra, Rochelle Zide, Fiona Fuerstner, Sonia Arova, Lydia Diaz Cruz, Frank Ohman, Judith Reece, Karen Batizi, Christine Henessey, Oleg Briansky, George Zoritch, Irina Kovalska, Edmund Novak, Claudia Cravey, Richard Dodd, Leslie Gearhart, Mariano Parra, Robert Davis, First Chamber Dance Co., Helgi Tomasson, Royes Fernandez, John Clifford, Jean-Paul Comelin, John Prinz, Marnee Morris, Karel Shimoff, Renee Estopinal, Christine Redpath, James Bogan, Marjorie Spohn, Douglas Hevenor

REPERTOIRE

"Swan Lake Act II," "Les Sylphides," "Giselle Pas de Deux," "Meditation from Thais," "Don Quixote Pas de Deux," "Spring Waters," "Black Swan Pas de Deux," "Blue Bird Pas de Deux," "Stars and Stripes Pas de Deux," "Dying Swan," "Mendelssohn Pas de Deux," "Sleeping Beauty Pas de Deux," "Nutcracker Pas de Deux," "Sylvia Pas de Deux," "Tchaikovsky Pas de Deux," "Coppelia Wedding Pas de Deux," "Glazounov Pas de Deux," "Le Corsaire," "Ribbon Dance," "Raymonda Variations," "Afternoon of a Faun," "Pas de Deux from Pas de Dix," "Pas de Trois '20's," "La Fille Mal Gardee Pas de Deux," "Night Shadow," "Le Combat," "Irish Fantasy," "Opus II," "Hungarica," "Les Deux," "Stravinsky Pas de deux," "Romantique," "The Skaters," "Romeo and Juliet Pas de Deux," "Esmeralda Pas de Deux," "Paganini Solo," "Slavonic Dancers Pas de Deux," "You Are Love," "Apollo," "Still Point," "Nutcracker Snow Scene Pas de Deux," "Valse Fantaisie"

Melissa Hayden, Jacques d'Amboise

David Drummond and Above: Edra Toth and Boston Ballet in "Giselle"

BOSTON BALLET COMPANY
Boston, Mass.
E. Virginia Williams, Artistic Director

Artistic Adviser, George Balanchine; Executive Director, Ruth G. Harrington; Ballet Mistress, Sydney E. Leonard; Conductor, Hugo Fiorato; Lighting, Jennifer Tipton, Thomas Skelton; General Manager, Margaret Prausnitz; Stage Manager, Aloysius Petruccelli; Sets, Helen Pond, Herbert Senn; Costumes, E. Virginia Williams, Cecilia Eller.

COMPANY

Jerilyn Dana, Geraldine Gagnon, Ellen O'Reilly, June Perry, Anamarie Sarazin, Edra Toth, Laura Young, Zirginia Zango, Tony Catanzaro, David Drummond, Alfonso Figueroa, Samuel Kurkjian, Warren Lynch, Robert Pierce, Robert Steele, Anthony Williams Nina Bator, Jeanne Churchill, Veronica Fell, Domini Lynch, Stephanie Marini, Susan Nivert, Cecily, Travesky, Reva Willdorf, Valerie Windsor, Bonnie Wyckoff, Frederic Alexson, Nicholas de Simone, Mark Held, Walter Kaiser, James Lewis, Alphonse Poulin, George Vegas, Diane Bryan, Sandra Feinberg, Elise Ingalls, Mathew Ingemie, Stephanie Moy, Kathy Murphy, James Reardon, Kathryn Sullivan, Helen Taylor, Leslie Woodies
GUEST ARTISTS: Earle Sieveling, Louis Falco, Violette Verdy, Edward Villella, Natalia Makarova, Ted Kivitt

REPERTOIRE

"Minotaur" (Carter, Butler), "Coppelia" (Delibes, Williams after Ivanov), "Missa Brevis" (Kodaly, Kurkjian), "Nutcracker" (Tchaikovsky) "Swan Lake Act II," "Allegro Brillante," "Suspicion" (Matsumura, Ichinohe), "Stars and Stripes" (Sousa, Balanchine), "Peter and the Wolf" (Prokofiev, Kurkjian), "Persephone" (Pearl Lang), "Valse Creole" (Geoffrey Holder), "Graduation Ball," "Giselle" (Adam, Romanoff after Sergueff), "Serenade" (Tchaikovsky, Balanchine), "La Source Pas de Deux" (Delibes, Balanchine), "Donizetti Variations" (Donizetti, Balanchine)
PREMIERE: "The Gamete Garden" (Michael Kamen, Louis Falco), "Speed Zone" (Hindemith, Kurkjian), "Dolly Suite" (Gabriel Faure, John Taras)

John Lindquist Photos

153

Karoly Barta *Jack Mitchell Photo*

BIRMINGHAM CIVIC BALLET
Birmingham, Ala.
Karoly Barta, Director

Choreographer-Ballet Master, Karoly Barta; Assistant, Martha Manners: Technical Director, John Kitchens; Assistant, Tom Gillespy; Lighting, Gil Rogers; Costumes, Chanyce Bergeron, Shannon Shultz, Kathryn Anderson; Press, Susan Foy

COMPANY

Cheryl Card, Gayla Davis, Lisa Gholson, Paul Greenlee, Neeka Guined, Pam Howard, Diana Larsen, Jobeth Norris, Kathy Padgett, Nikki Parrish, Hanie Randolph, Andrea Schwartz, Lori Sumner, Carolyn Thomas, Nanci Turner, Carlos White, Barbara Woodley, Cathy Zahumensky, Ginger Batcheler, Laura Gilbert, Cynthia Gray, Lori Guesman, Lyn Guesman, Adele Wilson
GUEST ARTISTS: Luis Rivera, Adonis Puertas

REPERTOIRE

"Nutcracker Pas de Deux" (Tchaikovsky, Petipa), "Black Swan Pas de Deux" (Tchaikovsky, Fernandez after Petipa), and premieres of "Classical Symphony" (Prokofiev, Barta), "Moonlight Sonata" (Beethoven, Barta), "Adagio for Strings" (Barber, Barta), "Fairy Doll" (Bayer, Barta), "Serenade in G" (Mozart, Barta), "Variations on America" (Ives, Barta), "El Amor Brujo" (DeFalla, Barta)

BRIANSKY BALLET
Binghamton, N. Y.
Oleg Briansky, Director

Choreographers, Oleg Brinsky, Mireille Braine; Ballet Master, Andre Pap; Production Manager, William Brandow, Sets and Costumes, John Braden

COMPANY

Jon Benoit, Rebecca Frampton, Kathy Gallagher, Christina Ham, Helen Heineman, Roger Petersen

REPERTOIRE

"Aquatic" (Griffes), "Pas de Six" (Verdi), "Raggedy Rag" (Orff), "Games" (Blacher), "Black Swan Pas de Deux," "Entrada" (Byrd-Orff), "Don Quichotte" (Minkus), "Queen Mab" (Berlioz), "Is It True What They Say About....," (Arnold)
PREMIÈRES: "Swan Lake Act II" (Tchaikovsky, Briansky after Petipa), "Snowflakes Scene from Nutcracker" (Tchaikovsky, Briane)

Right Center: Briansky Ballet
in "Raggedy Ann"

Sylvester Campbell, Sandra Fortune
in "Le Corsair" (Capitol Ballet)

CAPITOL BALLET COMPANY
Washington, D. C.

Artistic Directors, Doris Winifred Jones, Claire H. Haywood; Choreographers, Norman Walker, Sylvester Campbell Gerard Sebbritt, Louis Johnson, Doris Jones; Designers, Ronald Truitt, Quay Quay Truitt, Claire Haywood, Bernard Johnson; Press, Jewel Shepherd, Janise Colbert

COMPANY

PRINCIPALS: Sandra Fortune, Leroy Cowan
SOLOISTS: Maria Newby, Richard Moten
CORPS DE BALLET: Deborah Sullivan, Joyce Mattison, Beverly Butler, Nancy Hanson, Lauri Fitz, Rodney Green, Charles Pace, York Van Nixon
GUEST ARTISTS: Sylvester Campbell, Gerard Sebbritt, Raven Wilkinson, Arthur Mitchell, Bernard Stanley, Louis Johnson, Robert Davis

REPERTOIRE

"Le Corsaire" (Drigo), "Nutcracker" (Tchaikovsky), "Don Quixote" (Minkus, Petipa), "Raymonda" (Tchaikovsky), "Romantique Pas de Deux" (Rossini, Jack Carter), "Folk Impressions" (Gould, Louis Johnson), "Profiles" (Rachmaninoff Jones), "Haitien Tragedy" (Art Blackey, Claude Thompson), "Bach for Six" (Bach, Jones), "Stephen Foster Suite" (Foster, Jones), "Blue Guitar" (Minotti, Jones), "Gospel Songs" (Mahalia Jackson Jones), "Peter and the Wolf" (Prokofieff, Jones)
PREMIERES: "Pocahontas" (Elliott Carter, Doris W. Jones), "Intermezzo" (The Nice, Louis Johnson), "To Fire the Flame" (Negro Spirituals, Doris W. Jones), "Flair" (Gustave Holst, Doris W. Jones)

154

Jennifer Britton, Cookie Sloman, Ann Simpson
Sergent, Julianne Kemp, Brenda Taylor in "The
Greek Room" (Charleston Ballet)

CHARLESTON BALLET
Charleston, West Virginia
Andre Van Damme, Artistic Director

Choreographer, Andre Van Damme; Costumes,
Maggy Van Damme; Sets, Ellie Schaul, A. Benoni;
Rehearsal Assistant, Julianne Kemp; Stage Managers,
Elward Baker, Strauss Wolfe; President, Robert Martens

COMPANY

SOLOISTS: Andre Van Damme, Ann Simpson Sergent,
Julianne Kemp, Jennifer Britton, Mary Molle Skidmore,
Cookie Sloman, Monique Van Damme, Pam Wolfe,
Brenda Taylor
CORPS DE BALLET: Norma Brathor Adkins, Angel
Louden, Debby Nutter, Kim Pauley, Amy Pittman, Ann
Robertson, Donna Williams, Carl Berlin, Jr., Salem
Jackson, James W. Taylor, Jr., William McDowell

REPERTOIRE

"Iberia" (Selected), Premieres of "Joan of Arc" in two
acts (Gustav Mahler-Karl Hartmann, Andre Van
Damme), "The Greek Room" (Albert Roussel, Van
Damme)

CHARLESTON CIVIC BALLET
Charleston, S. C.
Don Cantwell, Director

Choreography and Costumes, Don Cantwell; Sets,
James N. Sellers, Jr., Don Cantwell

COMPANY

Elizabeth Pitts, Cathy Myers, Kristine Pierce, Grace
Freeman, Cheryl Pierce, Emmalee Mishoe, Celeste Con-
lon, Cecelia Forrest, Martha League, Sharon Tapp,
Merran Funderburg, Lena Kordonis, Nancy Salerni,
Elizabeth Garfinkle, Ann Marie Osborne, Rachael
Woodruff, Brad Buchanan, Peter Theos

REPERTOIRE

"The Nutcracker" (Tchaikovsky, Cantwell after Ivanov),
Premieres of "Hotel Papilon" (Poulenc, Cantwell), "Mat-
inees Musicales" (Britten, Cantwell), "Concerto" (Blanchard, Cantwell), "The Ballerina Bandit" (Rossini, Cantwell)

Right Center: Cathy Myers, Don Cantwell, Grace
Freeman in "Concerto"

CINCINNATI BALLET COMPANY
Cincinnati, Ohio
David McLain, Artistic Director

Assistant Artistic Director, David Blackburn; Music
Director, Carmon DeLeone; Choreographer, David
McLain; Lighting, Jay Depenbrock, David Eviston;
Costumes and Scenery, Andreas Nomikos, Henry Hey-
mann, Jay Depenbrock, Martha Berger; Stage Manager,
Roy Hopper; Wardrobe, Ruth Hopper, Joanne Burke;
Press, Toni Tobias; Sound, James C. Armstrong

COMPANY

SOLOISTS: Jane Wagner, David Blackburn, Barbara
Bogash, Joanne Burke, Karen Kuertz, Diana LoVerso,
Steffi MacFarlane, Claudia Rudolf, Susan Shtulman,
Lawrence Jones
CORPS DE BALLET: Sharon Cole, Linda Garner,
Nancy Gregory, Ellen Moritz, Alice Taylor, Deborah
Wilson, Paula Davis, Vivan Diller, Karl Lindholm

REPERTOIRE

"Antiche Arie E Danze" (Respighi), "Bluebird Pas de
Deux (Tchaikovsky, Sabline), "Concerto" (Poulenc),
"Dilemmas Moderne" (Carter), "Grand Waltz" (Tchai-
kovsky), "Lovers" (Rorem), "Minuet and Rondo"
(Haydn), "Night Soliloquies" (Barlow-Rogers-Hanson),
"Pas de Quatre" (Pugni, Markova), "Les Patineurs"
(Meyerbeer-Lambert, Martinez), "Romanza" (Arensky),
"Pas de Cinq from Sleeping Beauty" (Tchaikovsky),
"Nutcracker Suite" (Tchaikovsky), "Songs of Silence"
(Takacs), "2 X 2" (DeRopartz), "12 X 9 in 5" (Lutoslaw-
ski-DeLeone), "Winter's Traces" (Verdi)
PREMIERES: "Fandango" (Soler, Tudor), "Guitar Con-
certo" (Castelnuovo-Tedesco, McLain), "Morphosis"
(Palombo, McLain), "The Nutcracker Grand Pas de
Deux" (Tchaikovsky, Petipa-Markova)

Bob Gerding Photo

Cincinnati Ballet
in "Concerto' '

155

CIVIC BALLET OF SCOTTSDALE-PHOENIX
Scottsdale, Arizona

Artistic Directors, Ruth Sussman, Margaret Gisolo; Choreographers, Tom Holt, Beth Lessard, Ruth Sussman, Barbara Wolf; Ballet Mistresses, Barbara Benchoff, Gayla Crossman; Costumes, Donna Bartz, Charlene Bisch, Doreen Kennedy, Beth Lessard, Ruth Sussman, Barbara Wolf, D. Yamanouchi; Lighting, Jim Edmondson, Barry Koeb, Ruth Sussman, Barbara Wolf; Sets, Bobby Drover; Musical Consultant, Louise Kerr; Stage Managers, Mary Jane Bird, Pat Schultz

COMPANY

Amy Miller, Robin Chmelar, Stacey Hawkins, Paulette Taylor, John A. Packard, Penny Lawrence, Barbara Wolf, Michael Schwartz, Karen Sing, Tom Holt, Mary Jane Bird, Elizabeth Hackett, Jean Ellis, Diane-Marie Lemon, Charles Pavaroni, Patty Tang, Connie Traber, Karen Killgore, Kim Yamanouchi, and corps of 30.
GUEST ARTISTS: Diane Bradshaw, Terry Edlefsen, Richard Fein, Mark Mejia, James Morsky, Lori Rowan, Caprice Walker

REPERTOIRE

"Les Sylphides" (Chopin, Sussman), "Carnaval" (Schumann, Holt), "Dance Episodes from a Lorca Play" (Beth Lessard), "Peter and the Wolf" (Prokofiev, Sussman), "Nutcracker" (Tchaikovsky, Sussman), "Ballet Class" (Sussman), "Sarabande" (Muffat, Lessard), "Ars Poetica" (Vivaldi, Wolf), "L'Arlesienne Suite" (Bizet, Sussman), "Collage, 1971" (Hyman-Stockhausen-Cage, Lessard)

Paulette Taylor, John Packard, Penny Lawrence, Barbara Wolf, Michael Schwartz, Karen Sing in "Dance Episodes"

(Civic Ballet of Scottsdale - Phoenix)

COLORADO BALLET COMPANY
Colorado Springs, Colo.
Ilse Reese Gahart, Director

Principal Choreographer, Ilse Reese Gahart; Manager, Ben Gahart; Stage Manager, Bishop Nash

COMPANY

PRINCIPALS: Mona Ketchersid, LInda Murphy, Wes Williamson
SOLOISTS AND CORPS DE BALLET: Karen Hollingsworth, Debra Rich, Sybill Reese, Pamela Benson, Leslie Clark, Patricia Upton, Pamela Franker, Kim Arnn, Joanne McGraw
GUEST ARTISTS: Marcos Paredes, Geoffrey Thomas

REPERTOIRE

"Aurora's Wedding" (Tchaikovsky), "Ballet Classique" (Bach), "Concerto in F" (Gershwin), Graduation Ball" (Strauss), "Les Sylphides" (Chopin, Martinez after Fokine), "Scheherazade" (Rimsky-Korsakoff, "Firebird" (Stravinsky), "The Planets" (Holst), "Three-Cornered Hat" (DeFalla), "Toccata and Fugue" (Bach), "Cinderella" (Prokofiev)
PREMIERES: "Emperor Waltz" (Strauss, Gahart), "Four Hungarian Dances" (Brahms, Gahart)

Carl Brattin Photo

Colorado Ballet in "Emperor Waltz"

CONCERT BALLET GROUP
Tacoma, Washington
Jan Collum, Director

Choreographer, Jan Collum; Costumes, Mrs. Robert Loiland; Audio, Kearney Barton; Press, Mrs. M. S. Hampson

COMPANY

Barbara Anger, Julie Berger, Renee Bostic, Jomarie Carlson, Carla Crowley, Candi Crocker, Joan Everson, Laura Hoff, Elaine Kittinger, Marcie Little, Cheri Loiiland, Leslie Taylor, David Hitchcock, Blake Little, Dale Petersen, Lisa Marie Neal, Susan Bales, Jayne Rusu, Erin Walk, Donna Paul, Rachelle Allegro, Kim Muczynski

REPERTOIRE

"Youth-Ations" (Arnold), "Perfection" (Rosko, Carlson-Crocker-Everson), "Tapestry" (Electronic, Mary Staton), "The Clown" (Satie)
PREMIERES: "Saint Thomas" (Selected, Collum), "Wingborne" (Paul Creston, Jan Collum)

Jomarie Carlson, Marcia Little, Renee Bostick, David Hitchcock, Candi Crocker, Joan Everson in "Youth-Ations"

CONTEMPORARY CIVIC BALLET
Royal Oak, Michigan

Founder-Artistic Director-Choreographer, Rose Marie Floyd

COMPANY

Denise Smokoski, Richard Newman, Jan Hanniford, Debbie Smith, Leslie Bronson, Melinda Bronson, Mary Beth Ferkany, Denise Barnewold, Debbie Barr, Cindy Doyle, Ann Fisher, Alice Hlavaty, Margie Osburn, Susan Osburn, Kathleen Vander Velde, Michelle Gregory, Elena Maccarone, Julie Sasso, Shirley Acheson, Donna Belding, Karen Couturier, Mary Nissley, Christine Dupler, Carol Fenwick, Anne Parshall, Jane Shaffmaster, Susan Wallstrom, Grace Ward, Cindy Wenson

REPERTOIRE

"The Nutcracker Act II" (Tchaikovsky), "Les Sylphides" (Chopin), "Roumanian Rhapsody" (Enesco), "Conflict from Horoscope" (Lambert), "Oberon Overture" (von Weber), "La Forza del Destino" (Verdi), "Excerpts from Sleeping Beauty" (Tchaikovsky), "Soires Musicales" (Britten), Polovtzian Dances" (Borodin), "Holberg Suite" (Grieg, Ramon Segarra), "Ballet Parisienne" (Offenbach)

Richard Newman, Denise Smokoski
of Contemporary Civic Ballet

Duffy Photo

Dorothy Silverherz, Leslie Phillippe, Karen
Pannier and Conn. Valley Ballet in "Cinderella"

CONNECTICUT VALLEY REGIONAL BALLET COMPANY
Springfield, Mass.
Marguerite de Anguera, Artistic Director

Co-Director, Dorothy Silverherz; Guest Teachers, Jonathan Watts, William Burdick, William Hugg, Russel Fratto, Nelle Fisher.

COMPANY: names were not submitted

REPERTOIRE

"Prelude" (Choreography, Marguerite de Anguera), "Coppelia" (Delibes), "Cinderella" (Prokofiev, Fratto-Lauret), "Graduation Ball" (Strauss, Fisher after Lichine), "Unfinished Rhapsody" (Rachmaninoff, de Anguera), "Le Salle de Ballet" (de Anguera), "Rhythm Ritual" (Hugg), "Apres Le Bal" (Weber, de Anguera)

DALLAS CIVIC BALLET
Dallas, Texas
George Skibine, Artistic Director

Choreographers, George Skibine, Milenko Banovitch, Marjorie Tallchief, Gustave Mollajoli, Loyd Tygett; Conductors, Rudolf Krueger, Charles Blackman; Designers, Peter Hall, Peter Wolf; Stage Managers, Patricia Hyde, Jeannine Stegin, Lynn Satanford; Sound, B. W. Griffith, Jr.; Costumes, Pat White, Ellarose Sullivan; Lighting, Jeannine Stegin, Patricia Hyde, Frances Aronson; Ballet Master, Milenko Banovitch; Press, Eugene S. Lewis, Mildred Sale, Eldred Robinson; President, William G. Hardy.

COMPANY

SOLOISTS: Sharon Bowdich, Becky Burnett, Jane Evelyn Chalk, Cindy Jones, Maureen Kaplan, Lisa Boone, Kevin Brown, Jeff Butler, Don Greer, Kerry Kearns, Dennis Marshall, Sam McManus, Frederic Woolsey, Jr.
CORPS DE BALLET: Debbie Beckman, Denise Fuller, Bonnie Green, Susan Hinton, Vicki Lee, Leslie McPheeters, Mary McNulty, Jan Morris, Susan Perry, Sue Powers, Kim Smith, Cynthia Stevens, Michelle White, Pat Stroope
GUEST ARTISTS: Marjorie Tallchief, Claire Motte, Jean-Pierre Bonnefous, Milenko Banovitch, Nydia Neumayer, Rodolfo Lastra, Martha Terrizzano, Gustavo Mollajoli

REPERTOIRE

"Sketches" (Rossini, Mollajoli), "Combat" (DeBanfield, Dollar), "Shindig" (Gillis, Tygett), "Namouna" (Lalo, Banovitch), "Aurora's Wedding" (Tchaikovsky, Skibine and Tallchief after Petipa), "Firebird" (Minkus, Skibine after Petipa)
PREMIERE: "Cantata Profana" (Stravinsky, George Skibine; Costumes, Peter Hall)

Bobby Boone, Kevin Brown and Dallas Civic
Ballet corps in "Cantata Profana"

Dallas Metropolitan Ballet
in "Country Garden"

DALLAS METROPOLITAN BALLET
Dallas, Texas

Artistic Directors-Choreographers, Ann Etgen, Bill Atkinson; Costumes, Ouida; Stage Manager and Lighting, Jeannine Stegin

COMPANY

Becky Blair, Beth Bontempo, Kathy Chamberlain, Cheryl Hammer, Janella Houts, Susan Irons, Kevyn Jones, Peggy Judkins, Suzette Mariaux, Leslie Oeler, Gail Peters, Deanna Shanahan, Mitzi Smith, Ellen Tanner, Archie Esquivel, Chuck Flanders, Wayne Pitts, Bill Reaser, George Reed, Gary Tears, Gary Dyvbig, Ron Cundiff

REPERTOIRE

"Country Garden" (Grainger), "Workout" (Shostakovich), "Adagio for Seven and Two" (Gibson-Barber), "Coppelia" (Delibes), "Half-Time" (Gould), "Irish Suite" (Anderson)

DANCE REPERTORY COMPANY
New York, N. Y.
Richard Englund, Director

General Manager, Peter E. Obletz; Company Manager, Carlene Carroll; Ballet Mistress, Fiorella Keane; Stage Managers, Robert Freund, Haskell Fitz-Simons; Musical Advisor, David Bryant

COMPANY

Emily Adams, Delphine Del Bello, Ellen English, Marianne Handy, Everest Mayora, Ilene Strickler, John Gardner, Antonio Mendez, Charles Phipps, Paul Shoemaker, John Slothower, Don Winslow
GUEST ARTISTS: Gage Bush, Violette Verdy, Edward Villella

REPERTOIRE

"Ballade" (Scriabin, Sokolow), "Fete Galante" (Poulenc, Englund), "Hang It All" (Albinoni, Vislocky), "Icarus" (Matsushita, Hoving), "Impressions" (Schuller, Sanders), "In Games" (Copland, Noble), "La Malinche" (Lloyd, Limon), "Napoli" (Helsted-Paulli, Bournonville), "PI r2" (Varese, Lois Bewley), "Swan Lake Pas de Trois" (Tchaikovsky, Petipa)

John Slothower, Everest Mayora, Don Winslow,
Paul Shoemaker, Gage Bush, Antonio Mendez,
Emily Adams, Ellen English in "Divertisement"
(Dance Repertory Company)

George De Vincent Photo

DANCE THEATRE
Washington, D. C.
Erika Thimey, Director

Choreographer, Erik Thimey; Stage and Light Directors, Robert Babik, Guy LeValley; Narrator, Lee Reynolds

COMPANY

Clyde Barrett, Debra Berger, Miriam Cramer, Sally Crowell, Beatrice Davis, Carol Hamilton, E. Raye LeValley, Natalie Mulitz, Gregory Reynolds, Jo-Anne Sellars, Bobbi Seltzer, Gail Waterman

REPERTOIRE

"Noye's Fludde" (Britten), "Trip to Far Away Places" (Traditional), "The Gingham Dog and the Calico Cat" (de Boeck), "How the Rhinoceros Got His Skin" (de-Boeck), "Noisy Hello" (Butler)
PREMIERES: "Fanfare" (Schroeder), "Space Density" (Feldman), "The Rope" (Messiaen), "The Dissected Body Beautiful" (Butler)

Carol Hamilton, Sally Crowell, E. Raye LeValley,
Gail Waterman in "The Rope" (Dance Theatre)

Bruce Davidson Photo

Dancers' Workshop Company

DANCERS' WORKSHOP COMPANY
San Francisco, California
Ann Halprin, Artistic Director

Manager, Xavier Nash; Subjunctive Syzygial Environmentalis, Patric Hickey; Sound, Richard Friedman; Press, John Muto

COMPANY

Bo Conley, Alicia deNajera, Louise Graf, Fletcher Hall, Ann Halprin, John Hopkins, Ray Jackson, Suzanne Jackson, Xavier Nash, Clint Shelby, Pamela Young.

REPERTOIRE

PREMIERES: "New Time Shuffle" (Bo Conley, Ann Halprin and Group), "Invocation of the Cement Spirit" (Richard Friedman, Ann Halprin and Group), "Kadosh" (Fletcher Hall, Ann Halprin and Group)

DAYTON CIVIC BALLET
Dayton, Ohio
Josephine Schwarz, Artistic Director

Founder-Choreographer, Josephine Schwarz; Associate Directors, Bess Saylor, Jon Rodriguez; Costumes, Hermene Schwarz, Juan Carlos; Lighting and Technical Director, Penelope Curry; Wardrobe Mistress, Barbara Trick

COMPANY

Heidi Albrecht, Deborah Anderegg, Gloria Bailen, Amy Danis, Reine Duell, Cheryl Heckman, Syrena Irvin, Linda Lloyd, Lynn Moon, Pamela Moore, Bess Saylor, Julia Schweller, Kathleen Trick, Jill Wheeler, Donna Wood, Joe Duell, Timothy Graves, Jeff Gribler

REPERTOIRE

"Archaic Fragments" (Haines), "Flower Festival Pas de Deux" (Pugni, Bill Martin-Viscount), "Sugarplum Fairy from the Nutcracker" (Tchaikovsky), "Happening" (Penderecki, Bess Saylor), "Strauss Waltz" (Strauss, Jon Rodriguez), "Modern Demonstration" (Schumann), "Ballet Demonstration" (Schumann), "Ophelia" (Stravinsky, Saylor), "Danses Concertantes" (Stravinsky, Fernand Nault), "Vivaldiana" (Vivaldi, Rodriguez), "Cinderella" (Prokofiev, Rodriguez), "Fall into Winter" (Britten, Saylor), "I Watched Myself Grow Up" (Wasson), "Concerto Barroco" (Bach, Balanchine), "Concertino (Pergolesi, Pauline Koner)," "The Wheat Maiden" (Delibes)
PREMIERES: "Homage to Georg Friderich" (Handel, Rodriguez), "The Journey" (Shostakovich, Saylor), "there are no roses in my garden" (Penderecki, Rodriguez), "Celebrations" (Vivaldi, Yuriko)

Walter Kleine Photo

"Cinderella--Then--"
Dayton Civic Ballet

DELTA FESTIVAL BALLET
New Orleans, Louisiana
Joseph Giacobbe, Artistic Director

Associate Artistic Director, Maria Giacobbe; Guest Choreographers, Bill Martin-Viscount, Fiorella Keane, Andra Corvino; Sets, Julie Bouy; Press, Mrs. Earl V. Magri, Jr.; Technical Director, Sidney Trest

COMPANY

Carol Messmer, Gwen Delle Giacobbe, Denise Oustalet, Mary Leech, Maria Alessandra, Sandra Clay, Charlene Royer, Donna Roach, Toni Ann Alessandra, Susan Roach, Janice Roth, Lise Antoinne, Sandra Bolding, Melanie Montalto, Pam O'Neill, Donna Maria Terrebonne, Lylee Oddo, Cheryl Patin, Dawn Russo, Juanita Spizale, Sue Ellen Stewart, Cheryl Trapani, Jerel Hilding, Joseph Giacobbe, Mike Herrington, Marla Bernadas, Pam Boudreaux, Anne Benoit, Patricia Alexander, Melanie Kohout, Providence Grillot, Alexis Alexander
GUEST ARTISTS: Lupe Serrano, Ted Kivitt, Helgi Tomasson, Elisabeth Carroll, Ralph Davis, Richard Rholdon, Edmund LaFosse, Terry Fontenot, Patrick Swayze, David Fleming, Doug Douglas

REPERTOIRE

"Swan Lake Act II" (Tchaikovsky, Giacobbe after Ivanov), "Cimarosiana" (Cimarosa, Bill Martin-Viscount), "Aurora's Wedding" (Tchaikovsky, Keane after Petipa), "Pas de Quatre" (Pugni, Corvino after Dolin), "Nutcracker Act II" (Tchaikovsky), "Flower Festival Pas de Deux" (Helsted-Paulli, Martin-Viscount after Bournonville), "Parades and Patriots" (Sousa), "Swan Lake Peasant Pas de Deux" (Tchaikovsky)
PREMIERES: "Contrast" (Leonard Bernstein, Joseph Giacobbe), "Saddles and Sashes" (Aaron Copland, Joseph Giacobbe)

David Sandberg Photo

Elisabeth Carroll, Helgi Tomasson and Festival Delta Ballet in "Aurora's Wedding"

DETROIT CITY BALLET
Detroit, Michigan
Marjorie Hassard, Artistic Director

Co-Directors, Betty Bandyk, Kay Bliss, Myra Halsig, Mirdza Lemanis, Enid Ricardeau, Rene Russell; Stage Manager, Enid Ricardeau; Lighting, David Craig; Accompanist, John Wojnar; Wardrobe, Betty Bandyk; Press, John Herzog

COMPANY

Elizabeth Bolton, Eileen Herzog, Noreen Ellen Keros, Zoe Ann Keros, Sandra Kort, Karen Latham, Laura Nevejans, Alice Stephens, Terry Tempinski, Heidi Watson, Elizabeth Bird, Carol Bowen, Aloysia Busuttel, Dail Carter, Mary Cusmano, Pat Damian, Janet Darragh, Keith Dulla, Nancy Griffin, Lisa Herzog, Christina Hintzen, Patricia Johnson, Theresa Kennedy, Michelle LaPorte, Hayne LaRose, Alison Lewandowski, Isabel Matyszewski, Karen Mills, Renee Parent, Louise Poske, Libby Rogoff, Donna Tucci, Jennifer Vigor
GUEST ARTISTS: Joanne Danto, Linda Di Bona, Michael Lopuszanaki, Bill Martin-Viscount

REPERTOIRE

"Conversations" (Corelli-Barbirolli, Hug), "Rhythm Ritual 3-3/4" (Hug), "Concerto" (Mendelssohn, Dollar), "The Intruder" (Delibes, Michael Lopuszanaki), "Debussy Suite" (Debussy, Marjorie Hassard), "LaRonde" (Bizet, Alex Martin), "Rumanian Rhapsody" (Enesco, Yurek Lazowski), "Allegro Largo" (Bach, Ron Sequoio), "Soires Musicales" (Britten, Dollar), "Scaramouche" (Milhaud, Dollar), "Pas de Douze" (Mozart, Dollar), "Cimarosiana" (Cimarosa, Martin-Viscount), "Pastorale" (Milhaud, Dollar), "Concerto Grosso" (Vivaldi, Jon Rodriguez)

Detroit City Ballet in "Pastorale"

DISCOVERY DANCE GROUP
Houston, Texas
Camille Long Hill, Director

Choreography, Camille Long Hill; Assistant Director, Betty Morgan; Lighting and Costume Design, Camille Long Hill

COMPANY

PRINCIPALS AND SOLOISTS: Vickie Anders, Evelyn Etie, Erwin Gibson, Brian McAnally, Cheryl McCollough, David Quintero
CORPS DE BALLET: Chris Benton, Debbi Busby, Linda Castillon, Debbi Curry, Debbi Dickenson, Beth Ezzell, Donna Johnson, Kathleen Parker, Lynn Reynolds, Terri Ribble, Hope Stephens, Pam Stockman

REPERTOIRE

"Triangle" (Bernstein), "Deserts" (Lewis), "Jazz Bit," "Of Chains, Fire, and Hope" (Mingus), "Inhibitions" (Mingus), "Night Is For Dreaming" (Bernstein), "2 Degrees East, 3 Degrees West" (Lewis), "Sounds of Silence" (Arranged by Don Sebesky), "Sea Visions" (Garson), "Four Faces of Love" (Fanidi), "Nirvana" (Mann), "Search" (Bartok), "Habitat" (Copland, Patricia Williams), "The Matriarch" (Ingle, Gus Giordano)
PREMIERES: "Pas de Six" (Villa-Lobos, Hill), "Six Plus Two" (Stevens, Hill), "Yesterday, Today and Tomorrow" (Fripp-Sinfield-McDonald, Hill)

Robert Daly Photo

Discovery Dance Group in "Pas de Six"

DICK ANDROS THEATRE ARTS CENTER
Brooklyn, N. Y.
Dick Andros, Director

Choreographer, Dick Andros; Stage Manager and Lighting, Marvin Schoenberg; Costumes and Press, Gloria Rosenthal

COMPANY

Carole Campolo, Madeline O'Connell, Anne Hernandez, Ellyn Rosenthal, Mindy Toback, Annice Bernstein, Beth Darchi, Suzanne Seltzer, Andrea Havelin, Amy Paulin, Judy Janz, Stephanie Darchi, Anna Krueger, Karen Ackerman, Cynthia Goldson
GUEST ARTISTS: Judith Siegfried, Patrick Stines

REPERTOIRE

"Dance Suite" "Surprise Symphony," "Enchanted Mask," "Grand Tarantella," "Fiesta," "Jazz Suite"
PREMIERE: "Broadway--Then and Now" (Selected, Dick Andros)

Leslie Leon Photo

Carol Purcell, Judith Siegfried, Dick Andros, Roberta Solomon and corps in "Theme and Variations"

ELIZABETH CITY BALLET
Elizabeth City, N. C.
Penelope Martin, Artistic Director

Artistic Director-Choreographer, Gene Hammett; Drama Director, Penny Martin; Costumes, Angelique Martinez, Penny Martin; Sets, B. E. and Lucinda Richardson,Marjory Sawyer; Lighting, Hunt Thomas; Guest Teachers, Francesca Corkle, William George, Richard Gibbs, Terri Vigilante, Glenn White

COMPANY

SOLOISTS: Betty Bell, Katrina Midgett, Cindy Richardson, Patti Sawyer, Dorothy Thomas, Ashley Thompson, Dorothy White
CORPS DE BALLET: Cindy Anderson, Stephanie Anderson, Margaret Bell, Lisa Bulliner, Signe Albertson, Felicia Allen, Tammy Byrum, Becky Crutchley, Debbi Hartzog, Ellen Hessey, Jenny Houtz, Kathy Houtz, Cheryl Jones, Barbara Kepchar, Linda McPherson, Debbi MacMorris, Jeanna Marshall, Ellen Meekins, Cynthia Pharr, Barbie Pierce, Susan Ray, Kathy Sawyer, Hope Simmons, Lisa Wagner, Laura West, Becky White, Ann Williams, Erisha Williams, Mary Sue Wright
GUEST ARTISTS: Kathleen Caton, Carol Sue Dodd, Lorraine Graves, Sandra Johnson, Star McNeela, Richard Prewitt, David Wright

REPERTOIRE

"Alice" (Kabalevsky, Hammett), and premiere of "Classroom Dancer" (Prokofiev, Hammett)

Ann Williams, Cindy Richardson, Ellen Hessey
in "Alice" (Elizabeth City Ballet)

EMPIRE STATE BALLET COMPANY
Eden, N. Y.
Barbara Striegel, Director

Choreography, Barbara Striegel; Technical Director, Claudia Gurbacki; Lighting, John Ebling; Press, Mary Lou Vogt

COMPANY

Michele Grazier, Thomas Banasiak, Nancy Scalice, Katherine Bottiau, Edmund Wronski, Paul Sperrazza, Joseph Trembly, Suzanne Pulk, Carolyn Pulk, Tina Ebling,Deborah Ebling, Jill Strawbrich, Mary Ann Samuelson, Penny Palcic

REPERTOIRE

"Sleeping Beauty," "Fire and Ice," "Gaite Parisienne," "Coppelia," "Birth of a Beat," "Graduation Ball," "The Wild Ones," "Shades of Jade," "Petrouchka," "Afternoon of a Faun," "Ballet Militaire," "Polonaise," "Scheherra Jazz," "Ballet Americana," "Song of the Nightingale," "Afro-American "Concerto," "La Valse," "Apollo," "Leader of the Muses," "I Got Rhythm," "Black Sound, Red Sound," "Fireworks"

Empire State Ballet

ELMIRA-CORNING BALLET
Elmira, N. Y.

Founder-Artistic Director-Choreographer, Mme. Halina; Musical Conductors, Fritz Wallenberg, Theodore Hollenbach; Technical Director,Floyd Lutomski; Guest Choreographers, Val Deakin, Henry Danton, Laura Tuffel, James DeBolt, Rochele Zide

COMPANY

PRINCIPALS AND SOLOISTS: Ginger Fancher, Steve Dickinson, Ilonka Lutumski, Marily Haradon
CORPS DE BALLET: Roxanne Starry, Linda Wood, Sharon Tagliaferi, Debra Salmirs, Katherine Brown, Meredith Horton, Cathy Bailey, Catherine Peelle,, Gina Dick, Tina Dick, Elizabeth Minier, Sally Thyer, Carmella Berry, Debra Burgett, Jennie Bowes, Cecilia Pineo, Patrick Vete, Pat Goldsmith
GUEST ARTISTS: Carmen Mathe, Martin Fredmann, Eleanor D'Antuono, Ramon Segarra, James DeBolt, Seija Simonen, Rochele Zide, Sonia Taverner, Richard Beatty, William Glassman, Ellen Everett

REPERTOIRE

"The Wooden Prince" (Bartok), "Sleeping Beauty" (Tchaikovsky), "Coppelia" (Delibes), "Bayadere" (Adam, Denton), "Mozartiana" (Mozart, DeBolt), "Nutcracker" (Tchaikovsky), "Cinderella" (Prokofiev, Deakin), "Hat Trick" (Bohlme, Deakin)

Elmira-Corning Ballet
in "La Bayadere"

FAIR LAWN BALLET COMPANY
Fair Lawn, N. J.
Mae Picinich, Director

Choreographer, Mae Picinich; Ballet Mistress, Laurie Picinich

COMPANY

Thirty dancers
(names not submitted)
GUEST ARTISTS: Donna Silva, Frank Bays, Richard Holden

REPERTOIRE

"The Nutcracker," "Sleeping Beauty," "Swan Lake Act II," "Giselle Act II," "Coppelia," "Les Sylphides," "Humoresque," "Waltz from Serenade for Strings"

Right: Sophie Rivera, Mariano Garcia, Audrey Ross in "Les Sylphides"

Jay York Photo

Kathy Bliss, Shane Manley in "Summer Waltzes" (Fresno Civic Ballet) Above: Fresno Ethnic Dancers in "Sones de Mariache"

162

FRESNO DANCE REPERTORY ASSOCIATION
Fresno, Calif.
Karl Murray, Artistic Director

President, Benjamin Amirkhanian; Production Manager, Gaylaird Bissell; Music Supervisor, Roger Heffner
SPONSOR OF THE FOLLOWING COMPANIES:

FRESNO CIVIC BALLET

Director-Choreographer, Clare Lauche Porter; Associate Director, Joan Vickers Coffey; Choreographers, Joan Vickers Coffey, Karl Murray; Costumes, Jeanne; Sets, Gerald Dias, Jerry McGonagel; Conductor, Guy Taylor

COMPANY

Kathy Bliss, Tina Bologna, Terese Cenci, Kathleen Coffey, Regine Hoffmann, Susan Jones, Deborah Keuster, Robin Laikam, Karen McCoy, Kathy Mulligan, Donna Sonnenburg, Ellen Taylor, Sandra West, Cindy Willis, Fred Bologna, Jorge Ledesma, Michael Lepper, Shane Manley, Michael Tatum

REPERTOIRE

"Bartered Bride Dances" (Smetana, Porter-Sorina), "Bach on Stage" (Bach, Coffey), "Dancers West" (Newman, Murray), "La Fille Mal Gardee" (Herold, Coffey-Porter), "Once Upon A Time" (Grieg-Coffey), "Inscape" (Copland, Murray), "Encounter" (Berg, Porter), "Nutcracker" (Tchaikovsky, Coffey-Porter), "Boite a Joujoux" (Debussy, Coffey-Porter), "Histoire du Soldat" (Stravinsky, Murray)

FRESNO CIVIC CONTEMPORARY DANCE COMPANY

Director, Sara Dougherty; Choreographers, Sara Dougherty, Brooke Hunter

COMPANY

Jean Arnold, Wendy Balch, Fred Brooks, Shelly Cushman, Yolanda Demeteiff, Jane Dougherty, Diane Ferrari, Karen Fife, Barbara Fleming, Robert Gravelle, Dennis Howell, Betsy Jones, John Mandeville, Michael Magarian, Mary Mossette, Erica Oravetz, Sherry Polzin, Debbie Poochigian, Gary Rodriguez, Lorraine Ramos, Eustachia Rojas, Stephanie Sliger, Jeanne Smiley, John Sullivan, Joyce Unamoto, Ann Williams

REPERTOIRE

"Dimension IV" (Weinstein, Dougherty), "Volition" (Partch, Hunter)

FRESNO CIVIC ETHNIC DANCERS

Rivie Slupsky, Coordinator
Active Ethnic Dance Groups: Armenian, East Indian, Greek, Hawaiian, Irish, Japanese, Mexican, Scottish, Spanish, Phillipine, Yogoslav

GUS GIORDANO DANCE COMPANY
Chicago, Illinois
Gus Giordano, Director

Choreography, Gus Giordano; Costumes and Lighting, Mort Kessler

COMPANY

Gus Giordano, Jim Kolb, Debbi Hallak, Joellyn Speros, Debbie Kisor, Julie Walder

REPERTOIRE

"The Matriarch" (Ingle), "Jazz Triology" (Prince), "Dance Lecture" (Blomquist), "Movement Withheld, Movement Exploded" (Sounds and Percussion)
PREMIERES: "Call of the Drum--Napoleonic Dances" (Traditional, Giordano), "Time Trip" (Albinoni-Bach-Tchaikovsky, Giordano), "Dance Decades" (Selected, Giordano)

Sylvian Ofiara Photo

Right: Jim Kolb, Joellyn Speros, Debbie Hallak in "Jazz Trilogy"

Joanne Crum, Betty Church, Debby Harrison in "Cinderella" (Hampton Roads Ballet)

HAMPTON ROADS CIVIC BALLET COMPANY
Hampton, Virginia

Directors, Edgerton and Muriel Shelley Evans; Designers, John Clark, Pat Masonis, Bary Beaven; Wardrobe, Peggy Alvis, Stage Managers, C. O. Seaman, Margie Wallace; Choreographers, Edgerton and Muriel Shelley Evans.

COMPANY

Kitty Alvis, Lee Beaven, Susan Bragg, Heather Byrne, Michelle Cawthorn, Betty Church, Joanne Crum, Darcy Evans, Laura Ann Forbes, Ginger Gunter, Kathleen Harmon, Debbie Harrison, Kathy Sue Joynes, Faith Ann McErlean, Stephanie Messick, Jackie Quinn, Cynthia Richardson, Toni Seaman, Laurie Sherman, Coco Sheffield, Elizabeth Tolley, Tracey Troth, Virginia Vaughan, Jamee West, Kay Wiatt, Susan Woodland, Al Broyles, Danny Gunter, Ronnie Gunter, Eddie Lowder, John Strock

REPERTOIRE

"Cinderella" (Prokofiev), "Les Sylphides" (Chopin, Ann Parson after Fokine), "Crown Jewels" (d'Auber), "French Suite" (Chabrier-Poulenc-Faure, Lisa Evans), "Les Patineurs" (Meyerbeer), "Goldilocks" (Svenson), "Mozart cum Sextus" (Mozart), "Spectre de la Rose" (Von Weber, Beatric Bene), "Folk Dances" (Traditional)

HARTFORD BALLET COMPANY
Hartford, Conn.
Joseph Albano, Artistic Director

Founder-Choreographer, Joseph Albano; Technical Director, James Hodson; Lighting, Mollie Friedel, Beverly Emmons; Sets and Costumes, Russell Methany, Michael P. Duffy, Leo Meyer; Costumes, Gini Kleinan, J. Herbert Callister, Jack MacAnally; Costumer, Mary Wolfson; Press, Lois Reiner

COMPANY

Julia Frederick, Judith Gosnell, Merle Holloman, Paul Russell, Clare Bader, Judie Bringhurst, Leslie Craig, Joyce Karpiej, Enid Lynn, Kathleen O'Connell, Jon Carrell, Rudy D'Angona, Armando Zettina

REPERTOIRE

"The Nutcracker," "The Minister's Black Veil" (Frink), "Nowhere A Go Go" (Compiled), "The Lady of Tearful Regret" (Flanagan), "Suite for Symphonic Strings" (Harrison), "Ives and Me" (Ives), "Ballet Egyptien" (Luigini), "Introduction and Allegro" (Ravel), "The Mystery" (Floyd), "Divertissement" (Ibert)

Julia Frederick and Hartford Ballet in "Carmen"

HARTFORD MODERN DANCE THEATRE
Hartford, Conn.
Joseph Albano, Artistic Director

Director-Choreographer, Enid Lynn; Technical Director, James Hodson; Lighting, Mollie Friedel, Beverly Emmons; Costumer, Mary Wolfson; Assistant Administrator, Carol Luckman; Press, Lois Reiner

COMPANY

Enid Lynn, Deborah Brody, Linda Dorvel, Kathleen Fletcher, Debi Gale, Merle Holloman, Janet Johnson, Jon Carrell, Richard Moore, John Perpener, John Simone

REPERTOIRE

"Nowhere A Go Go" (Compiled, Albano), "Concerto Grosso No. 1" (Block, Albano), "Dover Beach" (Barber, Enid Lynn), "Piece for One or More Dancers" (Anthony Gnazzo, Lynn), "The Moth and the Star" (Weidman), "Meatwaves Studies" (Edward Miller, Lynn) premiered March 1971.

David Robbins Photo

Jon Carrell, Leslie Craig, Linda Dorvel, John Perpener, Janet Johnson in "Meatwaves Studies" (Hartford Modern Dance Theatre)

HOUSTON BALLET
Houston, Texas
Nina Popova, Artistic Director

Ballet Master, Michael Lland; Managing Director, Allen Thompson; Production Manager, Robb Grace; Stage Manager, Richard Jones; Costumer, Brauna Ben-Shane; Accompanist, Rachael P. Pitcock; Press, Bob Adams Associates

COMPANY

Judith Aaen, Anthony Sellers, Genzi Broughton, Aurelio Garcia, James Karlow, Mary Lynn, Lou Martin, Shirley McMillan Martha Pietz, Jennifer Potts, Sara Reynolds, Gilbert Rome, Sheryl Rowland, John Scott, Gary Snider, Charles Ward, Kathleen Weiss, Betty Wichterich

REPERTOIRE

'Tchaikovsky Pas de Deux" (Balanchine), "Nutcracker Grand Pas de Deux" (Tchaikovsky, Ivanov), "Flower Festival Pas de Deux" (Helsted-Paulli, Bournonville), "Protee" (Debussy, Lichine), "Bachianas Brasilieras" (Villa-Lobos, Sanders), "Opus '65" (Macero, Sokolow), "Caprichos" (Bartok, Ross), "Impressions" (Klee-Schuller, Sanders), "Design with Strings" (Tchaikovsky, Taras), "Pas de Dix" (Glazounov, Balanchine), "Workout" (Schostakovitch, Etgen-Atkinson)

Ed Stewart Photo

Judith Aaen, Anthony Sellers
in "Le Corsaire" (Houston Ballet)

HUNTSVILLE BALLET THEATRE
Huntsville, Alabama
Imogen Stooke Wheeler, Artistic Director

Imogen Stooke Wheeler, Artistic Director

Principal Choreographer, Imogen Stooke Wheeler; Technical and Lighting, Tom DeWille, Michael Sweigart; Sound, D. W. Gates; Co-ordinator, Miriam Hoyle Gates; Rehearsal Coaches, Sue Diseker, Sherri Smith, Sally Edwards

COMPANY

PRINCIPALS: Laura Gates, Michael Sweigart
SOLOISTS: Vicki Davis, Lisa Daniel, Sally Edwards, Sue Diseker, Sherri Smith, Janis Link, Beth Ennis, Ronnie Cleghorn

REPERTOIRE

Full length "Nutcracker," "La Sylphide," "Les Sylphides," "Reverie," "Swan Lake Act II," "Giselle," "Facade Act I," "Concerto," "Legend," "Matinee Musicales," "Match Girl," "Nimbus," "Opus 6 Plus 1," "Romance," "Serenade," "Valse Romantique," "Roads of Tomorrow," "Valse" (choreographer, Barnett), "Biljane" (choreographer, Dragde), "Reverie" (choreographer, Bolm), and Pas de Deux from "Aurora's Wedding," "Corsair," "Don Quixote."

Michael Sweigart, Laura Gates
(Huntsville Ballet Theatie)

HUNTSVILLE CIVIC BALLET COMPANY
Huntsville, Alabama
Loyd B. Tygett, Artistic Director

Choreographer, Loyd B. Tygett; Company Manager, Helen Herriott; Lighting, Ben Nation; Sound, Levin Soule; Stage Managers, Judy McClay, Jim Blanche; Press, Helen Herriott

COMPANY

Linda Soule, Audrey Powe, Hugh Bigler, Caitilin Dickerson, Pam Robinson, David Herriott, Kelly McClay, Phoebe Stone, Mary Pulles, Rene Sevigny, Jodi Stephens, Debbie Katz, Cindy Leonard, Dale May, Cheryl Baswell, Carol Riggins, Melanie Hollis, Anne Brigham, Cynthia Gray, David Brown, Daniel Katz, Kathy Horton, Doris Scott, Elise Glickman, Gala Phillips, Keren Bibb, Amy Lubowicki, Laura Lubowicki, Karen Simmons, Patti Davoren, Kerrie Morgan, Cathy Hutson, Kim Manning, Elaine Everman, Susan Morrison

REPERTOIRE

"Masquerade" (Khachaturian), "Under the Toadstools" (Meyerbeer), "Bach Suite" (Bach, Achille Vienneau), "Wing Shadow" (Vienneau), "The Comedians" (Kabalevsky), "Nutcracker," "Midsummer Vigil," "Aurora's Wedding," "Shindig"
PREMIERES: "Peter and the Wolf" (Prokofiev), "La Boutique Fantasque" (Rossini-Respighi), "Four Up a Trio" (Poulenc, Judith Pointer), opera ballets for "Aida," "Faust," "Romeo and Juliet," and "Orfeo"

Right: Linda Soule, Craig Reinhart, Brad Burks, Loyd Tygett in "Boutique Fantasque"

Dom Orejudos, Peggy Powell in "This Persistent Image" (Illinois Ballet)

INNER CITY REPERTORY DANCE COMPANY
Los Angeles, California
Donald McKayle, Artistic Director

Choreographer, Donald McKayle; Company Manager, Bruce Feldman; Lighting, Orville "Doc" Ballard; Setting and Costumes, Donald McKayle, Deena Burkett, Normand Maxon; Technical Supervisor, Lupre Autajay; Sound, Federico Bernache; Stage Managers, Annette Ensley, Jeanne Joe; Founding Directors, Janet Collins, Donald McKayle, Jaime Rogers.

COMPANY

Ron Bush, Carolyn Dyer, Barry D'Angelo, Maria Gahva, Ken Ganado, Jerry Grimes, Bill Landrum, Jackie Landrum, Lee Lund, Ruby Millsap, Delila Moseley, Juleste Salve, Michele Simmons, Roy Smith, Dan Strayhorn, Leslie Watanabe

REPERTOIRE

"Daughters of Eden" (Bloch), "Rainbow 'Round My Shoulder" (Arranged by Robert DeCormier, Milton Okun), "Sojourn" (Jolivet), "District Storyville" (Freitag)

ILLINOIS BALLET
Chicago, Illionis

Directors, Richard Ellis, Christine Du Boulay; Associate Director-Resident Choreographer, Dom Orejudos; Business Manager, Leon L. Bram; Press, Marilyn Rasmussen-Adams; Technical Director, William Ploeger

COMPANY

PRINCIPALS: Peggy Powell, Susan Kirby, Juanita Lopez, Jennifer Hartz, Dom Orejudos
CORPS DE BALLET: Nancy Mikota, Jocelyn Lorenz, Dana Mott, Deborah Chernin, Diane Vrettos, Robert Pfeil, Heidi Ellison, Donald Greene, Christine Brenkus
GUEST ARTIST: Elisabeth Herskind

REPERTOIRE

"The Stone Medusa" (Villa-Lobos, Orejudos), "Pas de Quatre" (Pugni, Dolin), "Songs of a Wayfarer" (Mahler, Orejudos), "Coppelia Act II" (Delibes, Ivanov), "Valse-Fantaisie" (Glinka, Hy Somers)
PREMIERE: "This Persistent Image" (Prokofiev, Dom Orejudos)

Lyn Smith Photo

Bill Landrum and Inner City company in "District Storyville"

Jacksonville Ballet Theatre company

JACKSONVILLE BALLET THEATRE
Jacksonville, Florida
Dulce Anaya, Artistic Director

Founder-Choreographer, Dulce Anaya; President, Buddy Sherwood; Press, Melitta Cohn; Costumes, Phil Phillips; Sound Rush Bullock; Guest Choreographer, Haydee Gutierrez

COMPANY

PRIMA BALLERINA: Dulce Anaya
Gilberto Almaguer, Regla Angulo, Anne Brown, Patricia Burton, Charmion Clark, Jeff Fancek, Mary Catherine Haut, Lisa Heide, Lisa Kaufman, Billye-Kay Kersey, Lisa Nice, Elaine Pennywitt, Lisa Permenter, Betty Vogl, Harriet Webb, Annette Menard, Sharon Campbell, Beth Ennis, Kathy Katibah, Sharon Kelly, Teena Lockermann, Wendy James, Leslie Snow, Cindy Goldsmith
GUEST ARTISTS: Adolfo Andrade, Alexei Yudenich, Ramon Segarra, Sonia Diaz, Haydee Gutierrez, Hilda Maria Reverte, Jeremy Anderson

REPERTOIRE

"Nutcracker" (Tchaikovsky, Anaya after Petipa), "Giselle" (Adam, Anaya after Coralli), and premieres of "Aria" (Stravinsky, Gutierrez), "Concerto" (Grieg), "Overture" (Schubert), "Fledermaus" (Strauss), "Marriage of Figaro" (Mozart), "Tarantella" (Rossini)

KANSAS CITY BALLET COMPANY
Kansas City, Missouri
Tom Steinhoff, Director

Founder-Artistic Adviser, Tatiana Dokoudovska; Guest Choreographer, Zachary Solov; Production Manager, Dory DeAngelo; Ballet Mistress, Vicki Reid; Conductor, Jay Decker; Lighting, Harry Silverglat, Jr.; Costumes, Mrs. Robert Rosenburg; Press, Mrs. Paul Hunt; Pianist, Dr. Gerald Kemner

COMPANY

PRINCIPALS: Shirley Weaver, Tom Steinhoff, Elizabeth Hard
SOLOISTS: Kathleen Shriner, Lanny Lea, Jean Sandquist, Angela Smith, Judy Gillespie, Vicki Bouckhout
CORPS DE BALLET: Elaine Andalikiewicz, Lisa Cromwell, Debby Ferguson, Pamela Fink, Carol Powick, Mary Giudici, Lesley Hanes, Tamara Klein, Cathy Eberhart, Kathy Labovsky, Kay Moseley, Karen Shore, Janice Merlo, Viktoria Smith, Kateri Terns, Gail Yates, Don Smith, Erik Smith
GUEST ARTISTS: Jacques d'Amboise, Melissa Hayden, Merril Ashley, Christine Redpath

REPERTOIRE

"Ages of Innocence," "Rhapsody" (Gershwin, Solov), "Sylvia Pas de Deux" (Delibes), "Celebration" (Delius-Debussy, Solov), "You Are Love" (Jerome Kern, Jacques d'Amboise)

Shirley Weaver, Tom Steinhoff in "Celebration"
(Kansas City Ballet)

LAKE CHARLES BALLET SOCIETY
Lake Charles, La.
Ida Winter Clarke, Artistic Director

Conductor, Don Wilder; President, Della Krause Thielen; Artistic Adviser, Mrs. William B. Coleman; Technical and Sound Adviser, George Kaough; Assistant Director, Sarah Quinn Jones; Choreographer, Ida Winter Clarke.

COMPANY

Mary Ferguson, Sarah Quinn Jones, Stacy Sherman, Lynette Roy, Amire Planche, Cissie Clarke, Julie Kaough, Martin Golson, Cheryl Teague, Linda Richards
GUEST ARTIST: Ramon Segarra

REPERTOIRE

"Fiddle Tunes," "Nutcracker Act II," "Mrs. Tubby's Traveling Circus" (Respighi-Rossini), "Papillons" (Shumann), "Pas de Quatre" (Pugni), "Gran Pas de Deux from Don Quixote" (Minkus, Natalie Krassovska after Petipa), "West by Southwest" (Gould), "Grand Tarantella" (Gottschalk, Richard Englund), "Capriccios" (Mendelssohn, Englund), "Valses Nobles" (Schubert), "Les Patineurs" (Meyerbeer), "La Guitarina" (Haydn, Ron Sequoio), "Peter and the Wolf" (Prokofiev), "Images of the Dance" (Mozart), "Holberg Variations" (Grieg, Segarra), "Divertissement D'Adam" (Adam, Segarra)

Lake Charles Ballet in "The Nutcracker Snowflake Ballet"

Odile de Witte, Hal O'Neal and Laguna
Beach Ballet in "Festa"

LAGUNA BEACH CIVIC BALLET COMPANY
Laguna Beach, Calif.
Lila Zali, Artistic Director

Founder-Choreographer, Lila Zali; General Director, Douglas Reeve; Assistant Directors, Barbara Stuart, Hal O'Neal; Ballet Mistress, Kathy Jo Kahn; Technical Directors, Carl Callaway, Zachary Malaby; Wardrobe Mistress, Myrth Malaby; Press, Sally Reeve

COMPANY

Damara Bennett, Barbara Byrnes, Odile de Witte, Louise Frazer, Michael Hillman, Kathy Jo Kahn, Mary Catherine Kaminski, Carrie Kneubuhl, Molly Lynch, Kathy Mason, Kristi Moorhead, Hal O'Neal, Gregory Osborne, Robert Petel, Lansing Reid, Michaele Rhodes, Lisa Robertson, Mary Sayers, Dee Dee Schlarb, Hope Sogawa, Belinda Smith, Steve Smith, Cynthia Tosh, Sandra Winieski, Gene Wilkes, Charles Colgan
GUEST ARTIST: Edward Villella

REPERTOIRE

"Visions Fugitive" (Prokofiev), "Grand Adagio from Paquita" (Minkus, Petroff), "The Enchanted Toy Shop" (Bayer), "Moods of Ancient Russia" (Arensky), "Octet" (Vivaldi), "Dream" (Bartok), "Swan Lake Act II" (Tchaikovsky, Zali), "Peter and the Wolf" (Prokofiev), "Nutcracker" (Tchaikovsky), "Ballet Portraits 18th Century" (Corelli), "Arabesque and Exercise in Four Dimensions" (Bach), "Ballad of the Sheriff and the Schoolmarm" (Copland, Hal O'Neal), "The Emperor's Clothes" (Francaix, O'Neal), "La Fille Mal Gardee" (Herold), "Chopiniana" (Chopin, Petroff), "Cinderella" (Prokofiev), "Les Pas de Quatre" (Bugni), "Capriole Suite" (Warlock)
PREMIERES: "Hansel and Gretel" (Humperdinck, Zali), "Stone Flower" (Prokofiev), "Carnival Tutu" (Milhaud, Ford), "Boxed" (Telemann-Ravel, Sweet), "Festa" (Adam-Burgmuller)

LOS ANGELES FESTIVAL BALLET
Los Angeles, Calif.
Eva Lorraine, Artistic Director

Founder-Choreographer, Eva Lorraine; Press, Hal Weiner

COMPANY

Anne Gough, Teresa Gomez, Karen Mitsunaga, Kathy Johnson, Grace Fedele, Joyce Lee

REPERTOIRE

"Gloriana Dream", "The Swan, " "Sleeping Beauty Variations," "Love's Dream," "Grand Finale"

Eva Lorraine and corps of Los Angeles Festival
Ballet rehearse "Glorianna"

Lyn Smith Photo

Linda Kostalik, Melanie Adam in "The Sisters"
(Los Angeles Dance Theatre)

LOS ANGELES DANCE THEATRE
Los Angeles, Calif.
Eugene Loring, Artistic Director

Director, Paul Gleason; General Manager, Richard Schottland; Director of Art and Production, Robert Fletcher; Press, Ricky Harris; Stage Managers, Jerry Rice, Lee Sailer; Wardrobe, Mary Belanger; Sound, Michael Gleason; Sets, and Costumes, Robert Fletcher, Donald Bradburn, Renate Druks, Andrea Attie; President, Sanford R. Goodkin; Conductor, Maurice Allard; Production Coordinator, John Elliott

COMPANY

Melanie Adams, Thomas Anthony, Noli Belanger, Susan Bonsvvor, Robin Diamond, Carol Fisher, Debra Hadley, Ann Marie Hansen, Alphonso Hidalgo, Mariko Hoshino, David Kresser, Linda Kostalik Jacqueline Sailer, Allen Schafer, Jeri Sparkman, Jackie Smith, Thomas Stanton, Charlene Van Pelt, Mary Lynn Waterman

REPERTOIRE

"Dance Is a Language," "Bath Towel Bagatelle," "Cavalcade of Dance," "Prisms" (Poulenc), The Sisters" (Ruggles), "Folk Dances of a Mythical Country" (Allard-Loring-Beaver & Krause)

LOUISIANA BALLET
New Orleans, Lousiana
Gayle Parmelee, Artistic Director

Choreographer, Gayle Parmelee; Composer-Musical Adviser, Charles Sens; Accompanists, Viola Eskew, Julia Costa; Musical Director, Milton Scheuermann, Jr.; Designer, John Scheffler; Stage Manager, Clyde Mayeux

COMPANY

Alden Adams, Voorhees Authement, Sandra Baranovics, Stephen Baranovics, Myra Brahney, Katherine Davis, Rebecca Denton, Craig Franko, Janet Haylo, Charles Lee, Fong Lee, Clyde Mayeux, Julianne Nice, Sylvia Sandberg, Mary Wichterich

REPERTOIRE

"Comus, A Masque," "The Nutcracker" (Tchaikovsky), "Blue Bird Pas de Deux" (Tchaikovsky), "Musette" (Gluck), "Green Grass"

David Sandberg Photo

Charles Lee in "Comus"
(Louisiana Ballet)

LOYOLA UNIVERSITY BALLET
New Orleans, Louisiana
Lelia Haller, Director

Choreographer, Lelia Haller; Musical Director, Joseph Herbert; Costumes, Miki Steiger; Stage Director, Bill Murphy

COMPANY

SOLOISTS: Bobbe Baron, Patricia Leclercq, Joan Casey, Karen Pederson, Barbara Jo Pontecorvo, John Latour, Richard Rholden, Frank Baltazar, Sal Mustacchia
CORPS DE BALLET: Arlene Albert, Ann Anoult, Terri Chaplain, Maureen Duschene, Kat Eichmann, Dawn Guillot, Pamela Trest, Ann Prattini, Lori Zulke, Pat Alexander, Judy Quave, Patricia Rosche, Dawn Russe, Carol Archer, Janet Comer, Sue Katz, Angelina Law, Sally McQuitty, Cheryl Hein, Doris Richards, Joyce Sharp
GUEST ARTISTS: Rene Toups, John Britton, Douglas Dawes, Thomas Springler, David Albers, Melvin Day, Flora Hood, Peggy O'Connell, Paula Konen, Victoria Butt, Donna Blair

REPERTOIRE

"Swan Lake," "Gaite Parisienne," "Boutique Fantastique," "Rhapsody in Blue," "Pineapple Poll," "American in Paris," "Gayne Suite," "Capriccio Italien," "Stars and Stripes," "Slavonic Dances," "Polka and Fugue"
PREMIERES: "Jazz Ballet" (Art Wiggins, Lelia Haller), "Incantations and Dance" (John Barnes Chance, Lelia Haller)

Maureen Duschene, Lori Zuehlke, Ann Arnoult, Dawn Guillot, Patricia Rosche, Kathy Porter of Loyola Ballet

MACON BALLET GUILD
Macon, Georgia
Gladys Lasky, Artistic Director

Choreographer, Gladys Lasky; President, George C. Oetter; Sets, Joseph H. Todd; Costumes, Gladys Lasky; Lighting, E. C. McMillan; Stage Director, B. Catherwood; Stage Manager, T. M. Northington; Sound, Gordon Andrews, Angus Domingos; Press, Elizabeth Drinnon

COMPANY

SOLOISTS: Alice Ann Domingos, Susan Dorsey, Melissa Fletcher, Lucy Holliday, Cheryl Andrews, Jody Beck, Leslie Bowen, Judy Friedel, Beth Oetter, Roger Britts, Steve Ewing
CORPS DE BALLET: Susan Bloodworth, Sara Broome, Carol Colston, Lauren Drinnon, Jane Espy, Janet George, Cathy Hess, Jeni Massenburg, Natalie Norton, Elizabeth Tinker
GUEST ARTISTS: Natalia Makarova, Ted Kivitt

REPERTOIRE

"Konservatoriet" (Paulli, Bournonville), "Pas de Quatre" (Pugni-Perrot, Lester), "Swan Lake Act III" (Tchaikovsky, Petipa), "Patterns" (Pop, Dolores Segler)

Walter Elliott Photo

Alice Ann Domingos, Susan Dorsey, Melissa Fletcher, Lucy Holliday in "Pas de Quatre"
(Macon Ballet)

MARGALIT OVED & COMPANY
Los Angeles, Calif.
Margalit Oved, Director

Choreography, Margalit Oved; Costumes, Malcolm McCormick; Lighting, Penelope Leavitt; Technical Director, David Hart; Stage Managers, Laura Gindi, Lynn Hachten

COMPANY

Margalit Oved, Ilana Herson, Nancy Ichino, David Drexler, Nina Watt, Dorothy Levens, Buddy Sperber, Maralyn Scherr, Betzi Roe, Wanda Evans, Lorraine Perez, Judy Hoddy

REPERTOIRE

"Gestures of Sand" (film by Allegra Fuller Snyder), "Aabbii--My Father" (Eliyahou Shasha, Oved), "Spring", "Landscape" (Music and choreography, Margalit Oved)

Lyn Smith Photo

Margalit Oved Company in "Landscape"

Cecil J. Thompson Photo

MARIETTA CIVIC BALLET
Marietta, Georga
Iris Antley Hensley, Artistic Director

Choreographer, Iris Antley Hensley; Assistant Director, Marilyn Gaston; Assistant Choreographer Diane Bennett

COMPANY

SOLOISTS: Diane Bennett, Marilyn Gaston, Becky Greenlee, Sharon Hildreth, Iris Hensley, Dot Dunaway CORPS DE BALLET: Nancy Atherton, Tammy Bryant, Kathy Bullard, Elizabeth Eros, Katie Groves, Katherine Kelley, Kathy Johnson, Suzanne MacIntyre, Debbie Mauldin, Dawn McBrayer, Kenslea Motter, Teresa Nation, Joy Railey, Elizabeth Ramsden, Valerie Vreeland, Diana Whipkey, Wynn Wise, Susan Wood, Patty Youngblood, Susan Hall

REPERTOIRE

"Variations Serieuses," "Marzipan," "Free for All"

Left: Sharon Hildreth, Valerie Vreeland, Susan Hall in "Marzipan"

MARIN CIVIC BALLET
San Rafael, California
Leona Norman, Director

Assistant Director, Jody White; Music Director, Dan Scarlett; StageDirector, Charles Hoeppner; Wardrobe Mistress, Betty Lucas; Press, Phyllis Thelen; President, Mrs. Carl G. Brimmekamp

COMPANY

Laurie Merryman, Lori Crichton, Cynthia Harvey, Becky Jones, Kathy McCormick, Charles Perrier, Jane Thelen, Rocky White, Carol Brannan, Nancy Jones, Martha Fietz, Debbie Farb, Jody Marvin, Doreen Singer, Karry Burcham, Laura Przetak

REPERTOIRE

"Rustic Wedding" (Goldmark, Marc Wilde), "Golden Moments of Ballet" (Guckenheimer Sour Kraut Band, Leona Norman), "Clown Alley" (Prokofiev, Wilde), "Gymnopedies" (Satie, Ron Guidi), "The Gap" (Villa-Lobos, Dennis Carey), "Twink" (Mozart, Ron Poindexter), "One Fine Day" (Copland, Charles Perrier), "Les Sylphides" (Chopin), "Nutcracker" (Tchaikovsky), "Paquita" (Minkus), "Pas de Deux from Don Quixote" (Minkus), "Black Swan Pas de Deux" (Tchaikovsky, Petipa), "Peasant Pas de Deux" (Adam), "Miss Margaret" (Goldsmith, Wilde)

Marin Civic Ballet in "The Gap"

McLEAN BALLET COMPANY
McLean, Virginia
Molly Vick, Director

Choreographers, Molly Vick, Barbara Theusen; Costumes, Mary Nelson; Lighting, Richard Smith; Coordinator, and President, Eugene Threadgill

COMPANY

PRINCIPALS: Marilyn Stedman, Patricia Heubusch, Vincent Jones, Patricia Barry, Angela Scimonelli
CORPS DE BALLET: Jennifer Vick, Barbara Birdt, Alexandra Deane, Julie Helleary, Joellen Brassfield, Jan Warden, Cheryl Dicks, Terri Roberts

REPERTOIRE

"History in Hats" (David Arnold, Molly Vick), "Skylarkin'" (Holtz, Barbara Theusen), "Dance on a Spot" (Bizet, Theusen), "Court Scenes" (Gretry, Vick)
PREMIERES: "Mobile" (Gershwin, Vick), "Preludes" (Bowles, Vick)

Left: Vincent James, Patricia Heubusch, Marilyn Stedman in "Mobile"

MIAMI BALLET
Miami, Florida
Thomas Armour, Artistic Director

Founder-Choreographer, Thomas Armour; President, Louisa Hofmann; Co-Directors, Martha Mahr, Renee Zintgraff, Robert Pike; Musical Director, Peter Fuchs; Stage Director, Demetrio Menendez

COMPANY

Annemarie Amanzio, Billie Ann Berg, Betsy Bergner, Linda Bonanno, Lydia Bonanno, Rio Cordy, Sally Danovitz, Lisa Cott, Caren de Marco, Mary Doane, Roslyn Dunn, Kathleen Essex, Mary Fellman, Debbie Friedman, Lynn Huck, Diane Guminski, Gloria Gaither, Elizabeth Green, Jennifer Grose, Susan Jaffe, Dana Knowlton, Nanette Loren, Anne McDonough, Elizabeth McEmber, Gloria McKinley, Donna Mecurio, Cynthia Ann Roses, Tina Osborne, Sheila Schwarzbart, Cynthia Williamson, Miriam Suraz, Mike Carter, Mark Goldweber, Bill Boyle, Kerry Roland, Armand Rivas, Richard Rock, Randy Parrot, Kris Nagle, Steve Schlairet
GUEST ARTISTS: Karena Brock, Alba Calzada, Jean-Paul Comelin, Anita Dyche, Stefan Grebel, Royes Fernandez, Frederic Franklin, Gail Israel, Ted Kivitt, Patricia Neary, Ronald Newman, Andrea Price, Judy Reece, Victoria Leigh, Lupe Serrano, Robert Scevers, Violette Verdy, Edward Villella

REPERTOIRE

"Giselle" (Adam, Corelli-Perrot), "Farewell" (Strauss, Jean-Paul Comelin), "Hoe Down" (Don Gillis, Robert Pike), "Pas de Quatre" (Pugni, Martha Mahr), "Imagery" (Donizetti, Mahr), "Ballet Suite" (Levin, Armour), "Les Sylphides" (Chopin, Fokine), "Swan Lake Act II" (Tchaikovsky, Ivanov), "Prince Igor" (Borodin, Fokine), "Papillons" (Schumann, Armour), "Pantomime for Lovers" (Mozart, Armour), "Symphonic Variations" (Franck, Mahr), "Ambivalence" (Bach, Armour), "Concerto" (Gershwin, Beatrice La Verne), "Divertimenti" (Mozart, Pike), "Slavonic Dances" (Dvorak, Armour), "Pas de Trois" (Thomas, Mahr), "3001" (Holst, Pike), "La Sylphide" (Lovenskjold, Bournonville)

Nanette Loren, Rio Cordy, Richard Rock in "3001" (Miami Ballet)

MILWAUKEE BALLET COMPANY
Milwaukee, Wisconsin
Jury Gotshalks, Artistic Director

Choreographer, Enrique Martinez; Resident Choreographer, Myron H. Nadel; Artistic Adviser, Lupe Serrano; Musical Director, Edmund Assaly; President, Mrs. Roberta Boorse; Designer, Stuart Johnson; Costumes, James Hook; Lighting, Don Thomas; Stage Manager, Helen Adelt

COMPANY

Eva Baenen, Josie Baenen, A. J. Brothers, Jeanine Buckstead, Diana Byer, Judy Feather, Daiva Gestautas, Jury Gotshalks, K. Henley Hirschbein, Nancy Haas, Ellen Holmes, Peggy Hurley, Chris Komar, Romanie Kramoris, Isabel Kralj, Juris Krisans, Vanda Ludeks, Stephen Lockser, Myron Howard Nadel, Charles Neal, Kathryn Moriarty, Jo-Jean Retrum, Robin Reseen, Merilyn Rutzky, Gary Schaaf, Barbara Smith, Sandy Turner, Lynne Weber, Maris Wolff, Sandra Yacona, Harry Zummach, Robert Jorge, James Bartz, Matthew Karr, Jori Clark, Susan Davis, Carol Delk, Susan Earnest, Terri Palabrica, Kathy Ploetz, Sarah Skeeba, Marlis Moldenhauer, Monica Wilant
GUEST ARTISTS: Lupe Serrano, Cynthia Gregory, Ted Kivitt, Naomi Sorkin, Ian Horvath

REPERTOIRE

"Polovetsian Dances from Prince Igor" (Borodin, Gotshalks after Fokine), "Coppelia" (Delibes, Enrique Martinez after St. Leon), "Les Sylphides" (Chopin, Martinez after Fokine), "The Combat" (De Banfield, Martinez-Serrano after Dollar), "Huapango" (Moncayo, Martinez)
PREMIERE: "The Hill" (Anton Dvorak, Myron Howard Nadel)

Naomi Sorkin, Ian Horvath, Susan Davis and Milwaukee Ballet in "Les Sylphides"

Bil Leidersdorf Photo

Paul Hagen Photo

Minnesota Dance Theatre Company
in "Terminal Point"

MURRAY LOUIS DANCE COMPANY
New York, N.Y.
Murray Louis, Artistic Director

Choreography, Murray Louis; Technical Director, James Van Abbema, Costumes, Frank Garcia; Administrative Director, Betty Young; Managing Director, Murray Farr; Company Manager, Charles Ziff

COMPANY

Murray Louis, Michael Ballard, Anne Ditson, Les Ditson, Helen Kent, Marcia Wardell

REPERTOIRE

"Chimera" (Nikolais), "Proximities" (Brahms), "Interims" (Foss), "Intersections" (Farberman), "Calligraph for Martyrs" (Nikolais), "Bach Suite," "Landscapes" (Walker)
PREMIERES: "A. D. Opus XLIV" in three acts: Personnae(Free Life Communications), Continuum(Corky Siegel), Disguise(Siegel-Nikolais)

MINNESOTA DANCE THEATRE
Minneapolis, Minn.
Loyce Houlton, Director

Choreographer, Loyce Houlton; Technical Director, John Linnerson; Music Director, David Voss; Ballet Mistress, Sylvia Bolton; Repertory Assistant, Becky Halmers; Press, Carol Cisek, Susan Pochapsky

COMPANY

Jon Benson, Sylvia Bolton, Bobby Crabb, Marianne Greven, Becky Halmers, Peter Hauschild, Kathy Hollenhorst, Lise Houlton, Dana Luebke, Erin Luebke, Frances Machala, Sandra Machala, Phyllis Patalas, Roberta Stiehm, Andrew Thompson, Susan Thompson, David Voss, Larry White
GUEST ARTISTS: Kent Hatcher, Valentina Pereyaslavec, Rochelle Zide, William Dollar, David Lichine, Brian Shaw, Michael Uthoff

REPERTOIRE

"Audition" (Dorati), "Bazaarque" (Sananta), "La Creation" (David Lichine), "Chronicles" (Bartok), "Earthsong" (Copland), "Untitled, Unfinished Dinner Divertissments" (Tommasini-Scarlatti), "La Fille Mal Gardee" (Hertel, Zide after Nault), "Graduation Ball" (Dorati-Strauss, Lichine), "Imprecis" (Ibert), "The Killing of Sister Creamcheese" (Zappa), "November Steps" (Takemitsu), "Nutcracker Fantasy" (Tchaikovsky), "Pas de Trois from Paquita" (Minkus, Zide after Petipa), "Present Laughter" (Roussel), "Raymonda Act III" (Glazounov, Zide after Petipa), "La Recontre" (Sauguet, Lichine), "Les Sylphides Suite" (Chopin, Zide after Fokine), "Tactus" (Stravinsky)," "Tenderplay" (Sibelius, Uthoff), "Troth" (Brown), "The Twisted Tree" (Tippett)
PREMIERES: "April" (Ravel, Houlton), "Bold and Brassy" (Bach, Houlton), "Bone Lonely" (Barry, Houlton), "Caprice" (Schubert, Houlton-Zide), "Gaje Rom" (Vivaldi, Houlton), "Insects and Lovers" (Bloch, Houlton), "Slaughter on Tenth Avenue" (Rogers, Houlton), "Terminal Point" (Cage, Houlton), "293.6" (Webern, Houlton), "Les Patineurs" (Meyerbeer, Brian Shaw after Ashton), "Le Combat" (deBanfield, Dollar)

Jack Mitchell Photo

Murray Louis Dance Company
in "Calligraph for Martyrs"

NEW ENGLAND DANCE THEATRE
Boston, Mass.
Toby Armour, Artistic Director

Choreographer, Toby Armour; Production, Lois Ginandes; Technical Director, Chip Largman; Sound, Ezra Sims

COMPANY

Toby Armour, Lolo Beckwith, Lois Ginandes, John Houston, Christina Jackmauh, Chip Largman, Bruce de St. Croix, Marlene Wallin, Rachel Whitman

REPERTOIRE

"Brick Layers," "Abalone Company"

Tim Freeman Photo

Toby Armour, Marlene Wallin in "Abalone Co."
(New England Dance Theatre)

NATIONAL BALLET
Washington, D. C.
Frederic Franklin, Artistic Director

Co-Artistic Director, Ben Stevenson; General Manager, Ralph Black; Principal Conductor, Ottavio deRosa; Associate Conductor, Campbell Johnson; Stage Production Manager, Ralph Hoffmann; Costumer, May Ishimoto; Assistant Manager, Harry Baernstein III

COMPANY

PRINCIPALS: Marilyn Burr, Susan Casey, Lydia Diaz Cruz, Luis Fuente, Reese Haworth, Gerard Sibbrett
SOLOISTS: James Capp, Joanne Danto, Michelle Lees, Kenneth Lipitz, Sheryl McKechnie, Edward Myers, Ronald Newman, Judith Rhodes, Elizabeth Risen, Raymond Serrano, Fredric Strobel
CORPS DE BALLET: Mariana Alvarez, Charlotte Belchere, Zelma Bustillo, Nancy Davis, Susan Frazer, Mary-Win Hardy, Dianna Marks, Kirk Peterson, Andrea Price, Jane Roseman, Stuart Sebastian, Susan Smith, Patricia Sorrell, Michelle White, Rory Woomansee
GUEST ARTISTS: Margot Fonteyn, Edward Villella, Ivan Nagy, Violette Verdy, Desmond Kelly

REPERTOIRE

"Raymonda" (Glazounov, Balanchine-Danilova), "La Sylphide" (Lovenskjold, Bournonville), "Serenade" (Tchaikovsky, Balanchine), "Warm-Up" (Barnwell, Franklin), "Tribute" (Franck, Franklin), "Flower Festival in Genzano Pas de Deux" (Helsted, Bournonville) "Touch and Go" (Abramson, Deakin), "Swan Lake Act II" (Tchaikovsky, Petipa-Ivanov), "Giselle" (Adam Coralli-Perrot), "Les Sylphides" (Chopin, Fokine), "The Shakers" (Humphrey), "Tchaikovsky Pas de Deux" (Balanchine), "Four Temperaments" (Hindemith, Balanchine, "Don Quixote Pas De Deux" (Minkus, Petipa), "Coppelia" (Delibes, Sergeyev-St. Leon), "Black Swan Pas de Deux" (Tchaikovsky, Petipa), "Cinderella" (Prokofiev, Stevenson), "Out of Darkness" (Hindemith, Comelin), "Idylle" (Herald, Comelin), "La Sonnambula" (Rietti-Bellini, Balanchine), "Con Amore" (Rossini, L. Christensen), "Dance Brillante" (Glinka, Franklin), "Tango Chikane" (Norgaard-Gade, Flindt), "Homage" (Gounod, Franklin), "Nutcracker" (Tchaikovsky, Danilova-Franklin), "Creation of the World" (Milhaud, Bolender), "Paquita" (Minkus, Eglevsky), "The Witch Boy" (Salzedo, McDowell), "Seeds" (Kodaly, Lopuszanski)

Shirley Nottingham Photos

Margot Fonteyn in "Cinderella"
Top Right: "Concerto Barocco"

Luis Fuente, Marilyn Burr in "Cinderella" Above:
Gerard Sibbritt, Lydia Diaz Cruz in "Witch Boy"

172

NEW JERSEY DANCE THEATRE
Mountainside, N. J.
Alfredo Corvino, Artistic Director

Choreographer, Alfredo Corvino; Assistant to Director, Toni Lacativo; Ballet Mistress, Sonya Dobrivinskaya; Costumes, Gail Rae; Business Director, Gail Rae; Stage Manager, Verne Fowler; Sets, Norman Cohen

COMPANY

100 dancers from Guild studios throughout New Jersey
GUEST ARTISTS: Christine Sary, Ali Pourfarrokh, Karen Kryche, Dorothy Fiore, Andra Corvino, Edillio Ferrara, Miriam Welch

REPERTOIRE

"Nutcracker" (Tchaikovsky, Corvino after Ivanov), "Pas de Quatre" (Pugni, Corvino after Dolin), "Spanish Dance" (Tchaikovsky, Dobrivinskaya), "Pas de Deux from Don Quixote" (Minkus, Petipa), "Waltz of the Flowers" (Tchaikovsky, Corvino after Ivanov), "Summer" (Glazounov, Vivers), "Dance of the Hours" (Dobrovinskaya), "Les Patineurs" (Meyerbeer-Lambert, Charles Kelley after Ashton), "Mission Accomplished" (Primrose, Kelley)
PREMIERES: "Foyer at the Rue de la Pelitier")Mozart, Vivers), "Napoleon Era Court Dances" (Vivers), "Wedding Festival"

Miriam Welch, Ali Pourfarrokh, Edilio Ferraro and New Jersey Dance Theatre company in "Nutcracker"

NEWBURGH BALLET GUILD
Vails Gate, N. Y.
Fred Douglass deMayo, Artistic Director

Choreographers, Marya Kennett, Tom Adair, Fred Douglass deMayo, E. Schneider; Costumes, Joanna Denisar, Sue Axtell; Lighting, James Cole

COMPANY

PRINCIPALS: Barbara Ellias, Judy Coleman
SOLOISTS AND CORPS: Alicia Gilkey, Adele Wright, Laura Psychas, Fern Kushner, Geoffrey Alexander, Garry Boehm, Quiedo Carbone, Peter Sarvis, Kim Kozaczek, Dom Pidone
GUEST ARTISTS: Andre Eglevsky, Daryl Gray

REPERTOIRE

"Peter and the Wolf" (Prokofiev), "Pas de Deux from Nutcracker, Carnaval, Don Quixote," "Pas de Trois" (Minkus), "Stars and Stripes" (Kay), "Orchestre Vivant" (Britten), "The Skaters" (Meyerbeer), "Zodiac" (Bartok), "Divertimento" (Mozart), "Love Waltzes" (Brahms)

Left: Quiedo Carbone, Barbara Ellias in "Don Quixote Pas de Deux"

NIAGARA FRONTIER BALLET
Buffalo, N. Y.
Kathleen Crofton, Artistic Director

Associate Director, Frank Bourman; General Manager, Russell R. Rokahr; Production Manager and Lighting, Malcolm Waters; Stage Manager, E. O. Larson

COMPANY

PRINCIPALS: Jeanne Armin, William Glassman, Peter Mallek, Tatsuo Sakai
SOLOISTS: Wendy Barker, Mary Barres, Ruth Perez, Sanson Candelaria, Robert Schnurr, Victor Vargas, Antoni Zalewski
GUEST ARTISTS: Paul Sutherland, Patricia McBride, Edward Villella

REPERTOIRE

"Les Biches" (Poulenc, La Nijinska), "Brahms Variations" (Brahms, La Nijinska), "Chopin Piano Concerto" (Chopin, La Nijinska), "Aurora's Wedding" (Tchaikovsky, Petipa), "Swan Lake Act II" (Tchaikovsky, Ivanov), "Grand Divertissement from Nutcracker Act II" (Tchaikovsky)
PREMIERES: "Graduation Ball" (Strauss, Lichine), "Le Combat" (de Banfield, Dollar), "Carnaval" (Schumann, Alicia Markova after Fokine), "La Sylphide" (Loveskjold, Hans Brenaa after Bournonville), "California Legend" (Kremski, Ana Ricarda)

Niagara Frontier Ballet

Linda Bogsrud, William Martin in "Classical Symphony" (Norfolk Civic Ballet)

OLYMPIA BALLET COMPANY
Olympia, Washington
Virginia Woods, Artistic Director

Choreographers, Virginia Woods, Ulla Fleming, A. Webster Bair, Mildred Keller; Conductors, C. Henry Howard, Gerald Wagner; Art Director, Ray Gilliland; Costumes, Mabelle Shaw; Props, Shirley Joachim; Mrs. Jim Evans, President; Press, Cherle Schmid.

COMPANY: 15 to 20 (names not submitted)

REPERTOIRE

"Nutcracker" (Tchaikovsky, Woods after Petipa), "Cinderella" (Prokofiev, Woods), "Wizard of Oz" (Various, Woods), "Gayne" (Katchaturian, Flemming), "Madame Butterfly" (Puccini, Woods)
PREMIERES: "Ciraporu" (Villa-Lobos, Woods), "The Seasons" (Wagner, Woods), "The Letter" (Wagner, Woods), "Heloise" (Wagner, Woods)

Jennifer Van Dijk, Wayne Payne, Vickie Evans in "Heloise" (Olympia Ballet)

NORFOLK CIVIC BALLET
Norfolk, Virginia

Artistic Directors, Major Burchfield, Gene Hammett, Penny Martin; Artistic Adviser, Perry Brunson; Choreographers in residence, Gene Hammett, Teresa Martinez, Musical Director, Trudy Hoffer; Drama Director, Penny Martin; Sets, Norrie and Penny Martin; Costumes, Angelique Martinez, Penny Martin; Lighting, Joseph Leonard; Press, Robin Selkin

COMPANY

PRINCIPALS: Linda Bogsrud, William Martin
SOLOISTS: Kathy Caton, Carol Sue Dodd, Lorraine Graves, Sandra Johnson, Richard Prewitt, Heidi Robitshek, Sherri Wisoff, David Wright
CORPS DE BALLET: Patsy Bailey, Sherron Black, Teresa Coleman, Terri Gardner, Cynthia Hal, Regina Helmer, Julianna Holm, Star McNeela, Mitzy McNeely
GUEST ARTISTS: Frank Bays, Francesca Corkle, William George, Richard Gibbs, Gregg Hoffman, Diane Orio, Eileen O'Rourke, Donna Silva, Glenn White

REPERTOIRE

"Pas de Trois from Swan Lake" (Tchaikovsky, Petipa), "La Favorita" (Donizetti, Hammett), "La Corsaire" (Drigo, Hammett), "To Glenn Miller, With Love" (Miller, Hammett), "Spring Waters" (Rachmaninov, Messerer), "Pas de Trois Miniature Act II Bayaderka" (Minkus, Hammett), "Nutcracker Act II" (Tchaikovsky, Petipa)
PREMIERES: "Classical Symphony" (Prokofiev, Hammett-Brunson), "Punch and Judy" (Stranger, Hammett-Martin), "Espana" (Chabrier, Martinez), "Love Story" (Lai, Hammett), "Alice's Dream" (Kabalevsky-Anderson, Hammett-Martin)

Bartlett Warren, Lisa Peck, Janet Glassman, Randy April, Laurinda Finelli, Pam Fallon (Northern Westchester Dance Company)

NORTHERN WESTCHESTER DANCE COMPANY
Bedford, N. Y.
Elizabeth Rockwell, Director

Manager, Claire Miller; Choreographers, Manuel Alum, Margot Fargnoli, Evan Williams, Elizabeth Rockwell; Conductor, Bernard LaDue; Designer, Harold Witherspoon; Sound, Richard April

COMPANY

PRINCIPALS: Lisa Peck, Pam Fallon, Bartlett Warren
SOLOISTS AND CORPS DE BALLET: Randy April, Laurinda Finelli, Janet Glassman, Sally Solinger, Terry Lehman, Merry Melvin, Pam Fletcher, Debby Scott
GUEST ARTISTS: Randall Faxon, Pamela Fiala, Evan Williams

REPERTOIRE

"Palomas" (Oliveras, Alum), "The Green Child" (Stravinsky, Rockwell), "Jazz Suite" (Brubeck, Rockwell)
PREMIERES: "The Unicorn, the Gorgon, and the Manticore" (Menotti, Rockwell), "Burnt Weenie Sandwich" (Frank Zappa, Rockwell), "The Abyss" (Judy Collins, Margout Fargnoli), "Adrift: Born by Metaphysical Circus" (Bach, the U.S.A., Evan Williams)

Alan Howard, Sally Streets in "Manolete"
(Pacific Ballet)

PENINSULA CIVIC BALLET COMPANY

Newport News, Virginia

Artistic Directors, Gene Hammett, Penny Martin; Choreographer, Gene Hammett; Drama Director, Penny Martin; Costumes, Joan Gorman, Penny Martin; Scenery, Dick Ivy

COMPANY

SOLOISTS: Karen Dearborn, Julianna Holm, Susan Hubbard
CORPS DE BALLET: Anna Marie d'Antonio, Cheryl Branscombe, Alexis Brown, Angelique Crawford, Melanie Davis, Amy Gorman, Cathy Harris, Stephanie Hollingsworth, Jennifer Jones, Mary Leath, Suzanne Lyon, Shelley Martin, Darlene Moon, Louisa Sargent, May Shumate, Nancy Smith, Ann Suttle, Leslie Suttle
GUEST ARTISTS: Sherron Black, Linda Bogsrud, Kathleen Caton, Carol Sue Dodd, Terri Gardner, William George, Lorraine Graves, Sandra Johnson, Heidi Robitshek, Sherri Wisoff, David Wright

REPERTOIRE

"Ecole de Ballet" (Offenbach), "Bartered Bride" (Smetana), and premieres of "Pied Piper" (Chapman, Hammett), "Sylvia Pas de Deux" (Delibes, Hammett)

Karen Dearborn, Susan Hubbard
(Peninsula Civic Ballet)

PACIFIC BALLET COMPANY

San Francisco, Calif.
Alan Howard, Artistic Director

General Manager-Choreographer, Alan Howard; Assistant to Manager, Beatrice T. Brooks; Business Manager, Susan Brown; Stage Manager, Glen Naratomi; Lighting, David Arrow; Costumes, Don Ransom, Dom Orejudos; Sets, Don Ransom, Cliff Gonzaler, Dom Orejudos

COMPANY

PRINCIPALS: Sally Streets, Alan Howard
SOLOISTS: Carolyn Goto, Marilyn Knowles, Gina Ness, Sally Stallings, Kyra Alexandra, Cindy Cox, Dudley Brooks, Les Boday, Fred Johnston, Antonio Mendes, Gilbert Chun
GUEST ARTISTS: Antoinette Sibley, Anthony Dowell

REPERTOIRE

Full length "Nutcracker" (Tchaikovsky), "Pas de Quatre" (Pugni, Dolin after Perrot), "Afternoon of a Faun" (Debussy, Marc Wilde), "Screenplay" (Mingus, Job Sanders), "Espana" (Rodrigo, Howard), "Harp Pas de Deux" (Grandjany, Howard), "Hungarian Variations" (Brahms, Howard), "Songs of a Wayfarer" (Mahler, Dom Orejudos), "Serenade a Quatre" (Dvorak, Carlos Garvajal), "Simple Symphony" (Britten, Jack Johannes)
PREMIERES: "Baroque Variations" (Bach-Vivaldi-Quantz, Alan Howard), "A La Foire" (Shostakovitch, Dom Orejudos), "The Charioteer" (Barber, Orejudos)

Kathryn Adam, Linda Arnold and members of
Premiere Dance Arts Company

PREMIERE DANCE ARTS COMPANY

Denver, Colorado
Gwen Bowen, Artistic Director

Founder-Choreographer, Gwen Bowen; Sets, John O'Brien; Lighting, Kathleen Caldwell, John O'Brien; Wardrobe Mistresses, Margaret Lenhart, Norma Lanier, Velma Rommel; Board Chairman, Mile Chetterbock; Guild Chairman, Jessie Gorringe

COMPANY

Kathryn Adam, Dixie Locklin Turnquist, John O'Brien, Mark Schneider, Debra Danos, Mary Gorringe, Keith Kimmel, Joyce Rider, Sheila Rommel, Patti Brath, Daniel Greenwald, Debra Norblom
GUEST ARTIST: John Landovsky

REPERTOIRE

"La Boutique Fantasque" (Rossini-Respighi), "Carnival of the Animals," "Danse Macabre" (Saint-Saens, Smith), "La Favorita" (Donizetti, Landovsky), "LeRoy Anderson Suite," "The Little Match Girl" (Tchaikovsky), "Lovers Three" (Wolf-Ferrari, Schneider), "Moldavian Suite" (Traditional, Landovsky), "The Not-So-Classical-Classical Ballet Suites 1 and 2" (Shostakovich, Schneider), "Nowhere to Now" (Prince), "Planet for Sale" (Selected), "Romeo and Juliet Balcony Scene" (Prokofiev, Cranko-Landovsky), "Sorcerer's Apprentice" (Dukas), "Witches Sabbath" (Verdi, Crane)
PREMIERES: "Echo and Narcissus" (Kenner, Bowen), "The Baptism" (Selected, Bowen), "Grand Tarantelle" (Gottschalk-Kay, Schneider), "Hannakah, Festival of Lights" (Selected, Bowen), "Jazz Collage" (Santana, Schneider), "Rustic Wedding" (Goldmark, Bowen), "The Skaters" (Meyerbeer-Lambert, Schneider)

PENNSYLVANIA BALLET
Philadelphia, Pa.
Barbara Weisberger, Artistic Director

Artistic Associate and Resident Choreographer, Robert Rodham; Music Director, Maurice Kaplow; Regisseur, Edward Caton; Ballet Mistress, Fiona Fuerstner; Assistant Ballet Mistress, Nadine Revene; Lighting, Jennifer Tipton

COMPANY

PRINCIPALS: Alba Calzada, Jean-Paul Comelin, Fiona Fuerstner, Hilda Morales Dando, Ross Parkes, Robert Rodham, Barbara Sandonato, Alexei Yudenich
SOLOISTS: Kathryn Biever, Patrick Frantz, David Kloss, Michelle Lucci, Judith Reece, Gretchen Warren
CORPS DE BALLET: Carolyn Anderson, Roger Bigelow, Kathleen Callaghan, Marilyn Shaune, Linda Dingwall, Svea Eklof, Phillip Carman, Marcia Darhower, Dane LaFontsee, Ben Lokey, Ellen Federov, Laura Gurdus, Rebecca McLain, Rudy Menchaca, Carmela Martinelli, Gary Masters, Marjorie Philpot, Ramon Rivera, Gary Moore, Ellen Parker, Maria Stylianos

REPERTOIRE

"Fugitive Visions" (Prokofiev, Job Sanders), "Idylle" (Louis Herold, Jean-Paul Comelin), "Journeys" (Anton Webern, John Butler), "Nutcracker," "Carmina Burana," "Serenade," "Concerto Barocco," "Pas de Dix," "Trio," "Cavalier Variations" (Brahms, Rodham)
PREMIERES: "Mass for Today" (Pierre Henry, Gyles Fontaine), "L'Attente" (Henry, Fontaine), "Spookride" (Chopin-Sims, James Waring), "Lumina" (Andrew Rudin, Raymond Broussard), "Ballade" (Gabriel Faure, Jean-Paul Comelin), "Vibrations" (Jonathan Tunick, Peter Gennaro), "Summernight" (Arnold Scheonberg, Job Sanders), "Les Sylphides" (Chopin, Alexandra Danilova after Fokine)

Jack Mitchell Photos

Right: Robert Rodham, Barbara Sandonato, Ross Parkes in "Carmina Burana" Above: "Concerto Barocco"

Barbara Sandonato, Alexei Yudenich in "Scotch Symphony"

Alba Calzada in "Les Sylphides"

PITTSBURGH BALLET THEATRE
Pittsburgh, Pa.
Nicolas Petrov, Artistic Director

Founder-Choreographer, Nicolas Petrov; Guest Choreographers, Ruth Page, Frederick Franklin, Vitale Fokine; Ballet Master, Kenneth Johnson; Ballet Mistresses, Jane Hillyer, Patricia Klekovic; Conductor, Dr. Michael Semanitzky; Executive Producer, S. Joseph Nassif; Production Manager, W. Valentine Mayer; Costumes and Sets, Henry Heymann; Lighting, Sam Gossard; Press, Paula Bern; Stage Managers, Richard A. Edwards, Joseph W. Franze, Barbara Allenberger

COMPANY

PRINCIPALS: Patricia Klekovic, Kenneth Johnson, Jayne Hillyer
SOLOISTS: Marion Petrov, John Occhipinti, Candace Itow, Joseph Kacamon, Hernan Perez-Porter, Jean Gedeon,
Charon Battles, Debby Benvin, Susan Bock, Lynn Carvell, Susan Carvell, Amy Chomas, Jane Crawford, Karl Daniels, Peggy Domer, Richard Fox, Lois Friedlander, Jean Gedeon, Rosemary Gleeson, Patricia Greenwood, Christine Hankes, Robin Hular, Rodney Irwin, Joseph Jutek Kacamon, Pamela Klare, Remus Marcu, Faith Marino, Joanna Mauer, Joann McCarthy, Shea Mihm, Susan O'Leary, Kathy Pierini, Hernan Perez-Porter, Paddy Toon de Perez-Porter, Karen Prunczik, Christine Ratay, Sharmayne Reffert, Eugene Richards, Roland Roux, Ronald Schave, William Sterner, Edward Stewart, Susan Stone, Sheila Waldrep, Leonard Weitershausen,
Jan Bruce Weshler, Diane White, Richard White, Mary Grace Wuenschell, Susan Zelenak
Leslie Anderson, Susan Belli, Barbara Bradshaw, Don Bradshaw, Denise Corbin, Paul Greeno, Mary Alice Kunel, Scott Mastro, Debora Perkins, Tammy Saloom, Mary Rose Saxman, Cheryl Sherman, Joel Sherman, Maxine Sherman, Kathleen Spine, Gracie Trink, Cindy Weidner, Sylvia Ziemianski
GUEST STARS: Violette Verdy, Edward Villella, Bill Martin-Viscount, Joyce Cuoco
PERMANENT GUEST ARTIST: Alexander Filipov

REPERTOIRE

"Nutcracker" (Tchaikovsky, Ivanov-Petrov), "Swan Lake" (Tchaikovsky, Petipa-Petrov), "Vistor from Pittsopolis" (Badings, Petrov), "Die Fledermaus" (Strauss, Page), "Carmen" (Bizet, Page), "Les Sylphides" (Chopin, Fokine), "The Merry Widow" (Lehar, Page), "Peter and the Wolf" (Prokofiev, Petrov), "Night on Bald Mountain" (Moussorgsky, Petrov), "Walpurgis Nacht" (Gounod, Petrov), "Tempi Variations" (Bach, Ethel Winter), "Suite de Danses Moldaves" (Golperin, Petrov), "Gopak" (Golperin-Khatchaturian, Petrov), "Motion in Emotion" (Oliveros, Petrov), "Spectre de la Rose" (von Weber, Fokine), and Pas de Deux from "Corsaire" (Drigo, Petipa), "Don Quixote" (Minkus, Gorsky), "Esmeralda" (Pugni, Jules Perrot, "Idyllis" (Hertel, Jean-Paul Comelin), "Mosaics" (Howard Hanson, Giles Fontaine), "Le Plus Que Lente" (Debussy, Kenneth Johnson), "Raymonda" (Glazounov, Balanchine), "Spring Waters" (Rachmaninoff, Asaf Messerer), "William Tell" (Rossini, Bournonville), "Gayne" (Khatchaturian, Petrov), "Dying Swan" (Saint-Saens, Fokine)

Top Right: Patricia Klekovic, Kenneth Johnson in "Walpurgis Nacht" Below: Jayne Hillyer, oAnn McCarthy, Bill Martin-Viscount in "Swan Lake"

Violette Verdy, Edward Villella and corps
in "Nutcracker"

SAVANNAH BALLET GUILD
Savannah, Georgia

Choreographer - Ballet Master, Don Cantwell; Directors, Rosalie Cotler, Hilda DeLaGuardia, Doris Martin, Lillian O'Donovan, Madeleine Walker; Sets and Costumes, Don Cantwell

COMPANY

Anne Smith, Susan Murray, Lillian O'Donovan, Barbara Duffy, Eileen Peterson, Terri Lawless, Sue Smith, Marsha Pike, Patricia Strang, Helen Keating, Cindy Huber, Natalie Walker, Corbett Coleman

REPERTOIRE

Premieres of "Capriol Suite" (Warlock), "Ballerina Bandit" (Rossini), "Waltz Configurations" (Tchaikovsky), "Visions Fugitives" (Prokofiev), "The Comedians" (Kabalevsky)

Patricia Strang, Sue Smith, Dianne Quante, Barbara Herman, Marsha Pike, Natalie Walker of Savannah Ballet

REPERTORY DANCE THEATRE
Salt Lake City, Utah

Associate Managers, Don S. Anderson, Donald Michaelis; Lighting and Production Manager, M. Kay Barrell; Costumes, Ron Hodge; Stage Manager, Larry N. Hopp; Adviser, Virginia Tanner Bennett; Press, Sherryn Barrell

COMPANY

Kay Clark, Bill Evans, Gregg Lizenbery, Kathleen McClintock, Joan Moon, Eric Newton, Ruth Jean Post, Manzell Senters, Linda C. Smith, Karen Steele, Tim Wengerd, Lynne Wimmer
GUEST ARTISTS: Betty Jones, Elizabeth Waters, Ethel Winter

REPERTOIRE

"Age of Innocence" (Collage, Winter), "Castor and Pollux" (Partch, Waters), "Chant" (Cage-Harrison, Wengerd), "Concerto Grosso in D Minor" (Vivaldi, Limon), "Earth" (Gerhardt, Sanasardo), "Enchantment" (Traditional, Senters), "Fatal Birds" (Ginastera, Sanasardo), "Five Dances" (Pezel, Moon), "The Initiate" (Bacewicz-Durko, Butler), "Interim" (Badings, Evans), "Lyric Suite" (Berg, Sokolow), "Night Scene" (Shostakovich, Wengerd), "Nocturne" (Moondog, McKayle), "Passengers" (Farber), "Quintet" (Wengerd, Wengerd), "Salt Lake City" (Ashley, Clark), "Steps of Silence" (Vieru, Sokolow), "Tricycle" (Roldan-Harrison, Post), "Tropic Passion" (Milhaud, Evans), "When Summoned" (Subotnick, Evans)
PREMIERES: "Dorian Horizon" (Takemitsu, Wengerd), "Diamond" (McKechnie, Smith), "For Betty" (Vivaldi, Evans), "Grasslands" (Feldman, Wengerd), "Mrs. Thing" (Collage, Senters), "Tin Tal" (Misra, Evans)

Tim Wingerd, Linda C. Smith in "When Summoned" (Repertory Dance Theatre)

ROYAL WINNIPEG BALLET
Winnipeg, Canada
Arnold Spohr, Artistic Director

Musical Director, Carlos Rausch; Associate Directors, Gwynne Ashton, Richard Rutherford; Balletmaster, Eugene Slavin; Press, Linda Litwack; General Manager, J. Sergei Sawchyn; Assistant, James R. Cameron; Production Director, Peter Hawkins; Business Manager, Gloria P. Samoluk; Technical Director, John Stammers; Stage Manager, Tom Schweitzer; Wardrobe, Doreen Macdonald; Pianist, Linda Lee Thomas; Costumes, Stanley Simmons, Suzanne Mess, Jean Robier, William Chappell, Sue le Cash, Doreen Macdonald, Thomas Pritchard

COMPANY

PRINCIPALS: Christine Hennessy, Alexa Mezincescu, Alexandra Nadal, Walter Bourke, Winthrop Corey, Tony Hulbert
SOLOISTS: Teresa Bacall, Ana Maria de Gorriz, Maria Lang, Shirley New, Jennifer Sholl, Dick Foose, Terry Thomas
CORPS DE BALLET: Madeleine Bouchard, Patrick Crommett, Attila Ficzere, Peter Garrick, Frank Garoutte, Veronica Graver, Laura Gray, Michael Manning, James Mercer, Petal Miller, Louise Naughton, Edward Traskowski
GUEST ARTISTS: Annette av Paul, Patrice Bart, Francesca Zumbo

REPERTOIRE

"Aimez-Voux Bach?" (Bach, Macdonald), "Black Swan Pas de Deux" (Tchaikovsky, Petipa), "Donizettiana" (Donizetti, Bolender), "Fall River Legend" (Gould, deMille), "Five over Thirteen" (Freedman, Macdonald), "The Golden Age" (Pitot-Rossini, deMille), "Labyrinth" (Somers, Butler), "Meadow Lark" (Haydn, Feld), "Moncayo I" (Moncayo, Contreras), "Grand Pas de Deux from The Nutcracker" (Tchaikovsky, Nureyev), "Pas D'Action" (Von Suppe, Macdonald), "Pastiche" (Alonso-Soutullo, Jose Ferran), " Les Patineurs" (Meyerbeer, Ashton), "Rose Adagio from Sleeping Beauty" (Tchaikovsky, Slavin after Petipa), "Spring Waters" (Rachmaninoff, Messerer), "The Still Point" (Debussy, Bolender), "Variations" (Gershwin, Paddy Stone)
PREMIERES: "A Ballet High" (Lighthouse, Macdonald), "Canto Indio" (Chavez, Macdonald), "Concert Fantasy" (Tchaikovsky, Clifford), "The Shining People of Leonard Cohen" (Cohen, Macdonald)

Madeleine Bouchard, Edward Traskowski in "Ballet High" Above: Madeleine Bouchard, Attila Ficzere in "The Shining People of Leonard Cohen"

SACRAMENTO CIVIC BALLET
Sacramento, Calif.
Barbara Crockett, Director

Choreographers, Barbara Crockett, Dom Orejudos, Robert Gladstein, Brynar Mehl, Dick Ford; Ballet Masters, Myron Curtis, Brynar Mehl; Conductors, Harry Newstone, John Coppin, Daniel Geeting; Designers, Harry Demas, Russell Hartley, Dick Ford, Dom Orejudos, Leonard Weisgard; Stage Manager, Bruce Kelley; Costume Coordinator, Marjorie Bader

COMPANY

PRINCIPALS: Leslie Crockett, Tom Reed
SOLOISTS: Roberta Bader, Michele Alcala, Lind Brune, Beata Garner, Ron Ruge
CORPS DE BALLET: Cynthia Marvik, Heidi Yund, Margaret Luther, Vincella Zaccone, Melinda Dobson, Gina Greco, Maryann Anderson, Paula Kirchubel, Donna Geyen, Joyce Stockdale, Suzann Siler, Alan Weddle
GUEST ARTISTS: Barbara Hamblin, John Hiatt, John Nelson, Christopher Fair, Craig Smith, Jone McCarthy, Don Weissmuller, Earl Riggins, Emily Byrne

REPERTOIRE

"Nutcracker" (Tchaikovsky, Crockett-Christensen), "La Ronde" (Rossini, Crockett), "The Changelings" (Butterfield Blues Band, David Wood), "Ballet Portraits" (18th Century, Corelli-Lila Zali), "Songs of a Wayfarer" (Mahler, Orejudos), "Younger Sister" (Rodrigo, Ford), "Vivaldi Concerto" (Vivaldi, Gladstein), "Swan Lake Act II" (Tchaikovsky, Alan Howard after Petipa)
PREMIERES: "Caprice" (Vivaldi, Crockett), "A Fragment" (Handel, Mehl)

Sacramento Civic Ballet members
in "Songs of a Wayfarer"

ST. LOUIS CIVIC BALLET
St. Louis, Missouri
Stanley Herbertt, Artistic Director

Choreographers, Stanley Herbertt, Allan Miles, Gerri Stretz; Conductors, Leonard Slatkin; Stage Manager, Glenn Hoffman; Ballet Mistresses, Betty McRoberts, LaVerne Meyering; Wardrobe, Vi Cowell

COMPANY

Carol Basch, Patty Corday, Denise Devereux, Millie Garvey, Carol Kolafa, Leah Kreutzer, Linda McFarland, Barbara Meyer, Karen Moore, Kim Reifschneider, Cozy Sanders, Eva Schmelzel, Sally Silverman, Jaris Waide, Kyle Wehmueller, John Callahan, Mike Michael
GUEST ARTIST: John Stephen Jenkins

REPERTOIRE

"Nutcracker" (Tchaikovsky), "Umbilicus" (Contemporary), "Rossiana" (Rossini), "The Man Who Invented Music" (Gillus), "Songs of Love and Rain" (Rorem), "Spectrum" (Rachmaninoff, Mildred Caskey), "3 X 5" (Drigo, Mavis Ray), "Caprice" (Tchaikovsky), "Bolero" (Ravel), "The Pad" (Contemporary), "Concerto 2" (Rachmaninoff, Socrates Birsky), "Masquerade" (Khachaturian, Allan Miles), "Commedietta" (Ibert-Kabalevsky), "Les Petits Riens" (Mozart), "Cradle Song" (Rozsa, Gerri Stretz), "History of Dance from Jig to Jet"

Rader Studio Photo

Linda Kintz, John Callahan, Millie Garvey
of St. Louis Civic Ballet

ST. MARK'S DANCE COMPANY
Washington, D. C.
Mary Craighill, Director

Founder-Choreographer, Mary Craighill; Associate Director, Rosetta Brooks; Technical Directors, Harry Morse, John Boykin; Costume Designer, Carmen Schein; Manager, Helen Daniel

COMPANY

Kathleen Bannon, Rosetta Brooks, Mary Craighill, Randy Hill, Katherine Laqueur Larson, Paul Ricci, Ernest Thompson, Barbara Thuesen

REPERTOIRE

"Blue Memory" (Duke Pearson), "World Full of Grey" (Oscar Brown, Jr.), "Stages of Man" (Selected), "Liturgical Symphony" (Honegger), "Rejoice Mass" (Herbert Draesul)
PREMIERE: "Passacaglia in C Minor" (Bach)

Roland L. Freeman Photo

St. Mark's Dance Company

SAN FRANCISCO BALLET
San Francisco, Calif.
Lew Christensen, General Director

Choreographer, Lew Christensen; Musical Director, Earl Bernard Murray; Choreographers, Richard Carter, Robert Gladstein, Jocelyn Vollmar; Guest Choreographers, John Butler, Michael Smuin, John Clifford; Ballet Master, Antony Valdor; Company Manager, Patricia TeRoller; Press, Lucille Toepfer; Production Manager, Richard Carter; Wardrobe, Patricia Bibbins; Designers, Robert O'Hearn, Tony Duquette, Chuck Arnett, Robert Darling, Rouben Ter-Arutunian, Paul Crowley, Marcos Paredes, William Pitkin

COMPANY

PRINCIPALS: Virginia Johnson, Lynda Meyer, Jocelyn Vollmar, Leo Ahonen, Philippe Arrona, Robert Gladstein
SOLOISTS AND CORPS DE BALLET: Sandra Adamson, Soili Arvola, Bruce Bain, Lroi Brody, Michael Cappara, Gardner Carlson, Joan DeVere, Donald Eryck, Deborah Macejunas, Scott Hanlon, Barbarajean Martin, Laurence Matthews, Sara Maule, Theodore Nelson, Anita Paciotti, Allyson Segeler, Daniel Simmons, Geoffrey Thomas, Rick Van Winkle, Christina Williams, Kerry Williams, Susan Williams
GUEST ARTISTS: Matti Tikkanen, Violette Verdy

REPERTOIRE

"Beauty and the Beast" (Tchaikovsky), "Caprice" (Von Suppe), "Con Amore" (Rossini), "Il Distratto" (Haydn), "Dances Concertantes" (Stravinsky), "Divertissement d'Auber" (Auber), "Fantasma" (Prokofiev), "Filling Station" (Thomson), "Jest of Cards" (Krenek), "Jinx" (Britten), "Le Corsaire Pas de Deux" (Drigo, Ahonen after Gorsky), "Night in the Tropics" (Gottschalk, Clifford) "Nutcracker" (Tchaikovsky), "Original Sin" (Lewis), "Pas de Six" (Lumbye), "Schubertiade" (Schubert, Smuin), "Serenade" (Tchaikovsky, Balanchine), "Symphony in D" (Boccherini), "Variations de Ballet" (Glazanov, Christensen-Balanchine)
PREMIERES: "Split" (Subotnick, John Butler), "Jon Lord: Both Sides Now" (Lord, Gladstein), "Airs de Ballet" (Gretry, Christensen), "Classical Symphony" (Prokofiev, Ahonen)

BALLET '70
San Francisco Ballet
Lew Christensen, General Director

Ballet Master, Antony Valdor; Company Manager, Patricia TeRoller; Production Manager, Richard Carter; Press, Lucille Toepfer; Assistant Manager, Timothy Duncan

COMPANY

Various Artists from the parent company

REPERTOIRE

"Games in 4/4 Time" (Krenek-Korngold-Berg, Jocelyn Vollmar), "Three Movements for the Shorthaired" (John Lewis, Lew Christensen), "Scherzo Mechanique" (Stravinsky, Bruce Bain), "Dark Vigil" (Barber, Antony Valdor), "Sun Did Not Rise" (Beethoven, Leo Ahonen), "Music Box" (Marcello, Don Eryck), "Tanssinen" (Minkus, Leo Ahonen)
PREMIERES: "Coup d' Essai" (Ravel, John McFall), "Dialogues in Jazz" (Brubeck, Antony Valdor), "Tapestry" (Tchaikovsky, Jocelyn Vollmar), "Introspections" (Varese, Susan Williams), "Afternoon Revival" (Satie, Rick Van Winkle), "Danse Dvorak" (Dvorak, Don Eryck), "Firebird Pas de Deux" (Stravinsky, Bruce Bain)

James Armstrong Photos

Top Left: Jocelyn Vollmar, Daniel Simmons, Michael Cappara, Robert Gladstein, Bruce Bain in "Filling Station" Below: Daniel Simmons, Theodore Nelson, Laurence Matthews, Susan Williams in "Con Amore"

Kerry Williams, Robert Gladstein in "Con Amore"

Geoffrey Thomas, Sara Maule in "Jon Lord" and above

Richard Rader, Debra Fasting
in "The Match Girl" (Tampa Ballet)

TANCE JOHNSON
AND COMPANY
San Francisco, Calif.
Tance Johnson, Artistic Director

Choreographer, Tance Johnson; Musical Director, Carl Sitton; Costumes, Constance Iwerson; Lighting, Tracy St. John; Press, Lois Zanich

COMPANY

PRINCIPALS: Tance Johnson, Doris Pellet, Nemesio Perades
CORPS: Helen Dannenberg, Michele Berne, Susan Brown, Jean Isaacs, Richard Burgess, Sammy Fair, Irene Asturias

REPERTOIRE

"Incantation," "Introspections," "Jungle Walk," "Les Rendezvous," "Baroque Suite," "Tea Talk," "Trisagion I & II," "Opus Breve," "Egghead & Cookie," "Theatre Piece--Chimera," "Opus 12" (Vivaldi)
PREMIERE: "Amuck" (Art Blakely, Tance Johnson)

Right: Tance Johnson in "Antic Dance"

Adela Clara, Miguel Santos
(Theatre Flamenco)

TAMPA BALLET THEATRE
Tampa, Florida
Frank Rey, Artistic Director

Associate Director, Richard Rader; Costumes, Betty Lee Rey; Sets, William and Jean Eckart; Production Supervisor, Helen Gonzalez; Lighting, Sydne Morris; Stage Manager, A. C. Spanton, Jr.; Press, Betty Poe; Choreography, Frank Rey

COMPANY

Renee LaFountain, Sandi Wargo, Beverly Gonzalez, Jinkey Gleaton, Suzanne Spanton, Debra Fasting, Sheri Brockmeier Sherry Johnson, Joan Taylor, Debbi Gallo, Marilyn Eady, Dawn Kersey, Cyndee Tennant, Lark Morse, Kay Baker, Danny Wever, Janice Briggs, Julie Beronda, Marilyn Poe, Keren Poe, Teil Rey, Jill Jennings, Roxane Cardoso, Lyn Wilson, Libby Luxon, Cindi Thomas, Cathy Wood, Veronica Reynolds, Donna Jordan, Allen Luxon, Janice Poe, Mary Frances Karau, Zellene Rutledge, Jeanne Talty, Johana Hernandez, Mary Brie, Kim Harvil, Melissa Jetton, Kari Wilson

REPERTOIRE

"Cinderella" (Mozart), "The Heartless Princess" (Prokofiev), "Ballerina" (Delibes), "A Child Is Born" (Prokofiev), "Ice Skaters" (Anderson), "Swan Lake" (Tchaikovsky, Barzel after Petipa), "Shostakovich Ballet Suite" (Shostakovich, Stigler), "Gypsy Potpourri" (Traditional, Sagi), "And When She Was Good" (Prokofiev), "Accented Variations" (Gershwin, Rader)
PREMIERES: "Classical Dissention" (Saint-Saens, Rader), "Concerto for Young People" (Rodgers-Hammerstein, Betty Rey), "Kaleidoscope" (Hayman, Rey), "Match Girl" (Chopin, Rey)

THEATRE FLAMENCO
San Francisco, Calif.
Adela Clara, Artistic Director

Assistant Director, Miguel Santos; Stage Manager, and Lighting, Allan Gross; Ballet Master, Guillermo de Oro; Choreography, Adela Clara, Miguel Santos

COMPANY

PRINCIPALS: Adela Clara, Miguel Santos
SOLOISTS: Ana Gabriela, Jose Vega, Emilio Osta
CORPS: Lourdes Rodrigues, Carmen Granados, Marietta Tardeo, Roberto Salas, Enrique Sanchez (narrator)
GUEST ARTISTS: Dini Roman, Ernesto

REPERTOIRE

"Mosaico Sevillano," "Playera," "La Guitarra," "Balada de la Placeta," "Alegrias de Cadiz," "Gitanerias," "Romance de la Pena Negra," "La Cana," "Orgia," "Rondalla," "Tiempos de Goya," "Soleares," "Sacromonte," "Juerga Flamenca"
PREMIERES: "Tiempos de Goya," "Rondalla"

Melissa Hicks, Renee Meyer, Gail Gregory
in "The Nutcracker" (Tulsa Civic Ballet)

UCLA DANCE COMPANY
Los Angeles, Calif.
Carol Scothorn, Director

Choreographers, Valerie Bettis, Lotte Goslar, Carol Scothorn, Marion Scott; Music Supervision, Pia Gilbert; Lighting, Doris Einstein Siegel; Costumes and Scenery, Malcolm McCormick; Technical Director, David Hart,: Stage Managers, Penelope Leavitt, Janet Hoag, Ilene Goldstein: Sound, Steve Neal, Ronalee Brosterman

COMPANY

Annie Bailey, Barbara Ball, Sherill Boutte, Marilyn Cameron, Joanne DeVerona, Lynn Hachten, Kathy Herrman, Judy LeVeque, Lorne MacDougall, George McClain, Susan Morton, Gretchen Phillips, Cynthia Pinney, Barbara Stiles, Antoinette Scinocca, Jerry Steinberg, Robert Small, Bob Thorneycroft

REPERTOIRE

"On Ship" (choreography, Valerie Bettis), "Metamorphoses" (Pia Gilbert), "Twelve Rites of Passage" (Ken Heller, Carol Scothorn), "Ends and Odds: Jig (Traditional), (Cupid), (Jack McKenzie), (Valsette), (William Ussachevsky), (No Waltz), (Pia Gilbert), (Lovely) (Arranged), Finale (Carl Orff)" choreographed by Lotte Gosler
PREMIERE: "The Abyss" (Krzysztof Penderecki, Marion Scott) on March 5, 1971.

Right: "The Abyss"

TULSA CIVIC BALLET
Tulsa, Oklahoma

Founders-Artistic Directors-Choreographers, Roman Jasinski, Moscelyn Larkin; Conductor, Franco Autori; Sets, Albert Martin, Jerry Harris; Technical Director, M. M. Donley; Costumes, Moscelyne Larkin

COMPANY

SOLOISTS: John Ashton, Cynthia Crews, Kevin Donnelly, Gail Gregory, Melissa Hicks, Roman L. Jasinski, Renee Meyer, Charles Ellis, Bob Barnes, Penny Martin
CORPS DE BALLET: Kim Bell, Mary Bennison, Matt Bridwell, Carla Chalmers, Karyne Cottingim, Barbara Crews, Kim Davis, Diane Deller, Diane Edwards, Melinda Edwards, Denny Sue Gilmore, Dana Hill, Merik Hollis, Kris Johnson, Sharon Kolker, Denise Lyons, Shela McAulay, Cindy McConahy, Cynthia McConahy, Mary Beth Minor, Necole Newbolt, Erica Pitts, Cinda Potter, Darcy Reynolds, Jerianne Roberts, Lisa Sherry, Susan Spoon, Laura Sutter, Edward Tuell
GUEST ARTISTS: Marjorie Tallchief, Milenko Bandovitch

REPERTOIRE

"Swan Lake Act II" (Chaikovsky, Petipa-Ivanov), "Giselle" (Adam, Corelli-Perrot), "Les Sylphides" (Chopin, Fokine), "Icare" (Fuerst, Jasinski), "Nutcracker Suite" (Tchaikovsky, Larkin-Jasinski), "Snow Country" (Tchaikovsky, Larkin-Jasinski), "Afternoon of a Faun" (Debussy, Jasinski), "Copelia Act III" (Delibes, Larkin-Jasinski after Sergeyev), "Firebird" (Stravinsky, Larkin-Jasinski after Fokine), "Jeux d'Enfants" (Bizet, Jasinski), "Pas de Quatre" (Pugni, Larkin after Dolin), "Prince Igor" (Borodin, Larkin-Jasinski), "Prodigal Son" (Prokofiev, Jasinski), "Ballet Parisienne" (Offenbach, Larkin-Jasinski), "Peter and the Wolf" (Prokofiev, Lazowski), "Fantastic Toyshop" (Rossini, Jasinski), "Stars and Stripes" (Sousa, Jasinski), "Spectre of the Rose" (Weber, Fokine), "Nutcracker" (Tchaikovsky, Larkin-Jasinski)
PREMIERES: "Mozartiana" (Mozart, Jasinski), "Eurhythmics" (Debussy, Jasinski), "Rhapsodic Variations" (Enesco, Jasinski), "Concerto" (Mendelssohn, Larkin), "Minkus Ballet Suite" (Minkus, Jasinski), "Variations on a Polish Theme" (Arranged by Yura Lazowski, Jasinski), "Brahms Symphony" (Brahms, Jasinski), "Soiree Musicales" (Britten, Jasinski), "Concerto" (Gershwin, Larkin), "Waltz Suite" (Strauss, Jasinski), "Projection 067-24-9041" (Barber, Larkin), "Le Foret Enchante" (Mendelssohn, Jasinski), "Scotch Suite" (Rossini, Jasinski), "Khatchaturiana" (Khachaturian, Jasinski), "Four Moons" (Ballard, Jasinski-Terekhov-Skibine-Hightower)

VALENTINA OUMANSKY DRAMATIC DANCE ENSEMBLE
Hollywood, California
Valentina Oumansky, Artistic Director

Choreography, Valentina Oumansky; Costumes, Beatrice Wood, Carol Funai, Peggy Jones, Madeleine Marrineau, Pablo Picasso, Tom Pierson; Lighting, Fred Allan

COMPANY

Valentina Oumansky, Diana Black, Marilyn Carter, Carol de la O, Connie Levy, Reiko Sato, Kazuko Smith, Tim Hill, Bill Hogerheiden

REPERTOIRE

"Conversations in Silence and Sound," "Adoration," "Homage to the Southwest Indian," "With Apologies to Aesop," "The Horse," "In the Hills," "El Popol Vuh," "Facade," "Gazals"

"El Popol Vun" (Valentina Oumansky Company)

VIRGINIA BEACH CIVIC BALLET
Virginia Beach, Va.

Artistic Directors, Gene Hammett, Penny Martin; Choreographers, Gene Hammett, Major Burchfield, Teresa Martinez; Costumes, Angelique Martinez, Penny Martin; Sets, Norrie and Penny Martin; Lighting, Maynard Allen

COMPANY

SOLOISTS: Sherron Black, Teresa Coleman, Terri Gardner, Dana Weber
CORPS DE BALLET: 11 senior and 20 junior members
GUEST ARTISTS: Arturo Azito, Gary Chryst, Charles Kennedy, Stanley Kostkowski, William Martin, Terri Vigilante, Marguerite Wesley, Glenn White, David Wright

REPERTOIRE

"Night on Bald Mountain" (Moussorgski), "Grande Tarantella" (Gottschalk), "Alice" (Kabalevsky), "Ecole de Ballet" (Offenbach), "Pas de Trois" (Gounod), "Gaite Parisienne" (Offenbach), "Nutcracker Act II" (Tchaikovsky), all choreography by Gene Hammett

Dail's Studio Photo

Sherron Black (Virginia Beach Ballet)

WESTCHESTER BALLET COMPANY
Ossining, N. Y.
Iris Merrick, Artistic Director

Choreographer, Iris Merrick; Musical Director, Stephen Simon; Costumes, Jacqueline Stoner; Press, Dorothy Meinel, Arvil Largiader

COMPANY

PRINCIPALS: Sue Crapanzano, Jan Rosenthal, Rhona Kastle, Charles Brideaux, Monica Serrichio
CORPS DE BALLET: Lenore Meinel, Nancy Long, Cathy Rosenthal, Deborah Musikar, Vivian Crapanzano, Jasmon Crawford, Amy Stoner, Lynn Gandal, Elizabeth Wedge, Donna Jakeway, Elizabeth Whitely, Ann Stipicevic, Gilda Aronson, Paula Wandzilak, Elizabeth Raver, Cathy Rusch, Pamela Natkin, Tracie Holmes, Claire Kelley, John Slothower, John Fogarty, Maureen Moriarty
GUEST ARTISTS: Ellis Winters, John Pierre Frohlich, Jacques Cesbron

REPERTOIRE

"Romeo and Juliet" (Tchaikovsky), "Cinderella" (Prokofiev), "Holiday" (Anderson), "Le Retour" (Kabalevsky), "Sleeping Beauty" (Tchaikovsky), "Caprice" (Shostakovich), "Emperor Valse" (Strauss) "Peter and the Wolf" (Prokofiev), "Nutcracker" (Tchaikovsky), "East of the Sun" (Grieg), "Seasons" (Chausson), "The Tailor and His Love" (Rossini-Britten), "Cry Baby Dolls" (Kabelevsky), "Come What May" (Riisager), "Star Maiden" (McDowell), "Swan Lake Act II" (Tchaikovsky), "Dream Toy Shop" (Rossini), "Summer Day" (Prokofiev), "Secret River" (Leyden)
PREMIERE: "Suite of Schubert Dances of Isadora Duncan" directed by Julia Levien.

Left Center: Shawn Stuart, Christine Sherry in "Il Commedia"

Al Horton Photo

WEST VALLEY BALLET
Los Gatos, Calif.

Co-Directors, Paul E. Curtis, Jr., Shawn Stuart; Ballet Mistress, Elizabeth Neumann; General Manager, Ursula Millett; Company Manager, Gail Salvaggio; Press, Barbara Carpenter; Technical Director, Robert Finocchio; Sets, Robert Vala; Costumes, Carolyn Cassady, Shawn Stuart; Musical Director, Richard Williams

COMPANY

PRINCIPALS: Nancie Berridge, Paul Curtis, Gloria Vauges Mohr, Shawn Stuart
SOLOISTS: Colette Bischer, Susan Cody, Nancy Colahan, Lucie Dean, Tricia Edwards, Yvonne Lee, Jacqualine Pagani, Christine Sherry
ENSEMBLE: Kristen Anderson, Angela Berquist, Meredith Clark, Mary DeVries, Claire Egan, Carolyn Kennedy, Cecile LaCara, Dorothy Lazara, Denise Messier, Anne Munemitsu, Candice Patrick, Sharon Smith, Tanya Styblo, Toncred Styblo, Melinda Wilder, Guyla-Fay Yoak, Sharon Sylva, Diane Flory, Phyllis Nagle, Elaine Todd, Craig Anderson, Philip Clyde, Keith Gouger, Buddy King, Gene Norton, Robert Norton
GUEST ARTISTS: Paula Del Osso, Florin Luball, Marietta Tardeo

REPERTOIRE

"Petite Suite" (Debussy, Stuart), "Romeo & Univac" (Shostakovitch, Neumann), "Les Sylphides" (Chopin, Gollner), "Le Voyage" (Henri, Curtis), "Raymonda Variations" (Glazounov, Curtis), "Peter and the Wolf" (Prokofiev, Stuart), "Tchaikovsky Serenade" (Tchaikovsky, Bartholomew), "Zarzuela" (Chueca, Stuart), "Concierto Andaluz" (Rodrigo, Stuart), "La Taberna Flamenca" (Traditional, Clara), "Les Valses Russes" (Tchaikovsky, Neumann-Curtis-Stuart), "Nutcracker" (Tchaikovsky, Curtis), "Rokoko Jazz" (Cicero, Mohr), "Dragonflies" (Kikuoka, Stuart), "Swan Lake Act II" (Tchaikovsky, Curtis), "Gat 1" (Shankar-Menuhin, Curtis), "Romeo and Juliet Pas de Deux" (Prokofiev, Curtis), "Auber Pas de Trois" (Auber, Curtis), "West Side Story Dance Suite" (Bernstein, King), "Pas de Quatre" (Pugni, Romanoff), "Il Commedia" (Britten, Stuart), "Les Millions d'Arlequin" (Drigo, Mann), "Coppelia Variations" (Delibes, Curtis)

Curt Meinel Photo

West Valley Ballet in "Shubert Dances of Isadora Duncan"

183

| Leo Ahonen | Salvatore Aiello | Joseph Albano | Frances Alenikoff | Dick Andros |

BIOGRAPHIES
OF DANCERS AND CHOREOGRAPHERS

ADAIR, TOM. Born in Venus, Tex. Joined American Ballet Theatre in 1963, elevated to soloist in 1966.

ADAMS, CAROLYN. Born in NYC Aug. 16, 1943. Graduate Sarah Lawrence Col. Studied with Schonberg, Karin Waehner, Henry Danton, Wishmary Hunt, Don Farnworth. Member of Paul Taylor Co. since 1965.

ADAMS, DIANA. Born in Stanton, Va. Studied with Edward Caton, Agnes de Mille. Made professional debut in 1943 in "Oklahoma!" Joined Ballet Theatre in 1944, NYC Ballet in 1950. Now ballet mistress-teacher at School of American Ballet, NYC.

AHONEN, LEO. Born June 19, 1939 in Helsinki, Finland. Studied at Kirov Theatre, Scandinavian School of Ballet. Joined company and rose to guest artist with it, and appeared with Bolshoi Ballet. Joined National Ballet of Holland as dancer and ballet master; Royal Winnipeg Ballet in 1966; San Francisco Ballet in 1968.

AIELLO, SALVATORE. Born Feb. 26, 1944 in NY. Attended Boston Conservatory. Studied with Danielian, Stanley Williams, Rosella Hightower. Professional debut with Joffrey Co. in 1964, subsequently with Donald McKayle, Pearl Lang, Patricia Wilde, Alvin Ailey, Harkness Ballet, and in Bdwy musicals. Joined Royal Winnipeg Ballet 1971.

AILEY, ALVIN. Born Jan. 5, 1931 in Rogers, Tex. Attended UCLA. Studied with Lester Horton, Hanya Holm, Martha Graham, Anna Sokolow, Karel Shoo, and Charles Weidman. Debut in 1950 with Lester Horton Dance Theatre, and became choreographer for company in 1953. Bdwy bow in 1954 in "House of Flowers." Formed own company in 1958 and has toured US and abroad.

AITKEN, GORDON. Born in Scotland in 1928. Joined Saddler's Wells Ballet in 1954. Soloist with Royal Ballet.

ALBA, MARIA. Born in China of Spanish-Irish parentage. Began studies in Russian School of Ballet, Peking. Moved to Spain, studied with Regla Ortega, and La Quica. After professional debut in teens, became one of world's foremost Spanish dancers at 21. Toured with Iglesias Co., and Ballet Espagnol. With Ramon de los Reyes, formed company in 1964 that has toured US, S. America and Europe.

ALBANO, JOSEPH. Born Dec. 29, 1939 in New London, Conn. Studied with Vilzak, Legat, Bartholin, Hightower, Danielian, Graham, Weidman, and Limon. Performed with Charles Weidman Co., Ballet Russe, Martha Graham, Joos-Leeder, NYC Ballet. Founder-artistic Director-Choreographer of Hartford Ballet Co.

ALDOUS, LUCETTE. Born Sept. 26, 1938 in Auckland, N.Z. Studied at Royal Ballet School. Joined Rambert, London's Festival Ballet (1963). Royal Ballet (1966), Australian Ballet (1971).

ALENIKOFF, FRANCES. Born in NYC; graduate Bklyn Col. Studied with Graham, Limon, Horton, Anthony, Sanasardo, Humphrey, Sokolow, Barashkova, Dunham, Fort, Flores. Debut 1957. Since 1959 toured with own company, and as soloist. Has choreographed Bdwy musicals.

ALEXANDER, ROD. Born Jan. 23, 1922 in Colo. Studied with Cole, Holm, Maracci, Riabouchinska, Horton, Castle. Debut with Jack Cole Dancers, then in Bdwy musicals before forming own company and becoming choreographer for Bdwy and TV.

ALLEN, JESSICA. Born Apr. 24, 1946 in Bryn Mawr, Pa. Graduate UCol., NYU. Made debut in 1970 with Jean Erdman Dance Theatre. Also appeared with Gus Solomons, Matt Maddox.

ALONSO, ALICIA. Born Alicia Martinez in Havana; married Fernando Alonso. Studied with Federova, and Volkova, and at School of American Ballet. Made debut in musicals. Soloist with Ballet Caravan 1939-40, Ballet Theatre 1941, and in 1948 formed own company in Havana. One of world's greatest ballerinas.

ALUM, MANUEL. Born in Puerto Rico in 1944. Studied with Neville Black, Sybil Shearer, Martha Graham, Mia Slavenska. Joined Paul Sanasardo Company in 1962, and is its assistant artistic director. Has appeared with The First Chamber Dance Quartet, and American Dance Theatre Co. Also teaches and choreographs.

ALVAREZ, ANITA. Born in Tyrone, Pa. in 1920. Studied with Martha Graham, and appeared with her company 1936-41. Since 1942 has appeared in Bdwy musicals.

ANAYA, DULCE. Born in Cuba; studied with Alonso, at School of Am. Ballet; joined Ballet Theatre at 15, Ballet de Cuba where she became soloist. In 1957 was prima ballerina of Stuttgart Opera before joining Munich State Opera Ballet for 5 years, Hamburg Opera for 3. Returned to US and joined Ballet Concerto.

ANDERSSON, GERD. Born in Stockholm in 1932. Pupil of Royal Swedish Ballet, and Lilian Karina. Joined company in 1948; became ballerina in 1958.

ANDROS, DICK. Born in Oklahoma City, March 4, 1926. Trained with San Francisco Ballet, American Theatre Wing, Ballet Arts, Met Ballet, Ballet Theatre, Ballet Russe. Has appeared with San Francisco Ballet, Irene Hawthorne, Marian Lawrence, John Beggs, Eve Gentry, Greenwich Ballet, Lehigh Valley Ballet, and Dance Originals. Now choreographs and operates own schoool in Brooklyn.

ANTONIO. Born Antonio Ruiz Soler in 1922 in Seville, Spain. Studied with Realito, Pericet, and Otero. Made professional debut at 7. Became internationally famous with cousin Rosario as "The Kids From Seville." Formed separate companies in 1950's, his becoming Ballets de Madrid. Made NY debut in 1955 and returned periodically.

ANTONIO, JUAN. Born May 4, 1945 in Mexico City. Studied in Mexico City, and with Xavier Francis, Am. Ballet Center, Ballet Theatre School. Made debut in 1963 in Mexico with Bellas Artes,NY debut in 1964 with Ballet Folklorico, subsequently danced with Glen Tetley, Louis Falco, Pearl Lang, Gloria Contreras, and Jose Limon.

ANTUNEZ, OSKAR. Born Apr. 17, 1949 in Juarez, Mex. Studied with Ingeborg Heuser, and at Harkness School. Joined Harkness Ballet in 1968. Joined Les Grands Ballets Canadiens in 1968.

APINEE, IRENE. Born in Riga, Latvia where she began training at 11. Moved to Canada; founded school in Halifax. Became leading dancer with National Ballet of Canada, and in 1956 became member of Les Ballets Chiriaeff, now Les Grands Ballets Canadiens. Soloist with Ballet Theatre in 1959. Rejoined Les Grands Ballets in 1965.

ARMIN, JEANNE. Born in Milwaukee, Aug. 4, 1943. Studied with Ann Barzel, Stone and Camryn, Ballet Russe, and in Paris with Mme. Nora. Made debut with Chicago Opera Ballet in 1958, later joined Ballet Russe (1959) and American Ballet Theatre (1965). Has appeared on Bdwy in "13 Daughters."

ARMOUR, THOMAS. Born Mar. 7, 1909 in Tarpon Springs, Fla. Studied with Ines Noel Armour, Preobrajenska, Egorova. Debut with Ida Rubenstein, followed by Nijinska's company, Ballet Russe, Ballet Russe de Monte Carolo. Founder-Artistic Director Miami Ballet.

AROVA, SONIA. Born in 1927 in Sofia, Bulgaria. Studied with Preobrajenska; made debut in 1942 with International Ballet Co., subsequently appearing with Ballet Rambert, Met Opera Ballet, Petit's Ballet, Tokyo-Kamaki Ballet, Ballet Theatre, Ruth Page Ballet Co., Norwegian State Opera Ballet.

ARPINO, GERALD. Born on Staten Island, NY. Studied with Mary Ann Wells, May O'Donnell, Gertrude Shurr, and at School of American Ballet. Made debut on Bdwy in "Annie Get Your

Annette av Paul　　**Frank Ashley**　　**Gladys Bailin**　　**Bruce Becker**　　**Margaret Beals**

Gun." Toured with Nana Gollner-Paul Petroff Ballet Russe; became leading male dancer with Joffrey Ballet, and NYC Opera. Currently choreographer and assistant director of Joffrey Ballet and co-director of American Ballet Center.

ARTHUR, CHARTHEL. Born in Los Angeles, Oct. 8, 1946. Studied with Eva Lorraine, and at American Ballet Center. Became member of Joffrey Ballet in 1965.

ARVOLA, SOILI. Born in Finland; began ballet studies at 8; joined Finnish Ballet at 18. Joined San Francisco Ballet in 1969.

ASAKAWA, TAKAKO. Born in Tokyo, Japan, Feb. 23, 1938. Studied in Japan and with Martha Graham. Has appeared with Graham Co., and with Alvin Ailey, Donald McKayle, and Pearl Lang, and in revival of "The King and I."

ASHLEY, FRANK. Born Apr. 10, 1941 in Kingston, Jamaica. Studied with Ivy Baxter, Eddy Thomas, Neville Black, Martha Graham. Has appeared with National Dance Theatre of Jamaica, Helen McGehee, Pearl Lang, Martha Graham, Yuriko, Eleo Pomare. Also choreographs.

ASHTON, SIR FREDERICK. Born in Guayaquil, Ecuador, Sept. 17, 1906. Studied with Massine and Marie Rambert. Joined Ida Rubinstein Co. in Paris in 1927, but soon left to join Rambert's Ballet Club for which he choreographed many works, and danced. Charles Cochran engaged him to choreograph for his cabarets. In 1933 was invited to create works for the newly formed Vic Wells Co. and in 1935 joined as dancer and choreographer. Moved with company to Covent Garden, and continued creating some of world's great ballets. Was knighted in 1962; first man so honored for services to ballet. After serving as associate director of Royal Ballet, became its director with the retirement of Dame Ninette de Valois in 1963. Retired in 1970.

ASTAIRE, FRED. Born Frederick Austerlitz in Omaha, Neb. May 10, 1899. Began studying at 5; was in vaudeville with sister Adele at 7; Bdwy debut in 1916 in "Over The Top." Appeared in many musicals and films.

ATWELL, RICK. Born July 29, 1949 in St. Louis, Mo. Studied with Dokoudovsky, Mattox, Krassovska, and Wilde. Joined Harkness Ballet in 1967 after appearing in several musicals.

av PAUL, ANNETTE(Wiedersheim-Paul). Born Feb. 11, 1944 in Stockholm. Studied at Royal Ballet School, and made professional debut with Royal Opera House Ballet. Appeared with Royal Winnipeg Ballet before joining Harkness Ballet in 1966.

AYAKO. (See Uchiyama, Ayako).

BABILEE, JEAN. Born Jean Gutman in 1923 in Paris. Studied at School of Paris Opera. In 1945 became premiere danseur in Les Ballet des Champs-Elysees. Toured with own company. Guest artist with ABT.

BAKER-SCOTT, SHAWNEEQUA. Born in Bronx; attended Hunter Col., CCNY. Studied with Holm, Humphrey-Weidman, NDG, Ailey, Beatty, Holder, Clarke, Graham. Debut 1952 with Donald McKayle, subsequently with Destine, New Dance Group, Ailey, Marchant, Dancers Theatre Co., Eleo Pomare.

BAILIN, GLADYS. Born in NYC Feb. 11, 1930. Graduate Hunter Col. Studied with Nikolais and joined his company in 1955. Has also appeared with Murray Louis and Don Redlich.

BALANCHINE, GEORGE. Born Georges Malitonovitch Balanchivadze in St. Petersburg, Russia on January 9, 1904. Graduate of Imperial School of Ballet. Made debut in 1915 in "Sleeping Beauty." Began choreographing while still in school. Left Russia in 1924 to tour with own company. Became associated with Diaghilev in Paris where he choreographed more than 10 works. Thence to Copenhagen as Ballet Master of Royal Dutch Ballet, then joined newly formed Russes de Monte Carlo. Formed Les Ballets in 1933 and toured Europe. Invited to establish school in NY, and in 1934 opened School of American Ballet, followed by American Ballet Co. Choreographed for Met (1935-8), a number of Bdwy musicals, and for such companies as Original Ballet Russe, Sadler's Wells Theatre Ballet, Ballet Russe de Monte Carlo, Ballet Theatre, and Ballet Society. Formed NYC Ballet which premiered in 1948, and won international acclaim under his direction and with his brilliant choreography.

BALLARD, MICHAEL. Born July 17, 1942 in Denver, Colo. Studied with Nikolais and Louis at Henry Street Playhouse, and made professional debut with Alwin Nikolais Co. in 1966. Joined Murray Louis Co. in 1968.

BARKER, JOHN. Born in Oak Park, Ill., Nov. 20, 1929. Studied at Chicago U., and with Bentley Stone, Walter Camryn, Margaret Craske, Antony Tudor, Pierre Vladimiroff, Anatole Oboukoff, Valentina Pereyaslavic, and Maria Nevelska. Made professional debut with Page-Stone-Camryn Co. in 1951. Has appeared with Chicago Opera Balliet, Juilliard Dance Theatre, and Jose Limon Co.

BARNARD, SCOTT. Born in Indianapolis; graduate Butler U. Studied with George Verdak, William Glenn. Appeared in musicals before joining Joffrey Ballet.

BARNETT, DARRELL. Born Sept. 24, 1949 in Miami, Okla. Attended Okla U. Studied with Mary Price, Ethel Winter, Betty Jones, Martha Graham. Debut in 1970 with Ethel Winter, subsequently with Yuriko, Mary Anthony, Pearl Lang, Erick Hawkins.

BARNETT, ROBERT. Born May 6, 1925 in Okanogan, Wash. Studied with Nijinska, Egoroba, Preobrajinska, and at School of American Ballet. Made debut with Original Ballet Russe; joined NYC Ballet in 1950; Atlanta Ballet in 1958, and its director from 1963. Choreographs and operates own school.

BARANOVA, IRINA. Born in Petrograd, Russia in 1919. Studied with Olga Preobrajenska. Soloist with Opera; Ballet Russe 1932-40; ballerina with Ballet Theatre 1941-2. More recently has been appearing in plays and musicals, and teaching at Royal Academy.

BARTA, KAROLY. Born in Hungary. Debut there at 11 with folk ensemble. Studied at Hungarian State Ballet Inst.; performed with Budapest opera and ballet. First choreographic work at 15. Joined Hungarian National Folk Ensemble before emigrating to U.S. in 1957. Attended Met Opera Ballet, and Stone-Camryn School. Joined Chicago Opera Ballet, and continued to choreograph for various groups. Co-founder of Hungarian Ballets Bihari for which he dances and choreographs, and is director of Birmingham Civic Ballet.

BAUMAN, ART. Born in Washington, D.C. Studied at Juilliard, Met, and Martha Graham schools. Has danced with Lucas Hoving, Paul Sanasardo, Charles Weidman. Has choreographed numerous works, and teaches.

BAYS, FRANK. Born June 6, 1943 in Bristol, Va. Attended King Col. Studied with Perry Brunson, and at Am. Ballet Center. Professional debut with American Festival Ballet in 1964, then joined Joffrey Ballet in 1965.

BEALS, MARGARET. Born Mar. 5, 1943 in Boston. Studied with Mattox, Graham, Sanasardo, Slavenska. Has appeared in musicals, and with Valerie Bettis, Jean Erdman, Pearl Lang, Jose Limon, and Paul Sanasardo. Also choreographs, and performs in concert.

BEATTY, TALLEY. Made professional debut in Bdwy musicals. Joined Ballet Society in 1947. Has more recently toured and given solo performances, and formed own company for which he choreographs.

BECKER, BRUCE. Born May 28, 1944 in NYC. Graduate Utah State U. Studied at O'Donnell-Shurr, Graham, and Don Farnworth studios. Debut 1961 with Norman Walker, subsequently on Bdwy, with Tamiris-Nagrin, Limon, O'Donnell; joined Batsheva in 1969.

BECKLEY, CHRISTINE. Born Mar. 16, 1939 in Stanmore, Eng. Studied at Royal Ballet School, joined company and advanced to solo artist.

BELHUMEUR, CHANTAL. Born Mar. 20, 1949 in Montreal, Can. Studied with Graham, Les Grandes Ballets Canadiens and became member 1965; joined Eleo Pomare in 1971.

BELIN, ALEXANDRE. Born Apr. 3, 1948 in Mulhouse, France. Made debut in 1966 with Les Grandes Ballets Canadiens.

BENJAMIN, FRED. Born Sept. 8, 1944 in Boston. Studied with Elma Lewis, ABT, Claude Thompson, Talley Beatty. Has danced in musicals, with Boston Ballet, and Talley Beatty Co. Also teaches and choreographs.

BENJAMIN, JOEL. Born Feb. 21, 1949 in NYC. Attended Juilliard, Columbia; studied with Alwin Nikolais, Martha Graham, and at American Ballet Center. Made debut in Paris in 1963. Formed own company in 1963.

Henry Berg

Valerie Bettis

Robert Beswick

Karena Brock

Robert Blanksh▮

BENNETT, CHARLES. Born in Wheaton, Ill. Studied with Bentley Stone; made debut with Ruth Page's Ballet before joining American Ballet Theatre. Member of NYC Ballet before formation of First Chamber Dance Quartet, now First Chamber Dance Co.

BENTLEY, MURIEL. Born in NYC. Studied with Tomaroff, Tarasoff, Swoboda, Fokine, Ruth St. Denis, Dolin and at Met Opera School. Made debut with Ruth St. Denis in 1931. Has appeared with Jose Greco 1936-7, at Met 1938-9; joined Ballet Theatre in 1940. Has since danced with Jerome Robbins' Ballets: U.S.A.

BERG, BERND. Born Nov. 20, 1943 in East Prussia. Began training at 11 in Leipzig. Joined Stuttgart Ballet in 1964; became soloist in 1967.

BERG, HENRY. Born in Chicago, Apr. 4, 1938. Studied with DeRea, Morrelli, Lew Christensen. Made professional debut with Ballet Alicia Alonso in 1958, subsequently joining San Francisco Ballet (1962), and Joffrey Ballet (1967).

BERGSMA, DEANNE. Born Apr. 16, 1941 in South Africa. Studied with Royal Ballet and joined company in 1958. Became soloist in 1962, principal in 1967.

BERIOSOVA, SVETLANA. Born Sept. 24, 1932 in Lithuania. Came to U.S. in 1940; studied at Vilzak-Shollar School. Made debut with Ottawa Ballet Co. in 1947. Appeared with Grand Ballet de Monte Carlo in 1947, and Met Opera in 1948. Joined Sadler's Wells in 1950, and became star ballerina in 1954 with Royal Ballet.

BESWICK, BOB. Born Nov. 11, 1945 in San Francisco. Studied with Cunningham, Sokolow, Waring, Louis, Bailin, Nikolais. Made debut in 1967 with Utah Repertory Dance Theatre, subsequently with Nikolais Co. Choreographer and teacher.

BETTIS, VALERIE. Born in 1920 in Houston, Tex. Studied with Hanya Holm. Debut with Miss Holm's company in 1937, and as a choreographer in 1941. Subsequently appeared as dancer-choreographer for several Bdwy productions, and own company that toured U.S. and abroad. Teaches in own studio in NYC.

BEWLEY, LOIS. Born in Louisville, Ky. Studied with Lilias Courtney. Made debut with Ballet Russe de Monte Carlo; subsequently with ABT, Ballets U.S.A., NYC Ballet.

BHASKAR. Born Bhaskar Roy Chowdhury in Madras, India, Feb. 11, 1930. Studied with G. Ellappa. Made debut in Madras in 1950 as concert dancer with own company which he brought to NYC in 1955. As dancer and/or choreographer, has appeared on Bdwy, and internationally; teaches.

BIEVER, KATHRYN. Born May 9, 1942 in Bryn Mawr, Pa. Studied at Ballet Russe School, Pa. Ballet School. Made debut in 1964 with American Festival Ballet before joining Pennsylvania Ballet.

BIRCH, PATRICIA. Born in Englewood, NJ. Studied at School of Am. Ballet, Cunningham, and Graham schools. Made debut with Graham company. Has appeared in concert, on Bdwy, and with Donald Saddler, Valerie Bettis. Also choreographs.

BLACKSTONE, JUDITH. Born May 10, 1947 in Iowa City, Iowa. Studied with Donya Feuer, Paul Sanasardo, Mia Slavenska, Karoly Zsedenyi. Debut with Sanasardo Co. in 1958.

BLAIR, DAVID. Born in Yorkshire, Eng. in 1932. Trained at Royal Ballet School. Subsequently joined its company, rising to principal dancer in 1955. Honored by Queen Elizabeth with title Commander of the Order of the British Empire.

BLANKSHINE, ROBERT. Born Dec. 22, 1948 in Syracuse, NY. Studied at American School of Ballet. Professional debut in 1965 with Joffrey Ballet which he left in 1968. Joined Berlin Opera Ballet in 1970.

BOLENDER, TODD. Born in Canton, O. in 1919. Studied with Chester Hale, Vilzak, and at School of American Ballet. Soloist with Ballet Caravan in 1937, Littlefield Ballet in 1941; founder-director of American Concert Ballet in 1943; joined Ballet Theatre in 1944, Ballet Russe de Monte Carlo in 1945. First choreography in 1943. Became dancer-choreographer for Ballet Society, and has continued to choreograph for various companies; was director of Cologne and Frankfurt Opera Ballets.

BORIS, RUTHANNA. Born in 1918 in Brooklyn. Studied at Met Opera School, with Helene Veola, and Fokine. Member of American Ballet in 1935, Met soloist in 1936, and premiere danseuse 1939-43. Joined Ballet Russe de Monte Carlo in 1943. Has choreographed a number of works. Now teaches.

BORTOLUZZI, PAOLO. Born May 17, 1938 in Genoa, Italy. Debut 1958 with Italian Ballet. Joined Bejart Ballet in 1960, rising to principal dancer.

BOUTILIER, JOY. Born in Chicago, Sept. 30, 1939. Graduate of U. Chicago. Studied at Henry St. Playhouse, and with Angelina Romett. Debut with Nikolais in 1964, subsequently with Mimi Garrad, Phyllis Lamhut, and Murray Louis. Has choreographed and appeared in own concerts.

BOWMAN, PATRICIA. Born in Washington, D.C. Studied with Fokine, Mordkin, Legat, Egorova, and Wallman. Ballerina at Roxy and Radio City Music Hall, with Mordkin Ballet in 1939, Ballet Theatre in 1940, and appeared with Chicago Opera, Fokine Ballet, and in musicals and operettas. Now teaches.

BRADLEY, LISA. Born in Elizabeth, N.J. in 1941. Studied at Newark Ballet Academy, American Ballet Center, and with Joyce Trisler. Appeared with Garden State Ballet before joining Joffrey Ballet in 1961. Invited to study classic roles with Ulanova. Currently with First Chamber Dance Co.

BRASSEL, ROBERT. Born Nov. 3, 1944 in Chicago. Attended Ind. U., American Ballet Center. Joined Joffrey Ballet in 1965, ABT in 1968.

BRIANSKY, OLEG. Born in Brussels in 1929. Studied with Katchourovsky, Gsovsky, Volkova. Joined Les Ballet des Champs-Elysees; became lead dancer in 1946. Subsequently with Ballets de Paris, London Festival Ballet, Chicago Opera Ballet. Formed own company, and teaches.

BROCK, KARENA. Born Sept. 21, 1942 in Los Angeles. Studied with Lanova, Lichine, Riabouchinska, DuBoulay, and Branitska. Danced with Natl Ballet of Netherlands before joining American Ballet Theatre in 1963. Became soloist in 1968. Has also appeared in musicals and films.

BROWN, CAROLYN. Born in Fitchburg, Mass. in 1927. Graduate of Wheaton College. Studied with Marion Rice, Margaret Craske, Antony Tudor and Merce Cunningham. Professional debut with Cunningham in 1953 and now appears in almost entire repertoire of the company in roles she created. Has choreographed "Balloon" and "Car Lot."

BROWN, KELLY. Born Sept. 24, 1928 in Jackson, Miss. Studied with Bentley Stone, Walter Camryn. Made professional debut with Chicago Civic Opera Ballet in 1946; soloist with Ballet Theatre (1949-1953). Has since appeared in films, musicals, and on TV.

BROWN, SANDRA. Born Jan. 6, 1946 in Ft. Wayne, Ind. Studied with Tudor, Craske, Graham, Limon. Made debut in Juilliard concert in 1967, subsequently dancing with DTW, James Clouser, James Waring, and Lucas Hoving.

BRUHN, ERIK. Born Oct. 3, 1928 in Copenhagen, Den. Attended Academie of Royal Danish Theatre, and received training with Royal Danish Ballet with which he made his professional debut in 1947. Became its leading male dancer, and has appeared on tour with the company, and as guest soloist with all leading companies throughout the world. For brief period was a principal dancer with American Ballet Theatre, and is now a permanent guest artist. Is considered one of world's greatest classical dancers. Appointed Director of Ballet of Royal Swedish Opera in 1967.

BUCHTRUP, BJARNE. Born Aug. 11, 1942 in Copenhagen. Studied with Birger Bartholin, Leon Danielian. Appeared in musicals before joining West Berlin Ballet Co. in 1963. Danced with Manhattan Festival Ballet (1965-66) and joined American Ballet Theatre in 1967.

BUIRGE, SUSAN. Born in Minneapolis, June 19, 1940. Graduate of U. Minn. Studied at Juilliard, Henry St. Playhouse, Conn. College. Made professional debut with Nikolais Co. in 1964. Has

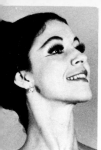
Zelma Bustillo

Bjarne Buchtrup

Carolyn Carlson

William Christensen

Diana Cartier

also appeared with Murray Louis, Mimi Garrard, Bill Frank, Juilliard Dance Ensemble, and Jose Limon. Also choreographs, and teaches.

BURKE, DERMOT. Born Jan. 8, 1948 in Dublin, Ire. Studied at Royal School of Dance. Appeared with Royal Concert Group before joining Joffrey Company in 1966.

BURR, MARILYN. Born Nov. 20, 1933 in New South Wales. Studied at Australian Ballet School; made debut with Ntl. Ballet Co. in 1948. Joined London Festival Ballet in 1953 as soloist; became ballerina in 1955. Joined Hamburg State Opera Co. in 1963. Has danced with Natl. Ballet of Wash.

BUSSEY, RAYMOND. Born March 8, 1946 in Pawtucket, R.I. Studied with Perry Brunson, Tupine, and at Joffrey School. Made professional debut with American Festival Ballet in 1962. Joined Joffrey Company in 1964.

BUSTILLO, ZELMA. Born in Cartagena, Columbia, but came to NYC at 6. Graduate of High School of Performing Arts. Appeared with Thalia Mara's Ballet Repertory, at Radio City Music Hall, with American Festival Ballet, Joffrey Ballet Co.(1965), National Ballet (1970).

BUTLER, JOHN. Born in Memphis, Tenn., Sept. 29, 1920. Studied with Martha Graham and at American School of Ballet. Made debut with Graham company in 1947. Appeared in Bdwy musicals before becoming choreographer. Formed own company with which he toured.

CAMRYN, WALTER. Born in Helena, Mont. in 1903. Studied with Bolm, Maximova, Swoboda, Novikoff, and Muriel Stuart. Appeared with Chicago Civic Opera Ballet, Page-Stone Ballet, and Federal Theatre as premier danseur and choreographer. Teacher at Stone-Camryn School, Chicago. Has choreographed more than 20 ballets.

CARAS, STEPHEN. Born Oct. 25, 1950 in Englewood, N.J. Studied at American Ballet Center, School of American Ballet. Made debut in 1967 with Irene Fokine Co. Joined NYC Ballet in 1969.

CARLSON, CAROLYN. Born in Oakland, Calif., Mar. 7, 1943. Graduate of U. Utah. Studied at San Francisco Ballet School, and Henry St. Playhouse. Professional debut in 1965 with Nikolais Co. Has also appeared with Murray Louis, and in New Choreographers Concert.

CARROLL, ELISABETH. Born Jan. 19, 1937 in Paris. Studied with Sedova, Besobrasova. Made debut in 1952 with Monte Carlo Opera Ballet; joined Ballet Theatre in 1954, Joffrey Ballet in 1962, and Harkness Ballet in 1964.

CARTER, RICHARD. Became principal male dancer of San Francisco Ballet in 1958. With wife, Nancy Johnson, performed in more than fifty countries around the world. Was director and premier danseur of the San Diego Ballet Co. for which he created 14 ballets. Now with San Francisco Ballet.

CARTER, WILLIAM. Born in 1936 in Durant, Okla. Studied with Coralane Duane, Carmalita Maracci. Joined American Ballet Theatre in 1957, NYC Ballet in 1959. Helped to organize and has appeared since 1961 with First Chamber Dance Quartet.

CARTIER, DIANA. Born in Philadelphia. Studied with Tudor, Doubrouska, Balanchine, Joffrey, Griffith, and Brunson. Made professional debut in 1960 with Met Opera Ballet in "Orfeo," subsequently joining John Butler, NYC Opera Ballet, Zachary Solov, and Joffrey Ballet since 1961.

CASEY, SUSAN. Born in April 1949 in Buffalo, N.Y. Studied at Ballet Russe, and Harkness Schools, and with Kravina, Danielian, Shollar, Vilzak, and Volkova. Joined American Ballet Theatre in 1965; became its youngest soloist in 1969.

CATANZARO, TONY. Born Nov. 10, 1946 in Bklyn. Studied with Norman Walker, Sanasardo, Danielian, Lillian Moore, Lang, Joffrey, Jaime Rogers. Debut 1968 in musicals; subsequently appearing with Norman Walker, Harkness Youth Ballet, NJ Ballet, Boston Ballet; joined Joffrey in 1971.

CATON, EDWARD. Born in St. Petersburg, Russia, Apr. 3, 1900. Studied at Melidova's Ballet School, Moscow, and made professional debut in 1914. Joined Max Terptzt Co.(1918), Ourkransky-Pavley Co. (1919), Pavlova (1924), Chicago Opera Ballet (1926),

American Ballet (1934), Catherine Littlefield (1935), Mikhail Mordkin (1938), Ballet Theatre (1940), retired in 1942 to become teacher and choreographer.

CEBRON, JEAN. Born in Paris in 1938. Made debut in 1956 in London. Joined Joos Folkwangballet. Tours world in concert.

CESBRON, JACQUES. Born May 10, 1940 in Angers, France. Studied at Paris Opera Ballet School, and joined company in 1958. Member of Harkness Ballet before becoming soloist with Pennsylvania Ballet in 1966.

CHAMBERLAIN, BETTY. Born Nov. 10, 1949 in Madison, Wisc. Studied with Armour, LaVerne, Nault, Skibine, and at ABT. Joined American Ballet Theatre in 1969.

CHAMPION, GOWER. Born in Geneva, Ill., June 22, 1920. After appearing in vaudeville, night clubs, and on Bdwy, made debut as choreographer for "Lend An Ear" in 1946. Is now in great demand as choreographer and director of musicals, and films.

CHASE, LUCIA. Born March 24, 1907 in Waterbury, Conn. Studied at Theatre Guild School, and with Mikhail Mordkin. Became member of his company and danced title role in "Giselle" in 1937. Was principal dancer with Ballet Theatre when it was founded in 1939. In 1945 became co-director with Oliver Smith of American Ballet Theatre. In recent years has appeared only with her company in "Fall River Legend," "Swan Lake," and "Las Hermanas."

CHAUVIRE, YVETTE. Born Apr. 22, 1917 in Paris. Studied at Paris Opera School. Appeared with Paris Opera Ballet, London Festival Ballet, Royal Ballet (1959). In 1963 appointed director of Paris Opera Ballet School.

CHIRIAEFF, LUDMILLA. Born in 1924 in Latvia. Began training at early age in Berlin with Alexandra Nicolaieva. Joined de Basil's Ballets Russe, was soloist with Berlin Opera Ballet, and prima ballerina at Lausanne Municipal Theatre. Opened own academy in Geneva and choreographed for Ballet des Arts, Geneva. Moved to Canada in 1952 and organized own company, ultimately leading to her being founder and artistic director of Les Grands Ballets Canadiens.

CHOUTEAU, YVONNE. Born in Ft. Worth, Tex. in 1929. Studied with Asher, Perkins, Vestoff, Belcher, Bolm, at Vilzak-Shollar School, School of American Ballet. Made debut as child in American Indian dance company at Chicago's 1933 Fair. Joined Ballet Russe de Monte Carlo in 1943. Now teaches, makes guest appearances, and is Co-Director of Okla. Civic Ballet.

CHRISTENSEN, HAROLD. Born in Brigham City, Utah. Studied with Balanchine. Appeared with Met Opera Ballet (1934), Ballet Caravan, San Francisco Opera Ballet, San Francisco Ballet. Retired to teach and direct San Francisco Ballet School.

CHRISTENSEN, LEW. Born in 1906 in Brigham City, Utah. Studied with uncle Lars Christensen at American School of Ballet. Performer and choreographer since 1934, on Bdwy, for Met Opera, Ballet Caravan, American Ballet Co., and NYC Ballet. In 1938, with brothers Harold and William, founded San Francisco Ballet; has been general director since 1951.

CHRISTENSEN, WILLIAM. Born Aug. 27, 1902 in Brigham City, Utah. Studied with uncle Lars Christensen, Nescagno, Novikoff, and Fokine. Made debut with Small Ballet Quartet in 1927, subsequently becoming choreographer, ballet master, director and teacher. With brothers Harold and Lew, formed San Francisco Ballet which he directed until 1951 when he established School of Ballet at U. of Utah. Is director-choreographer for Utah Civic Ballet which he organized in 1952, now Ballet West.

CHRISTOPHER, ROBERT. (formerly Robert Hall) Born Mar. 22, 1942 in Marion, Md. Studied with Harry Asmus, Vincenzo Celli, Celo Quitman. Made debut in 1960 with National Ballet of Venezuela; subsequently with Stuttgart Ballet, ABT, Anne Wilson, Valerie Bettis, Sophie Maslow; currently soloist and ballet master for Garden State Ballet, and appears with Downtown Ballet.

Ivy Clear   **Vernon Coffman**   **Lillian Coleman**   **Jean-Paul Comelin**   **Colleen Corkré**

CHRYST, GARY. Born in LaJolla, Calif. Studied with Walker, Hoving, Limon, Jaime Rogers, Nina Popova, ABC. Debut at 16 with Norman Walker, subsequently with McKayle, Washington Ballet, NYC Opera, before joining Joffrey Ballet in 1968.

CLARE, NATALIA. Born in Hollywood, Calif. Studied with Nijinska, Egorova; joined Basil's Ballet Russe, then Markova-Dolin Co., Ballet Russe de Monte Carlo. In 1956, established school in North Hollywood, and founded Ballet Jeunesse for which she is artistic director and choreographer.

CLARKE, THATCHER. Born Apr. 1, 1937 in Springfield, Ohio. Made professional debut with Met Opera Ballet in 1954, subsequently joined Ballet de Cuba, Ballet Russe de Monte Carlo, San Francisco Ballet, and American Ballet Theatre. Has appeared in several musicals.

CLAUSS, HEINZ. Born Feb. 17, 1935 in Stuttgart. Studied at Stuttgart Ballet School, and with Balanchine. Joined Stuttgart Ballet in 1967 after appearing at Zurich Opera Ballet, and in Hamburg.

CLEAR, IVY. Born in Camden, Maine, Mar. 11, 1948. Studied at Professional Children's School, and School of American Ballet. Made professional debut in 1963 with NYC Ballet. Soloist with Joffrey Ballet from 1965 to 1969.

CLIFFORD, JOHN. Born June 12, 1947 in Hollywood. Studied at American School of Dance and School of American Ballet. Appeared with Ballet of Guatemala and Western Ballet before joining NYCity Ballet in 1966. Soloist since 1969. Has choreographed 6 works for the company.

CLOUSER, JAMES. Born 1935 in Rochester, N.Y. Studied at Eastman School of Music, Ballet Theatre School. Joined ABT in 1957, Royal Winnipeg Ballet in 1958, rising to leading dancer in 1959, subsequently choreographed, composed and designed for it, and became ballet master and assistant director. Has appeared in concert, taught, and tours with wife Sonja Zarek.

COCKERILLE, LILI. Born in Washington, D.C. Studied at Fokine School, Wash. School of Ballet and School of American Ballet. Made professional debut with NYC Ballet in 1963, joined Harkness Ballet in 1964, Joffrey Co. in 1969.

COFFMAN, VERNON. Born Dec. 5, 1947 in Tucson, Ariz. Studied with Lew and Harold Christensen. Made professional debut with San Francisco Ballet in 1964. Joined Joffrey Ballet in 1966, and American Ballet Theatre in 1967.

COHAN, ROBERT. Born in NYC in 1925. Soloist with Martha Graham Co. Opened own school in Boston, joined faculty of Harvard's Drama Center, made solo tours here and abroad, taught in Israel and choreographed for Batsheva Co. Now director of London Contemporary Dance Theatre.

COLE, JACK. Born in 1913 in New Brunswick, N.J. Began studies and made professional debut with Ted Shawn and His Men Dancers. Has choreographed for and appeared on Bdwy and in Hollywood films.

COLEMAN, LILLIAN. Born Nov. 21, 1949 in NYC. Attended SUNY, Harkness School. Made debut with New Dance Group.

COLL, DAVID. Born Mar. 20, 1947 in Chelsea, Mass. Studied with Vilzak, Nerden, Van Muyden, Fallis, Christensen. Made debut in 1965 with San Francisco Ballet. Joined American Ballet Co. in 1969, ABT in 1970.

COLLIER, LESLEY. Born Mar. 13, 1947 in Kent, Eng. Studied at Royal Academy of Dancing, Royal Ballet School. Joined Royal Ballet in 1965.

COLLINS, JANET. Born in New Orleans in 1917. Studied with Carmalita Maracci, Bolm, Lester Horton, Slavenska and Craske. Appeared in solo concerts before becoming premiere danseuse of the Met Opera Ballet (1951-54). Now teaches.

COMELIN, JEAN-PAUL. Born in France; studied at Cons. of Music and Art; made debut with Paris Opera Ballet in 1957. Soloist for London Festival Ballet in 1961, principal in 1962. Joined National Ballet in 1966.

CONDODINA, ALICE. Born in Philadelphia; graduate of Temple U. Studied with Tudor, Zaraspe, Danielian, and at Met Opera Ballet, Ballet Theatre, and American Ballet Schools.

Danced with Ruth Currier, Lucas Hoving, Sophie Maslow, Jack Moore, and Jose Limon Companies. Director-choreographer for own company since 1967.

CONRAD, KAREN. Born in 1919 in Philadelphia. Made debut with Littlefield Ballet (1935-7), subsequently with Mordkin Ballet, and Ballet Theatre. Retired in 1946 and opened school in Atlanta.

CORKLE, FRANCESCA. Born Aug. 2, 1952 in Seattle, Wash. Studied with Virginia Ryan, Perry Brunson, Robert Joffrey. Joined Joffrey Ballet in 1967.

CORKRE, COLLEEN. Born in Seattle, Wash. and began training at 4. Debut with Chicago Opera Ballet. Dancer and choreographer for several musicals. Formed own company that tours every season.

COWEN, DONNA. Born May 2, 1949 in Birmingham, Ala. Studied with Gage Bush, Richard Englund, School of American Ballet, Joffrey. Made debut in 1968 with Huntington Dance Ensemble; joined Joffrey Ballet in 1969.

CRAGUN, RICHARD. Born in Sacramento, Cal. Studied in London's Royal Ballet School and in Denmark. Joined Stuttgart Ballet in 1962 and quickly emerged as principal.

CRANE, DEAN. Born Jan. 5, 1932 in Logan, Iowa. Made professional debut at 14 as aerialist with Pollock Circus. Studied with Nimura, Dokoudovsky, Tudor and Petroff. Became first dancer and choreographer with Ballet Arts Co. Has also appeared on Bdwy and in clubs.

CRANKO, JOHN. Born in Rustenberg, S. Africa in 1927. Studied at Sadler's Wells. Before becoming choreographer, appeared with Capetown Ballet 1944-5, and Sadler's Wells 1946-7. Appointed director of Stuttgart Ballet in 1961.

CRASKE, MARGARET. Born in England. Studied with Cecchetti. Appeared with Diaghilev Ballets Russes, de Valois group. Became Ballet Mistress for Ballet Theatre in 1946, subsequently joined Met Opera Ballet School staff and became its assistant director. Currently with Manhattan School of Dance.

CRISTOFORI, JON. Born in Buzzard's Bay, Mass., and began training at 15. Became lead student dancer in National Ballet of Wash., and toured with it until joining Joffrey Ballet. Left in 1969.

CROLL, TINA. Born Aug. 27, 1943 in NYC. Bennington Col. graduate. Studied with Cunningham, Fonaroff. Debut 1964 in Kaufmann Hall. Has danced and choreographed for DTW since 1965.

CROPLEY, EILEEN. Born Aug. 25, 1932 in London. Studied with Sigurd Leeder, Maria Fay, Martha Graham, Don Farnworth. Made debut in 1966 with Paul Taylor Co.

CUNNINGHAM, MERCE. Born in Centralia, Wash. Studied at American School of Ballet. Professional debut as soloist with Martha Graham in 1940; with company through 1945. Began choreographing in 1946; in 1952 formed own company that has toured extensively every year. Teaches in his NYC studio.

CURRIER, RUTH. Born in 1926 in Ashland, Ohio. Studied with Doris Humphrey and Elsa Kahl. Made debut in 1949 with American Dance Festival. Soloist with Jose Limon Co. 1949-63. Since 1956 has been director-choreographer for own company which has toured U.S. Also teaches.

d'AMBOISE, JACQUES. Born in 1934 in Dedham, Mass. Joined NYC Ballet at 15 after 7 years at School of American Ballet, and rapidly rose to premier danseur in 1953. Has appeared in films and on TV and choreographed.

DANIAS, STARR. Born Mar. 18, 1949 in NYC. Studied at School of Am. Ballet. Debut 1968 with London Festival Ballet, subsequently joined Joffrey Ballet in 1970.

DANIELIAN, LEON. Born Oct. 31, 1920 in NYC. Studied with Mordkin and Fokine. Made debut as dancer with Mordkin Ballet in 1937. Has appeared with Original Ballet Russe, Ballet Russe de Monte Carlo, Ballet Theatre, Ballet-des Champs Elysees, and San Francisco Ballet. Was choreographer-director of Ballet de Monte Carlo. Now with American Ballet Theatre School.

DANIELS, DANNY. Born in 1924 in Albany, N.Y. Studied with Thomas Sternfield, Jack Potteiger, Vincenzo Celli, Elisabeth

| lexandra Danilova | James DeBolt | Carmen DeLavallade | Fred deMayo | Michael Denard |

Anderson-Ivantzova, Anatole Vilzak. Appeared in musicals, as soloist with orchestras, and Agnes de Mille Dance Theatre before becoming choreographer for TV and Bdwy musicals.

DANILOVA, ALEXANDRA. Born Nov. 20, 1906 in Peterhof, Russia. Graduate of Imperial School of Ballet, and became member of company. Subsequently with Balanchine's company, Les Ballet Russes de Diaghilev, Ballet Russe de Monte Carlo (both de Basil's and Massine's). Made NYC debut in 1948 at Met with Massine's company. Has appeared with and choreographed for NYC Ballet. In 1954 formed and toured with own company The Concert Dance Group. Was choreographer for Met in 1961-62. Now teaches.

D'ANTUONO, ELEANOR. Born in 1939 in Cambridge, Mass. Danced with Ballet Russe de Monte Carlo for 6 years before joining Joffrey Ballet in 1960. Became member of American Ballet Theatre in 1961; principal since 1963.

DAVIS, ROBERT. Born March 13, 1934 in Durham,N.C. Studied at Wash. School of Ballet, and with Fokine, Franklin, and Joffrey. Debut in 1960 and has appeared as principal dancer with Washington Ballet, National Ballet of Canada, and Joffrey Ballet. Is also director and choreographer.

DE BOLT, JAMES. Born in Seattle, Wash. Studied with Marian and Illaria Ladre, and at U. Utah. Professional debut with Seattle's Aqua Theatre. Joined Joffrey Ballet in 1959, and subsequently with NYC Opera Ballet, joined NYC Ballet in 1961, Manhattan Festival Ballet in 1965. Is also a costume designer and choreographer. Re-joined Joffrey Co. in 1968.

DELANGHE, GAY. Born Aug. 21, 1940 in Mt. Clemens, Mich. Studied at Severo School. Professional debut in 1960 and toured with "The Dancemakers." Choreographer, performer and teacher since 1965. Joined Lucas Hoving Co. in 1967.

de LAPPE, GEMZE. Born Feb. 28, 1922 in Woodhaven, Va. Attended Hunter Coll. and Ballet Arts School. Studied with Duncan, Fokine, Nimura, Caton, and Nemtchinova. Has appeared with Ballet Theatre and Agnes de Mille Dance Theatre and in Bdwy productions.

de LAVALLADE, CARMEN. Born March 6, 1931 in Los Angeles. Attended LACC, and studied with Lester Horton. Professional debut with Horton Dance Theatre. Bdwy debut in 1954 in "House of Flowers." Has appeared with various companies, including John Butler, Met Opera, de Lavallade-Ailey, Donald McKayle, and Ballet Theatre.

DELZA, SOPHIA. Born in NYC. Studied in China. Professional debut in 1953 in program of Chinese dances. Has toured world in concert, and been choreographic consultant for Met Opera, Lincoln Rep. Theatre, and Bdwy musicals.

de MAYO, FRED DOUGLASS. Studied at Abbey Theatre, and with Fokine, Youskevitch, Pereyaslavec, and in Paris with Preabrajenska. Appeared with National Ballet, Met. Opera Ballet. Now teacher-choreographer for Newburgh Ballet which he founded; co-director of Kingston Ballet School.

de MILLE, AGNES. Born in NYC in 1909. Graduate of UCLA. Studied with Kosloff, Rambert, Karsavina, Tudor, Sokolova, Caton, Craske, Stroganova, and Dolmetsch. Debut in 1928 in own dance compositions and toured with them in Europe. Became leading choreographer for Bdwy. Created first ballet "Black Ritual" for Ballet Theatre in 1940. In 1953 organized Agnes de Mille Dance Theatre which toured U.S. Has choreographed for Ballet Russe de Monte Carlo, and Royal Winnipeg Ballet.

DENARD, MICHAEL. Bor Nov. 5, 1944 in Dresden, Germany. Studied in Toulouse and Paris. Has appeared with Berlin Opera, and Paris Opera Ballets, and guest artist with Bejart, ABT(1971).

DENVERS, ROBERT. Born Mar. 9, 1942 in Antwerp. Studied with Nora Kiss, Tania Grantzeva, Peretti; joined Bejart's Ballet in 1963.

DeSOTO, EDWARD. Born Apr. 20, 1939 in The Bronx. Attended Juilliard, AADA, New Dance Group Studio. Danced with Gloria Contreras, Judith Willis, Sophie Maslow, Art Bauman, Valerie Bettis, before joining Limon Co. in 1966.

DESTINE, JEAN-LEON. Born in Haiti, March 26, 1928. Attended Howard U. Made professional debut at Jacob's Pillow in 1949. Formed own company and has toured U.S., Europe, and Japan.

DIAMOND, MATTHEW. Born Nov. 26, 1951 in NYC. Attended CCNY. Debut in 1967 with Matteo and the Indo-American Dance Co. Subsequently with Norman Walker, NYC Opera, Louis Falco.

DOKOUDOVSKY, VLADIMIR. Born in 1922 in Monte Carlo. Studied with Preobrajenska; made debut at 13; became soloist with Ballet Russe de Monte Carlo, Mordkin Ballet, Ballet Theatre. Premier danseur with Original Ballet Russe (1942-52). Has choreographed several ballets. Now teaches.

DOLIN, ANTON. Born Sydney Francis Patrick Chippendall Healey-Kay in Slinfold, Sussex, Eng. July 27, 1904. Studied with Astafieva, Nijinska. With Diaghileff Company 1921-9, principal dancer with Sadler's Wells 1931-5, Ballet Russe 1939, 1946-8. Founder, director, and dancer with Markova-Dolin Co. 1935-8, 1945, 1947-8. Danced, restaged, and choreographed for Ballet Theatre from inception to 1946. 1949 organized and danced with London Festival Ballet until 1961. Currently artistic adviser of Les Grands Ballets Canadiens.

DOLLAR, WILLIAM. Born in 1907 in East St. Louis, Mo. Studied with Fokine, Mordkin, Balanchine, Vladimiroff, and Volinine. Lead dancer with Philadelphia Opera, American Ballet 1936-7, Ballet Caravan 1936-8, Ballet Theatre 1940, American Ballet Caravan 1941, New Opera Co. 1942, Ballet International 1944, ballet master for American Concert Ballet 1943, Ballet Society 1946, Grand Ballet de Monte Carlo 1948, NYC Ballet. Has choreographed many works, and teaches.

DONN, JORGE. Born Feb. 28, 1947 in Buenos Aires. Attended School of Teatro de Colon. Appeared in musicals before joining Bejart Ballet in 1963, rising to leading male dancer.

DOUGLAS, SCOTT. Born June 16, 1927 in El Paso, Tex. where he made his professional debut at 9. Studied with Lester Horton and Ruth St. Denis. Appeared with San Francisco Ballet, Ballets U.S.A., John Butler Co., Ballet Theatre, Nederlands National Ballet, and Glen Tetley Co.

DOWELL, ANTHONY. Born in London in 1943. Studied with June Hampshire, entered Royal Ballet School at 10. Debut as hunter in "Swan Lake" at Covent Garden Opera House. Joined Sadler's Wells Opera Ballet, and joined Royal Ballet in 1961. Is now a principal.

DOYLE, DESMOND. Born June 16, 1932 in South Africa. Joined Royal Ballet in 1951. Became soloist in 1953; is now a principal and teacher.

DRAPER, PAUL. Born 1909 in Florence, Italy. Began studies at early age, and became tap soloist, elevating it to ballet-tap concert form. Made debut in 1932 in London. Continues to give solo performances, teaches, and is photographer.

DRIVER, SENTA. Born Sept. 5, 1942 in Greenwich, Conn. Graduate Bryn Mawr, Ohio State U. Studied with Don Farnworth, and at O'Donnell-Shurr Studio. Joined Paul Taylor Company in 1967.

DU BOULAY, CHRISTINE. Born in 1923 in Ealing, Eng. Trained at Sadler's Wells Ballet School. Soloist with International Ballet before joining Sadler's Wells. Settled in U.S. in 1950, and with husband, Richard Ellis, became founders and directors of Illinois Ballet Co.

DUBREUIL, ALAIN. Born in Monte Carlo, Mar. 4, 1944. Studied at mother's ballet school until awarded scholarship at Arts Educational School (1960). Joined London Festival Ballet in 1962 and became soloist in 1964.

DUDLEY, JANE. Dancer-choreographer. Born in NYC in 1912. Studied with Martha Graham, Hanya Holm, Louis Horst. Leading dancer with Graham Co. (1937-44). With Sophie Maslow and William Bales, formed concert Dance Trio. Retired in 1954 to teach.

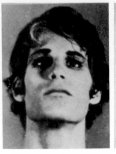

James Dunne   Michael Ebbin   Richard Englund   Robert Estner   Royes Fernand

DUNCAN, JEFF. Born Feb. 4, 1930 in Cisco, Tex. Attended N. State Tex. U., studied with Holm, Nikolais, Limon, Cunningham, Schwetzoff, Tomkins, Joffrey. Assistant to Doris Humphrey and Anna Sokolow. Professional debut 1952 at Henry St. Playhouse. Has appeared with New Dance Group, Juilliard Dance Theatre, Anna Sokolow, Jeff Duncan Dance Co., and is founder-director of Dance Theatre Workshop. Has also appeared in Bdwy musicals.

DUNHAM, KATHERINE. Born June 22, 1912, in Chicago. Debut with Chicago Opera Co. in 1933. Bdwy debut 1940 in "Cabin In The Sky." Formed own company for which she choreographed; toured with it in 1943, and subsequently in 57 other countries. Founded Katherine Dunham School of Cultural Arts in NYC in 1943.

DUNNE, JAMES. Born in Waldwick, NJ. Studied with Irene Fokine, and at School of American Ballet, Harkness House. Joined Harkness Ballet for 4 years, then Joffrey Ballet.

EBBELAAR, HAN. Born Apr. 16, 1943 in Hoorn, Holland. Studied with Max Dooyes and Benjamin Harkarvy. Danced with Nederlans Dans Theater before joining American Ballet Theatre in 1968 as soloist; promoted to principal in 1969, Dutch Ntl. Ballet (1970).

EBBIN, MICHAEL. Born June 5, 1945 in Bermuda. Studied at Patricia Gray's, National Ballet, American Ballet Center, and Harkness schools. Has danced with Eleo Pomare, Cleo Quitman, Australian Dance Theatre, Anna Sokolow, Talley Beatty, and Rod Rodgers companies, and appeared on Bdwy.

EDWARDS, LESLIE. Born Aug. 7, 1916 in Teddington, Eng. Studied with Marie Rambert and at Sadler's Wells School. Debut 1933 with Vic-Wells Ballet, subsequently joining Ballet Rambert, Royal Ballet. Now teaches and makes guest appearances.

EGLEVSKY, ANDRE. Born in Moscow Dec. 21, 1917. Received training in France. At 19 joined Rene Blum's Ballet de Monte Carlo. Came to U.S. in 1937, and after appearing with all major companies, joined Ballet Theatre. In 1947 appeared with Grand Ballet du Marquis de Cuevas. In 1950 joined NYC Ballet Co. and danced leading male roles until 1958, also created "Scotch Symphony" and other ballets for the company. In 1955, with his wife, prima ballerina Leda Anchutina, opened school in Massapequa, L.I., and in 1960 formed local classical ballet company which he directs.

EISENBERG, MARY JANE. Born Mar. 28, 1951 in Erie, Pa. Attended Hunter, New School. Studied at Graham, ABT, Harkness schools. Debut 1969 with John Tetley, subsequently with Keith Lee, Contemporary Dance Ensemble, Louis Falco.

ELLIS, RICHARD. Born 1918 in London. At 15 joined Vic-Wells Ballet which became Sadler's Wells Ballet. Important member of company until 1952. After touring U.S. with company in 1949-50, settled in Chicago. With wife, Christine Du Boulay, became founders and co-directors of Illinois Ballet Co.

ENCKELL, THOMAS. Born in Helsinki, Finland, Oct. 14, 1942. Studied with Margaret Craske. Professional debut with Met Opera Ballet in 1962. Joined Finnish Natl. Opera Ballet in 1965, and Manhattan Festival Ballet in 1966.

ENGLUND, RICHARD. Born in Seattle, Wash. Attended Harvard, Juilliard. Studied with Tudor, Graham, Volkova. Appeared with Limon, Met Opera, Ntl Ballet of Canada, ABT, and in musicals. Currently teaches and choreographs.

ENTERS, AGNA. Dancer, choreographer and mime was born in 1907 in NYC. Created own style of dance and pantomime that she has performed all over the world. Is also a writer and painter.

ERDMAN, JEAN. Born in Honolulu, Hawaii. Graduate of Sarah Lawrence College (1938). Studied at Bennington, American School of Ballet, Hisamatsu, Martha Graham, Pukui and Huapala Hawaiian Dancers. Professional debut 1938 with Martha Graham, and as a choreographer in 1942. Organized own company in 1950, and made annual tours through 1960. World tour 1963-5 with "The Coach With The Six Insides" which she conceived and staged. Now head of NYU Dance Dept.

ESTELLE & ALFONSO. Born in NY; trained with Haakon, Mattox, Juarez, LaSylphe, Nettles, Chileno, Wills, Thomas. Toured widely as team. Currently operate school on Poughkeepsie, N.Y., and artistic directors for Mid-Hudson Regional Ballet.

ESTNER, ROBERT. Born in North Hollywood, Calif. Attended Los Angeles City Valley Jr. Col. Studied with Robert Rossalatt, Natalie Clare, Andre Tremaine, Carmalita Maracci, and at ABC. Appeared with Ballet Concerto, Pacific Ballet, Ballet La Jeunesse, before joining Joffrey Co.

EVERETT, ELLEN. Born in Springfield, Ill. Studied in Chicago and School of American Ballet. Professional debut 1958 with Ruth Page's Chicago Opera Ballet. Soloist with American Ballet Theatre. Has also appeared on Bdwy.

FADEYECHEV, NICOLAI. Born in Moscow in 1933. Studied at Bolshoi School and joined company in 1952; became soloist in 1953, and subsequently premier danseur.

FAISON, GEORGE. Born Dec. 21, 1945 in Washington, DC. Attended Howard U. Studied with Louis Johnson, Claude Thompson, Alvin Ailey, Dudley Williams, Elizabeth Hodes. Appeared on Bdwy and with Universal Dance Experience (1971).

FALCO, LOUIS. Born in NYC; studied with Limon, Weidman, Graham, and at American Ballet Theater School. Has danced, choreographed, and toured with Jose Limon. Co., choreographed for other groups, and own company.

FALLIS, BARBARA. Born in 1924 in Denver, Colo. Moved to London in 1929. Studied at Mona Clague School, Vic-Wells and Vilzak-Shollar Schools. Debut 1938 in London. With Vic-Wells Ballet 1938-40; Ballet Theatre in 1941; Ballet Alicia Alonso (1948-52), NYC Ballet (1953-58). Now teaches.

FARBER, VIOLA. Born in Heidelberg, Ger., Feb. 25, 1931. Attended American U. and Black Mt. College. Studied with Katherine Litz, Merce Cunningham, Alfredo Corvino, and Margaret Craske. Professional debut 1952 with Merce Cunningham, subsequently appearing with Paul Taylor, and Katherine Litz. More recently, choreographing, and guest artist with Merce Cunningham.

FARRELL, SUZANNE. Born Roberta Sue Ficker 1945 in Cincinnati. Began ballet studies in Cincinnati, subsequently attending School of American Ballet. After 15 months joined NYC Ballet, and became a princial dancer in 1965. Joined National Ballet of Canada in 1970, Bejart (1970).

FAXON, RANDALL. Born Sept. 26, 1950 in Harrisburg, Pa. Studied with Elizabeth Rockwell, Martha Graham, Paul Sanasardo, Alfredo Corvin, and at Juilliard. Debut 1969 with Ethel Winter; joined Lucas Hoving in 1970.

FEIGENHEIMER, IRENE. Born June 16, 1946 in NYC. Attended Hunter Col. Studied with Holm, Graham, Cunningham, ABC. Debut 1965 with Met Opera Ballet, subsequently danced with Merry-Go-Rounders, Ruth Currier, Anna Sokolow, Cliff Keuter, Don Redlich.

FELD, ELIOT. Born 1943 in Brooklyn. Studied with Richard Thomas and at School of American Ballet. Appeared with NYC Ballet, and on Bdwy before joining American Ballet Theare in 1963. Co-founder (1969), director, dancer, and choreographer for American Ballet Co.

FERNANDEZ, ROYES. Born June 15, 1929 in New Orleans. Studied with Lelia Hallers and Vincenzo Celli. Appeared with Ballet Russe, Markova-Dolin, Ballet Alicia Alonso, de Cuevas' Ballet, before joining Ballet Theatre. Premier danseur since 1957. Has appeared with several companies as guest artist.

FIBICH, FELIX. Born May 8, 1917 in Warsaw, Poland; attended dance and theatre schools, and made professional debut there in 1936. Became dancer-choreographer in 1939. Formed own company that has toured widely with Israeli and Chassidic dances.

FIFIELD, ELAINE. Born in Sydney, Aust. Studied at Sadler's Wells, RAD. Debut 1948 with Sadler's Wells. Co., subsequently appeared with Royal Ballet, Australian Ballet.

Laura Foreman   Felix Fibich   Julia Frederick   Flemming Flindt   Fiona Fuerstner

FILIPOV, ALEXANDER. Born Mar. 19, 1947 in Moscow. Studied at Leningrad Kirov School. Debut with Moiseyev Ballet, defected and appeared with Pa. Ballet, Eglevsky Ballet, ABT(1970).

FITZGERALD, HESTER. Born Oct. 1, 1939 in Cleveland, O. Trained with Nedjedin, Levinoff, and at Ballet Russe. American, and Ballet Theatre schools. Debut with Ballet Russe 1956; subsequently with NYCity Ballet, American Ballet Theatre, and Harkness Ballet.

FLINDT, FLEMMING. Born 1936 in Copenhagen. Entered Danish Royal Ballet School at 10; became member at 18. Invited by Harald Lander to appear in London; returned to Danish Ballet and became leading dancer before joining Paris Opera as danseur etoile, and began to choreograph. Ranks among world's greatest male dancers, and has achieved recognition as choreographer. Became director of Royal Danish Ballet in 1966.

FONAROFF, NINA. Born in NYC in 1914. Studied with Martha Graham, at School of American Ballet. Danced with Graham company 1937-46 before forming own company in 1945. Is now teacher-choreographer.

FONTEYN, MARGOT. Born May 18, 1919 in Surrey, Eng. Began training at 14 with Astafieva, and a few months later entered Sadler's Wells School. Solo debut with company in 1934 in "The Haunted Ballroom." In 1935, succeeded to ballerina roles of Markova. Unrivaled in roles of Aurora and Chloe. Made Dame of British Empire by Queen Elizabeth. Guest star of Royal Ballet, and considered Prima Ballerina Assoluta of the world.

FOREMAN, LAURA. Born in Los Angeles. UWisc. graduate. Danced with companies of Tamiris-Nagrin, Marion Scott, Harriet Anne Gray, Ann Halprin. Director of Laura Foreman Dance Company; Founder/Director of Choreographers Theatre/ChoreoConcerts; director New School Dance Dept.

FOSSE, BOB. Born in Chicago June 23, 1927. Appeared in musicals before becoming outstanding choreographer for Bdwy, films, and TV.

FOWLER, TOM. Born Feb. 18, 1949 in Long Beach, Cal. Graduate UCin. Studied with David Howard, Claudia Corday, David McLean, Margaret Black, Richard Thomas, Harkness House. Debut 1971 with American Ballet Company.

FRACCI, CARLA Born Aug. 20, 1936 in Milan, Italy. Began training at 8 at La Scala with Edda Martignoni, Vera Volkova, and Esmee Bulnes. Became prima ballerina of La Scala in 1958; joined London Festival Ballet as guest artist. Now permanent guest artist with American Ballet Theatre.

FRANKEL, EMILY. Born in NYC. Studied with Weidman, Holm, Graham, Craske, Tudor, and Daganova. Professional debut 1950. Founder, director, choreographer, and dancer with Dance Drama Co. since 1955. Has made 8 transcontinental tours, a State Dept. sponsored tour of Europe, and British Arts Council tour of England and Scotland.

FRANKLIN, FREDERIC. Born in Liverpool, Eng. in 1914. Studied with Legat, Kyasht, and Pruzina. Made debut as child dancer; went to London at 17; appeared in music halls, night clubs, and musicals before joining Markova-Dolin Co. 1935-7. Premier danseur with Ballet Russe de Monte Carlo from 1938; became its ballet master in 1944. Artistic adviser ABT (1961). Since 1962 Director of National Ballet, Wash., D. C.

FREDERICK, JULIA. Born in Boston. Studied and performed with Boston Ballet, Harkness Ballet, NYC Ballet. Also danced with Pennsylvania Ballet, Garden State Ballet, and NYC Opera Co. Resident soloist with Hartford Ballet.

FREEDMAN, LAURA. Born July 7, 1945 in NYC. Graduate Bennington Col. Studied with Graham, Cunningham, Zena Rommett. Debut 1967 with Merry-Go-Rounders, subsequently with Batsheva Dance Co. (1968)

FREEMAN, FRANK. Born July 16, 1945 in Bangalore, India. Studied at Royal Ballet School. Joined company in 1963.

FUENTE, LUIS. Born in 1944 in Madrid where he began studies at early age. Joined Antonio's Ballets de Madrid in 1963; Joffrey Ballet 1964-1970, National Ballet(1967).

FUERSTNER, FIONA. Born Apr. 24, 1936 in Rio de Janeiro. Attended San Francisco State College, Studied at San Francisco Ballet School (debut with company in 1952), School of American Ballet, Ballet Rambert, Royal Ballet School, Ballet Theatre School. Has danced with Les Grands Ballets Canadiens, San Francisco, NY City Center, and Philadelphia Opera ballet companies. Principal dancer with Pennsylvania Ballet.

GABLE, CHRISTOPHER. Born 1940 in London, began studies at Royal Ballet School. At 16 joined Sadler's Wells Opera Ballet, and next year Covent Garden Opera Ballet. In 1957 became member of Royal Ballet and at 19 advanced to soloist. Retired in 1967 to act.

GAIN, RICHARD. Born in Belleville, Ill. Jan 24, 1939. Studied with Lalla Baumann, and Martha Graham. Professional debut with St. Louis Municipal Opera, followed by musicals. Became member of Graham Co. in 1961, also danced with Jazz Ballet Theatre, Lotte Goslar, Sophie Maslow, and Pearl Lang, and formed concert group "Triad" that performed in NY and on tour. Joined Joffrey Co. in 1964; ABT in 1967.

GARRARD, MIMI. Born in Gastonia, N.C. Attended Sweet Briar College. Studied at Henry St. Playhouse, with Julia Barashkova, Angelina Romett. Has appeared with Alwin Nikolais and Murray Louis companies, and own company for which she choreographs.

GARTH, MIDI. Born in NYC. Studied with Francesca de Cotelet, Sybil Shearer, Louis Horst. Has choreographed and performed solo concerts in NY and on tour. Also teaches.

GARY, M'LISS. Born Nov. 8, 1951 in Lisbon, Port. Graduate Ntl. Ballet Academy. Studied with Oleg Tupine, Richard Thomas, Barbara Fallis. Debut 1969 with National Ballet, joined American Ballet Co. in 1971.

GAYLE, DAVID. Born July 10, 1942 in Yorkshire, Eng. Appeared in Covent Garden opera ballets before joining Royal Ballet. Left in 1970 to teach in Buffalo.

GENNARO, PETER. Born 1924 in Metairie, La. Studied at American Theatre Wing. Debut with Chicago San Carlo Opera 1948, and Bdwy bow same year. After several musicals and TV, choreographed "Seventh Heaven" in 1955. Is much in demand as dancer and choreographer for television.

GENTRY, EVE. Born Aug. 20 in Los Angeles. Used own name Henrietta Greenhood until 1945. Studied with Holm, Graham, Humphrey, Weidman, Tamiris, Barashkova, at Ballet Arts-Studio, and American Ballet Center. Debut with Hanya Holm. Since 1949, director-choreographer-soloist with own company.

GERMAINE, DIANE. Born July 5, 1944 in NYC. Studied with Martha Graham, May O'Donnell, Norman Walker, Paul Sanasardo. Debut with Sanasardo in 1963. Has appeared in concert with Norman Walker, and teaches.

GEVA, TAMARA. Born 1908 in St. Petersburg, Russia. Studied at Maryinsky Theatre. Joined Diaghilev. Came to U.S., signed by Ziegfeld, subsequently appeared in musicals and films, and with American Ballet.

GIELGUD, MAINA. Born Jan. 14, 1945 in London. Studied with Karsavina, Idzikovski, Egorova, Gsovsky, Hightower. Debut 1961 with Petit Ballet, subsequently with Ballet de Marquis de Cuevas, Miskovitch, Grand Ballet Classique, joined Bejart Ballet in 1967.

GILPIN, JOHN. Born in 1930 in Southsea, Eng. Was child actor; joined Ballet Rambert in 1945, London's Festival ballet 1950, becoming artistic director and principal dancer. Guest artist with ABT and Royal Ballet. Resigned as artistic director Festival Ballet but remains premier danseur.

GIORDANO, GUS. Born July 10, 1930 in St. Louis. Graduate U.Mo. Debut at Roxy NYC, 1948, subsequently appeared in musicals, on TV before becoming choreographer. Currently director of Giordano Dance Studio in Evanston, Ill., and his own company.

Gus Giordano

Erika Goodman

Miguel Godreau

Janice Groman

Nicholas Gunn

GLADSTEIN, ROBERT. Born Jan. 16, 1943 in Berkeley, Calif. Attended San Francisco State College, and studied at San Francisco Ballet School. Became member of San Francisco Ballet in 1960 and choreographed 13 ballets. Joined American Ballet Theatre in 1967, became soloist in 1969. Rejoined SF Ballet 1970.

GLASSMAN, WILLIAM. Born 1945 in Boston and began dance studies at 7. Scholarship to School of American Ballet. Studied with Alfredo Corvino and Margaret Craske. Appeared in musicals, with NYC Opera, and on TV, before joining American Ballet Theatre in 1963. Promoted to soloist in 1965. Now with Niagara Frontier Ballet.

GLENN, LAURA. Born Aug. 25, 1945 in NYC. Graduate Juilliard. Joined Limon Company in 1964. Has also performed with Ruth Currier, Sophie Maslow, Valerie Bettis, and Contemporary Dance Sextet.

GLUCK, RENA. Born Jan. 14, 1933. Juilliard graduate. Studied with Graham, Tudor, Horst, Blanche Evans. Founding member of Batsheva Dance Co. in 1963. Also choreographs.

GODREAU, MIGUEL. Born Oct. 17, 1946 in Ponce, P.R. Studied at Joffrey Ballet Center, School of American Ballet, Ballet Russe, and with Martha Graham. Debut 1964 with First American Dance Co., subsequently with Ailey, McKayle, and Harkness Ballet. After appearing on Bdwy, organized and danced with own company in 1969. Returned to Ailey Co. in 1970.

GOLLNER, NANA. Born 1920 in El Paso, Texas. Studied with Kosloff. Soloist with American Ballet 1935, de Basil's Ballet Russe 1935-6, Blum's Ballet Russe 1936-7, Ballet Theatre 1939-48. Only American to achieve rank of ballerina in foreign country.

GOODMAN, ERIKA. Born Oct. 9 in Philadelphia. Trained at School of American Ballet, and American Ballet Center. Debut with NYCity Ballet 1965. Appeared with Pa. Ballet, and Boston Ballet before joining Joffrey Ballet in 1967.

GOPAL, RAM. Hindu dancer, came to U.S. in 1938, and with own company has toured world as its soloist. Operates own school.

GORDON, MARVIN. Born in NYC. Graduate of Queens College. Studied with New Dance Group, Met Opera Ballet, Graham, Humphrey, and Weidman. Appeared on Bdwy and TV, and in concert with Doris Humphrey, and Pearl Lang. Choreographed before becoming founder-director of Ballet Concerts, a group that has appeared in NY and on tour throughout the U.S.

GOSLAR, LOTTIE. Born in Dresden, Ger. Studied at Mary Wigman School. Toured Europe as dance mime before coming to U.S. in 1937. Formed own pantomime company for tours of U.S. and Europe. Also teaches.

GOTH, TRUDY. Born in Berlin in 1913. Studied with Kreutzberg and Ballet Joos. Came to U.S. in 1940 and studied with deMille, Limon, Celli. Founded Choreographers' Workshop in 1946. Currently writes on dance events.

GOVRIN, GLORIA. Born Sept. 10, 1942 in Newark, N.J. Studied at Tarassof School, American Ballet Academy, School of American Ballet. Joined NYC Ballet in 1957. Promoted to soloist at 19.

GOYA, CAROLA. Born in NYC. Studied with Fokine, Otero, LaQuica, Maria Esparsa. Danced with Met Opera before solo debut as Spanish dancer in 1927. Appeared with Greco before partnership with Matteo in 1954.

GRAHAM, MARTHA. Born in 1893 in Pittsburgh. Studied at Denishawn School of Dance; made debut with its company in 1919, and danced with them until 1923. First choreographed and appeared in NYC in a program of 18 original works in 1926, followed by annual concerts until 1938. A founder of Bennington (Vt.) Dance Festival where she staged several premieres of her works. Formed own company with which she has made numerous successful tours throughout world. Founded Martha Graham School of Contemporary Dance in 1927, and remains its director. Has created over 100 dances.

GRANT, ALEXANDER. Born Feb. 22, 1925 in Wellington, New Zealand. Entered Sadler's Wells School in 1946, and five months later joined company. Has created more major roles than any other male dancer with Royal Ballet.

GRECO, JOSE. Born Dec. 23, 1919 in Montorio-Nei-Frentani, Compobasso, Italy. Studied with Mme. Veola in NYC, Argentinita and La Quica in Madrid. Debut as soloist in 1935 with Salmaggi Opera Co. Partner with La Argentinita 1943-4, Pilar Lopez 1946-8, before organizing own company in 1949, with which he has become internationally famous.

GREENFIELD, AMY. Born July 8, 1940 in Boston. Studied with Graham, Cunningham, Fonaroff, Robert Cohan, American Ballet Center. Made debut in 1965. Has appeared in concert and with DTW.

GREGORY, CYNTHIA. Born July 8 in Los Angeles where she studied with Lorraine, Maracci, Panaieff, and Rossellat. Danced with Santa Monica Civic Ballet, LA Civic Light Opera, in 1961 joined San Francisco Ballet, subsequently SF Opera Ballet, and American Ballet Theatre in 1965; became principal in 1968.

GREY, BERYL. Born in Highate, England, in 1927. Began studies at Sadler's Wells Ballet School, and at 15 danced "Swan Lake" with its company. Left in 1957 but returned for guest appearances. Appointed in 1966 to head Arts Education School, London.

GRIFFITHS, LEIGH-ANN. Born Dec. 5, 1948 in Johannesburg, SA. Studied at Royal Ballet School. Joined Stuttgart Ballet in 1968.

GRIGOROVICH, YURI. Born in Leningrad in 1927. Graduated from Leningrad Ballet School and became one of leading soloists with Kirov Co. In 1964 became choreographer for Moscow Bolshoi Ballet Co.

GROMAN, JANICE. Born in New Britain, Conn. Joined NYC Ballet at 16. Later with ABT, and First Chamber Dance Quartet.

GUNN, NICHOLAS. Born Aug. 28, 1947 in Bklyn. Studied with Ellen Segal, Helen McGeehee, June Lewis, Don Farnworth. Debut with Paul Taylor Co.

GUTELIUS, PHYLLIS. Born in Wilmington, Del. Studied with Schwetzoff, Tudor, Graham. Joined Graham Company in 1962. Has appeared on Broadway and with Glen Tetley, Yuriko, Sophie Maslow, John Butler.

GUTHRIE, NORA. Born Jan. 2, 1950 in NYC. Studied with Marjorie Mazia, Martha Graham. Professional debut 1970 with Jean Erdman Co.

GUZMAN, PASCHAL. Born in Arecibo, PR. Attended Harkness, National Ballet, Graham, Dalcroze schools. Debut 1964 with National Ballet, subsequently with Baltimore Ballet, Washington Dance Repertory, Penn. Ballet, New America Ballet, Ballet Concerto, Downtown Ballet.

HAAKON, PAUL. Born in Denmark in 1914. Studied at Royal Danish Ballet School, with Fokine, Mordkin, and at School of American Ballet. Debut with Fokine in 1927. Danced and toured with Anna Pavlova. Became premier danseur with American Ballet in 1935. Appeared in musicals and nightclubs. In 1963 became ballet master and instructor of Jose Greco Co.

HAMILTON, PETER. Born in Trenton, N.J. Sept. 12, 1915. Attended Rutgers. Danced in Broadway musicals before becoming choreographer and teacher.

HAMMONS, SUZANNE. Born Aug. 26, 1938 in Oklahoma City. Attended San Francisco Ballet, American Ballet Center, and Harkness schools. Debut in 1958 with San Francisco Ballet; subsequently joined Harkness, and Joffrey Ballet companies.

HANITCHAK, LEONARD R., JR. Born July 24, 1944 in Oklahoma City. Studied with Ethel Butler, Graham, and Cunningham. Has danced with DTW, and Rudy Perez Co.

HANKE, SUSANNE. Born in 1948 near Berlin. Studied with Anneliese Morike, Anne Woolliams, and at Royal Ballet School. Debut 1963 in Wuerttemberg State Theatre Ballet. Joined Stuttgart Ballet in 1966.

HARPER, LEE. Born Nov. 10, 1946 in Hickory, NC. Juilliard graduate. Studied with Tudor, Limon, Koner, Lindgren, Cunningham, Fallis. Debut 1969 with Pearl Lang, subsequently with James Cunningham, Alvin Ailey.

HARPER, MEG. Born Feb. 16, 1944 in Evanston, Ill. Graduate of U.Ill. Studied with Merce Cunningham and made professional debut with his company in 1968.

| Meg Harper | Randal Harris | Dyane Harvey | Phillip Hoffman | Kathryn Horne |

HARRIS, RANDAL. Born in Spokane, Wash. Attended Pacific Lutheran U. Studied with Joffrey, Edna McRae, Jonathan Watts, ABC. Joined Joffrey Ballet in 1970.

HART, JOHN. Born in London in 1921. Studied with Judith Espinosa, and at Royal Acad. Joined Sadler's Wells in 1938, and rose to principal. Became Ballet master in 1951, asst. director in 1962.

HARVEY, DYANE. Born Nov. 16, 1951 in Schenectady, NY. Studied with Marilyn Ramsey, Paul Sanasardo. Appeared with Schenectady Civic Ballet, Dance Uptown, Miguel Godreau, Eleo Pomare, Movements Black, Story Time Dance Theatre.

HASH, CLAIRE RISA. Born May 18, 1946 in Norwich, Conn. Studied at U Colo. and NYU. Debut 1970 with Jean Erdman Co.

HAUBERT, ALAIN. Born in NYC. Attended UUtah. Studied with Helen Averell, Raoul Pause, Kira Ivanovsky, Dorothy Dean, Alan Howard, William Griffith. Debut with Monterey Peninsula Ballet, subsequently with Pacific Ballet, ABT, Joffrey Ballet.

HAWKINS, ERICK. Born in Trinidad, Colo. Studied at School of American Ballet. Appeared with American Ballet 1934-7, Ballet Caravan 1936-9, and with Martha Graham, before becoming choreographer, teacher, and director of his own company.

HAYDEE, MARCIA. Born in 1940 in Rio de Janeiro. Studied at Royal Ballet School, London. Debut with Marquis de Cuevas Ballet. Joined Stuttgart Ballet in 1961, becoming its prima ballerina.

HAYDEN, MELISSA. Born Mildred Herman in Toronto, Can. April 25, 1923, where she received early training before becoming charter member of NYC Ballet. Has appeared with National Ballet of Canada, Ballet Theatre, and Royal Ballet. In great demand as educator and lecture-demonstrator. Has also appeared on Bdwy.

HAYMAN-CHAFFEY, SUSANA. Born Jan 31, 1948 in Tenterden, England. Studied at Sadler's Wells School, and with Lepeshinskaya, Graham, Cunningham. Made debut in 1968 with Merce Cunningham.

HAYWARD, CHARLES SUMNER. Born May 2, 1949 in Providence, R.I. Attended Juilliard. Debut in 1968 with Jose Limon Company.

HELPMANN, ROBERT. Born April 9, 1909 in Mt. Gambier, Austl. Attended King Alfred College; studied with Laurent Novikov. Professional debut in musicals in Austl., in 1933 joined Sadler's Wells (Now Royal Ballet) School, and rose to soloist from 1933-50. Became choreographer, and created ballet "Hamlet" in 1942. Recently has devoted time to acting, directing, guest performances, and directing Australian Ballet.

HERBERTT, STANLEY. Born in Chicago in 1919. Studied with Tudor, Caton, Ivantzova. Member of Polish Ballet, Littlefield, Chicago and San Carlo Opera Ballets before joining Ballet Theatre in 1943. Founder-Director of St. Louis Ballet. Also teaches and choreographs.

HERMANS, EMERY. Born June 25, 1931, in Seattle. Studied with Vaunda Carter, and at Henry St. Playhouse. Debut 1968 with Nikolais Co. Has danced with Carolyn Carlson, Al Wunder, and in own works.

HIGHTOWER, ROSELLA. Born 1920 in Ardmore, Okla. Studied at Perkins School. Appeared with Ballet Russe de Monte Carlo 1938-41, Ballet Theatre 1941-5, Markova-Dolin 1946, Original Ballet Russe 1946-7. Now teaches in Cannes and makes guest appearances.

HILL, CAROLE. Born Jan. 5, 1945 in Cambridge, Eng. Studied at Royal Ballet School and made debut with Royal Ballet Co. in 1962.

HILL, MARTHA. Born in East Palestine, O. Graduate Columbia, NYU. Debut with Martha Graham (1929-31). Director of Dance, Bennington (1934-42), NYU(1930-51), Juilliard since 1951. Founder Conn.Col. School of Dance and Am. Dance Festival.

HINKSON, MARY. Born in Philadelphia, March 16, 1930. Graduate of U. Wisc. Studied with Graham, Horst, Shook, June Taylor, Schwezoff. Professional debut with Graham Co. in 1952, and still appears as soloist with them. Also danced with John Butler, NYC Opera, and NYC Ballet Co.

HOCTOR, HARRIET. Born in Hoosick Falls, N.Y. Studied with Tarasov, Chalif, Dolin, Legat. Danced in vaudeville, theater, and films before opening own school in Boston in 1941, where she teaches.

HODES, STUART. Born in 1924. Studied with Graham, Lew Christensen, Ella Daganova, and at School of American Ballet. Leading dancer with Graham (1947-58), appeared in Bdway musicals, and as soloist in own works. Choreographer and instructor with Harkness Ballet. Now teaches.

HOFF, ALEXIS. Born Aug. 31, 1947 in Chicago. Studied with Melba Cordes, Betty Gour, Edna MacRae, and at Stone-Camryn School. Made debut with Chicago Lyric Opera Ballet in 1961. Joined Harkness Ballet in 1965, becoming soloist in 1968.

HOFF, STEVEN-JAN. Born June 24, 1943, in Hilversum, Holland. Studied at Amsterdam Academie of Dance. Appeared in musicals before joining American Ballet Theatre in 1966. Became soloist in 1969. Joined Garden State Ballet 1970.

HOFFMAN, PHILLIP. Born in Rochester, NY. Attended Miami Dade Jr. Col. Studied with Thomas Armour, and at Harkness House, ABC. Joined Joffrey Ballet in 1969.

HOGAN, JUDITH. Born Mar. 14, 1940 in Lincoln Neb. Studied with Martha Graham. Made debut with Bertram Ross in 1964. Danced with Glen Tetley Co. before joining Graham Company in 1967.

HOLDEN, STANLEY. Born in London, Jan. 27, 1928. Studied with Marjorie Davies/Romford. Made professional debut in 1944. With Royal Ballet until 1969. Now teaches, and makes guest appearances.

HOLDER, CHRISTIAN. Born in Trinidad. Studied in London, and with Martha Graham, Bella Malinka, ABC. Joined Joffrey Ballet.

HOLDER, GEOFFREY. Born in Port-of-Spain, Trinidad, Aug.1, 1930. Attended Queens Royal College. With brother's dance company in Trinidad, later its director. With his company, made first U.S. appearance in 1953. Besides touring, and giving annual concerts with his group, has appeared on Bdwy, with Met opera, and John Butler Co., also choreographs and designs.

HOLM, HANYA. Born in 1898 in Worms-am-Rhine, Germany. Attended Hoch Conserv., Delcroze Inst., Wigman School of Dance. U.S. debut with own company in 1936, followed by annual performances and transcontinental tours. Came to U.S. in 1931 to found N.Y. Wigman School of Dance which became her school in 1936. Has choreographed musicals and operas in U.S. and London.

HOLMES, GEORGIANA. Born Jan.5, 1950 in Vermont. Studied with Pauline Koner, Duncan Noble, Job Sanders, Boston School of Ballet. Debut 1969 with Norman Walker; subsequently with Pearl Lang, Louis Falco, Paul Sanasardo.

HORNE, KATHRYN. Born in Ft. Worth, Tex., June 20, 1932. Studied with Margaret Craske, Antony Tudor. Professional debut 1948 with Ft. Worth Civic Opera Ballet. Appeared with American Ballet Theatre as Catherine Horn (1951-56), a principal dancer Met. Opera Ballet (1957-65), Manhattan Festival Ballet (1963-8), also ballet mistress and teacher for MFB.

HORVATH, IAN. Born in Cleveland, O., June 3, 1945. Studied with Danielian, Joffrey. Appeared in musicals on Bdwy, and on TV, before joining Joffrey Ballet. With ABT from 1967, became soloist in 1969.

HOVING, LUCAS. Born in Groningen, Holland. Attended Dartington Hall, and Kurt Jooss School. Professional debut with Kurt Jooss Ballet in 1942. Has appeared with Graham, Limon companies, and with his own. Has also appeared in Bdwy musicals.

HOWARD, ALAN. Born in Chicago. Studied with Edna MacRae and in Europe. Joined Ballet Russes de Monte Carlo in 1949 and became premier danseur. Appeared with NYC, and Met Opera Ballets before being appointed director of Academy of Ballet in San Francisco. Founded and is artistic director of Pacific Ballet.

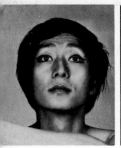

Al Huang **Lone Isaksen** **Finis Jhung** **Edith Jerell** **Louis Johnso**

HOWELL, JAMES. Born in Yakima, Wash. Attended UWash. Studied with Else Geissmar, Martha Graham, Doris Humphrey, Mary Wigman, Margaret Craske, Alfredo Corvino, Robert Joffrey. Original member of Joffrey Ballet.

HUANG, AL. Born in Shanghai, came to U.S. in 1955. Attended Oregon State U., Perry-Mansfield School, graduate UCLA and Bennington. Studied with Carmelita Maracci. Appeared with Lotte Goslar before forming own co., with which he tours when not teaching.

HUJER, FLOWER. Born in Hollywood, Calif. Studied with Theodore Kosloff, Charles Weidman. Has toured in solo concerts and choreographs.

HUNTER, JENNY. Born Aug. 20, 1929 in Modesto, Calif. Studied with Merce Cunningham, Charles Weidman, Marjorie Sheridan. Debut 1951 with Halprin-Lathrop Co. With Dancers' Workshop Co. until 1958 when she left to found, direct, and choreograph for own company, Dance West.

HYND, RONALD. Born in London, April 22, 1931. Studied with Marie Rambert, Angela Ellis, Volkova Idzikowski, and Pereyaslavec. Professional debut 1949 with Ballet Rambert. Joined Royal Ballet in 1951, and graduated from corps to principal dancer.

INDRANI. Born in Madras, India. Studied with Pandanallur Chokkalingam Pillai, Sikkil Ramaswami Pillai, Devas Prasad Das, Narasimha. First dancer to present Orissi classic dance outside India. Tours extensively in solo and with company.

ISAKSEN, LONE. Born Nov. 30, 1941 in Copenhagen where she studied with Edithe Feifere Frandson. Accepted in Royal Danish Ballet School at 13. In 1959 joined group organized by Elsa Marianne Von Rosen and Allan Fredericia, and shortly elevated to soloist. In 1961 studied at Joffrey's American Ballet Center, and appeared with his company. In 1965 joined Harkness Ballet, and became one of its principal dancers until 1970, when she joined Netherlands Ntl. Ballet.

ISRAEL, GAIL. Born in Paterson, N.J. Studied with Alexandra Fedorova. Rose to soloist with Ballet Russe before joining American Ballet Theatre in 1962.

JACKSON, DENISE. Born in NYC; attended ABC. Danced with NYC Opera Ballet, joined Joffrey Ballet in 1969.

JAMISON, JUDITH. Born in 1944 in Philadelphia. Studied at Judimar School, Phila. Dance Acad., Joan Kerr's School, Harkness School, and with Paul Sanasardo. Debut 1965 with ABT. Joined Ailey Co. in 1965. Harkness Ballet in 1966, and rejoined Ailey in 1967.

JAYNE, ERICA. Born Aug. 8, 1945 in Amersham, Eng. Studied at Royal Ballet School, RAD. Debut 1962 with Royal Opera Ballet. Currently principal with Les Grands Ballets Canadiens.

JEANMAIRE, RENEE ZIZI. Born 1924 in Paris. Studied at L'Opera de Paris with Volinine, and with Boris Kniaserf. Debut with Ballet de Monte Carlo in 1944. Joined Ballet Russes de Colonel de Basil(1945-47), Petit's Ballets de Paris in 1948. Has appeared in musicals and films.

JENNER, ANN. Born March 8, 1944 in Ewell, Eng. Began studies at 10 with Royal Ballet School. Debut with Royal Ballet in 1962. Became soloist in 1966, principal in 1970.

JERELL, EDITH. Studied with Antony Tudor, Margaret Craske, Dokoudovsky, Brenna, Pereyaslavec, Joffrey, Popova, Gentry, Norman Walker, Nona Schurman, Nancy Lang, Lazowski, Dunham, and Nimura. Appeared with Met Opera Ballet as principal or solo dancer for 10 years. Is now teacher, concert and guest artist.

JHUNG, FINIS. Born May 28, 1937 in Honolulu where he began training. Graduate of U. Utah. Appeared on Bdwy before joining San Francisco Ballet in 1960. Advanced to soloist then joined Joffrey Ballet in 1962. Joined Harkness Ballet as soloist in 1964.

JILLANA. Born in 1936 in Hackensack, N.J. After studying from childhood at School of American Ballet, joined NYC Ballet in teens, rising rapidly to ballerina. With ABT(1957-8) returned to NYCB(1959). Retired in 1966. Is active in teaching and touring U.S.

JOFFREY, ROBERT. Born Dec. 24, 1930 in Seattle, Wash. Began studies with Mary Ann Wells, later attended School of American Ballet, and studied with May O'Donnell and Gertrude Shurr. Professional debut as soloist with Petit's Ballets de Paris. Appeared with O'Donnell company, and taught at High School of Performing Arts and Ballet Theatre School before starting his own American Ballet Center in 1950. Formed first company in 1952 that was resident co. of NY Opera, and made tours in his own works in the U.S. and abroad. Reorganized group appeared in 1965 and has been internationally acclaimed. Is now City Center Company.

JOHNSON, BOBBY. Born Oct. 26, 1946 in San Francisco. Studied at Harkness House, and with Joffrey, Mattox, Jack Cole, Fokine. Has appeared on Bdwy and with Fred Benjamin Co.

JOHNSON, LOUIS. Born in Statesville, N.C. Studied with Doris Jones, Clara Haywood, and at School of American Ballet. Debut with NYC Ballet in 1952. Appeared in musicals, before forming, choreographing for, and dancing with own group. Teaches, and is on staff of Negro Ensemble Co.

JOHNSON, NANCY. Born in 1934 in San Francisco. Studied with Harold and Lew Christensen at San Francisco Ballet School, eventually becoming principal dancer of SF Ballet Co. With Richard Carter, toured world, appearing in fifty nations. Prima ballerina with San Diego Ballet Co.

JOHNSON, PAMELA. Born in Chicago where she studied with Richard Ellis and Christine Du Boulay. Made debut with their Illinois Ballet Co. Joined Joffrey Ballet in 1966.

JOHNSON, RAYMOND. Born Sept. 9, 1946 in NYC. Graduate Queens Col. Studied with Alwin Nikolais, Murray Louis, Gladys Bailin, Phyllis Lamhut. Debut 1963 with Nikolais, joined Murray Louis in 1968. Also teaches and choreographs.

JONES, BETTY. Born in 1926 in Meadville, Pa. Studied with Ted Shawn, Alicia Markova, La Meri, Doris Humphrey, and Jose Limon. Debut 1947 with Limon Co. and toured world with it. Has own lecture-performance, and teaches master classes throughout U.S. Has appeared in Bdwy musicals.

JONES, MARILYN. Born Feb. 17, 1940 in Newcastle, Australia. Studied with Tessa Maunder, Lorraine Norton, Royal Ballet School. Debut 1956 with Royal Ballet, subsequently with Borovansky Ballet, Marquis de Cuevas, London Festival, and Australian Ballet.

JORGENSEN, NELS. Born in New Jersey in 1938. Studied with Rose Lischner, and toured with her co. before beginning studies at School of American Ballet in 1935. Appeared in musicals and on TV before joining Joffrey Ballet as soloist in 1958. Now artistic director Louisville Civic Ballet.

KARNILOVA, MARIA. Born in Hartford, Conn., Aug. 3, 1920. Studied with Mordkin, Fokine, Charisse, and Craske. First appeared with Met corps de ballet (1927-34). Became soloist with Ballet Theatre, and Met Opera Ballet. Recently in several Bdwy musicals.

KATAYEN, LELIA. Born in NYC; studied with Francesca de Cotelet, Sybil Shearer, Nanette Charisse, Joseph Pilates. In 1960 formed Katayen Dance Theatre Co. for which she is director-choreographer. Head of Southampton College Dance Dept.

KAYE, NORA. Born Nora Koreff in NYC in 1920. Studied at Ballet School of Met Opera, and with Michel Fokine. Debut at 7 with Met's children's corps de ballet. Joined American Ballet Theatre as soloist in 1940 and NYC Ballet in 1950. Now assistant to her husband, choreographer Herbert Ross.

KEHLET, NIELS. Born in 1938 in Copenhagen where he began studies at 6, subsequently going to Royal Danish Ballet School. Teachers include Vera Volkova, Stanley Williams, Nora Kiss, and Melissa Hayden. First solo at 16 in Royal Danish Ballet's "Sleeping Beauty." Made concert tour of Africa, and guest artist with de Cuevas' Ballet, and London Festival Ballet.

KELLY, DESMOND. Born in 1945 in Bulawayo, Rhodesia. Studied at London's Royal Acad. Joined London Festival Ballet, becoming principal in 1963, subsequently with New Zealand Ballet, Zurich Opera Ballet, National Ballet 1968, Royal Ballet as principal in 1970.

Allegra Kent　　　**Jane Kosminsky**　　　**Nathalie Krassovska**　　　**La Meri**　　　**Masami Kuni**

KELLY, GENE. Born Aug. 23, 1912 in Pittsburgh. Graduate of U. Pittsburgh. Teacher and choreographer before appearing in Bdwy musicals and films. Currently choreographing and directing films.

KELLY, KAREN. Born Feb. 1, 1951 in Philadelphia. Trained at Thomas-Fallis School. Debut 1969 with American Ballet Co.

KENT, ALLEGRA. Born 1938 in Los Angeles where she began her studies. At 13 went to School of American Ballet, and 2 years later joined NYC Ballet. Quickly rose to one of company's leading ballerinas.

KENT, LINDA. Born Sept. 21, 1946 in Buffalo, N.Y. Juilliard graduate. Studied with Graham, Limon, Sokolow, Craske, Corvino, Tudor. Joined Alvin Ailey Co. in 1968.

KESSLER, DAGMAR. Born in 1946 in Merchantville, New Jersey. Studied with Thomas Cannon. Joined Pennsylvania Ballet in 1965, Hamburg State Opera in 1966, and London's Festival Ballet in 1967.

KIDD, MICHAEL. Born in NYC Aug. 12, 1919. Attended City College, and School of American Ballet. Studied with Blanche Evan, Ludmilla Scholler, Muriel Stewart, and Anatole Vilzak. Appeared as soloist with Ballet Caravan in 1938, and with Eugene Loring Co. Solo dancer with Ballet Theatre (1942-47), before becoming popular choreographer for musicals and films.

KINCH, MYRA. Born in Los Angeles. Graduate of U.of Calif. Solo and Concert dancer, and choreographer of satirical ballets. Also teaches.

KING, BRUCE. Born in Oakland, Calif. Graduate of U.of Calif. and NYU. Studied at Holm, Met Opera Ballet and Cunningham Schools. Debut 1950 with Henry St. Playhouse Dance Co. Toured with Merce Cunningham and is choreographer and teacher.

KIRKLAND, GELSEY. Born in 1953 in NYC. Joined NYC Ballet in 1968, promoted to soloist in 1969.

KIRPICH, BILLIE. Born in NYC, graduate of NYU. Studied with Graham, and at American School of Ballet. Debut 1942 with Pittsburgh Dance Co. Has appeared with New Dance Group, City Center Opera Ballet, on TV, and in musicals.

KITCHELL, IVA. Born in Junction City, Kan., March 31, 1912. Appeared with Chicago Opera Ballet before making solo debut as dance satirist in 1940. Has continued as concert artist and teacher.

KIVITT, TED. Born in Miami, Fla., Dec. 21, 1942. Studied with Alexander Gavriloff, Thomas Armour, Jo Anna Kneeland, and George Milenoff. Debut 1958 in night club revue. Appeared in Bdwy musicals before joining American Ballet Theatre in 1961. Elevated to soloist in 1964, principal dancer in 1967.

KOESUN, RUTH ANN. Born May 15, 1928 in Chicago. Studied with Swoboda, Nijinksa, Tudor, and Stone-Camryn. Debut with Ballet Theatre in 1946, and became one of its principal dancers. Retired in 1968 but makes guest appearances.

KOLPAKOVA, IRINA. Born in 1933 in Leningrad. Studied with Kirov company and made debut at 18. Elevated to principal ballerina. Now prima ballerina for Leningrad Kirov Co.

KOMLEVA, GABRIELLA. Member of Leningrad Kirov Ballet. Guest artist with Bolshoi Ballet.

KONDRATYEVA, MARINA. Born Feb. 1, 1933 in Kazan, Russia. Enrolled in Bolshoi School in 1943; graduated into company in 1951. One of company's principal ballerinas.

KONER, PAULINE. Born 1912 in NYC. Studied with Michel Fokine, Michio Ito, and Angel Cansino. Solo concert debut in 1930; has toured in concert and with own company annually since. Has appeared with Limon, and been successful choreographer and teacher.

KOSMINSKY, JANE. Born in Jersey City, N.J. in 1944. Attended Juilliard, CCNY. Debut 1960 with May O'Donnell. Joined Paul Taylor Company in 1965. Has appeared with Helen Tamiris, Daniel Nagrin, and Norman Walker.

KRASSOVSKA, NATHALIE. Born in Leningrad in 1918. Studied with Preobrajenska, Fokine, Massine, Balanchine, and Nijinska. Prima ballerina with Ballet Russe de Monte Carlo and London Festival Ballet. Currently teaches and dances with Dallas Civic Ballet, and appears with other companies as guest artist.

KRIZA, JOHN. Born Jan. 15, 1919 in Berwyn, Ill. Attended Cicero Jr. Coll., Stone-Camryn School, and studied with Dolin, Vladimeroff, Perejaslavec, Tudor, and Craske. Danced with WPA Ballet 1938-9, joined American Ballet Theatre in 1940, becoming one of its most popular soloists. Currently its assistant director.

KRONSTAM, HENNING. Born in Copenhagen in 1934. Studied at Royal Danish Ballet School and joined company in 1952. Became premier danseur in 1956. Has appeared as guest artist with many companies.

KRUPSKA, DANIA. Born Aug. 13, 1923 in Fall River, Mass. Studied at Ethel Phillips, and Mordkin Ballet Schools. Began dancing at 6 in Europe as Dania Darling. On return to U.S., joined Catherine Littlefield Ballet. Became member of American Ballet Co. in 1938. More recently has been busy as choreographer.

KUNI, MASANI. Started career in Japan at 13. Gained international fame in solo recitals throughout Europe. Graduate of German Dance College, and studied with Mary Wigman and Max Terpis. Has taught and choreographed in Berlin, London, Copenhagen, Italy, Argentina, and Israel. Is currently director of Kuni Inst. of Creative Dance in Tokyo and Los Angeles.

LAERKESEN, ANNA. Born in 1942 in Copenhagen. Studied at Royal Danish Ballet School and joined company in 1959. Became soloist in 1961.

LAING, HUGH. Born in 1911 in Barbados, B.W.I. Studied in London with Craske and Rambert. Long career with Ballet Rambert, and Ballet Theatre, before joining NYC Ballet in 1950. Now a commercial photographer.

LA MERI. Born Russell Meriwether Hughes in Louisville, Ky., May 13, 1899. Professional debut in 1928. Annual tours throughout world until 1957. Established Ethnologic Dance Center and Theater in 1943, which she closed in 1956, and retired in 1960. Has written several books on dance, and teaches. Organized Festival of Ethnic Dance 1970.

LAMHUT, PHYLLIS. Born Nov. 14, 1933 in NYC where she began her studies in Henry St. Settlement Playhouse. Also studied with Cunningham, and at American Ballet Center. Debut in title role of Nikolais' "Alice in Wonderland." In 1957 gave concert of own works, and has appeared with Murray Louis. In addition to dancing, teaches and choreographs.

LAMONT, DENI. Born in 1932 in St. Louis,Mo. Appeared in musicals before joining Ballet Russe de Monte Carlo in 1951, Ballet Theatre 1953, NYC Ballet in 1954, now soloist.

LANDER, TONI. Born June 19, 1931 in Copenhagen, and studied there with Leif Ornberg, and in School of Royal Danish Ballet. Became member of its company at 17. In 1951, joined Paris Opera Ballet. Later joined London Festival Ballet for 3 years then Ballet Theatre Francais. In 1960 becoming principal ballerina. Re-joined Royal Danish 1971.

LANDON, JANE. Born Jan. 4, 1947 in Perth, Australia. Attended Royal Ballet School, London. Joined company in 1963 rising to principal dancer in 1969. Member of Stuttgart Ballet in 1970.

LANG, HAROLD. Born Dec. 21, 1920 in Daly City, Calif. Debut with SF Opera Co., subsequently dancing with Ballet Russe de Monte Carlo, and Ballet Theatre. More recently has appeared in musicals, and teaches.

LANG, PEARL. Born May 29, 1922 in Chicago, Attended U. of Chicago, and studied at Frances Allis, Martha Graham, American Ballet, Nenette Charisse, and Vicente Celli Schools. Debut with Ukrainian Folk Dance Co. in 1938, subsequently appearing with Ruth Page, Martha Graham companies before forming her own. Became active choreographer and teacher, and has appeared on Bdwy.

LANNER, JORG. Born Mar. 15, 1939 in Berlin. Studied with Kurt Jooss, Nora Kiss, Menia Martinez. Debut 1958 in Ballet Babilee; joined Bejart in 1959.

195

| Jose Limon | Judith Lerner | Eugene Loring | Katherine Litz | Woytek Lowski |

LAPZESON, NOEMI. Born in Buenos Aires, Argentina, June 28, 1940. Studied at Juilliard, and with Corvino, Tudor, Limon, Nikolais, and Graham. Debut in Buenos Aires in 1955. Has appeared with Yuriko, Sophie Maslow, Helen McGehee, Bertram Ross, and Martha Graham. Has appeared in several musicals, and teaches.

LARSEN, GERD. Born in Oslo in 1921. Studied with Tudor. Debut with London Ballet, followed with Ballet Rambert, International Ballet, Sadler's Wells (now Royal) becoming soloist in 1954. Also teaches.

LATIMER, LENORE. Born July 10, 1935 in Washington, DC. Graduate Juilliard. Joined Jose Limon Co. in 1959. Has appeared with Valerie Bettis, Anna Sokolow. Also teaches.

LAYTON, JOE. Born May 3, 1931 in NYC. Studied with Joseph Levinoff. Bdwy debut in 1947. After many musicals, joined Ballet Ho de George Reich in Paris (1945-5). Returned to NY and has become popular director and choreographer.

LECHNER, GUDRUN. Born Nov. 7, 1944 in Stuttgart, Ger. Studied at Stuttgart, and Royal Ballet School, London. Debut 1962 with Stuttgart Ballet.

LEDIAKH, GENNADI. Born in 1928 in Russia. Entered Bolshoi School in 1946, and was graduated into company in 1949.

LEE, ELIZABETH. Born Jan. 14, 1946 in San Francisco. Studied with Harriet DeRea, Wilson Morelli, Richard Thomas. Debut 1964 with Pennsylvania Ballet. Joined American Ballet Theatre in 1967, American Ballet Co. 1969.

LEE, KEITH. Born Jan. 15, 1951 in the Bronx. Studied at Harkness, and Ballet Theatre Schools. Has danced with Norman Walker, Harkness Youth Co., ABT, and own company.

LEIGH, VICTORIA. Born July 3, 1941, in Brockton, Mass. Studied with Georges Milenoff and at JoAnna-Imperial Studio. Debut 1958 with Palm Beach Ballet. Joined American Ballet Theatre in 1961, and became soloist in 1964.

LERNER, JUDITH. Born in Philadelphia, Dec. 30, 1944. Attended Hunter, College, American Ballet School, Ballet Theatre School, and studied with Nenette Charisse and Antony Tudor. Debut as soloist with Eglevsky Ballet in 1961, and joined American Ballet Theatre same year.

LEVINE, MICHELLE. Born Jan. 24, 1946 in Detroit Mich. NYU graduate. Studied with Nenette Charisse, Gladys Bailin, Jean Erdman. Made debut in 1970 with Erdman Co.

LEVINS, DANIEL. Born Oct. 7, 1953 in Ticonderoga, N.Y. Studied at High School of Performing Arts, NY School of Ballet. Made debut in 1969 with American Ballet Co.

LEWIS, DANIEL. Born July 12, 1944 in Bklyn. Juilliard graduate. Joined Limon Co. in 1963. Has appeared with Ruth Currier, Felix Fibich, Anna Sokolow companies.

LEWIS, JAMES J. Born July 30, 1946 in Denver, Colo. Graduate UMich. Studied with Sandra Severo; Debut 1969 with Boston Ballet. Joined American Ballet Co. in 1970.

LICHINE, DAVID. Born in 1910 in Rostov on the Don, Russia. Studied with Egarova, and Nijinska. Joined Ballet Russe, and appeared with Ballet Theatre before becoming choreographer. Now teaches.

LIEPA, MARIS. Born July 27, 1930 in Riga, Latvia. Studied at Riga, and Bolshoi schools. Joined Bolshoi in 1961, quickly rising to principal.

LIMON, JOSE. Born Jan. 12, 1908 in Culiacan, Mexico. Studied at Humphrey-Weidman Co., and with Tudor. Became soloist before forming own company for which he dances and choreographs.

LINDEN, ANYA. Born Jan. 3, 1933 in Manchester, Eng. Studied in U.S. with Theodore Koslov, entered Sadler's Wells School in 1947; joined company (now Royal) in 1951; ballerina in 1958. Now retired.

LINDGREN, ROBERT. Born in 1923 in Vancouver, Can. Studied with Vilzak, Swoboda, Preobrajenska. Joined Ballet Russe in 1942, NYC Ballet in 1957. Retired to teach.

LINN, BAMBI. Born in Brooklyn, April 26, 1926. Studied with Mikhail Mordkin, Helen Oakes, Hanya Holm, Agnes de Mille, and Helene Platava. Debut 1943 in "Oklahoma!" Subsequently danced with Ballet Theatre, Met Opera Ballet, Dance Jubilee Co., and American Ballet Co.

LISTER, MERLE. Born in Toronto, Can., where she began training and had own dance troupe. After moving to NYC, organized dance company in 1964 with which she has appeared in NY and on tour. Is also a teacher.

LITZ, KATHERINE. Born in 1918 in Denver, Colo. Studied with Humphrey, Weidman, Horst, Platova, Thomas. Debut with Humphrey-Weidman Co. in 1936. Soloist with Agnes de Mille Co. (1940-42), and in Bdwy musicals. Debut as choreographer in 1948 in Ballet Ballads, followed by solo and group works. Also teaches.

LLAND, MICHAEL. Born in Bishopville, SC. Graduate USCar. Studied with Margaret Foster. Debut 1944 in "Song of Norway." Joined Teatro Municipal Rio de Janeiro (1945), ABT (1948) rising to principal in 1957. Ballet Master Houston Ballet (1968), ABT (1971).

LOMBARDI, JOAN. Born Nov. 18, 1944 in Teaneck, NJ. Parsons graduate. Studied with Raoul Gelebert, Igor Schwezoff, Paul Sanasardo, Richard Thomas. Debut 1967 with Sanasardo Co. Has appeared with NYC Opera Ballet, and John Butler.

LORING, EUGENE. Born LeRoy Kerpestein in Milwaukee in 1914. Studied at School of American Ballet, and with Balanchine, Muriel Stuart, Anatole Vilzak, and Ludmilla Schollar. Debut 1934 in "Carnival." Subsequently danced with Met Opera Ballet, and Ballet Caravan, for whom he choreographed and starred in "Billy The Kid." Has become a leading choreographer for all mediums. Owns and operates American School of Dance in Hollywood.

LORRAYNE, VYVYAN. Born April 20, 1939 in Pretoria, South Africa. Entered Royal Ballet School in 1956 and company in 1957. Became principal in 1967.

LOSCH, TILLY. Born in Vienna, Aust., Nov. 15, 1907. Studied ballet with Vienna State Opera, later becoming its premiere danseuse. Toured Europe as dance soloist, and with Harold Kreutzberg. Joined Balanchine Ballets in Paris, and later formed own company "Les Ballets." In addition to choreographing, has appeared on Bdwy and is successful painter.

LOUIS, MURRAY. Born Nov. 4, 1926 in NYC. Graduate of NYU. Studied with Alwin Nikolais, and made debut in 1953. Has appeared annually since in concerts and on tour with Nikolais, and own company, for which he also choreographs. Co-director of Chimera Foundation for Dance.

LOUTHER, WILLIAM. Born in Brooklyn. Attended Juilliard. Studied with Kitty Carson, Martha Graham, May O'Donnell, Antony Tudor, Gertrude Schurr. Debut with O'Donnell Co. in 1958. Has appeared in musicals, and in Donald McKayle Co. Joined Graham Co. in 1964.

LOWSKI, WOYTEK. Born Oct. 11, 1939 in Brzesc, Poland. Studied in Warsaw and Leningrad. Debut 1958 with Warsaw Ballet, joined Bejart Ballet in 1966.

LOYD, SUE. Born May 26, 1940 in Reno, Nev. Studied with Harold and Lew Christensen, Vilzak, Scolar, Danielian, Zerapse, Bruson, and Joffrey. Debut with San Francisco Ballet in 1954. Joined Joffrey Ballet in 1967.

LUBOVITCH, LAR. Born in Chicago; attended Art Inst., UIowa, Juilliard, ABT School, and studied with Martha Graham, Margaret Black. Debut 1962 with Pearl Lang, subsequently with Glen Tetley, John Butler, Donald McKayle, Manhattan Festival Ballet, Harkness, before forming own company. Also designs and choreographer.

LUCAS, JONATHAN. Born Aug. 14, 1922 in Sherman, Tex. Graduate of Southern Methodist U. Studied at American Ballet School. Debut 1945 in "A Lady Says Yes," followed by many Bdwy musicals. Became choreographer in 1956.

LUDLOW, CONRAD. Born in Hamilton, Mont. in 1935. Began studies in San Francisco, and became member of its ballet company where he attained rank of soloist before joining NYC Ballet in 1957.

| Lar Lubovitch | Sue Loyd | Nicholas Magallanes | Enid Lynn | Peter Martins |

LUPPESCU, CAROLE. Born April 18, 1944 in Brooklyn. Attended Ind. U. Studied at Met Opera Ballet School. Joined Pennsylvania Ballet in 1964. Has performed with Ballet Rambert.

LYNN, ENID. Born in Manchester, Conn. Studied with Joseph Albano, Martha Graham, Sigurd Leeder. Ballet Mistress for Hartford Ballet, Director-Choreographer for Hartford Modern Dance Theatre.

LYNN, ROSAMOND. Born Dec. 31, 1944 in Palo Alto, Calif. Studied with Bill Griffith, Vincenzo Celli, Richard Thomas, Patricia Wilde. Debut 1964 with Philadelphia Lyric Opera, subsequently with ABT (from 1965), Alvin Ailey Co.(1970)

MacDONALD, BRIAN. Born in 1928 in Montreal, Canada where he began choreographing for television. In 1958 became choreographer for Royal Winnipeg Ballet; and commuted to Norwegian and Royal Swedish Ballets where he held positions as director. Joined Harkness Ballet as director in 1967, left in 1968.

MacLEARY, DONALD. Born in Inverness, Scot., Aug. 22, 1937. Trained at Royal Ballet School. Joined company in 1954, became soloist in 1955 and premier danseur in 1959. Has partnered Beriosova on most of her appearances.

MacMILLAN, KENNETH. Born in 1930 in Scotland. Studied at Sadler's Wells and joined company (now Royal) in 1948. Debut as choreographer with Sadler's Wells Choreographers' Group in 1953 with "Somnambulism." Subsequently created dances for Theatre Ballet, Royal Ballet, American Ballet Theatre, Royal Danish, Stuttgart, and German Opera Ballets. Perhaps most famous are "Romeo and Juliet" and "The Invitation." Director Royal Ballet 1970.

MADSEN, EGON. Born 1944 in Copenhagen. Appeared with Pantomime Theatre and Scandinavian Ballet before joining Stuttgart Ballet in 1961. Promoted to soloist in 1963.

MADSEN, JORN. Born Dec. 7, 1939 in Copenhagen. Studied at Royal Danish Ballet School; joined company in 1957; appointed soloist in 1960. Guest with Royal Ballet in 1965. Now retired.

MAGALLANES, NICHOLAS. Born in Chihuahua, Mex. Studied at School of American Ballet. Danced with Littlefield Ballet, American Ballet Caravan, Ballet Russe de Monte Carlo. Principal dancer with NYC Ballet from its inception in 1946.

MAGNO, SUSAN. Born in 1946 in Melrose, Mass. Studied with Margaret Craske, Alice Langford, Virginia Williams. Appeared with Boston Ballet before joining Joffrey Ballet in 1965.

MAHLER, RONI. Born in NYC in 1942. Studied with Maria Swoboda and at Ballet Russe School. Debut with Ballet Russe de Monte Carlo in 1960. Joined National Ballet in 1962 and became leading soloist in 1963. Joined ABT as soloist in 1969.

MAKAROVA, NATALIA. Born in 1940 in Leningrad. Studied at Kirov School and joined company in 1959. Had triumph with her first "Giselle" in 1961. Defected in 1970 and joined ABT as principal, making her debut in "Giselle."

MANN, BURCH. Born in Texas; Studied with Adolph Bolm, Mordkin, and Fokine. Operates studio in Pasadena, Calif. Organized "Burch Mann Concert Group" that has become The American Folk Ballet.

MARCEAU, MARCEL. Born March 22, 1923 in Strasbourg, France. Studied with Charles Dullen and Etienne Decroux. Debut with Barrault-Renaud Co. in 1946. In 1947 formed own company, and among other works, presented "Bip" with whom he has become identified. Subsequently toured Europe, and U.S.

MARCHOWSKY, MARIE. Dancer-choreographer. Studied with Martha Graham; became member of company 1934-40. With own company, and as soloist, performing own choreography, has appeared in U.S. and abroad.

MARKOVA, ALICIA. Born Lilian Alice Marks in London, Dec. 1, 1910. Studied with Seraphine Astafieva and Enrico Cecchetti. Appeared with Diaghileff Ballet (1925-9), Vic-Wells Ballet (1932-5), Markova-Dolin Ballet (1935-7), Monte Carlo Ballet Russe (1938-41), prima ballerina Ballet Theatre (1941-5). Original Ballet Russe 1946, Markova-Dolin Co. (1947-8), co-founder and prima ballerina London Festival Ballet (1950-2), and has appeared as guest artist with companies throughout the world. Director of Met Opera Ballet 1963-9. Teaches at UCinn.

MARKS, BRUCE. Born in NYC, in 1937 and studied at Met Opera School of Ballet with Tudor and Craske. Joined Met Opera Ballet in 1957, rising to rank of first dancer; joined American Ballet Theatre in 1961 as a principal dancer, and is currently premier danseur with the company. Appeared as guest in 1963 with Royal Swedish Ballet, and in 1965 with London Festival Ballet. Joined Royal Danish Ballet in 1971.

MARKS, J. Born in Los Angeles, Feb. 14, 1942. Founder of San Francisco Contemporary Dancers Foundation. Has choreographed over 200 works. Founder-Director of First National Nothing.

MARSICANO, MERLE. Born in Philadelphia. Studied with Ethel Phillips, Mordkin, Ruth St. Denis, Mary Wigman, Martha Graham, Louis Horst. Debut with Pennsylvania Opera. Since 1952 has presented own program of solos which she choreographs.

MARTIN, KEITH. Born June 15, 1943 in Yorkshire, Eng. Joined Royal Ballet School in 1958 and company in 1961. Appointed soloist in 1967.

MARTIN, YON. Born Sept. 12, 1945 in Washington, DC. Studied with Erika Thimey, Paul Sanasardo, and at Washington School of Ballet. Debut with Dance Theatre of Wash. Joined Sanasardo Co. in 1966.

MARTINEZ, ENRIQUE. Born 1926 in Havana, Cuba where he studied with Alonso and danced with Ballet Alicia Alonso. In addition to appearing with American Ballet Theatre has created several ballets, and in 1964 served as ballet master of Bellas Artes Ballet de Mexico.

MARTINS, PETER. Born 1947 in Copenhagen. Trained at Royal Danish Ballet School and joined company in 1965. Granted leave to appear with NYC Ballet. Joined company in 1970.

MARTIN-VISCOUNT, BILL. Born in Winnipeg, Can. Began study at 12 with Royal Winnipeg Ballet, subsequently studied at Royal Ballet, American Ballet Theatre, and Bolshoi Schools. Joined Royal Winnipeg Ballet in 1959; took leave to appear with London Festival Ballet, and returned in 1962.

MASLOW, SOPHIE. Born in NYC where she studied with Blanche Talmund, and Martha Graham. Joined Graham company and became soloist. Debut as choreographer in 1934. Joined Jane Dudley, William Bales to form Dudley-Maslow-Bales Trio. Helped found American Dance Festival at Conn. College. Has choreographed and appeared in many of her works. On Board of Directors and teaches for New Dance Group Studio.

MASON, KENNETH. Born April 17, 1942 in Bartford, Eng. Attended Royal Ballet School and joined company in 1959. Became principal in 1968.

MASON, MONICA. Born Sept. 6, 1941 in Johannesburg, S.A. Studied at Royal Ballet School, and joined company in 1958, rising to soloist, and principal in 1967.

MASSINE, LEONIDE. Born in Moscow, Aug. 9, 1896. Studied at Imperial Ballet School and with Domashoff Checchetti, and Legat. Discovered by Diaghilev; joined his company in 1914; became principal dancer and choreographer; Ballet de Monte Carlo 1932-41; Ballet National Theatre 1941-4, organized Ballet Russe Highlights 1945-6; subsequently appearing as guest artist and/or choreographer with almost every important company, and in films.

MATHIS, BONNIE. Born Sept. 8, 1942 in Milwaukee, Wisc. Attended Juilliard. Studied with Tudor and Anderson. Performed with Radio City Ballet, Paul Taylor, Norman Walker, before joining Harkness Ballet, ABT (1971).

MATTEO (VITTUCCI). Born in Utica, N.Y. Graduate of Cornell. Studied at Met Opera School, with La Meri, LaQuica, Esparsa, Azuma, Guneya, Balasaraswati. Member Met Opera Ballet (1947-51); solo debut in 1953; formed partnership with Carola Goya in 1954. Teaches, and organized Indo-American Dance Group with which he appears.

Kay Mazzo   Donald McKayle   Arthur Mitchell   Meredith Monk   Francisco Moncion

MATTOX, MATT. Born Aug. 18, 1921 in Tulsa, Okla. Attended San Bernardino College; studied with Ernest Belcher, Nico Charisso, Eugene Loring, Louis Da Pron, Evelyn Bruns, Teddy Kerr, and Jack Cole. Debut in 1946 in "Are You With It?," subsequently appearing in many musicals. First choreography in 1958 for "Say, Darling," followed by several Bdwy productions, and Met Opera Ballet.

MAULE, MICHAEL. Born in 1926 in Durban, S. Af. Studied with Vincenzo Celli and made debut in 1946 in "Annie Get Your Gun." Joined Ballet Theatre, then Ballet Alicia Alonso (1949-50), NYC Ballet (1950-53), Ballets: U.S.A. (1959), Ballet Ensemble (1960-61). In 1964 organized own touring group. Now teaches.

MAXIMOVA, YEKATERINA. Born in Russia in 1939. Entered Bolshoi School at 10, and joined company in 1958, rising to ballerina.

MAXWELL, CARLA. Born Oct. 25, 1945 in Glendale, Calif. Juilliard graduate; debut 1965 with Limon Co. (now soloist), also appears with Louis Falco, and in concert with Clyde Morgan.

MAZZO, KAY. Born Jan. 17, 1947 in Chicago. Studied with Bernadene Hayes, and at School of American Ballet. In 1961 appeared with Ballets U.S.A. before joining NYC Ballet corps in 1962, became soloist in 1965, ballerina in 1969.

McBRIDE, PATRICIA. Born Aug. 23, 1942, in Teaneck, N.J., and studied at School of American Ballet. Joined NYC Ballet in 1959 and attained principal dancer status before leaving teens, ballerina in 1961.

McGEHEE, HELEN. Born in Lynchburg, Va. Honor graduate of Randolph-Macon College. Studied at Graham School and joined company. Became first dancer in 1954. Among her choreographic works are "Undine," "Metamorphosis," "Nightmare," "Cassandra," and "Oresteia." Also teaches.

McKAYLE, DONALD. Born in NYC, July 6, 1930. Attended City College; studied at New Dance Group Studio, Graham School, with Nenette Charisse, Karel Shook, and Pearl Primus. Debut with New Dance Group in 1948, subsequently appeared with Dudley-Maslow-Bales, Jean Erdman, NYC Dance Theatre, Anna Sokolow, and Martha Graham. Formed own company in 1951, and in addition to choreographing, is a teacher.

McLERIE, ALLYN ANN. Born Dec. 1, 1926 in Grand'Mere, Can. Studied with Nemchinova, Caton, De Mille, Yeichi Nimura, Holm, Graham, and Forte. First performed in ballet corps of San Carlo Opera Repertoire Co. in 1942. Bdwy debut 1943 in "One Touch Of Venus" followed by many musicals.

MEAD, ROBERT. Born April 17, 1940 in Bristol, Eng. Studied at Royal Ballet School, and joined company in 1958. Made principal dancer in 1967.

MEDEIROS, JOHN. Born June 5, 1944 in Winston Salem, NC. Studied at Boston Cons., with Ailey, Beatty, and Segarra. Has appeared in musicals and with Alvin Ailey Co.

MEEHAN, NANCY. Born in San Gracisco. Graduate U. Cal. Studied with Halprin, Lathrop, Graham, and Hawkins. Debut 1953 with Halprin company. Joined Erick Hawkins in 1962.

MEISTER, HANS. Born in Schaffhausen on the Rhine. Studied at Zurich Opera Ballet School, and with Mme. Rousane. In 1956 joined Royal Ballet School, London. Joined National Ballet of Canada in 1957, and Met Opera Ballet in 1962. Now makes guest appearances.

MERCIER, MARGARET. Born in Montreal. Studied at Sadler's Wells School, graduating into company in 1954. Joined Les Grands Ballets Canadiens in 1958; Joffrey Ballet in 1963; Harkness Ballet in 1964.

MERRICK, IRIS. Born in 1915 in NYC. Studied with Fokine, Fedorova, Vladimiroff Decroux, Egorova. Is now director and choreographer of Weschester Ballet Co. which she founded in 1950.

MEYER, LYNDA. Born in Texas. Studied at San Francisco Ballet School and joined company in 1962. Became principal dancer in 1966.

MILLER, BUZZ. Born in 1928 in Snowflake, Ariz. Graduate of Ariz. State College. Debut 1948 in "Magdalena." In addition to Bdwy musicals, has appeared with Jack Cole Dancers, and Ballets de Paris, and active choreographer.

MINAMI, ROGER. Born in Hawaii, reared in Calif. Left Long Beach State College to attend Eugene Loring's American School of Dance. Became member of Loring's Dance Players, and now teaches in Loring's school.

MITCHELL, ARTHUR. Born in NYC in 1934. Studied at School of American Ballet. Joined NYC Ballet in 1955 and rapidly rose to soloist. Is now a principal. Was choreographer at Spoleta, Italy Festival for one season. Director of Dance Theatre of Harlem.

MITCHELL, JAMES. Born Feb. 29, 1920 in Sacramento, Calif. Graduate of LACC. Debut 1944 in "Bloomer Girl." Joined Ballet Theatre in 1950, subsequently danced with Met Opera Ballet, De Mille Dance Theatre, and in Bdwy productions.

MLAKAR, VERONIKA. Born in 1935 in Zurich, Switzerland. Appeared with Roland Petit Ballet, Ruth Page, Milorad Miskovitch, Janine Charat, John Butler, and Jerome Robbins before joining American Ballet Theatre in 1964.

MOFSIE, LOUIS. Born in NYC, May 3, 1936. Graduate of State U. of NY at Buffalo. Training on Hopi and Winnebago Indian reservations. Debut at 10. In 1950, organized, directed and appeared with own group performing native Indian dances, both in NYC and on tour.

MOLINA, JOSE. Born in Madrid, Spain, Nov. 19, 1937. Studied with Pilar Monterde. Debut 1953 with Soledad Mirales Co., subsequently joined Pilar Mirales, Jose Greco, and in 1962 premiered own company in the U.S. to national acclaim. Has since made several international tours.

MONCION, FRANCISCO. Born in Dominican Republic. Studied at School of American Ballet. Danced with New Opera Co., Ballet International, Ballet Russe de Monte Carlo, and Ballet Society which became NYC Ballet. Is now a principal. First choreographic work "Pastorale" performed by company in 1957. Is also a painter.

MONK, MEREDITH. Born Nov. 20, 1943 in Lima, Peru. Graduate of Sarah Lawrence. Studied with Tarassova, Slavenska, Cunningham, Graham, Mata and Hari. Debut 1964, subsequently choreographed for herself and company.

MONTALBANO, GEORGE. Born in Bklyn. Studied with Mme. Deinitzen, Natalia Branitska, ABC. Appeared with Westchester Ballet, in musicals, before joining Joffrey Ballet.

MONTERO, LUIS. Born in Granada in 1939. Debut at 15 with Mariemma company. Joined Pilar Lopez, then Jose Greco, Victor Albarez. Became first dancer with Jose Molina Bailes Espanoles in 1961; also choreographs from 1961.

MOONEY, ELINA. Born Nov. 28, 1942 in New Orleans. Attended Sara Lawrence Col. Studied with Evelyn Davis, Weidman, Cunningham, Tamiris, Sanasardo. Debut 1961 with Tamiris-Nagrin Co., subsequently with Weidman, Marion Scott, Paul Sanasardo, Cliff Keuter, Don Redlich, and own company.

MOORE, JACK. Born March 18, 1926 in Monticello, Ind. Graduate U. Iowa. Studied at Graham School, School of American Ballet, Conn. College School of Dance, and Cunningham Studio. Debut 1951, subsequently appeared in companies of Nina Fonaroff, Helen McGehee, Pearl Lang, Katherine Litz, Martha Graham, Anna Sokolow, and City Center Opera. Has also appeared in musicals, and in his own works annually since 1957. Has taught at Conn. College, Bennington, Juilliard, UCLA, and Adelphi.

MORALES, HILDA. Born June 17, 1946 in Puerto Rico. Studied at San Jaun Ballet School and American School of Ballet. Debut with NYC Ballet, then joined Pennsylvania Ballet in 1965. Guest with Les Grands Ballets Canadiens.

MORDAUNT, JOANNA. Born Feb. 13, 1950 in London. Trained at Royal Ballet School; joined company in 1968. Member of London Festival Ballet in 1970.

MORDENTE, TONY. Born in Brooklyn in 1935. Studied with Farnworth. Has appeared on Bdwy and TV, and been assistant to Gower Champion and Michael Kidd. Has also directed and choreographed musicals.

MORE, VICTORIA. Born in Los Angeles. Attended School of American Ballet. Debut with NYC Opera and joined Joffrey Ballet in 1969.

Jack Moore	Victoria More	Fernand Nault	Mary Ann Niles	Alwin Nikolais

MORGAN, CLYDE. Born Jan. 30, 1940 in Cincinnati. Graduate Cleveland State Col. Studied at Bennington, Karamu House, Ballet Russe, New Dance Group. Debut 1961 with Karamu Dance Theatre; joined Limon in 1965 (now soloist), also appears with Anna Sokolow, Pearl Lang, Olatunji, and in concert with Carla Maxwell.

MORGAN, EARNEST. Born Dec. 3, 1947 in Waihiwa, Hawaii. Attended NorthwesternU. Debut 1966 with Gus Giordano Co., subsequently in musicals before joining Paul Taylor Co. in 1969.

MOYLAN, MARY ELLEN. Born in 1926 in Cincinnati. Studied at School of American Ballet, and made debut at 16 as leading dancer in operetta "Rosalinda." Following year joined Ballet Russe de Monte Carlo as soloist. In 1950 became ballerina with Ballet Theatre. Retired in 1957.

MULLER, JENNIFER. Born Oct. 16, 1944 in Yonkers, NY. Graduate Juilliard. Studied with Limon, Graham, Lang, Tudor, Corvino, Craske, Horst, Sokolow. Has danced with Pearl Lang, Sophie Maslow, NYC Opera, Frances Alenikoff, Louis Falco. Member of Jose Limon Company since 1963. Also teaches.

MUNRO, RICHARD. Born Aug. 8, 1944, in Camberley, Eng. Trained at Hardie Ballet School. Debut with Zurich Opera Ballet, subsequently with London Festival Ballet, American Ballet Co. in 1969.

MUMAW, BARTON. Born in 1912 in Hazelton, Pa. Studied with Ted Shawn; debut with Shawn's company in 1931 and danced with group until it disbanded. Now makes guest appearances, teaches, and appears in musicals, and at Jacob's Pillow.

MURPHY, SEAMUS. Born in Hong Kong. Attended Juilliard. Appeared on Bdwy before forming own company. Also teaches.

MUSGROVE, TRACI. Born Feb. 7, 1948 in Carlysle, Pa. Graduate SMU. Studied with Graham, Limon, Hoving, Kuch, Yuriko. Debut 1970 with Yuriko, subsequently with Pearl Lang.

MUSIL, KARL. Born Nov. 3, 1939 in Austria. Studied at Vienna State Opera School; joined company in 1953; promoted to soloist in 1958. Has appeared as guest artist with many companies.

MUSSMAN, MARJORIE. Born Feb. 19, 1943 in Columbus, O. Attended Smith College, and Sorbonne, Paris. Studied with Reznikoff, Marmein, Limon, and Joffrey. Debut with Paris Festival Ballet in 1964, and US debut with Jose Limon in 1964. Member of Joffrey Ballet 1965. Currently with First Chamber Dance Co.

NAGRIN, DANIEL. Born in NYC, graduate of CCNY. Studied with Graham, Tamiris, Holm, and Sokolow. Debut in 1945 in "Marianne," followed by several Bdwy musicals, and choreography for Off-Bdwy productions. Now appears in solo concerts.

NAGY, IVAN. Born Apr. 28, 1943 in Debrecen, Hungary. Studied at Budapest Opera Ballet School and joined company. Came to U.S. and National Ballet in 1965. One season with NYC Ballet; joined ABT in 1968 as soloist. Became principal in 1969.

NAULT, FERNAND. Born Dec. 27, 1921 in Montreal, Can. Studied with Craske, Tudor, Preobrajenska, Volkova, Pereyslavic, Leese. Debut with American Ballet Theatre in 1944, for which he has been ballet master 20 years. Is artistic director of Louisville Civic Ballet, and associate artistic director of Les Grands Ballets Canadiens, Montreal.

NEARY, PATRICIA. Born 1942 in Miami, Fla. Studied with Georges Milenoff and Thomas Armour, at Natl. Ballet School, School of American Ballet. From 1962 was soloist with NYC Ballet until 1968. Now makes guest appearances. Co-director Berlin State Opera Ballet 1970.

NEELS, SANDRA. Born Sept. 21, 1942 in Las Vegas, Nev. Studied with Nicholas Vasilieff, Martha Nishitani, Richard Thomas. Debut with Merle Marsicano in 1962. Teacher at Cunningham School since 1965.

NERINA, NADIA. Born in 1927 in Cape Town, South Africa where she received her training. Joined Sadler's Wells Ballet, subsequently becoming one of its leading ballerinas. Now retired.

NEUMEIR, JOHN. Born Feb. 24, 1942 in Milwaukee. Studied at Stone-Camryn, and Royal Ballet (London) schools, and with Sybil Shearer, Vera Volkova. Debut 1961 with Sybil Shearer. With Stuttgart Ballet from 1963. Director Frankfurt Opera Ballet.

NICKEL, PAUL. Born in Detroit, Mich. Debut with NYC Ballet. Joined American Ballet Theatre in 1961 and became soloist in 1967.

NICHTINGALE, JOHN. Born Oct. 21, 1943 in Salisbury, Southern Rhodesia. Studied at London School of Contemporary Dance. Joined Paul Taylor Company in 1967.

NIKOLAIS, ALWIN T. Born Nov. 25, 1912 in Southington, Conn. Studied with Graham, Humphrey, Holm, Horst, Martin, and at Bennington Summer Dance School. Professional debut in 1939. Has designed, composed, and choreographed for own company that tours US and abroad. Was co-director of Henry St Playhouse School of Dance and Theatre. Now co-director of Chimera Foundation for Dance.

NILES, MARY ANN. Born May 2, 1933 in NYC. Studied with Nenette Charisse, Ernest Carlos, Frances Cole, and Roye Dodge. Appeared with American Dance Theatre in US and Europe. Was half of popular Fosse-Niles Dance Team that toured US and appeared in Bdwy musicals. Currently teaching, dancing and choreographing.

NILLO, DAVID. Born July 13, 1917 in Goldsboro, N.C. Debut with Ballet Theatre in 1940, then with Ballet Caravan, and Chicago Opera Ballet before appearing in and choreographing musicals.

NIMURA, YEICHI. Born in Suwa, Japan March 25, 1908. First appeared with Operetta Taza. Soloist Manhattan Opera House 1928. Choreographed for musicals and Met Opera. Currently teaches.

NOBLE, CHERIE. Born Dec. 11, 1947 in Philadelphia. Studied with Ethel Phillips, Michael Lopuszanski, Edmund Novak, Pa. Ballet School. Debut with Novak Ballet in 1961 before joining Pennsylvania Ballet in 1962.

NUCHTERN, JEANNE. Born in NYC, Nov. 20, 1939. Studied with Craske, and Graham. Debut 1965 in "The King and I" followed by appearances with Martha Graham, Yuriko, Sophie Maslow, and Bertram Ross.

NUREYEV, RUDOLF. Born Mar. 17, 1938 in Russia; reared in Tartary, Bashkir. Admitted to Kirov Ballet school at 17; joined its company and became premier danseur. Defected during its 1961 appearance in Paris. Invited to join Royal Ballet as co-star and partner of Margot Fonteyn. Has choreographed several ballets. Considered by many as world's greatest male dancer.

O'BRIEN, SHAUN. Born Nov. 28, 1930. Studied with Fokine, Schwezoff, Diaghilev, Balanchine, School of American Ballet. Debut 1944 with Ballet International, subsequently with Ballet for America, Grand Ballet de Monte Carlo, Ballet Da Cuba, Conn. Ballet, NYC Ballet from 1949.

O'DONNELL, MAY. Born in Sacramento Calif., in 1909. Debut with Estelle Reed Concert Group in San Francisco; lead dancer with Martha Graham Co. 1932-44. Formed own school and company for which she dances and choreographs.

OHMAN, FRANK. Born Jan. 7, 1939 in Los Angeles. Studied with Christensens in San Francisco, and appeared with SF Ballet. Joined NYC Ballet in 1962. Now soloist.

OLRICH, APRIL. Born April Oelichs in Zanzibar, E. Africa in 1931. Studied with Borovsky, and Tchernicheva. Joined Original Ballet Russe in 1944. Appeared on Bdwy.

ORIE, OHARA. Born June 18, 1945 in Tokyo. Studied at Tokyo Ballet School. Debut 1960 with Tokyo Ballet before joining Bejart Ballet.

ORIO, DIANE. Born Feb. 9, 1947 in Newark, N.J. Trained at Newark Ballet Academy, School of American Ballet, American Ballet Center. Joined Joffrey Ballet in 1968.

ORMISTON, GALE. Born April 14, 1944 in Kansas. Studied with Hanya Holm, Shirlee Dodge, and at Henry St. Playhouse. Debut 1966 with Nikolais Co.

ORR, TERRY. Born Mar. 12, 1943 in Berkeley, Calif. Studied at San Francisco Ballet School; joined company in 1959; American Ballet Theatre in 1965, now soloist.

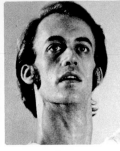

Diane Orio   Haynes Owens   Ruth Page   Stanze Peterson   Merle Park

OSATO, SONO. Born Aug. 29, 1919 in Omaha, Neb. Studied with Egorova, Oboukhoff, Caton, Bolm and Bernice Homes. Member of corps de ballet and soloist with Ballet Russe de Monte Carlo (1934-40), Ballet Theatre (1941-43), followed by Bdwy musicals.

OSSOSKY, SHELDON. Born Brooklyn, June 10, 1932. Attended Juilliard, and studied with Nikolais, Graham, Limon, Tudor, and Craske. Debut 1950, subsequently appeared in musicals and with Pearl Lang, Sophie Maslow, Fred Berke, and at Henry St. Playhouse.

OSTERGAARD, SOLVEIG. Born Jan. 7, 1939 in Denmark. Studied at Royal Danish Ballet School; joined company in 1957; appointed soloist in 1962.

OUMANSKY, VALENTINA. Born in Los Angeles; graduate of Mills college. Studied with Oumansky, de Mille, Vladimiroff, Horst, Cunningham, Graham, and Maracci. Debut with Marquis de Cuevas' Ballet International, subsequently appeared in Bdwy musicals, before devoting full time to choreography, concert work, and teaching.

OWENS, HAYNES. Born in Montgomery, Ala. Studied with Elinor Someth, Molly Brumby; appeared with Montgomery Civic Ballet. Attended ABC, and joined Joffrey Ballet in 1966.

PADOW, JUDY. Born Jan. 10, 1943 in NYC. Studied with Don Farnworth, Marvis Walter, Trisha Brown Schlicter, Ann Halprin. Has danced with Yvonne Rainer, and in own pieces.

PAGE, ANNETTE. Born Dec. 18, 1932 in Manchester, Eng. Entered Royal Ballet School in 1945, and joined company in 1950. Became ballerina in 1959. Has toured with Margot Fonteyn, and made guest appearances at Stockholm's Royal Opera. Retired in 1967.

PAGE, RUTH. Born in Indianapolis, Ind. Studied with Cecchetti, Bolm, and Pavlowa. Debut 1919 with Chicago Opera Co. Toured S. America with Pavlowa, leading dancer on Bdwy, and premiere danseuse with Met Opera. Debut with Diaghilev Ballet Russe, and Ballet Russe de Monte Carlo. Formed own company with Bentley Stone and toured US, Europe, and S. America for 8 years. In Chicago, has been first dancer, choreographer, director for Allied Arts, Grand Opera Co., Federal Theatre, Ravinia Opera Festival. Currently ballet director of both Chicago Opera Ballet and Lyric Opera of Chicago.

PANAIEFF, MICHAEL. Born in 1913 in Novgorod, Russia. Studied with Legat, Egorova. Debut with Belgrade Royal Opera Ballet, becoming first dancer in two years; later joined Blum Ballet, Ballet Russe, and Original Ballet Russe. Now has school and performing group in Los Angeles.

PAPA, PHYLLIS. Born Jan. 30, 1950 in Trenton, NJ. Studied at Joffrey, Harkness, and Ballet Theatre schools. Debut with Harkness Ballet in 1967. Joined ABT in 1968, Royal Danish Ballet 1970.

PARK, MERLE. Born in 1937 in Salisbury, Rhodesia. Joined Sadler's Wells (now Royal) Ballet in 1954, becoming soloist in 1958. Now a leading ballerina.

PARKES, ROSS. Born June 17, 1940 in Sydney, Australia. Studied with Valrene Tweedie, Peggy Watson, Audrey de Vos, Martha Graham. Debut 1959 with Ballet Francais. Has danced with Ethel Winter, Bertram Ross, Helen McGehee, Martha Graham, Sophie Maslow, Glen Tetley, Mary Anthony, Carmen de Lavallade, Jeff Duncan companies. Joined Pennsylvania Ballet in 1966.

PARKINSON, GEORGINA. Born Aug. 20, 1938 in Brighton, Eng. Studied at Sadler's Wells School. Joined Royal Ballet in 1957, became soloist in 1959. Now a principal ballerina.

PARKS, JOHN E. Born Aug. 4, 1945 in the Bronx. Studied at Juilliard. Teacher-dancer-choreographer for Movements Black: Dance Repertory Theatre. Joined Alvin Ailey Co. in 1970.

PARRA, MARIANO. Born in Ambridge, Pa., Mar. 10, 1933. Studied with La Meri, Juan Martinez, La Quica, and Luisa Pericet in Spain. Debut 1957. Has organized and appeared with own company in NYC and on tour.

PAUL, MIMI. Born in Nashville, Tenn., Feb. 3, 1943. Studied at Washington (D.C.) School of Ballet, and School of American Ballet. Debut 1960 in NYC Ballet in "Nutcracker." Joined ABT in 1969.

PEREZ, RUDY. Born in NYC. Studied with New Dance Group, Graham, Cunningham, Hawkins, Anthony. Artist-in-residence Marymount Manhattan Col., on faculty at DTW. Choreographer-Director Rudy Perez Dance Theatre.

PERRY, PAMARA. Born Feb. 8, 1948 in Cleveland, Ohio. Studied at School of American Ballet. Debut 1966 with Western Ballet Association of Los Angeles. With Eglevsky Ballet (1966-7), joined Joffrey Ballet in 1967. Retired in 1969.

PETERS, DELIA L. Born May 9, 1947 in NYC. Attended School of American Ballet. Joined NYC Ballet in 1963.

PETERSON, CAROLYN. Born July 23, 1946 in Los Angeles. Studied with Marjorie Peterson, Irina Kosmouska, Carmelita Maracci, and at School of American Ballet. Debut 1966 with NYC Ballet.

PETERSON, STANZE. Born in Houston, Tex. Has appeared with Syvilla Fort, Edith Stephen, Charles Weidman, Eve Gentry, and Gloria Contreras. In 1963 organized Stanze Peterson Theatre with which he has appeared in NYC and on tour.

PETIT, ROLAND. Born in Paris in 1924. Studied at Paris Opera School; became member of corps in 1939, and began choreographing. In 1945 was co-founder, ballet master, and premier danseur of Les Ballets des Champs-Elysees. In 1948 formed own company Les Ballets de Paris, for which he dances and choreographs.

PETROFF, PAUL. Born in Denmark; Studied with Katja Lindhart; Debut 1930 with Violet Fischer. Became premier danseur of de Basil's Ballet Russe; later joined Original Ballet Russe, Ballet Theatre (1943) and International Ballet. Now teaches.

PHIPPS, CHARLES. Born Nov. 23, 1946 in Newton, Miss. Studied with Graham, Cunningham, and at Ballet Theatre School. Debut 1968 with Pearl Lang, subsequently appearing with Louis Falco, Lucas Hoving.

PIERSON, ROSALIND. Born in Salt Lake City. Bennington graduate. Studied at Thomas-Fallis School, American Ballet Center. Has appeared with Ruth Currier, Charles Weidman, Ballet Concepts, Anne Wilson, DTW, Garden State Ballet.

PIKSER, ROBERTA. Born Sept. 3, 1941 in Chicago. Graduate UChicago. Studied with Erika Thimey, Paul Sanasardo. Debut 1951 with Dance Theatre of Washington; subsequently with Edith Stephen, Paul Sanasardo, Eleo Pomare.

PLATOFF, MARC. Born Marcel LePlat in Seattle, Wash. in 1915. Debut with de Basil's Ballet Russe; soloist with Ballet Russe de Monte Carlo 1938-42 and choreographed for them. As Marc Platt made Bdwy bow in 1943, subsequently appearing in and choreographing for films. Was director of Radio City Ballet.

PLEVIN, MARCIA. Born Oct. 26, 1945 in Columbus, O. Graduate UWisc. Studied with Lang, Graham, Cohan, Yuriko. Debut 1968 with Pearl Lang, subsequently with Sophie Maslow, New Dance Group, Ethel Winter.

PLISETSKAYA MAYA. Born in Russia in 1925. Began studies at Moscow State School of Ballet at 8 and joined Bolshoi company in 1943, rising to premiere danseuse. Internationally famous for her "Swan Lake." Awarded Lenin Prize in 1964. In addition to dancing with Bolshoi, is now teaching. Considered one of world's greatest ballerinas.

PLUMADORE, PAUL. Born Nov. 5, 1949 in Springfield Mass. Studied at NYU and with Kelly Holt, Jean Erdman, Nenette Charisse, Gladys Bailin. Debut 1969 with Katherine Litz, with Jean Erdman in 1970, and danced in concert.

POMARE, ELEO. Born in Cartagena, Colombia Oct. 22, 1937. Studied with Jose LImon, Luis Horst, Curtis James, Geoffrey Holder, and Kurt Joos. In 1958 organized and has appeared with the Eleo Pomare Dance Co. in NYC, abroad, and on tour in the US.

| Kathryn Posin | Andre Prokovsky | Pearl Primus | Lawrence Rhodes | Yvonne Rainer |

POPOVA, NINA. Born in 1922 in Russia. Studied in Paris with Preobrajenska and Egorova. Debut 1937 with Ballet de la Jeunesse. Later with Original Ballet Russe, Ballet Theatre, and Ballet Russe de Monte Carlo. Now Teaches.

POSIN, KATHRYN. Born Mar. 23, 1944 in Butte, Mont, Bennington graduate. Studied with Fonaroff, Cunningham, Graham, Thomas-Fallis. Debut with Dance Theatre Workshop in 1965. Also danced with Anna Sokolow, Valerie Bettis, Lotte Goslar, American Dance Theatre, and in own works.

POWELL, GRAHAM. Born in Cardiff, Wales, Aug. 2, 1948. Studied at Royal Ballet School; joined company in 1965, then Australian Ballet.

POWELL, ROBERT. Born in Hawaii in 1941, and graduate of High School of Performing Arts. Has been featured dancer with all major American modern dance companies, and appeared with NYC Opera Ballet. Currently soloist with Graham Co.

PRICE, MARY. Born May 20, 1945 in Fort Bragg, NC. Graduate UOkla. Studied with Mary Anthony, Martha Graham. Debut 1970 with Mary Anthony, subsequently with Pearl Lang, Richard Gain.

PRIMUS, PEARL. Born in 1919 in Trinidad, B.W.I. NY debut at YMHA in 1943, and first solo performance next year. Has since choreographed and performed in West Indian, African, and primitive dances throughout the world. Also teaches.

PRINZ, JOHN. Born in Chicago in 1945. Studied with Comiacoff, Allegro School, American Ballet Center, School of American Ballet. Joined NYC Ballet in 1964. Makes guest appearances with Ballet Spectacular and Eglevsky Ballet. Joined Munich Ballet, then ABT in 1970.

PROKOVSKY, ANDRE. Born Jan. 13, 1939 in Paris, and achieved recognition in Europe with Grand Ballet du Marquis de Cuevas and London Festival Ballet, and made world tour with "Stars of the French Ballet." Joined NYC Ballet as principal dancer in 1963. Joined London's Festival Ballet in 1967.

QUITMAN, CLEO. Born in Detroit. Attended Weinstein U. Studied with Martha Graham, Alfredo Corvino, Maria Nevelska. Formed NY Negro Ballet Co. that toured Europe. Has appeared with Joffrey Ballet and is founder-director-choreographer of Cleo Quitman's Dance Generale.

RADIUS, ALEXANDRA. Born July 3, 1942 in Amsterdam, Holland. Studied with Benjamin Harkarvy. Debut with Nederlands Dans Theatre in 1957. Joined American Ballet Theatre in 1968 as soloist. Became principal in 1969. Joined Dutch National Ballet in 1970.

RAINER, YVONNE. Born in 1934 in San Francisco. Studied with Graham, Cunningham, Halprin, Stephen. Has performed with James Waring, Aileen Passloff, Beverly Schmidt, Judith Dunn. Started Judson Dance Workshop in 1962, and choreographs for own company.

RALL, TOMMY. Born Dec. 27, 1929 in Kansas City, Mo. Attended Chouinard Art Inst. Studied with Carmelita Maracci, David Lichine, and Oboukhoff of School of American Ballet. Joined Ballet Theatre in 1944, and became soloist in 1945. Has appeared in musicals, films, and choreographed for TV.

RAPP, RICHARD. Born in Milwaukee, Wisc. Studied with Adele Artinian, Ann Barzel, School of American Ballet. Joined NYC Ballet in 1958; became soloist in 1961.

RAUP, FLORITA. Born in Havana, Cuba; attended school in Springfield, O. Has studied with Holm, Limon, Humphrey, Tamiris, and Julia Berashkova. Debut in 1951. Has appeared in concert with own group since 1953, in NYC and on tour.

REDLICH, DON. Born in Winona, Minn., Aug. 17, 1933. Attended U. Wisc., and studied with Holm, and Humphrey. Debut in 1954 musical "The Golden Apple," Has appeared in other musicals, with Hanya Holm, Doris Humphrey, Anna Sokolow, Murray Louis, John Butler, and in own concert program. Is also teacher and choreographer, and tours with own co.

REED, JANET. Born in Tolo, Ore., Sept. 15, 1916. Studied with William Christensen, Tudor, and Balanchine. Member of San Francisco Ballet 1937-41, Ballet Theatre 1943-6, NYC Ballet from 1949. Has been teaching since 1965.

REID, ALBERT. Born July 12, 1934 in Niagara Falls, N.Y. Graduate Stanford U. Studied with Nikolais, Cunningham, Lillian Moore, Richard Thomas, Margaret Craske. Debut 1959 with Nikolais Co. Since with Murray Louis, Erick Hawkins, Katherine Litz, and Yvonne Rainer.

REIN, RICHARD A. Born May 10, 1944 in NYC. Attended Adelphi U., School of Am. Ballet. Debut 1965 with Atlanta Ballet, subsequently with Ruth Page's Chicago Ballet, Pa. Ballet, joined ABT in 1970.

REMINGTON, BARBARA. Born in 1936 in Windsor, Can. Studied with Sandra Severo, School of American Ballet, Ballet Theatre School, Royal Ballet School. Joined Royal Ballet in 1959, followed by American Ballet Theatre, Joffrey Ballet.

RENCHER, DEREK. Born June 6, 1932 in Birmingham, Eng. Studied at Royal Ballet school and joined company in 1952, rising to soloist, and principal in 1969.

REVENE, NADINE. Born in NYC. Studied with Helene Platova. In musicals before joining Ballet Theatre. Subsequently member of NYC Ballet, prima ballerina of Bremen Opera in Germany, and First Chamber Dance Quartet.

REYES, RAMON DE LOS. Born in Madrid and started dancing at 9. Professional debut at 17 after studying with Antonio Marin. Formed own company and toured Spain, Europe, and US. Joined Ximenez-Vargas Co., later Roberto Iglesias Co. as leading dancer. With Maria Alba, formed Alba-Reyes Spanish Dance Co. in 1964.

REYN, JUDITH. Born Dec. 28, 1943 in Rhodesia. Studied at Royal Ballet School, London, and joined company in 1963. Member of Stuttgart Ballet since 1967.

RHODES, LAWRENCE. Born in Mt. Hope, W. Va., in 1939. Studied with Violette Armand. Debut with Ballet Russe de Monte Carlo. Joined Joffrey Ballet in 1960, Harkness Ballet in 1964. Became its diretor in 1969. Joined Netherlands National Ballet 1970.

RIABOUCHINSKA, TATIANA. Born May 23, 1916 in Moscow. Studied with Alexandre Volinin, and Mathilda Kchesinska. Debut in London in 1932. With Monte Carlo Ballet Russe de Basil (1933-43), Ballet Theatre, London Festival Ballet, Theatre Colon (Buenos Aires, 1946-47). Also appeared in musicals. Now teaches.

RICHARDSON, DORENE. Born in NYC, Oct. 5, 1934. Studied at NYU and Juilliard. Debut in 1953. In addition to musicals has appeared with Natanya Neumann, Sophie Maslow, Donald McKayle, and Alvin Ailey.

RICHARDSON, LARRY. Born Jan. 6, 1941 in Minerva, O. Graduate of Ohio State U. Studied with Louis Horst, Jose Limon. Has danced at Kauffman Hall, Hunter College, in musicals, and with Pearl Lang. Also choreographs.

RIVERA, ALONZO. Born Oct. 14, 1938 in Morelia, Michoacan, Mexico. Attended U. Michoacan. Studied with Sergio Franco, and Leon Escobar, and at Jacob's Pillow. Debut in 1952 and has toured the Americas with Leon Escobar since 1954.

RIVERA, CHITA. Born in 1933 in Washington, D.C. Studied at School of American Ballet. Has become popular star of musicals, and TV.

RIVERA, LUIS. Born in Los Angeles. Studied with Michael Brigante, Martin Vargas, Luisa Triana, Mercedes & Albano, Alberto Lorca. Appeared with several companies before forming his own.

ROBBINS, JEROME. Born Oct. 11, 1918 in NYC. Attended NYU. Studied with Daganova, Platova, Loring, Tudor, New Dance League, and Helen Veola. Debut in 1937 with Sandor-Sorel Co. Subsequently in musicals before joining Ballet Theatre in 1940, for which he first choreographed "Fancy Free." Joined NYC Ballet Co. in 1949 and became its associate artistic director in 1950. Formed Ballets: U.S.A. which toured Europe and US in 1958, 1959, 1961. Has choreographed and directed many Bdwy productions and ballets.

Nancy Robinson

Herbert Ross

Shirley Rushing

Donald Saddler

Brunilda Ruiz

ROBERSON, LAR. Born May 18, 1947 in Oakland, Calif. Attended Cal. State College, and Graham School. Debut 1968 with Sophie Maslow Company. Joined Graham Company in 1969. Also appeared with Pearl Lang.

ROBINSON, CHASE. Born in Panama City, Fla. Graduate of Fla. State U. Studied with Aubry Hitchins, Don Farnsworth. Debut in 1956. Has since appeared with Natl. Ballet of Canada, Joffrey Ballet, Limon, Graham, Lang, Butler, Cunningham, and Hoving. Also teaches.

ROBINSON, NANCY. Born Aug. 28, 1945 in Los Angeles. Studied with Andre Tremaine, Michael Panaieff, San Francisco Ballet, joining company in 1960, becoming soloist in 1964. Joined American Ballet Theatre in 1967, Joffrey Co. in 1968.

RODGERS, ROD. Born in Detroit where he began his studies. Member of Erick Hawkins Dance Co., and dance supervisor of Mobilization for Youth project. Has also appeared in concert of own works.

RODHAM, ROBERT. Born Sept. 2, 1939 in Pittston, Pa. Studied with Barbara Weisberger, Virginia Williams, and at School of American Ballet. Joined NYC Ballet in 1960. Was ballet master, choreographed, and appeared with Pennsylvania Ballet from 1963.

RODRIGUEZ, ZHANDRA. Born Mar. 17, 1947 in Caracas, Ven. Debut 1962 with Ballet National Venezuela; joined American Ballet Theatre in 1968.

ROMANOFF, DIMITRI. Born in Tsaritzin, Russia. Came to US in 1924 to attend Stanford U. and take ballet lessons with Theodore Kosloff. First dancer with American Ballet Theatre when it was organized in 1940. Now directs ballet school in San Jose, Calif.

ROMERO, RAFAEL. Born Apr. 2, 1945 in Puerto Rico. Studied at School of American Ballet, Natl. Ballet, and American Ballet Center. Has appeared with Ballets de San Juan, Westchester Ballet, Pilar Gomez, National Ballet, Joffrey Ballet, NYC Opera Ballet (1970).

RON, RACHAMIM. Born Nov. 15, 1942 in Cairo. Studied with Gertrude Kraus, Donald McKayle, Glen Tetley, Pearl Lang, Martha Graham. Debut 1963 with Batsheva Dance Co. of Israel. Joined Donald McKayle Co. in 1967 and Martha Graham in 1968. Re-joined Batsheva 1970.

ROOPE, CLOVER. Born 1937 in Bristol, Eng. Studied at Royal Ballet School and joined company in 1957. Debut as choreographer in 1958. Choreographer in residence at Jacob's Pillow in 1965. Has also appeared with Helen McGehee.

ROSARIO. Born Rosario Perez in Seville in 1920. Cousin of Antonio with whom she achieved international fame. Studied with Realito. With Antonio, became known as "The Kids From Seville" and toured world together until they separated in 1952. Formed own ballet company, but changed to dance recitals. Has returned to guest star with Antonio and his Ballets de Madrid.

ROSS, BERTRAM. Born in Brooklyn in 1920. Leading male dancer of the Martha Graham Co., appears in almost every work in the active repertoire. Has appeared with own company and choreography. Teaches at Graham School, Juilliard, and Neighborhood Playhouse.

ROSS, HERBERT. Born May 13, 1927 in Brooklyn. Studied with Doris Humphrey, Helene Platova, and Laird Leslie. Debut in 1942-3 touring in Shakespearean repertory, and dancing debut in "Follow the Girls" in 1944, followed by several other musicals. In 1950 choreographed and appeared with Ballet Theatre in "Caprichos," subsequently choreographing for Bdwy musicals, Met Opera Ballet, American Ballet Theatre, and danced with own company in 1960.

ROSSON, KEITH. Born Jan. 24, 1937 in Birmingham, Eng. Studied at Royal Ballet School. Joined Covent Opera Ballet in 1954 and Royal Ballet in 1955. Became soloist in 1959, and principal dancer in 1966.

ROTANTE, THEODORE. Born Feb. 23, 1949 in Stamford, Conn. Studied with Nenette Charisse, Kelly Holt, Jean Erdman, Gladys Bailin, Matt Mattox, Donald McKayle. Debut in 1970 with Jean Erdman Dance Theatre.

RUDKO, DORIS. Born Oct. 18, in Milwaukee. Graduate of U. of Wisc. Studied with Humphrey, Weidman, Limon, Graham, Holm, Horst, Daganova, Platova, Joffrey, and Fonaroff. Debut on Bdwy in 1946 in "Shootin' Star". Concert performer and choreographer since 1947. Formed own company in 1957. Is also a teacher.

RUIZ, BRUNILDA. Born in Puerto Rico in 1936, reared in NYC. Studied with Martha Melincoff, and Robert Joffrey before joining his touring group in 1955, and his company in 1961. Appeared with Philadelphia and NYC Opera companies. Joined Harkness Ballet in 1964.

RUSHING, SHIRLEY. Born in Savannah, Ga. Attended Juilliard, Bklyn Col. Studied with May O'Donnell, Gertrude Shurr, Perry Brunson, Jose Limon, Tudor, Graham. Has appeared with Eleo Pomare, Rod Rodgers, Louis Johnson, Gus Denizulu.

SABLE, SHERRY. Born Sept. 4, 1952 in Philadelphia. Studied at Phila. Dance Academy, Graham School. Debut 1970 with Pearl Lang, subsequently with DTW Workshop, Richard Gain.

SABLINE, OLEG. Born in 1925 in Berlin. Studied with Preobrajenska, Egorova, Colinine, Ricaus; danced with Grand Ballet de Monte Carlo, l'Opera Comique Ballet, Grand Ballet du Marquis de Cuevas. Came to U.S. in 1958. Formed and toured with own group Ballet Concertante. Currently teaches.

SADDLER, DONALD. Born Jan. 24, 1920 in Van Nuys, Calif. Attended LACC. Studied with Maracci, Dolin, and Tudor. Debut in 1937, subsequently appearing with Ballet Theatre (1940-3, 1946-7), and in Bdwy musicals. First choreography "Blue Mountain Ballads" for Markova-Dolin Co. in 1948, followed by other ballets and musicals. Performed with own company in 1949. Became assistant artistic director of Harkness Ballet in 1946.

SANASARDO, PAUL. Born Sept. 15, 1928 in Chicago. Attended Chicago U. Studied with Tudor, Thimey, Graham, and Slavenska. Debut in 1951 with Erika Thimey Dance Theatre. Has appeared with Anna Sokolow, and Pearl Lang companies. In 1958 was founder-director of Studio For Dance, which is school for his own company that has presented concerts throughout the US, Canada, and BWI. Choreographer and dancer on TV. Director of Modern Dance Artists (NYC), and School of Modern Dance (Saratoga, NY).

SANDERS, JOB. Born in Amsterdam in 1929. Studied with Gavrilov, and at School of American Ballet. Debut with Ballet Society. Subsequently with Ballet Russe de Monte Carlo, ABT, Ruth Page's Ballet, American Festival Ballet, Netherlands Ballet, Netherlands Dance Theatre. Began choreographing in 1956.

SANDONATO, BARBARA. Born July 22, 1943 in Harrison, N.Y. Studied at Lorna London School, and School of American Ballet. Debut with NYC Ballet, danced with Gloria Contreras Co., before joining Pennsylvania Ballet in 1964.

SANTANGELO, TULY. Born May 30, 1936 in Buenos Aires. Studied at Opera Theatre, with Martha Graham, Alwin Nikolais. Debut 1956 with Brazilian Co., subsequently with Nikolais, Don Redlich (1970).

SAPIRO, DANA ROBIN. Born Jan. 2, 1952 in NYC. Studied with Karin Irvin, Joffrey, and at American Ballet Center. Debut 1970 with Joffrey Ballet.

SAPPINGTON, MARGO. Born in Baytown, Tex., July 30, 1947. Studied with Camille Hill, Matt Mattox, and at American Ballet Center. Debut with Joffrey Ballet in 1965. Also appeared in musicals, and choreographs.

SARRY, CHRISTINE. Born in Long Beach, Calif. in 1947. Studied with Silver, Howard, Maracci, Oumansky, Fallis, Thomas. Joined Joffrey Ballet in 1963, American Ballet Theatre in 1964, American Ballet Co.(1969).

SATO, SHOZO. Born May 18, 1933 in Kobe, Japan. Graduate Tokyo U. Debut with Classical Ballet in 1948. Has appeared around the world in concert and lecture demonstrations since 1964.

SAUL, PETER. Born Feb. 10, 1936 in NYC. Studied with Craske, Tudor, and Cunningham. Appeared with Met Opera Ballet 1956-7, International Ballet 1960-61, American Ballet

Barbara Sandonato   **Dana Sapiro**   **Ted Shawn**   **Suki Schorer**   **Tonia Shimin**

Theatre 1962-4, Les Grands Ballets Canadien 1964-5, Merce Cunningham 1966-7.

SCHANNE, MARGRETHE. Born in Copenhagen in 1921. Graduate of Royal Danish Ballet school, and joined its company in mid-1940's, rapidly rising to premiere danseuse and the epitome of the Bournonville style. Briefly joined Petit's Ballets des Champs-Elysses in Paris, and in 1947 made London debut with it before returning to Royal Danish Ballet where she became synonymous with "La Sylphide." Made NY debut in it in 1956, and danced it for her farewell performance in NY and Copenhagen in 1966. Now teaches.

SCHEEPERS, MARTIN. Born in 1933 in Arnheim, Holland. Studied with Georgi, Adret, Crofton, Lifar, Gsovsky, Kiss. Debut in 1948 with Amsterdam Opera. Joined Champs-Elysses and London Festival Ballets before American Ballet Theatre in 1960.

SCHORER, SUKI. Born in Cambridge, Mass. Attended U. Cal. Studied at San Francisco Ballet School and joined company. In 1959 joined NYC Ballet, becoming soloist in 1963, ballerina in 1969.

SCHULKIND, MARCUS. Born Feb. 21, 1948 in NYC. Graduate Goddard Col. Studied at Juilliard. Debut 1968 with Pearl Lang, then with Norman Walker, Felix Fibich, joined Batsheva in 1970.

SCOTT, MARION. Born July 24, 1922 in Chicago. Studied with Graham, Humphrey, Weidman, Horst, Tamiris, and Slavenska. Debut with Humphrey-Weidman Co. in 1942. Has danced with Tamiris company, and in 1964 formed own company for which she choreographs. Also teaches.

SEGARRA, RAMON. Born Nov. 26, 1939 in Mayaguez, P.R. Studied with Chaffee, Malinka. Moore, Pereyaslavec, Vilzak, Oboukoff, Vladimiroff, Eglevsky, and Zaraspe. Debut 1954 with Ballet Chaffee, subsequently appearing as soloist with May O'Donnell Co. (1956-8), Ballet Russe de Monte Carlo (1958-61), NYC Ballet (1961-4), National Ballet of Canada principal dancer from 1964. Joined Ailey Co. in 1970. Makes many guest appearances.

SEKH, YAROSLAV. Born in Ukrania in 1930. Entered Bolshoi School in 1949, and joined company in 1951. Became one of leading character dancers.

SELLERS, JOAN. Born Sept. 21, 1937 in NYC. Studied with Graham, Cunningham, Thomas, Fallis, Farnworth. Debut 1960 with Dance Theatre, subsequently with DTW, James Cunningham Co.

SERAVALLI, ROSANNA. Born March 9, 1943 in Florence, Italy. Trained and performed in Italy before joining American Ballet Theatre in 1963.

SERGAVA, KATHERINE. Born in Tiflis, Russia. Studied with Kchessinska, Fokine, Kyasht, Mendes. Danced with Mordkin Ballet, Ballet Theatre (1940), Original Ballet Russe. More recently has appeared in musicals.

SERRANO, LUPE. Born Dec. 7, 1930 in Santiago, Chile. Studied in Mexico City with Dambre and joined Mexico City Ballet Co. Organized Mexican Academy of Modern Dance. After studying with Celli and Tudor, performed with Ballet Russe, and Ballet Theatre since 1953. Has also appeared as guest artist with many companies.

SETTERFIELD, VALDA. Born Sept. 17, 1934 in Margate, Eng. Studied with Rambert, Karsavina, Waring, Cunningham. Debut with Ballet Rambert in 1955. Since with James Waring, Aileen Pasloff, Katherine Litz, David Gordon, Merce Cunningham.

SEYMOUR, LYNN. Born in 1939 in Wainwright, Alberta, Canada. Besides appearing as dramatic ballerina with Royal Ballet, has made guest appearances with Stuttgart, and Canadian National Ballet. Guest artist with Ailey Co. 1970-71.

SHANKAR, UDAY. Born in Udayapur, India, in 1902. Had such success helping his father produce Hindu plays and ballets, that Anna Pavlova requested his help, and he appeared with her in "Radha- Krishna." At her insistence, pursued dance career. Organized own company and toured U.S. in 1931, 1952, 1962, and 1968. Has been more responsible than any other dancer for arousing interest in Indian dance.

SHAW, BRIAN. Born in 1928 in Golcar, Yorkshire, Eng. At 14 entered Sadler's Wells School, and joined company 2 years later, becoming one of Royal Ballet's outstanding principal dancers.

SHAWN, TED. Born in Kansas City, Mo., Oct. 21, 1891, was first male dancer to achieve eminence in US. Attended U. of Denver. Studied with Hazel Wallack, and made professional debut in Denver in 1911. Next year in Los Angeles began to teach, choreograph, and produce. With 4 dancers, began coast-to-coast tour Jan. 1, 1914, during which met and married dancer Ruth St. Denis. Together founded Denishawn school and company which flourished for 17 years, and produced many important contemporary dancers. Made history with tours of America, Europe and Orient. In 1932, without St. Denis, turned attention to development of male dancers, and in 1933 started what is now the world renowned Jacob's Pillow Dance Festival. With his company of men dancers, toured US, Canada, Cuba, and Eng. until 1940 when selective service curtailed personnel. The Festival is adjunctive to school, The University of The Dance, where students must study ballet, modern, and ethnic dance. In 1957 Shawn was knighted by the King of Denmark. He has also written many books and articles on dance.

SHEARER, MOIRA. Born in Dunfermline, Scotland, Jan. 17, 1926. Studied with Legat and Preobrajenska; joined International Ballet at 15, transferring to Sadler's Wells and became ballerina in 1944. More recently has appeared on stage and films.

SHEARER, SYBIL. Born in Toronto, Can. Studied in France and Eng. Before forming and choreographing for own group, appeared with Humphrey-Weidman Co., and Theatre Dance Co. Also teaches.

SHELTON, SARA. Born Dec. 17, 1943. Studied at Henry St. Playhouse. Debut 1966 with Bill Frank Co., subsequently with Nikolais, Louis Murray companies.

SHERWOOD, GARY. Born Sept. 24, 1941, in Swindon, Eng. Studied at Royal Ballet School; joined company in 1961; Western Theatre Ballet 1965; London's Festival Ballet 1966; returned to Royal Ballet in 1967.

SHIMIN, TONIA. Born Sept. 16, 1942 in NYC. Attended Met Opera Ballet, Royal Ballet, Graham schools. Debut 1965 with Martha Graham, subsequently with Pearl Lang, Gus Solomons, Anna Sokolow, Mary Anthony.

SHIMOFF, KAREL. Born in Los Angeles where she began studies with Irina Kosmovska. Appeared with L.A, Junior Ballet and NYC Ballet's "Nutcracker" in L.A. in 1961. Studied at School of American Ballet, and joined NYC Ballet for 2 years, before returning as principal dancer with Ballet of Los Angeles.

SHULER, ARLENE. Born Oct. 18, 1947 in Cleveland, O. Studied at School of American Ballet, and American Ballet Centcr. Debut with NYC Ballet in 1960, and joined Joffrey Ballet in 1965.

SHURR, GERTRUDE. Born in Riga, Latvia. Studied at Denishawn, and with Humphrey, Weidman, and Graham. Has appeared with Denishawn Co., Humphrey-Weidman Concert Co., and Martha Graham. Now teaches.

SIBLEY, ANTOINETTE. Born in Bromley, Eng., Feb. 27, 1939. Studied at Royal Ballet School, and made debut with them in 1956, becoming soloist in 1959, then principal in 1960.

SIEGENFELD, BILLY. Born Oct. 15, 1948 in Mt. Vernon, NY. Graduate Brown U. Studied with Nikolais. Debut 1970 with Don Redlich Co., subsequently with Elina Mooney.

SIMON, VICTORIA. Born in 1939 in NYC. Studied at School of American Ballet, American Ballet Center, Ballet Theatre School. Joined NYC Ballet in 1958, promoted to soloist in 1963.

SIMONE, KIRSTEN. Born July 1, 1934 in Copenhagen. Studied at School of Royal Theatre; made debut with company in 1952, subsequently becoming principal dancer. Has appeared with Ruth Page Opera Ballet, Royal Winnipeg Ballet, Royal Swedish Ballet.

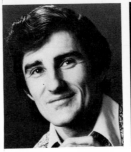

Earle Sieveling   Trinette Singleton   Michael Smuin   Anna Sokolow   Ben Stevenson

SIMONEN-SVANSTROM, SEIJA. Born in Helsinki, Finland, Sept. 7, 1935. Studied at Finnish Natl. Opera Ballet School, and with Nikitina, Baltazcheva, Semjonowa, Lopuchkina, Karnakoski, Stahlberg, Northcote, Franzel, and Craske. Debut 1952 with Helsinki Natl. Opera. Has appeared with Finnish Natl. Ballet, and London Festival Ballet.

SINGLETON, TRINETTE. Born in Beverly, Mass., Nov. 20, 1945. Studied with Harriet James, and at American Ballet Center. Debut with Joffrey Ballet in 1965.

SIZOVA, ALLA. Born in Moscow in 1939. Studied at Leningrad Ballet School. Joined Kirov Co. in 1958, and became its youngest ballerina.

SKIBINE, GOERGE. Born Jan. 17, 1920 in Russia. Studied with Preobrajenska, and Oboukhoff. Debut with Ballet de Monte Carlo in 1937, and with company until 1939. With Original Ballet Russe (1939-40), American Ballet Theatre (1940-1942), Marquis de Cuevas Grand Ballet (1947-56), Theatre National de 'Opera Paris (1956-64), and became artistic director of Harkness Ballet in 1964. Resigned in 1966. Currently works with regional companies.

SLAVENSKA, MIA. Born Mia Corak in 1916 in Yugoslavia. At 12 made debut and toured Europe with Anton Vyanc, subsequently appearing with Lifar and Dolin, and as prima ballerina with Ballet Russe de Monte Carlo, before forming own company Ballet Variant that toured Americas and Europe. Has worked with many regional companies, toured with Slavinska-Franklin Co. Currently teaches.

SLAYTON, JEFF. Born Sept. 5, 1945 in Richmond, Va. Attended Adelphi U. Studied with Merce Cunningham and made debut with his company in 1968.

SLEEP, WAYNE. Born July 17, 1948 in Plymouth, England. Attended Royal Ballet School, and was graduated into the company in 1966.

SMUIN, MICHAEL. Born Oct. 13, 1939 in Missoula, Mont. Studied with Christensen brothers, William Dollar and Richard Thomas. Joined San Francisco Ballet in 1957, and made choreographic debut in 1961. Has choreographed for Harkness and Ballet Theatre. A principal with American Ballet Theatre since 1969.

SOKOLOW, ANNA. Born in 1912 in Hartford, Conn. Studied with Graham and Horst. Became member of Graham Co. but left to form own in 1938. Internationally known as choreographer, and her works include many modern classics. Formed own Lyric Theatre Co. in Israel in 1962. Has taught at major studios and universities, and choreographed for Broadway, TV, and opera.

SOLINO, LOUIS. Born Feb. 7, 1942 in Philadelphia. Studied with Graham, O'Donnell, Schurr, Walker, Anthony, Farnworth. Has performed with Glen Tetley, Mary Anthony, Sophie Maslow, Norman Walker, Arthur Bauman, Seamus Murphy, and Jose Limon.

SOLOMON, ROBERT. Born Feb. 13, 1945 in The Bronx. Studied at Henry Street Playhouse. Has appeared with Henry Street Playhouse Company, and Nikolais.

SOLOMON, RUTH. Born June 10, 1936 in NYC. Studied with Jean Erdman and joined her company in 1957, still appears with her between teaching. Is now head of Dance-Theatre program at UCal. at Santa Cruz.

SOLOV, ZACHARY. Born in 1923 in Philadelphia. Studied with Littlefield, Preobrajenska, Carlos, Holm, and Humphrey and at American Ballet School. Debut with Catherine Littlefield Ballet Co. Later joined American Ballet, New Opera Co., Loring Dance Players, and Ballet Theatre. In 1951 became choreographer for Met Opera Ballet. Toured own company 1961-1962. Also appeared on Bdwy and with regional companies.

SOLOVYOV, YURI. Born in 1940. Graduated from Leningrad Ballet School and into Kirov Co. in 1958. Has become one of its leading soloists.

SOMBERT, CLAIRE. Born in 1935 in Courbevoie, France. A pupil of Brieux, made debut in 1950. Has appeared with Ballets de Paris, Ballets Jean Babilee, Miskovitch Co. Toured U.S. with Michel Bruel.

SOMES, MICHAEL. Born in 1917 in Horsley, Eng. Attended Sadler's Wells School; joined company in 1937, and became lead dancer in 1938. For many years, partner for Margot Fonteyn, and creator of many famous roles. In 1962 appointed assistant director of company, and still performs character roles.

SPOERLI, HEINZ. Born July 8, 1944 in Basel, Switz. Studied with Walter Kleiber; debut 1962 with Tradttheater, subsequently with Royal Winnipeg Ballet, Les Grands Ballets Canadiens (1968).

SPOHR, ARNOLD. Born in Saskatchewan, Can. Joined Winnipeg company in 1945, rapidly rising to leading dancer, and appeared in England partnering Alicia Markova. Began choreographing for company in 1950. In 1958 was appointed director of Royal Winnipeg Ballet Co. for which he still choreographs.

STACKHOUSE, SARAH. (formerly Sally). Born in Chicago, graduate of U. of Wisc. Studied with Arrby Blinn, Steffi Nossen, Perry-Mansfield School, John Begg, Limon, Graham, and Nagrin. Joined Limon company in 1959. Has also appeared with Alvin Ailey Co. Teaches at Julliard and Conn. College.

STARBUCK, JAMES. Born in Albuquerque, New Mex. Attended College of Pacific. Debut 1934 with Ballet Moderne, subsequently appearing with San Francisco Opera Ballet, Ballet Russe de Monte Carlo (1939-44). On Bdwy in musicals before first choreography for "Fanny." Has since choreographed and directed for theatre and TV.

STEELE, MICHAEL. Born in Roanoke, Va. Studied at American Ballet School, and made debut with NYC Ballet.

STEPHEN, EDITH. Born in Salamanca, NY. Studied with Doris Humphrey, Jose Limon, Mary Wigman, Rudolf Laban. Debut in 1962 with own company and choreography. Has toured US and Europe.

STEVENSON, BEN. Born April 4. Was principal dancer for many years with London's Festival Ballet. Retired to teach but makes guest appearances. Directed Harkness Youth Co. Now with National Ballet.

STEWART, DELIA WEDDINGTON. Born in Meridian, Miss. Studied at Ballet Arts Center, Ballet Theatre School, and International Dance School. Appeared in Bdwy musicals. Became director of Dixie Darling Dance Group. In 1963 when Mississippi Coast Ballet was founded, became its artistic director.

STIRLING, CRISTINA. Born May 22, 1940 in London. Trained at Audrey de Vos and Andrew Hardie School. Debut with Sadler's Wells Opera Ballet, subsequently with Netherlands Ballet, London Festival Ballet, American Ballet Co.

STONE, BENTLEY. Born in Plankinston, S. Dak. Studied with Severn, Caskey, Albertieri, Novikoff, and Rambert. After dancing in musicals, joined Chicago Civic Oprea, becoming permier danseur. Also danced with Ballet Rambert, Ballet Russe, and Page-Stone Ballet for which he choreographed many works.

STRIPLING, JAN. Born Sept. 27, 1947 in Essen, Ger. Studied with Volkova, Tudor, Jooss, Hoving, and Jean Lebron. Joined Stuttgart Ballet in 1963.

STROGANOVA, NINA. Born in Copenhagen, and studied at Royal Danish Ballet with Preobrajenska and Dokoudovsky. Appeared with Ballet de L'Opera Comique Paris, Mordkin Ballet, National Ballet Theatre, de Basil's Original Ballet Russe, Ballet Russe de Monte Carlo, and Danish Royal Ballet. Was co-director and ballerina of Dokoudovsky-Stroganova Ballet. Is now a teacher.

STRUCHKOVA, RAISSA. Born in 1925 in Moscow; graduate of Bolshoi School in 1944. Became soloist in 1946 with company; now a prima ballerina. Has appeared in almost every ballet performed by Bolshoi.

SUMNER, CAROL. Born in 1940 in Brooklyn. Studied with Eileen O'Connor and at School of American Ballet. Joined NYC Ballet, becoming soloist in 1963.

SUTHERLAND, DAVID. Born Sept. 18, 1941 in Santa Ana, Cal. Studied with Michel Panaieff, Aaron Girard. Debut 1959 with Ballet de Cuba. Joined Stuttgart Ballet in 1965.

SUTHERLAND, PAUL. Born in 1935 in Louisville, Ky. Joined Ballet Theatre in 1957, subsequently dancing with Royal Winni-

Britt Swanson

Robert Talmage

Sonia Taverner

Glen Tetley

Edra Toth

peg Ballet, and Joffrey Ballet. Rejoined American Ballet Theatre as soloist in 1964; Harkness in 1969, Joffrey 1971.

SUZUKI, DAWN. Born in Slocan, B.C., Can. Graduate of U. Toronto; studied at Canadian Royal Academy of Dance, Banff School, and Martha Graham School. Debut with Yuriko in 1967, followed by performances with Pearl Lang. Joined Graham Co. in 1968.

SVETLOVA, MARINA. Born May 3, 1922 in Paris. Studied with Trefilova, Egorova, and Vilzak. With Original Ballet Russe (1939-41), Ballet Theatre (1942), prima ballerina Met Opera Ballet (1943-50), NYC Opera (1950-52), own concert group (1944-58), and as guest with most important European companies. Artistic Director of Dallas Civic Ballet; choreographer for Dallas, Seattle, and Houston Operas.

SWAN, PAUL. Born in Nebraska in 1889. Largely self-taught. Has given solo concerts abroad and in US. Founder-Director of School of the Aesthetic Ideal. Continues to give weekly concerts.

SWANSON, BRITT. Born June 6, 1947 in Fargo, N Dak. Studied at SF Ballet Sch., NY School of Ballet. Debut 1963 with Chicago Opera Ballet, subsequently with SF Ballet, on Bdwy, with Paul Sanasardo, Paul Taylor (1969).

TALLCHIEF, MARIA. Born Jan. 24, 1925 in Fairfax, Okla. After studying with Bronislava Nijinska, joined Ballet Russe de Monte Carlo in 1942, and became leading dancer. In 1948 joined NYC Ballet as prima ballerina, and excelled in classic roles. Has appeared as guest artist with Paris Opera and other European companies. Retired in 1965.

TALLCHIEF, MARJORIE. Born on Indian reservation in Oklahoma in 1927. Studied with Bronislava Nijinska, and David Lichine. Debut with American Ballet Theatre in 1945, subsequently appearing with Marquis de Cuevas Ballet (1947-56), Theatre National Opera de Paris (1956-64), Bolshoi (1964), and joined Harkness Ballet in 1964. Resigned in 1966. Now teaches.

TALMAGE, ROBERT. Born in Washington, DC. Attended SF State Col. Studied with Eugene Loring. Appeared with Atlanta Ballet, in musicals, before joining Joffrey Ballet.

TARAS, JOHN. Born in NYC in 1919. Studied with Fokine, Vilzak, Shollar, and at School of American Ballet. Appeared in musicals and with Ballet Caravan, Littlefield Ballet, American Ballet, and Ballet Theatre with which he became soloist, ballet master, and choreographed first ballet "Graziana" in 1945. Joined Marquis de Cuevas' Grand Ballet in 1948. Returned to NYC Ballet in 1959 as assistant to Balanchine. Has created and staged ballets for companies throughout the world.

TAVERNER, SONIA. Born in Byfleet, Eng., in 1936. Studied at Sadler's Wells, and joined their company before moving to Canada where she became member of Royal Winnipeg Ballet, developing into its premiere danseuse.

TAYLOR, BURTON. Born Aug. 19, 1943 in White Plains, N.Y. Studied with Danielian, and at Ballet Theatre School. Debut with Eglevsky Ballet in 1959 before joining American Ballet Theatre, Joffrey Co. in 1969.

TAYLOR, JUNE. Born in 1918 in Chicago. Studied with Merriel Abbott. Debut in "George White's Scandals of 1931," subsequently appearing in other musicals. Choreographer for June Taylor Dancers and director of own school.

TAYLOR, PAUL. Born in Alegheny County, Pa., July 29, 1930. Attended Syracuse U., Juilliard Met Opera Ballet School and Graham School. Studied with Craske and Tudor. Member of Graham Co. for 6 years, and appeared with Merce Cunningham, Pearl Lang, Anna Sokolow, and NYC Ballet. In 1960 formed own company, and tours US and Europe.

TCHERINA, LUDMILLA. Born in Paris in 1925. Trained with d'Allesandri, Clustine, Preobrajenska. Has appeared with Monte Carlo Opera, Ballets des Champs-Elysees, Nouveau Ballet de Monte Carlo. Toured with own company, and has appeared in films.

TETLEY, GLEN. Born Feb. 3, 1926 in Cleveland, Ohio. Attended Franklin and Marshall College, and NYU graduate. Studied with Holm, Graham, Tudor, and Craske. Debut in 1946

in "On The Town," subsequently appeared with Hanya Holm (1946-9), John Butler (1951-8), NYC Opera (1951-66), Robert Joffrey (1955-6), Martha Graham (1957-60), American Ballet Theatre (1958-60), Ballets: USA (1960-1), Nederlands Dans Theatre (1962-5). Formed own company in 1961, and choreographs.

THARP, TWYLA. Graduate Barnard College. Studied with Collonette, Schwetzoff, Farnworth, Louis, Mattox, Graham, Nikolais, Taylor, and Cunningham. Debut with Paul Taylor in 1965. Has organized, choreographed, and appeared with own company in NYC and on tour.

THOMAS, ROBERT WILLIS, III. Born Mar. 5, 1948 in Iowa City. Studied with Anne Dirksen, and at Harkness School. Joined Harkness Ballet in 1968, Joffrey Ballet 1970.

THOMPSON, BASIL. Born in Newcastle-on-Tyne, Eng. Studied at Sadler's Wells. Joined Covent Garden Ballet in 1954, the Royal Ballet, ABT in 1960. Currently Ballet Master of Joffrey Ballet.

THOMPSON, CLIVE. Born in Kingston, Jamaica, BWI., Oct. 20. Studied with and joined Ivy Baxter's Dance Co. Attended Soohih School of Classical Dance, and University College of West Indies. In 1958 represented Jamaica at Federal Festival of Arts. Won Jamaican award for choreography and contribution to dance. Came to US in 1960, studied with Graham, and joined her company in 1961. Also appeared with Talley Beatty, Pearl Lang, Yuriko, Geoffrey Holder, and Alvin Ailey.

THORESEN, TERJE. Born in 1945 in Stockholm. Debut in 1959. Appeared with Royal Dramatic Theatre, Stockholm Dance Theatre, Syvilla Fort African Dance Group.

TIMOFEYEVA, NINA. Born in 1935 in Russia. Entered Leningrad Ballet School and graduated into Kirov Co. in 1953. Joined Bolshoi in 1956 and is a principal dancer.

TOMASSON, HELGI. Born in Reykjavik, Iceland. Studied with Sigridur Arman, Erik Bidsted, Vera Volkova, and American Ballet School. Debut in Copenhagen's Pantomine Theatre in 1958. In 1961 joined Joffrey Ballet; Harkness Ballet in 1964; NYC Ballet in 1970.

TOTH, EDRA. Born in 1952 in Budapest. Trained with Alda Marova, E. Virginia Williams. Joined Boston Ballet in 1965.

TOUMANOVA, TAMARA. Born in 1919. Protege of Pavlowa; danced first leading role with Paris Opera at 10; ballerina with Ballet Russe de Monte Carlo at 16. Joined Rene Blum Co. in 1939; returned to Paris Opera in 1947, and to London with de Cuevas Ballet in 1949. More recently making guest appreances and in films.

TRACY, PAULA. Born in San Francisco where she studied with Lew and Harold Christensen. Joined San Francisco Ballet in 1956. Joined American Ballet Theatre in 1967, now soloist.

TREURE, BARTHA (Tania Bari). Born May 7, 1936 in Rotterdam, Holland. Studied with Nora Kiss, Messerer, Gsovsky, Don Lurio in Paris. Debut 1955 with Bejart Ballet.

TRISLER, JOYCE. Born in Los Angeles in 1934. Graduate of Juilliard. Studied with Horton, Maracci, Tudor, Holm, Joffrey, Caton. Joined Horton Co. in 1951. Became member of Juilliard Dance Theatre, and performed with own group, for which she choreographed. Has also choreographed for musicals and operas. Now teaches.

TROUNSON, MARILYN. Born Sept. 30, 1947 in San Francisco. Graduated from Royal Ballet School and joined company 1966.

TUDOR, ANTONY. Born Aug. 4, 1908 in London. Studied with Marie Rambert, and made debut with her in 1930, when he also choreographed his first work. Joined Vic-Wells Ballet (1933-5), and became active choreographer. Formed own company,

London Ballet, in NY in 1938. In 1940 joined American Ballet Theatre as soloist and choreographer. Has also produced ballets for NYC Ballet, Theatre Colon, Deutsche Opera, and Komaki Ballet. Was in charge of Met Opera Ballet School (1957-63); considered one of world's greatest choreographers.

Patricia Turko   Martine Van Hamel   Michael Uthoff   Karin von Aroldingen   Edward Verso

TUPINE, OLEG. Born in 1920 aboard ship off Istanbul. Studied with Egorova and made debut with her company. Joined Original Ballet Russe in 1938, Markova-Dolin Co. in 1947, Ballet Russe de Monte Carlo in 1951, then formed own company. Now teaches.

TURKO, PATRICIA. Born May 22, 1942 in Pittsburgh. Studied at School of American Ballet. Danced with Pittsburgh and Philadelphia Opera companies and in musicals before joining Pennsylvania Ballet in 1964.

TURNEY, MATT. Born in Americus, Ga. Joined Martha Graham Co. in 1951. Has also danced with Donald McKayle, Alvin Ailey, Paul Taylor, and Pearl Lang.

TUROFF, CAROL. Born Jan 14, 1947 in New Jersey. NYU graduate; studied with Jean Erdman, Erick Hawkins. Debut 1968 with Hawkins Co., subsequently appearing with Jean Erdman, and in concert.

UCHIYAMA, AYAKO. Born in Japan in 1925. Began studies in Tokyo with Masami Kuni, Aiko Yuzaki and Takaya Eguchi. In 1950 organized Uchiyama Art Dance School. Awarded scholarship to study in US with Graham, Horst, Limon, Cunningham, Joffrey, Ballet Russe School, and Luigi's Jazz Center. Has given many concerts and recitals in Japan, and US under sponsorship of Japan and Asia Societies.

ULANOVA, GALINA. Born in Russia in 1910. Studied with Vagonova. Grauduate of Leningrad State School of Ballet. Joined Bolshoi Company and became Russia's greatest lyric ballerina. Now in retirement, but coaches for Bolshoi.

ULLEATE, VICTOR. Born in Spain. Studied with Rosella Hightower, Maria de Avila. Debut with Antonio. At 18 joined Bejart Ballet.

USHER, GRAHAM. Born in Beverley, Eng., May 23, 1938. Attended Royal Ballet School, and made debut with Royal Ballet in 1955. Is now a principal dancer.

UTHOFF, MICHAEL. Born in Santiago, Chile, Nov. 5, 1943. Graduate of U. Chile. Studied at Juilliard School of American Ballet, American Ballet Center, and with Tudor, and Limon. Debut with Limon's company in 1964. Appeared with American Dance Theatre before he joined Joffrey Ballet in 1965. Currently with First Chamber Dance Co.

VALDOR, ANTONY. Began career with Marquis de Cuevas Company, subsequently appearing with Jose Torres' Ballet Espagnol, Opera de Marseille, Theatre du Chatelet, Theatre Massimo de Palermo. Currently ballet master of San Francisco Ballet.

VALENTINE, PAUL. Born William Daixel, March 23, 1919 in NYC. Began career at 14 with Ballet Russe de Monte Carlo, subsequently as Val Valentinoff with Fokine Ballet, and Mordkin Ballet. Since 1937 has appeared in theatre, TV, and night clubs.

VAN DYKE, JAN. Born April 15, 1941, in Washington, DC. Studied with Ethel Butler, Martha Graham, Merce Cunningham, and at Conn. College, Henry St. Playhouse. Dancer-choreographer-director of Church St. Dance Co., and appeared with Dance Theatre Workshop.

VAN HAMEL, MARTINE. Born Nov. 16, 1945 in Brussels. Attended Ntl Ballet School of Canada. Debut 1963 with Ntl Ballet of Can. Guest with Royal Swedish Ballet, Royal Winnipeg Ballet, Joffrey Ballet, before joining ABT.

VASSILIEV, VLADIMIR. Born in Russia in 1940. Studied at Bolshoi School and joined company in 1958, becoming soloist in 1959.

VEGA, ANTONIO. Born in Huelva, Spain. Studied with Pericet and Antonio Marin. Has performed with Jose Molina, Luisillo, Mariemma, Antonio, and Jose Greco. Joined Ballet Granada in 1968 as soloist.

VERDON, GWEN. Born Jan 13, 1926 in Culver City, Calif. Studied various styles of dancing, including ballet with Ernest Belcher and Carmelita Maracci. Danced with Aida Broadbent company, and with Jack Cole. Became assistant choreographer to Cole on several films, before becoming star on Bdwy musicals.

VERDY, VIOLETTE. Born in Brittany, Dec. 1, 1933. Debut in 1944 with Roland Petit. Has appeared with major European ballet companies, including England's Royal Ballet, Petit's Co., and Paris Opera Ballet. Joined ABT in 1957, NYC Ballet in 1958 as a principal.

VERE, DIANA. Born Sept. 29, 1942 in Trinidad. Studied at Royal Ballet School; joined company in 1962; promoted to soloist in 1968, principal 1970.

VERED, AVNER. Born Feb. 3, 1938 in Israel. Debut 1965 with Bertram Ross, subsequently with Jose Limon, Pearl Lang.

VERSO, EDWARD. Born Oct. 25, 1941 in NYC. Studied with Vincenzo Celli. Appeared on Bdwy and with Ballets USA, before joining American Ballet Theatre in 1962, Joffrey Ballet in 1969.

VETRA, VIJA. Born Feb. 6 in Latvia. Studied in Vienna, and India. Debut 1945 in Burgertheatre, Vienna. Since 1955 has toured world in solo concerts, and teaches in own NY studio.

VIKULOV, SERGEI. Trained at Leningrad Ballet School. Joined Kirov Company in 1956.

VILLELLA, EDWARD. Born Oct. 1, 1936, in Bayside, Queens, N.Y. Began studies at School of American Ballet at 10. Graduate of Maritime College. Joined NYC Ballet in 1957, and rapidly rose to leading dancer. First male guest artist to appear with Royal Danish Ballet. Appeared in NYC Center productions of "Brigadoon," and on TV. Recently choreographed for NYC Ballet.

VODEHNAL, ANDREA. Born in 1938 in Oak Park, Ill. Studied at Ballet Russe School, and School of American Ballet, and with Semenova and Danilova. Joined Ballet Russe de Monte Carlo in 1957, and became soloist in 1961. Joined National Ballet in 1962 as ballerina.

VOLLMAR, JOCELYN. Entered native San Francisco Ballet School at 12 and joined company at 17 in 1943. Later with NYC Ballet, American Ballet Theatre, de Cuevas Ballet, and Borovansky Australian Ballet. Rejoined SF Ballet in 1957, and has choreographed several ballets.

VON AROLDINGEN, KARIN. Born July 9, 1941 in Germany. Studied with Edwardova, Gsovsky. Debut 1958 in Frankfurt. Joined NYC Ballet in 1961, soloist since 1967.

WAGNER, RICHARD. Born Jan. 30, 1939 in Atlantic City, N.J. Studied with Antony Tudor. Debut with Ballet Russe de Monte Carlo in 1957; joined American Ballet Theatre in 1960, and Harkness Ballet in 1964 as dancer and choreographer.

WAGONER, DAN. Born July 13, 1932 in Springfield, W Va. Attended U W Va. Studied with Ethel Butler, Martha Graham. Debut 1958 with Graham, subsequently with Merce Cunningham, Paul Taylor and in own choreography.

WALKER, DAVID HATCH. Born Mar. 14, 1949 in Edmonton, Can. Studied at Ntl Ballet School, Toronto Dance Theatre, Martha Graham. Debut 1968 with Ballet Rambert, London, subsequently with Donald McKayle, Lar Lubovitch, Martha Graham.

WALKER, NORMAN. Born in NYC in 1934. Studied at High School of Performing Arts. Appeared with May O'Donnell, Yuriko, Pauline Koner, and Pearl Lang. Began choreographing while in army, and afterward taught at Utah State U., and choreographed for musicals and festivals throughout US. Now appears with own company, and choreographs for it as well as others. Also teaches and artistic director of Batsheva Co.

WALL, DAVID RICHARD. Born in London, March 15, 1946. Attended Royal Ballet School, and made debut with company in 1962. Now a principal.

WALLSTROM, GAY. Born Mar. 9, 1949 in Beaumont, Tex. Studied at American Ballet Center and joined Joffrey Ballet in 1968.

WARREN, VINCENT. Born Aug. 31, 1938 in Jacksonville, Fla. Studied at Ballet Theatre School. Debut 1957 with Met Opera Ballet, subsequently with Santa Fe Opera, James Waring, Aileen Pasloff, Guatemala Ntl. Ballet, Penn. Ballet, Cologne Opera Ballet, Les Grands Ballets Canadiens.

Gay Wallstrom   Vincent Warren   Karla Wolfangle   John Wilson   Rebecca Wright

WATANABE, MIYOKO. Born in Japan and began training at 6. Joined all-girls Kabuki Troupe and became one of its leading performers. Came to US in 1960 as announcer-interpreter for Kabuki troupe, and remained to perform in concert and teach classic Japanese dances.

WATTS, JONATHAN. Born in 1933 in Cheyenne, Wyo. Studied with Joffrey, Shurr, and O'Donnell. Debut with Joffrey before joining NYC Ballet in 1954, Australian Ballet 1962, and Cologne Opera Ballet as premier danseur in 1965. Now director Am. Ballet Center.

WAYNE, DENNIS. Born in NYC; attended High School of Performing Arts. Debut with Norman Walker Co., joined Harkness Ballet then Joffrey Ballet.

WEBER, DIANA. Born Jan. 16, in Passaic, N.J. Studied at Ballet Theatre School. Joined ABT in 1962; became soloist in 1966.

WEIDMAN, CHARLES. Born July 22, 1901, in Lincoln, Neb. Studied at Denishawn School, with Frampton, and Humphrey. Debut with Martha Graham in "Xochitl." Toured with Denishawn Dancers for 8 years. In 1929, with Doris Humphrey, established school and concert company. In 1948, formed own company "Theatre Dance." Was choreographer for NYC Opera Co., and Bdwy productions. In 1960, established Expression of Two Arts Theatre with weekly performances.

WELCH, GARTH. Born April. 14, 1936 in Brisbane, Aust. Studied with Phyllis Danaher, Victor Gzovsky, Anna Northcote, Zaraspe, Martha Graham. Debut 1955 with Borovansky Ballet, subsequently with Western Theatre Ballet, Marquis de Cuevas Ballet, Australian Ballet (1962).

WELLS, BRUCE. Born Jan. 17, 1950 in Tacoma, Wash. Studied with Patricia Cairns, Banff School, School of American Ballet. Joined NYC Ballet in 1967, dancing soloist and principal roles since 1969.

WELLS, DOREEN. Born June 25, 1937 in London. Studied at Royal Ballet School and made debut with company in 1955, rising to ballerina.

WESCHE, PATRICIA. Born Oct. 13, 1952 in West Islip, NY. Attended American Ballet Theatre School. Debut 1969 with ABT.

WESLOW, WILLIAM. Born Mar. 20, 1925 in Seattle, Wash. Studied with Mary Ann Wells. Appeared on Bdwy and TV before joining Ballet Theatre in 1949. Joined NYC Ballet in 1958.

WHELAN, SUSAN. Born feb. 26, 1948 in NYC. Studied with Eglevsky, at Ballet Theatre, and Harkness schools. Joined Harkness Ballet in 1966, ABT (1971).

WHITE, FRANKLIN. Born in 1924 in Shoreham, Kent, Eng. After 3 years with Ballet Rambert, joined Royal Ballet in 1942. Is also well known as lecturer on ballet.

WHITE, GLENN. Born Aug. 6, 1949 in Pittsburgh, Calif. Studied at Norfolk Ballet Academy, American Ballet Center. Debut 1968 with NYC Opera, joined Joffrey Company in 1969.

WHITE, ONNA. Born in Nova Scotia. Debut with San Francisco Opera Ballet Co. Became assistant choreographer to Michael Kidd, and subsequently choreographer for several Bdwy, Hollywood, and London productions.

WHITENER, WILLIAM. Born Aug. 17, 1951 in Seattle, Wash. Studied with Karen Irvin, Mary Staton, Hector Zaraspe, Perry Brunson. Debut 1969 with City Center Joffrey Ballet.

WILDE, PATRICIA. Born in Ottawa, Can. in 1928 where she studied before joining Marquis de Cuevas' Ballet International and continuing studies at School of American Ballet. Joined NYC Ballet in 1950 and became one of its leading ballerinas, having danced almost every role in the company's repertoire. Director of Harkness School. Now teaches.

WILLIAMS, ANTHONY. Born June 11, 1946 in Naples, Italy. Studied with Virginia Williams and Joffrey. Debut 1964 with Boston Ballet. Joined Joffrey company 1968; rejoined Boston Ballet in 1969.

WILLIAMS, DANIEL. Born in 1943 in San Francisco. Studied with Welland Lathrop, Gloria Unti, May O'Donnell Gertrude Shurr, Nina Fonaroff, Wishmary Hunt, Paul Taylor. Joined

Taylor's company in 1963 and appears in most of its repetoire.

WILLIAMS, DUDLEY. Born in NYC where he began dance leessons at 6. Studied with Shook, O'Donnell, Tudor, Graham, and at Juilliard. Has appeared with May O'Donnell, Martha Graham, Donald McKayle, Talley Beatty, and Alvin Ailey.

WILSON, ANNE. Born in Philadelphia. Graduate of U. of Chicago. Studied with Fokine, Tudor, Weidman, Elizabeth Anderson, Etienne Decroux, and Heinz Poll. Debut 1940 with American Ballet Theatre. Also with Weidman company, and in 1964 formed own group. Noted for solo concert-lecture "The Ballet Story" which she has toured extensively.

WILSON, JOHN. Born in 1927 in Los Angeles. Studied with Katherine Dunham. Toured with Harriette Ann Gray, appeared in concert with own group, and Joyce Triler. Joined Joffrey Ballet in 1956, Harkness Ballet in 1964.

WILSON, SALLIE. Born Apr. 18, 1932 in Ft. Worth, Tex. Studied with Tudor and Craske. Joined American Ballet Theatre in 1959, and in 1963 was raised to principal dancer. Has also appeared with Met Opera and NYC Ballets.

WINTER, ETHEL. Born in Wrentham, Mass., June 18, 1924. Graduate of Bennington College. Soloist with Martha Graham Co. since 1964. Has taught Graham Method in various schools in Eng. and appeared as lecture-demonstrator. Her own choreography has received recognition, and is included in repetoire of Batsheva Co. Also appeared with NYC Opera, and Sophie Maslow.

WOLENSKI, CHESTER. Born Nov. 16, 1931 in New Jersey. Attended Juilliard, and American School of Ballet. Debut 1956 with Jose Limon, subsequently with Anna Sokolow, Donald McKayle, John Butler, American Dance Theatre, Juilliard Dance Theatre, Jack Moore, Bill Frank and Ruth Currier. Also appeared in musicals.

WRIGHT, REBECCA. Born Dec. 5, 1947 in Springfield, Ohio. Studied with David McLain and Josephine Schwarz. Joined Joffrey Ballet in 1966.

YOHN, ROBERT. Born Sept. 23, 1943 in Fresno, Calif. Studied at Fresno State Col., New Dance Group, and with Charles Kelley, Perry Brunson. Has appeared with New Dance Group, Bruce King, and joined Erick Hawkins Company in 1968.

YOUNG, GAYLE. Born Nov. 7, in Lexington, Ky. Began study with Dorothy Pring at U. Calif. Studied at Ballet Theatre School, and joined Joffrey Ballet. Appeared on Bdwy and with NYC Ballet before joining American Ballet Theatre in 1960. Became principal in 1964.

YOUSKEVITCH, IGOR. Born in Moscow in 1912. Studied with Preobrajenska. Debut in Paris with Nijinska company; joined De Basil's Ballet, then, Ballet Russe de Monte Carlo. In 1946 became premier danseur with Ballet Theatre. Currently operating own school in NYC.

YOUSKEVITCH, MARIA. Born Dec. 11, 1945 in NYC. Studied with father, Igor Youskevitch, and made debut with his company in 1963. Appeared with Met Opera Ballet before joining American Ballet Theatre in 1967.

YUDENICH, ALEXEI. Born July 5, 1943 in Sarajevo, Yugoslavia. Studied at Sarajevo Opera Ballet School, and made debut with company. Guest artist with Sagreb Opera Ballet before joining Pennsylvania Ballet in 1964 as principal dancer.

YURIKO. Born Feb. 2, 1920 in San Jose, Calif. Began professional career at 6 with group that toured Japan for 7 years. Studied with Martha Graham, and joined company in 1944, becoming soloist, and choreographer. Formed own company in 1948 with which she has appeared in NY and on tour. Also appeared in musicals.

ZAMIR, BATYA. Studied with Alwin Nikolais, Gladys Bailin, Phyllis Lamhut, Murray Louis, Bill Frank. Appeared with Nikolais, Murray Louis, Mimi Garrard, Rachel Fibish, Joy Boutilier, and in own concerts and choreography. Also teaches.

ZHDANOV, YURI. Born in Moscow in 1925. Began career at 12 before attending Bolshoi School. Joined company in 1944, became Ulanova's partner in 1951. Is now retired.

ZIDE, ROCHELLE. Born in Boston, Apr. 21, 1938. Studied with Hoctor, Williams, Pereyaslavec, Joffrey, Danielian, and at Ballet Russe School. Debut in 1954 with Ballet Russe de Monte Carlo, subsequently appearing with Joffrey Ballet (1958), Ballets USA (1961), American Dances (1963), NYC Opera Ballet (1958-63), Ballet Spectaculars (1963), and became ballet mistress of Joffrey Ballet in 1965.

ZIMMERMAN, GERDA. Born Mar. 26, 1937 in Cuxhaven, Ger. Studied with Georgi, Wigman, Horst, Zena Rommett. Soloist with Landestheater Hannover 1959-62. Choreographer from 1967. Solo recitals in US from 1967 and in Ger. Formed Kammertanz Theatre. Guest artist in residence at WashU. Teaches.

ZITO, DOROTHY. Born in Jersey City, NJ. Attended Juilliard. Studied at Graham, Harkness schools, and NY School of Ballet. Debut 1969 with New Dance Group, subsequently with Pearl Lang.

ZOMPAKOS, STANLEY. Born in NYC, May 12, 1925, Studied with Balanchine and at School of American Ballet. Debut 1942

with New Opera Co. In Bdwy musicals, with Ballet Russe de Monte Carlo (1945-7), NYC Ballet (1951-3), Boris-Hobi Co. (1954-6), and became artistic director of Charleston, S.C., Civic Ballet.

ZORINA, VERA. Born Eva Brigitta Hartwig, Jan. 2, 1917 in Berlin, Ger. Studied with Edwardova, Tatiana and Victor Gsovsky, Dolin, and Legat. Debut 1930 in Berlin. Toured with Ballet Russe de Monte Carlo (1934-6). Made NYC debut in "I Married An Angel" in 1938. Joined Ballet Theatre in 1943. Subsequently, appeared in Bdwy productions, and films.

ZORITCH, GEORGE. Born in Moscow in 1919. Studied in Lithuania, Paris, and NY, with Preobrajenska, Vilzak, Vladimiroff, and Oboukhoff. Debut 1933 with Ida Rubenstein Co. in Paris. Joined de Basil Ballet Russe in 1936, Ballet Russe de Monte Carlo in 1938, Grand Ballet du Marquis de Cuevas (1951-8), Marina Svetlova Co. (1961), and formed own company. Is favorite teacher and choreographer for regional ballet companies. Operates own school in Calif.

OBITUARIES

ARCHIBALD, WILLIAM, 53, dancer, choreographer, actor, playwright, died in NYC of hepatitis on Dec. 27, 1970. Made debut in 1939 with Humphrey-Weidman Co. Subsequently danced in many Bdwy productions, at the Roxy, on TV, and in night clubs before becoming writer. Two brothers and two sisters survive.

BOURMEISTER, VLADIMIR, 66, chief choreographer of the Stanislavsky and Nemirovich-Danchenko Musical Theatre, died in Moscow. "The Corsair," his first production, was staged in 1931, followed by among others "Merry Wives of Windsor," "Scheherezade," "Jeanne d'Arc," "Swan Lake," "Carnaval," "Straussiana," and "Snow Maiden." During his early years, had been leading soloist with Moscow Ballet Theatre.

BRAUN, ERIC, 46, Vienna-born principal with Ballet Theatre, died Oct. 27, 1970 of a heart attack while teaching a class in his dance school in Highland Park, Ill. Joined Ballet Theatre in 1945 and left in 1956. Became prominent as teacher and choreographer in Chicago, and was director of Phyllis Sabold Co. He was divorced from Ruth Ann Koesun.

CHACE, MARIAN. 73, former Denishawn dancer, teacher, and the nation's first dance therapist, died in Aug. 1970. Opened school in Washington, D. C. in 1930 and became interested in using rhythmic body action with the emotionally disturbed. She was invited to work at St. Elizabeth's Hospital. Became first president of American Dance Therapy Association.

COOPER, REX, 48, died of cancer Oct. 26, 1970 in Jackson, Miss. Joined Ballet Theatre in 1942, rising to soloist, then joined Met Opera Ballet, Markova-Dolin Co. After 1947 appeared in musicals, and taught. With his wife Albia Kavan, opened school in Jackson, Miss. and became director of Jackson Ballet. His widow and son survive.

DARLING, MAY, 63, former Ziegfeld dancer, and dance soloist, died March 23, 1971 in Chicago, where she had lived for many years.

GOLEISOVSKY, KASYAN YAROSLAVICH, 78, veteran Russian choreographer, died May 2, 1970. Joined Boshoi Theater Ballet in 1909, began choreographing in 1917 and won renown for short works, and founded Chamber Ballet in 1922. Fell into official disfavor under Stalin. Among his works are "Price Igor," "Joseph the Beautiful," "Spanish Dances," "Two Roses," "Visions Fugitives," "Scriabiniana," "L'Apres-Midi d'un Faune," and "Salome."

LEGAT, NADINE NICOLAEVA, 81, former Russian ballet dancer, and teacher, died Feb. 4, 1971 in Tunbridge Wells, Eng. Widow of Nicholas Legat, leading dancer of the St. Petersburg Imperial Ballet, she had continued the school they founded originally in London.

MANDIA, JOHN, 45, former NYC ballet dancer, died of a heart attack Aug. 11, 1970 in Berkeley, Calif., where he had gone to assist with rehearsals of "Still Point." He had danced a lead role in the 1956 production. After leaving NYC Ballet, was choreographer for Cologne and Frankfurt Opera houses in Germany. Also taught at Univ. of Wash. Surviving are his mother and 2 sisters.

MARMEIN, MIRIAM, dancer-teacher, died Aug. 17, 1970 in Schenectady, N.Y. after a long illness. Had appeared in vaudeville and concert with her sisters Irene and Phyllis. Later taught and choreographed in NYC and Massachusetts where she conducted a summer school.

ORTHWINE, RUDOLF, 76, inventor, printer, and publisher of Dance Magazine, died July 13, 1970 in NYC after a long illness. Born in Germany and came to U.S. at age 19. With Mikhail Mordkin organized Mordkin Ballet in 1935, and eventually it became Ballet Theatre. Several years later began publishing Dance Magazine. A daughter, brother and sister survive.

ROOS, NELL, 55, dancer, teacher, writer, died Aug. 24, 1970 in Amsterdam. She had been active in Dutch dance affairs for many years, and had taught and choreographed frequently in the U.S. She had been Netherlands correspondent for "Dance News" since 1960.

SOYER, IDA, 61, former modern dancer, died July 4, 1970 in her summer home in Hampton Bays, L. I. She had been a leading dancer with the Tamiris ballet and modern dance companies. Surviving are her husband, artist Moses Soyer, and a son.

STRAVINSKY, IGOR, 88, acclaimed as the greatest ballet composer of this century, died Apr. 6, 1971 in NYC. He had worked in every known musical form, but excelled in dance. Joined Diaghilev in Paris and composed his first masterpiece "Firebird." After its success in 1910 he turned out scores regularly for Diaghilev's Ballets Russes, including "Petrouchka," "The Rite of Spring"(Le Sacre du Printemps), and "Pulcinella," which have become classics. Moved to U. S. and became citizen in 1945. His second wife survives.

TIHMAR, DAVID, 61, former dancer, actor, director, died after a heart attack in Oklahoma City on Apr. 16, 1971. With Mia Slavenska in the 1940's toured with Slavenska-Tihmar Co. Appeared with Ballet Russe, and on Broadway, before becoming director for stock and regional theaters. Taught and directed Hasty Pudding shows at Harvard for four years. A sister and brother survive.

TOMSKY, ALEXANDER, 65, former dancer, choreographer, and company manager of the Bolshoi Ballet, died of a heart attack in Milan, Italy, on Sept. 28, 1970, while on tour with the company. Joined company as dancer in 1923 and was a soloist until retirement in 1954. He became director of the touring Stars of the Bolshoi, and choreographed for many companies around the world. His widow and two daughters survive.

VLADIMIROFF, PIERRE, 77, former dancer, and teacher, died Nov. 25, 1970 of a stroke in NYC. Became premier danseur of the Imperial Ballet of the Maryinsky Theater in 1915, and subsequently with Diaghilev's Ballet Russes. Joined Anna Pavlova's company as her partner in 1928 and remained until her death in 1931. Came to U. S. and joined faculty of School of American Ballet where he taught for 33 years until retirement in 1967. His widow, former ballerina Felia Doubrovska, survives.

INDEX